Lecture Notes in Information Systems and Organisation

Volume 20

More information about this series at http://www.springer.com/series/11237

Katia Corsi • Nicola Giuseppe Castellano •
Rita Lamboglia • Daniela Mancini
Editors

Reshaping Accounting and Management Control Systems

New Opportunities from Business Information Systems

 Springer

Editors
Katia Corsi
Sassari University
Sassari, Italy

Nicola Giuseppe Castellano
Macerata University
Macerata, Italy

Rita Lamboglia
Parthenope University of Naples
Naples, Italy

Daniela Mancini
Parthenope University of Naples
Naples, Italy

ISSN 2195-4968   ISSN 2195-4976   (electronic)
Lecture Notes in Information Systems and Organisation
ISBN 978-3-319-49537-8   ISBN 978-3-319-49538-5   (eBook)
DOI 10.1007/978-3-319-49538-5

Library of Congress Control Number: 2017935810

Printed on acid-free paper

This Springer imprint is published by Springer Nature
The registered company is Springer International Publishing AG
The registered company address is: Gewerbestrasse 11, 6330 Cham, Switzerland

Contents

Trends of Digital Innovation Applied to Accounting Information and Management Control Systems

D. Mancini, R. Lamboglia, N.G. Castellano, and K. Corsi

Abstract The period we live is known as the digital era. The way in which companies work and interact with each other has radically changed. The digitalisation of data, information and flows requires an additional effort of research, especially in the field of accounting information and management control systems, which are under-explored, in order to understand the potentiality, the benefits and the disadvantages of that kind of technologies. The research works published in this book are a selection of the best papers submitted at the Accounting Information Systems track of the XII Annual Conference of the Italian chapter of Association for Information Systems (ItAIS 2014), entitled "Reshaping Organizations through Digital and Social Innovation".

Keywords Accounting information systems • Digital innovation • Data management • Information systems architecture • Internal reporting • External reporting

1 Introduction

The research works published in this book are a selection of the best papers submitted at the XII Annual Conference of the Italian chapter of Association for Information Systems (ItAIS 2015), which was held in Rome in October, and entitled "Reshaping Organizations through Digital and Social Innovation". The volume contains 21 research works that were accepted at the conference after a double-blind review and were mainly presented at the Accounting Information Systems track.

D. Mancini (✉) • R. Lamboglia
Parthenope University of Naples, Naples, Italy
e-mail: daniela.mancini@uniparthenope.it; rita.lamboglia@uniparthenope.it

N.G. Castellano
Macerata University, Macerata, Italy
e-mail: nicola.castellano@unimc.it

K. Corsi
Sassari University, Sassari, Italy
e-mail: kcorsi@uniss.it

© Springer International Publishing AG 2017   1
K. Corsi et al. (eds.), *Reshaping Accounting and Management Control Systems*,
Lecture Notes in Information Systems and Organisation 20,
DOI 10.1007/978-3-319-49538-5_1

The book presents a collection of papers concerning the relationship between digital innovations (such as cloud, data mining, XBRL, digital platforms) and accounting and management information systems. The aim of the book is to contribute to the current debate, in Italian research community of accounting information systems, on the impact of digital technologies on accounting and management information systems that support control activities.

Business information system is usually defined as a mix of interrelated elements such as [1, 2]:

- Data, regarding corporate and environmental state, which are collected, organised and structured in databases.
- Methodologies, procedures and models to assure the effectiveness and efficiency of data processing and the reliability of information flows.
- Information technology infrastructures and tools and human resources as key elements to manage corporate information processes.
- Information, obtained from data processing, which aims to meet internal and external needs through consistent reporting systems.

With regard to the business information systems, the contributions in this book focus their attention on the accounting and management information systems which are dedicated to support manager's decision-making using accounting data as primary information sources. Some papers consider how new technologies could reshape the accounting and management information systems, enhancing their information potentialities and their ability to support decision-making processes, while other research studies show how managerial information needs affect and reshape the adoption of information technologies asking for more digitalisation.

Consistently with the key elements of business information systems, in order to highlight the impacts of digital innovations, the book is articulated in the following sections:

- Data management, in terms of data collection, data processing and sharing of a large amount of data.
- Information systems architecture, which refers to the structure of the information system, the integration and consistency of its components.
- Internal reporting, regarding the way in which financial and non-financial information is reported and shared, and how it generates knowledge to support management decision-making processes.
- External reporting, concerning the way in which financial and non-financial information is communicated and reported towards external stakeholders.

2   Data Management

The development of information technologies often represent a great opportunity for companies. With the passage of time, technological innovations have changed the way in which companies manage and process their information to support reliable decision-making processes, considering, for example, the importance of data warehouse architecture for the development of the business intelligence, or the relevance of multimedia technologies for the adoption of new form of economic and financial communication.

Every IT innovation requires research and studies in order to understand its potentiality and discover its practical implications for firms. Regarding accounting and management information systems, the most immediate impact of IT is on data management, i.e. the way in which companies manage data processing in order to obtain reliable information. Initially, automation helped companies to gain efficiency in the accounting data management for financial and administrive purposes, subsequently, some other benefits emerged as timeliness of information processes and reliability of information and reporting [1], and finally, some integration issues have been highlighted [3, 4]. Integration represents not only an implication of IT, but also a different way to see processes and organisation through IT.

Today firms live in a digitalised world and have to take into account digital technologies not only for strategic and competitive aims, but also for their implications on accounting information and management control systems. Many studies have investigated how digital technologies affect business models, competitive advantages and firms' approach to markets. Low attention is paid to the study of the implications of digital technologies on the way in which firms manage information and control activities for their competitive success. The investigation of the relationship between digital technologies and accounting information systems and management control processes is just at the beginning and requires greater attention.

Digitalisation is not only a technological innovation but implies a different philosophy in the way in which companies manage their business and processes. Some keywords characterise the philosophy of digital technology are ubiquity, openness and sharing [5]. Data and information have to be freely available and have to flow free and without restrictions among organisations or groups of people. Moreover, data and information come from collaboration and co-creation, i.e. a broader vision of firms business based on openness and engagement. Finally, data and information have to be organised and managed to facilitate sharing and re-using.

The most immediate impact of these technologies is on data management that is the process companies follow to collect, select, classify, process data and communicate and share information. In this section, we present four papers which deal with that topic.

Bruno et al. investigate the role of data management and data quality in credit risk control in small Italian banks. These kinds of banks use external databases to collect data for credit risk control; in fact, they outsource their information systems because of poor financial resources. The research highlights that the adoption of an outsourced data management improves the quality and quantity of data processed and determines an enhancement of the knowledge of the risk profile of banks' portfolio.

Trizio et al. develop a digital system to collect data for risk evaluation in three hospital laboratories. The research highlights how the integration between information technologies (sensor to monitor physical environmental conditions, data platform to collect different flows of data, etc.) and information systems (standardisation of languages, codification of risk type, etc.) are key elements to develop an information system able to collect flows of data from different hospitals and to forward them to a digital smart platform in order to evaluate the level of risk and the level of compliance with law and regulations.

The last two papers consider cloud computing and its impacts on firms as a non-traditional way to manage data and information.

Caldarelli et al. examine benefits and problems of cloud computing in small and medium enterprises during the implementation and the post-implementation phases. The study highlights that in the implementation phase some benefits emerge, as cost savings, flexibility and scalability of the information system, but for the firms examined, IT cost reduction is the most important factor during the decision-making processes. Regarding the post-implementation phase, the most important effects are a strong reduction of IT costs and energy savings, while there are no disadvantages.

The paper of Di Martino et al. takes into account the legal implication of cloud computing, especially in terms of privacy, as an obstacle for moving firms towards the cloud technology. The research proposes an interesting model useful to measure if the provider is compliant with law in terms of security, trust and privacy. The compliance model is based on two key technologies: XML and semantic-web.

3 Information Systems Architecture

Information Systems Architecture (ISA) seems to represent a relevant tool for the firms to achieve success in a period characterised by several digital innovations [6, 7].

New technologies arise from a combination of existing technologies and from the desire to accomplish new goals. To manage the complexity of innovation in the middle of technological change, an ISA constitutes a strategic tool that, properly orchestrated, can be used to link historical scope and future potentialities [7]. ISA is an instrument which permits to produce opportunities in the digital era for the creation of an innovation path. Whether companies will be able to transform innovation practices and leverage opportunities of digital technology depend, to a significant degree, on their ability to enrich new architectural perspectives that match with the opportunity afforded by digital technology.

In other words, firms need to have flexible business information systems to adapt them to new digital innovations. The flexibility of Information Systems to create business value depends, principally, on the flexibility of ISA [8]. For example, the possibility to modify subsidiary functionality, add supplemental functionality or introduce entirely new functionality could represent a potential solution to carry out a match between information systems and digital innovations [7].

ISA, as noted above, is playing a critical role in innovating a firm's business model towards e-business model. In general, business model means a realised business design to create business value based on business vision and strategy to deal with related concerned parties. On the other hand, e-business means business conducted by utilising methods brought by new IT. Concerning ISA, we have to deal with not only intra-organisational business architecture but also inter-organisational business architecture. Thus, we should seek to discuss ISA including the relationship between firms like banking, vendors, suppliers and shareholders and consider an extended ISA.

Considering its relevance, also the roles and skills of those actors involved when applying ISA are key success factors. It is a critical element to have senior executive aware of the benefits of ISA. However, this include not only the CIO and IT managers but also the CEO, COO and line-of-business managers. If the top management of a firm improves cognition with regard to ISA, the effect and the benefits of ISA will be higher [8].

Another central success factor is to have a governance model able to control processes, rules, standards and organisation structure, which are needed to drive the ISA initiatives. Even if firms have established ISA, they would not have maintained it without a Governance mechanism for a long time. It is necessary that ISA reflect the latest developments and support the collaboration and communication in which all stakeholders are involved. From an ISA point of view, Governance should take into consideration that it consists of IT principle, IT architecture, IT investment and management framework.

Thus, ISA effectiveness seems to depend upon the following perspectives:

- Developing a flexible architecture for Information Systems to process high data volume in an effective way.
- Developing an extended ISA to support collaboration and communication in which all stakeholders involved.
- Driving ISA cognition for senior management level.
- Creating a governance model to support the effectiveness development of ISA.

However, information system literature is almost silent on how digital innovation impacts on ISA. Information system literature rarely considers how ISA influences strategic choices of the firms and related IT deployments. This is unfortunate because changes in product architecture and organising logic reshape the landscape of information system strategy and use in firms. The digitalisation of physical products challenges some of the fundamental assumptions about architecture and organising logic.

In the last decade, information systems scholars have mainly analysed the impacts of digital innovation on firms' strategies, structures and process. Similar progresses have been made to understand the role of information technology in creating business value and developing sustainable competitive advantage [7, 9].

However, in the context of digital technologies literature shows that innovation influences architecture and, on the contrary, architecture shapes innovation. While some studies [10] analyse the impact of digital innovation on ISA, others [11, 12] examine the role ISA plays in the innovation process.

Among the few studies that analyse the impact of digital innovation on ISA, there is the research of Yoo et al.

In their study, Yoo et al. propose that digital innovation gave birth to a new type of architecture: the layered modular architecture. Authors conceive it "as an hybrid of the modular architecture of a physical product and the layered architecture of digital technology".

The modular architecture presents a framework by which a physical product can be decomposed into components that can be recombined. It permits "to reduce complexity and to increase flexibility in design by decomposing a product into loosely coupled components interconnected through specified interfaces" [9].

The layered architecture derives from the characteristics of digital technology and is considered as an important consequence of the digitalisation of product and services. This type of architecture consists of four layers: devices, networks, services and contents. The device layer is further articulated in physical machinery (e.g. computer and hardware) and logical capability (e.g. operating system). The role of logical capability layer is to offer a control and maintenance of the physical machine and to link the physical machine to other layers. Also the network layer can be further divided into physical transport (e.g. cables, transmitters) and logical transmission (e.g. network standards such as TCP/IP or peer to peer protocols). The service layer regards application functionality that directly serves users to create, manipulate, store and consume contents. The content layer contains data such as texts, sounds, images and videos that are stored and shared.

The layered modular architecture combines characteristics of the layered and the modular architecture adding other features: the generativity, "a technology's over-all capacity to produce unprompted change driven by large, varied and uncoordinated audiences" [13].

This means that the design of a component is not driven by the functional requirements created within the context of a given product. That is, components in a layered modular architecture are not product specific, but are defined "product agnostic".[1] In this regard, layers are coupled through standards and protocols shared by heterogeneous firms. For example, Google's designers cannot fully anticipate all the possible ways that Google maps as components will be used.

With a layered modular architecture, a digitised product can be at the same time a product and a platform. "For example, an iPad can be used as a complete product out of the box. Yet, as a platform, it enables other firms to invent novel components such as new applications and peripheral hardware accessories with which its basic functionality can be expanded" ([10]: 728). In a competitive era, firms use a layered modular architecture to produce digital product platforms, which can function as a new product, but at the same time can enable others to innovate upon using firm-

---

[1]"Google Maps, for example, consists of a bundle of contents (i.e. maps) and service (e.g. search, browse, traffic and navigation) layers with different interfaces (i.e. application programming interfaces). Though Google Maps can be used as a stand-alone product, it can simultaneously be used in a variety of different ways, bundled with a host of heterogenous devices such as desktop computers, mobile phones, televisions, cars, navigation systems, or digital cameras" ([10]: 728).

controlled platform resources. The generativity of a layered modular architecture represents the company's capability to project a product platform characterised by heterogeneous components that belong to different design hierarchies.

In this context, the new invention is distributed not only among firms of the same type but also across firms of different kinds. Furthemore, the firm's innovation activities influence reciprocally also other companies creating the image of "wake of innovation". Thus, the organising logic of a layered modular architecture is defined as "doubly distributed" ([10]: 730). It is distributed because the "main source of value creation is the generativity that comes from the unbounded mix-and-match capabililty of heterogeneous resources across layers". It is doubly distributed because "the control over product components is distributed across multiple firms and the product knowledge is distributed across heterogeneous disciplines and communities" [10: 730].

A large number of studies [11, 12, 14, 15] analyse, instead, the role ISA plays in the innovation process.

Some studies [14, 15] examine the role played by architecture for the success of the innovation process in a case where the new technology is the information infrastructure. In general, this research has revealed that architectures shape the way information infrastructure evolution is planned and managed.

These studies show how both the complexity levels of the architecture and the organising of the project activities concerning the number of the stakeholders involved influence the success of the innovation processes. More sophisticated and articulated architectures tend to form complex systems that are challenging to create in practice, require a high level of stakeholders coordination and may be too expensive to modify in future revisions [14]. On the contrary, more simplified architectures which follow a gradual growth and require the involvement of a number of stakeholders tend to create systems more flexible [16].

Grisot et al. (2014) analyse the role architecture plays in the success of the innovation process in a case where new technology is an information infrastructure and address what are the conditions for successful infrastructural innovations. From the case study analysis, the authors show architecture must have a level of modularisation that satisfies the needs for flexibility to modify the Information Infrastructure for the changes produced by new digital innovations.

Gaaloul et al.'s study focuses on the cloud technology and considers architecture as a good instrument to "analyse the current state of the enterprise and guard the cohesion and alignment between different aspects of an enterprise such as business process and their ICT". IT architecture is considered an imperative for businesses that want to successfully adopt cloud computing in a way that aligns to their business strategy.

The six papers selected in this section discuss information systems architecture considering the relationship with the following elements:

– Cloud technology
– Digital platforms
– Strategic management accounting

Two of the six papers analyse cloud technology but with two different scopes.

Candiotto and Candini study the impact of cloud infrastructure on value creation opportunities for companies that decide to apply this type of innovation, while Ficco and Rank propose a method for security controls selection for a cloud-based service. In both papers, ISA represents a relevant element to enable an effectiveness implementation and usage of the cloud infrastructure.

In particular, in the study of Candiotto and Gandini IT architecture represents a tool to create value, because it permits to identify and implement the organisation's strategic objectives for implementing cloud infrastructure from a technical point of view. The case studies analysed in the paper show that IT architecture represents one of the elements which differ between the firms and constitutes a relevant variable which influences the impact of cloud on value creation opportunities for companies. Therefore, similar projects from a technical point of view can lead companies to use cloud to improve their customer value proposition.

In the paper of Ficco and Rank, the relevance of the architecture for the success of cloud service implementation is analysed from another point of view. The focus of the paper is on the security controls for cloud service, defined as guidelines to identify and prioritise security actions which are effective against cyber threats. In this research, architecture represents one of the most important elements to be control, because it is used to implement cloud service and determine its real effectiveness.

Three of the six papers, instead, focus on another typology of digital innovation: the digital platforms.

Regarding the relationship between innovations and accounting and management information systems, all the case studies analysed in these papers highlight that the characterisitcs of digital platform influence the ISA.

In their paper, Bellini and Fiore present a platform able to gather the events occurring along the social media timeline and to build a tailored visualisation/ summarisation of these data with price movements of a given stock or index. According to the study of Yoo et al., it is possible to affirm that the necessity to development a new digital platform paves the way for a new architecture. The architecture of the digital platform consists of functional blocks covering all the phases of the social media data processing chain: data collection, deployment of different analysis and transformations and summarisation and visualisation. Similarly to the layered architecture, the TrendMiner architecture seems to be constituted of four layers: devices to monitoring different social media sources; networks; processing services; and contents coming from Twitter, news and financial markets. The processing services are classified into two groups depending on their usage in the processing life cycle. The first group performs the resources pre-processing regardless of any context of usage. The results produced by these components are stored in the data repository and serve as a base for subsequent data searching and browsing. The second group of services computes collective analytical information based on user-defined context and resources selection. Finally, a presentation layer service provides an abstraction over the actual data prior to its presentation to the financial (and also political) analyst (end user).

Corsi et al. investigate the contribution of digital platform to management control system. The case study analysed in the paper shows that digital platform has represented an opportunity to support and enhance the effectiveness of architecture understood as the structure of the information system, the integration and consistency of its components. In particular, regarding the structure of the information digital platform has permitted a more compliant and transparent information flow. As regards, instead, the integration and consistency of components, digital platform contains tools to share information, to manage information from an office to another, to publish and share ideas, objectives and information in a well-defined community and to organise and manage digital documents to improve efficiency in administrative processes.

Also the paper of Di Vaio and Varriale confirms this relationship. The adoption of an information technology platform in the Port Authorities has facilitated the data collection and the information management. In particular, the use of the information technology platform permits to develop an architecture of inter-organisational relationships system for the information and data sharing, which allows to connect many port users with minimal linkages.

Inghirami's paper focuses on the role of Strategic Management Accounting (SMA) and analyses the definition and the use of SMA in a medium-sized company. In this context, ISA seems to have a central role in the implementation of the SMA systems. Author highlights as the literature does not consider the implementation aspects of SMA systems and does not assess the potential related to Information Technology. Case study analysis confirms the initial hypothesis of the research, showing that a robust IT architecture is the only capable of collecting and processing information necessary for the implementation of the SMA.

4 Internal Reporting

Integration is still one of the keywords that characterises the studies on management control reporting. New competitive and technological challenges trigger a development in the managers' information needs. As a consequence, new variables deserve to be monitored and managed and the information systems have to be developed accordingly in order to fulfil the information gap.

A growing body of research proposes for example the inclusion in the management control system of variables representing sustainability, corporate social responsibility and environmental initiatives [17]. The integration of these new variables in the management reporting generally produces, among others, the following advantages [18]:

– Operationalisation of objectives.
– Broader managers and stakeholders' accountability.
– Intensified interactions with stakeholders.
– Formalisation of organisation beliefs.
– Improvement of internal communication.

The development of the information systems, though, may not be limited to the inclusion of new variables that need to be managed in order to achieve the strategic purposes. New techniques of data processing may also be particularly fruitful.

Recently, big data and business analytics have raised a remarkable interest among academics and practitioners, given the huge amount of data that Internet and mobile application as well as social media allow to produce and store.

Big data represent one of the hot trend of the 2010s, according to the IBM Tech Trends Report [19]. Companies are increasing their investments in techniques, information resources and competences related to big data, in order to get valuable insights into customers, employees, suppliers and all the other strategic partners that might support the creation of a durable competitive advantage.

Lainey [20] in 2001 attempted to describe in a framework the characteristics of the future information systems applications: volumes, velocity and variety. After a decade in 2012, these terms have represented the blocks on which Gartner Group created the definition of Big Data: *Big Data is high Volume, high Velocity, and/or high Variety information assets that require new forms of processing to enable enhanced decision-making, insight discovery and process optimization.*

According to Capgemini [21], companies use big data mainly to gain four kinds of advantages:

- Efficiency and cost focus.
- Growth of existing business streams.
- Growth through market disruption from new revenue streams.
- Monetisation of data itself, with the creation of new lines of business.

Opportunities for cost reduction may arise, for example, from a deep analysis of the supply chain as well as other operational processes whose value may not be perceived as relevant by the customers. But also risk management and fraud detection may represent a relevant source for cost reduction.

Several companies also employ big data techniques to deepen their knowledge about customers, in order to develop value propositions even more suitable in order to maximise the possibilities to generate revenues from the existing markets. The emerging customer needs may be discovered by sieving social media, clickstream data and other customer analytics, and the knowledge generated can drive innovative offerings and solutions. Also, the effectiveness of marketing and sales initiatives is particularly monitored.

Big data may also offer opportunities to create new revenues by a market disruption, that is, a change in the business model, driven by an increasing knowledge about customers which allows companies to propose additional and specific digital services.

Finally, data itself may represent a source of new revenues when the company who own them has the opportunity to sell them.

The research on big data involves the information science primarily, but also all the disciplines that have realised the potential of working with diverse and large datasets: health care, public health, education, public policy, government studies, marketing and retail, finance, etc. [22]. Some of the research streams in this field relate for example to data infrastructure (which particularly involves computer science and electrical engineering disciplines), Analytics, and Decision Support Systems, which is a more interdisciplinary field of studies and generally refers to the generation of knowledge and intelligence to support decision-making and strategic objectives.

The contributions collected in this section of the volume may be generally referred to the integration of new variables and methodologies in order to improve decision-making. The above mentioned topics are considered under quite different perspectives, but at the same time the papers present some common points. In particular, two papers refer to universities investigating the adoption of a new accounting system (Bonollo et al.) and the design of a performance measurement system aimed to signal, in particular, the criticalities impacting on the time needed by students to complete their bachelor's or master's degree (Giovanelli et al.).

Bonollo, Lazzini and Zuccardi Merli analyse the introduction of an accrual-based accounting system in Italian universities, traditionally characterised by a "cash- and commitment-based" accounting system. The new regulation aims to force universities to implement a responsibility accounting system in order to make the managers aware of an effective allocation of resources, strictly coherent with the institutional strategic purposes in the mid term.

Universities are also required to prepare a mandatory yearly budget referred to the overall organisation, in order to estimate the expected revenues and authorise the maximum level of expenses and investments accordingly. The budget is obtained by consolidating all the items referred to the peripheral administrative units, such as departments, research centres, service units and all the other relevant responsibility centres.

The hypothesis formulated is that the wide impacts produced by the regulatory innovations produce consequences not limited to the accounting system but as well on the distribution of roles and responsibilities among the players involved in the operating process and in their accounting representation.

In the paper, the administrative activities adopted to manage the research projects are described by comparing two universities which decided to adopt the new system earlier than when requested by law. The evidences collected support the above-mentioned assumption: the change in the accounting systems does not only require that technical problems are to be solved, but also organisational changes are involved. The changes require in particular a wider involvement and integration of competences and responsibilities between the actors operating in the central and peripheral administrative units. In particular, the integration occurs under three different perspectives:

- The accounting systems employed in the central and peripheral units.
- The responsibilities required for the accounting representation of the operational processes.
- The decision-making activities.

Giovanelli, Rotondo and Marinò develop a scorecard suitable to measure and control the most relevant factors affecting the students' career in a bachelor's or a master's degree, held by an Italian public university. The scorecard is designed with the intent to improve, as strategic purpose, the performance of didactic, which is a perspective deeply considered by the national Ministry of University, which in recent years developed to this purpose a specific didactic quality assurance system that universities have to be compliant with.

In the explorative study, the scorecard is designed considering either the legislative requirements and the main scientific contributions. The measure adopted to evaluate the overall success of the teaching activity is the average time needed by students to get their degree. Its determinants are classified by considering three stages of a student's career: the enrolment to the course of study, the intermediate stage, which covers all the graduation period, and the post-graduation stage.

The success during the enrolment stage is conditioned by all the actions that universities take to attract students strongly motivated and properly skilled, who are more likely to succeed in the challenge with the disciplines included in the course of study. The performance measured in this section of the scorecard is the result of all the initiatives adopted to attract new full-time or part-time students. Generally, the initiatives pertaining to the enrolment stage should require a rather low absorption in terms of financial resources.

During the intermediate stage, the productivity of students is monitored. The productivity is intended as the number of credits earned by the students during each term. The abandonment rate is also monitored. The measure used in a scorecard for a bachelor's degree should differentiate the results obtained during the first year, which is considered particularly critical for the newcomers. In the second and third year, the students' satisfaction referred to the specific disciplines and the mobility rates are also monitored. Specific measures are also considered for the last term of the bachelor's degree: the rate of students who graduate on time and their level of satisfaction are included in the scorecard.

In the third section of the scorecard, the student's post-graduation career is considered and all the alternative way-outs are measured: application to post-bachelor programmes or employment rate within 1 or 3 years from graduation.

Of course, the development of a suitable management accounting system is needed to measure the indicators included in the scorecard and the initiatives expected to produce an impact on them. This could represent a critical aspect especially for the collection of external data included in the third perspective of the scorecard.

A public environment is considered as well in the study of Obreja, Ross and Bednar. In particular, the authors summarise some reflections concerning the factors that may condition the successful implementation of intelligent agents in health care, considering the perspective of the several stakeholders.

An intelligent agent is a software which simulates the cognitive and judgement processes of the human brain to produce expert knowledge valid to support decision-making. As a difference from human brain, intelligent agents are able to process huge amounts of structured and unstructured data, finding interesting regularities which can support a wide range of information needs.

The authors base their reflections on a review of the literature and on case studies mainly sponsored by vendors of intelligent agents' software.

The implementation of an intelligent agent may be interesting for hospitals intended as socio-technical systems, in order to adopt an integrated thinking perspective and rationalise the data storage and the data flow among the several users (medical personnel, administrative staff, management board, etc.).

Under the administrative decision-makers' perspective, the adoption of intelligent agents is effective when an improvement in the standard quality of care or in the efficiency (being all other conditions equal) is allowed. Their adoption, on the other hand, may raise several ethical implications, particularly when intelligent agents are adopted as a diagnostic support.

Also the paper of Castellano and Del Gobbo contains some reflections about the adoption of intelligent agents, but the context of their research is different, since they refer to a private company. In particular, the authors intend to describe how organisational heterogeneity may influence the perceptions of the managers involved in the strategic planning, about the knowledge generated by the adoption of a data mining tool.

The tool—a Structured Neural Network (SNN)—is employed with a confirmative rather than an explorative approach. The information produced summarises the perceptions of customers about how the variables included in the business plan are relevant in order to improve the customer satisfaction and profitability, in turn.

The managers involved in the strategic planning are then free to express and share their opinions and knowledge about the key factors and the most suitable initiatives, and once the business plan is completed, they can test its reliability in the light of the information produced by the SNN. A requirement for the adoption of the SNN is that the strategic plan needs to be deployed through a causal map. The tool in particular allowes managers to measure the strength of the expected causal relation as perceived by customers.

The organisational heterogeneity, intended as the differences in the mix of characteristics of the managers (educational background, level of experience, "confidence with numbers"), may enable or hinder the perceived usefulness of the results obtained through the information tool.

The results provide slight evidence that the data mining tool may improve the strategic capability even when the managers do not hold similar competencies and educational background. The results also show that the successful adoption of the SNN has been positively conditioned by the mental attitude of the CEO that played a key role in determining the general acceptance of the results by all other managers and the effectiveness of information produced in driving decision-making.

5   External Reporting

In literature, several theories are used to provide theoretical explanation of external report, such as the agency theory, the political economy theory, the legitimacy theory, the stakeholder theory, the signalling theory and the proprietary costs theory [23]. According to Verrecchia [24], the starting point of every disclosure theory is the reduction of information asymmetry between insiders and outsiders. Particularly, the agency theory considers the disclosure as the main instrument to reduce the information asymmetry between principals and agents and to resolve agency problems. This theory was initially focused on the financial disclosure and the relationship between managers (agents) and shareholders (principals); it was subsequently extended to voluntary disclosure and applied to different contexts, as the public sector in which several agency relationships between the elected officials, managers and citizens take place.

In the last two decades, there was a growing emphasis on the corporate disclosure: in private sector, this is linked to the attempt of improving companies' governance after some scandals and during the crisis [25]; in public sector, this is linked to the continuing pressure to provide information on managers' activities and outcomes produced.

So, the external reporting has became a critical activity to acquire consensus and trust of outsiders, ensuring survival and success of a company. In this context, information technology increased, in several ways, information potentials, effectiveness and efficiency of the external reporting. The information technology, and particularly the growing importance of Internet, contributed to change many aspects of external reporting, both formal and substantial ones.

In recent years, a digital and open standardised language has been proposed and applied to financial reports of private companies: XBRL (eXtensible Business Reporting Language). This language aims to make financial data readable and understandable by any software, improving transparency and increasing the efficiency through savings in terms of time, costs, resources and risks of error. But the traditional report has also progressively increased its contents, communicating information on corporate social responsibility, ethics and environmental issues, intellectual capital and other information more closely linked to value creation and more useful for the decision-making process of stakeholders.

Internet increases the dissemination of information, their flexibility, versatility and timeliness, and it contributes to foster stakeholder involvement and, in terms of agency theory, increases accountability of agents and allows principals to control the agents' activities [26–28]. These advantages can exceed traditional disadvantages of e-disclosure, such as information overload, information accuracy and security issues.

Recently, companies need to move beyond the traditional use of the Internet, as a means of communication, and to embrace the new technologies, known as Web 2.0, social media. These regard collaborative tools such as social networks, blogs, wikis, which open up new potentials for disclosure and improve the relationship between companies and their stakeholders [5]. The new technologies are available for all the companies and are able to create a bidirectional communication: they amplify the pre-existing unidirectional communication system and generate a corporate dialogue, through active and real-time interactions between the entity and its stakeholders (collaboration) and through an implicit set of mutually beneficial outcomes (engagement) [29].

These new technologies are also very important in the public sector, as evidenced by four of the seven selected papers in this section. The public sector entities show great needs of increase and improve the disclosure for two reasons. Firstly, for corporate policy in order to create an engagement with citizens and to increase their participation in government, but also to enhance internal knowledge management. Secondly, for being compliant with recent legislative reforms and governmental initiatives aimed to increase transparency and accountability in public sector.

Bonson et al. (2012) show that the tools of web 2.0 have four different impacts in this field, improving (1) transparency, (2) policymaking, (3) public services and (4) knowledge management and cross-agency cooperation.

The seven papers selected in this section discuss the external reporting, focusing on several aspects which can increase the transparency and improve the efficiency and effectiveness of private or public companies disclosure. Particularly, they analyse the following main aspects:

– The AIS integration
– The new tools of mandatory and voluntary disclosure, some with particular attention to human capital information.
– Standard digital format, such as the XBRL.

Mancini and Lamboglia deal with the first topic. The authors firstly analyse the polyhedral concept of transparency in public sector, pointing out its different forms and several approaches of study in literature, and secondly they agree to a wide concept of transparency, including publication of information on website, accessibility, information effectiveness, usability and interactivity. Basing on the dynamic relationship between the transparency and ICT, the paper proposes an interesting theoretical framework to correlate the transparency effectiveness to different levels of AIS integration. Accepting that the integration of information system can be realised on data, communication networks connectivity and communication networks flexibility, the authors propose three different and progressively higher levels of integration: 1) Part Integration, 2) Full System Integration and 3) Full Information Integration. Similarly, the authors carry out a threefold distinction regarding the transparency: 1) Formal transparency (characterised only by information publication), 2) Quality transparency (characterised by a high level for "public information" and "Accessibility, information effectiveness and usability" but a low level for "Interactivity") and 3) Full transparency (with higher levels of all dimensions of transparency). The paper offers a usefulness model for the future researches, showing how higher levels of AIS integration contribute to improve the transparency, ensuring its effectiveness and interactivity.

Four papers focus on information that companies provide to the market through old and new tools such as Web 2.0, social media, blogs, etc., and conduct empirical researches in private and public sector.

Gesuele and Metallo, considering the increasing importance of e-disclosure in public sector (also confirmed by specific laws, e.g. Decree 10/2009 and Decree 33/2013), examine the determinants of mandatory and voluntary e-disclosure diffusion by Italian municipalities. This paper contributes to enrich the wide literature aimed to measure companies' disclosure. The authors, indeed, propose two new interesting indices for measuring mandatory disclosure, diffused through website, and voluntary disclosure, spread by social media such as Facebook and Twitter. In order to understand the factors influencing e-disclosure diffusion by municipalities, the authors identify several determinants concerning the environmental, political-social and economic status-based aspects of sampled municipalities. Findings from the data analysis, carried by statistical regressions, show that the size of the municipality (in terms of population) and citizens' wealth (in terms of the value of economic activity per capita) positively affect the use of website for information disclosure. The municipality's size influences also the usage of social media. The paper reveals particular results, which deserve a possible further study: the disclosure through social media is positively affected by the political position (in terms of political ideology of municipal ruling parties) but is negatively influenced by the geographical position and the municipalities' type.

The issue of e-disclosure in public sector is dealt also by Lepore and Pisano, but with a different perspective, considering the relationship between the e-disclosure and performance. This work starts from the assumption that e-disclosure, and particularly the diffusion of data performance through Internet, allows a social control, providing to citizens (that are the main lenders of public administrations) a more easy way to activate an evaluation process of how the public administration spends public money. This could increase the level of transparency and accountability and consequently improve the efficiency and effectiveness of management of local government authorities (LGA). The authors aim to test the dependence of the performance of public organisations by the e-disclosure but also by the media interest (as media and newspaper), which disclose the performance data to stakeholder, stimulating their social control and public opinion. This work represents a quantitative analysis carried out on 162 Italian local government authorities. Through a regression model, a performance index (financial autonomy) is correlated to e-disclosure and degree of media interest perceived by each LGA but also to other control variables. Even if the findings partially confirm the initial hypothesis, they are very interesting. The no significant relationship between perfomance and e-disclosure, emerging from analysis, suggests that higher level of e-disclosure does not necessarily generate greater accountability. This shows that the greater e-disclosure is only symbolic, associated more with a formal transparency than with accountability and consequently with social control. Conversely, the analysis shows a relevant role that media could have in stimulating a social control. These results could be very useful to improve the communication policies of local government authorities.

The other two papers, regarding the disclosure issue, focus on intellectual capital (IC) and especially on human capital (HC) reporting. This type of disclosure provides information on knowledge, capabilities, networks, operation processes, organisational relations, etc.: this is aimed to inform the stakeholders on company's ability to create value and to be socially responsible, generating trustworthiness with the market capital.

The first paper is more in line with those mentioned above because it is focused on information concerning human capital and transmitted through Web. In this work, the authors (Pisano, Lepore and Alvino) provide an interesting twofold methodological and cognitive contribution. Indeed, they propose a new index to measure human capital disclosure, more extensive than those already available in literature: it considers not only the stock of knowledge and human capabilities but also the human resource management practices. Examining the website of Italian listed companies and several documents presented there, the authors find a higher level of HC disclosure compared to previous studies and a greater amount of information in qualitative form. These findings are probably due to the wider index used in this work: this new index allows us to better understand the firms' behaviors regarding the information released on human capital, and it presents high potential for future research on this topic.

The second paper regarding the IC disclosure differs from the previous because it focuses on consequences of this disclosure on market capital and on firm's reputation. This paper provides a theoretical and operational contribution to the prevailing literature which mainly focuses on the quantity and quality of the IC information, disclosed by firms: this paper, indeed, aims to investigate if and how the IC management affects financial analysts' recommendation, helping managers to understand the positive and unintended effects of released voluntary information. The authors (Demartini, Panaro, Trucco) analyse the effect that IC performance disclosed has on the information risk, measured as the way in which the market is informed about the firm performance. The IC performance is examined in its three components (relational, human, structural capital), and the findings show that the human capital performance (represented by variables regarding average training, turnover of employees, training hours total) mostly affects, in a positive way, information risk of a company.

Last but not least, two papers in this section deal with the XBRL adoption. Both focus on the taxonomy XBRL issue, albeit in different contexts: one in public organisations, and the other in Italian industrial companies, which adopt IFRS.

Bonollo carries out a theoretical analysis to understand whether XBRL could be easily adopted by Italian public organisations. The authors examines the several benefits and critical aspects linked to XBRL adoption in public sector. Standard digital format for disclosure has many benefits, such as costs reduction, saving of time, and errors due to re-enter data in different reports; improvement of mandatory control; increase of transparency and accountability; support of development of e-government. Conversely, the main critical aspect in adopting XBRL in public sector is to define a standard classification system of financial information (XBRL taxonomy) for several different AISs used by organisations: just think of State central administration, Local governments administrations, Universities, local health-care organisations and others. In order to facilitate the XBRL adoption in aforementioned organisations, Bonollo considers the pros and cons of the existing coding systems used by organisations (e.g. SIOPE, Information System on Public Organisations' Operations; COFOG, Classification of the Functions of Government; The Integrated Chart of Accounts) to understand whether they could be used as a basis for the development of an XBRL taxonomy. From this comparative analysis, the author identifies the Integrated Chart of Accounts as the most appropriate coding system for this purpose. Its codes are sufficiently analytical and shared and it may offer a list of items for the XBRL taxonomy.

Fradeani et al. deal with the degree of compatibility the XBRL taxonomy for the companies adopting IFRS. This paper has an operational value: it represents a first step of a wider project launched in 2011 by XBRL Italy in order to assess the viability of IFRS XBRL taxonomy for communication needs of involved companies. The authors, through an empirical research, focus on two main and correlated problems: the translation and the possible extension of taxonomy. Indeed, the official translation does not imply the use of a specific terminology or a specific level of detail, and the possibility of extension of taxonomy represents a means to overcome this problem. At the basis of this work, we find the idea that the IFRS XBRL taxonomy, without resolving the problems of translation and allowing a possible extension, could represent an element of rigidity for IFRS financial disclosure, created to provide the more and better information to stakeholders. Finally, the authors propose a set of actions to be implemented within the project of XBRL Italy Group, in order to reach a certain consistency between the translation of the IFRS Bound Volume and the IFRS XBRL labels.

References

1. Marchi, L. (2003). *I sistemi informativi aziendali*. Milano: Giuffrè.
2. Oliviero, G., & Castellano, N. (2012). Information systems design for reporting and strategic purposes: Evidences from a case study. *Management Control, 3*, 69–93.
3. Marchi, L. (2011). Editoriale, Management control, 1.
4. Rom, A., & Rohde, C. (2007). Management accounting and integrated information systems: A literature review. *International Journal of Accounting Information Systems, 8*, 40–68.
5. Mancini, D. (2016). Accounting information systems in an open society. *Emerging Trends and Issues, Management Control, 1*, 5–16.
6. Montilva, J., Barrios, J., & Besembel, I. (2013) *A process model based on Enterprise Architecture for ICT management*. Latin American computing conference.
7. Henfridsson, O., Mathiassen, L., & Svahn, F. (2014). Managing technological change in the digital age: The role of architectural frames. *Journal of Information Technology, 29*, 27–43.
8. Kamogawa, T., & Okada, H. (2005). A framework for enterprise architecture effectiveness. *IEEE Xplore, 9*(4), 740–745.
9. Yoo, Y., Lyytinen, K., Boland, R., Berente, J., Gaskin, J., Schutz, D., & Srinivasan, N. (2010) *The next wave of digital innovation: Opportunities and challenges*. Report on the research workshop "Digital challenges in innovation research". http://ssrn.com/

10. Yoo, Y., Henfridsson, O., & Lyytinen, K. (2010). The new organizing logic of digital innovation: An agenda for information systems research. *Information Systems Research, 21*, 724–735.
11. Gaaloul, K., Yangui, S., Tata, S., & Proper, H. A. (2014). *Architecting access control for business processes in the cloud.* International workshop on advanced information systems for enterprises.
12. Grisot, M., Hanseth, O., & Thorseng, A. A. (2014). Innovation of, in, on infrastructures: Articulating the role of architecture in information infrastructure evolution. *Journal of the Association for Information Systems, 15*(Special Issue), 197–219.
13. Zittrain, J. (2006). The generative internet. *Harvard Law Review, 119*, 1974–2040.
14. Aanestad, M., & Jensen, T. (2011). Building nation-wide information infrastructure in healthcare through modula implementation strategies. *Journal of Strategic Information Systems, 20*(2), 161–176.
15. Hanseth, O., Bygstad, B., Ellingsen, G., Johannesen, L. K., & Larsen E. (2012). *ICT standardization strategies and service innovation in health care.* Thirty third international conference of information systems, Orlando.
16. Sahay, S., Monteiro, E., & Aanestad, M. (2009). Configurable politics and asymmetric integration: Health e-infrastructures in India. *Journal of the Association for Information Systems, 10*(5), 399–414. Special issue on e-infrastructure.
17. Johnson, M. P. (2015). Sustainability management and small and medium-sized enterprises: Managers' awareness and implementation of innovative tools. *Corporate Social Responsibility and Environmental Management, 22*(5), 271–285.
18. Kerr, J., Rouse, P., & De Villiers, C. (2015). Sustainability reporting integrated into management control systems. *Pacific Accounting Review, 27*(2), 189–207.
19. IBM. (2011, November 15). The 2011 IBM Tech trends report: The clouds are rolling in. . .is your business ready?
20. Lainey, D. (2001). 3D data management: Controlling data volume, velocity, and variety. http://blogs.gartner.com/doug-laney/files/2012/01/ad949-3D-Data-Management-Controlling-Data-Volume-Velocity-and-Variety.pdf
21. Capgemini. (2015). Big & fast data: The rise of insight-driven business.
22. Goes, P. B. (2014). Big data and IS research. *MIS Quarterly, 38*(3), III–VIII.
23. Khlifi, F., & Bouri, A. (2010). Corporate disclosure and firm characteristics: A puzzling relationship. *Journal of Accounting–Business and Management, 17*(1), 62–89.
24. Verrecchia, R. (2001). Essays on disclosure. *Journal of Accounting and Economics, 32*(1–3), 97–180.
25. Stewart, J., Asha, F., Shulman, A., & Ng, C. (2012). Governance disclosure on the internet: The case of Australian State Government Departments. *Australian Journal of Public Administration, 71*(4), 440–456.
26. Marston, C., & Polei, A. (2002). Corporate reporting on the internet by German companies. *International Journal of Accounting Information Systems, 5*(3), 285–311.
27. Gandia, J. L. (2008). Determinants of internet base corporate governance disclosure by Spanish listed companies. *Online Information Review, 32*(1), 791–817.
28. Tagesson, T., Blank, V., Broberg, P., & Collin, S. O. (2009). What explains the extent and content of social and environmental disclosures on corporate websites: A study of social and enviromental reporting in Swedish listed corporations. *Corporate Social Responsibility and Environmental Management, 16*, 352–364.
29. Bonsón, E., Torres, L., Royo, S., & Flores, F. (2012). Local e-government 2.0: Social media and corporate transparency in municipalities. *Government Information Quarterly, 29*, 123–132.

Data Quality and Data Management in Banking Industry. Empirical Evidence from Small Italian Banks

Elena Bruno, Giuseppina Iacoviello, and Arianna Lazzini

Abstract This chapter addresses the problems created by fragmentation of performance management systems, i.e. having different systems for storing, reporting and analysing data for different business functions, locations and units. These problems are the result of organizations focusing IT investment on systems that support the efficient day-to-day operations, making it difficult to access and use data to support management decision-making. Relevant data is likely to be spread over multiple databases in different systems, in multiple formats and even over multiple organizations.

Keywords Information technology • Credit quality • Standardization report • Credit risk • Asset quality

1 Introduction

With the rapid evolution of information and communication technologies (ITC), information systems (IS) have assumed a central importance in the organizational and functional structure of all kinds of business. The spread of technologies linked to the use of the Web has, moreover, favoured the redesigning of the very boundary lines of the company [1] which today appears increasingly open and connected with other entities and information systems.

In this context, the implementation of information systems capable of managing a plurality of information types coming from various information sources as well as

E. Bruno (✉) • G. Iacoviello
Department of Economics and Management, University of Pisa, Pisa, Italy
e-mail: elena.bruno@unipi.it; giuseppina.iacoviello@unipi.it

A. Lazzini
Department of Communication & Economics, University of Modena and Reggio Emilia, Modena, Italy
e-mail: arianna.lazzini@unimore.it

K. Corsi et al. (eds.), *Reshaping Accounting and Management Control Systems*,
Lecture Notes in Information Systems and Organisation 20,
DOI 10.1007/978-3-319-49538-5_2

the adoption of effective policies of information security assumes a crucial importance. The continuous and rapid changes in technologies, on the one hand, and the considerable operational, organizational and financial commitment, on the other, make this process extremely arduous. This is particularly important for banks which today have to meet new needs and challenges. On the supply side, it can be observed that, if the guarantee of secure and reliable services has always constituted a factor of primary importance, today it becomes one of the main components of competitive advantage.

From an operational point of view, the regulations require increasingly strict controls and the implementation of standardized, automated processes in order to manage better and reduce the various components of risk to which a bank is subject. The measurement and management of credit risk have in recent years assumed increasing importance in the process of risk management for financial institutions, also in the light of the recent crisis that has involved economies of many countries. Credit quality impairment has mainly affected small and medium-sized enterprises which constitute the life blood of the Italian productive system. The negative economic cycles that have involved Western economies in the last few years have made it very difficult for businesses to comply, in the agreed times, with the terms of finance contracts signed with financial intermediaries. In this context of credit risk aversion, there are important new developments of a regulatory character regarding the correct representation of impaired credit information.

The first concerns the introduction by the Bank of Italy of the "archive of the losses historically recorded on default positions" which requires the annual notification of losses suffered on non-performing loans (non-performing receivables, substandard, doubtful, restructured loans and expired and/or over-limit impaired exposures). Objects of detection are the exposure at the moment of default, any variation in the exposure, the value of the recoveries obtained, the costs connected with the recovery activities and information details relating to aspects such as technical form and system of guarantees. The second innovation regards the recent provisions of the International Accounting Standards Board (IASB) on the subject of the impairment test. Taking up again the cornerstone of prudence, which has always been central in the Italian system of financial reporting, but in the past underestimated in the international approach, there will be a change from the incurred loss model to the expected loss model with the aim of predicting losses in advance and avoiding their manifestation only in moments of crisis.

The activity of credit risk control is a critical and complex process that involves management at several levels and a multiplicity of business functions, primarily the function of risk management. As well as technical-quantitative skills, the employees performing the functions must possess transversal knowledge of the operating processes of the bank and soft skills such as independent judgement, critical spirit, authoritiveness and flexibility. The IS must perform a decisive role in ensuring that the process of risk management is prompt. Indispensable goals are the integration at group level of the information systems, the safeguarding of data quality and the structuring of the information flows and of the reporting activity so that important information reaches, promptly and at the appropriate time, the desk of whoever has to decide. The comparability of the data in time and space constitutes a critical aspect. It requires an activity of standardization which, today, cannot but be based on computerized processes and languages (see the paragraph 3).

Up to a decade ago, there had been very little standardization of regulatory reporting across the European Union. Standardized electronic formats and data models such as XBRL and Data Point Model (DPM) were only introduced by the Committee of European Banking Supervision in 2004 and the European Banking Authority shortly after. These standards, however, remained nonbinding until the introduction of the Single Supervisory Mechanism at the European Central Bank (ECB) in 2014 [2]. It is crucial to note that this is no longer just "the next step" in reporting, but rather represents a radical change in regulation and supervision. This is because prior initiatives to standardize regulatory reporting focus on how organizations exchange data (and thus mainly resulted in requirements for the need for Information Technology function). The enforcement of standards such as XBRL and DPM, however, affects functions of organizations' data collection and data compilation chains (and thus mainly results in requirements for business departments). This represents an example for the continuously growing demand for regulatory reporting within the financial industry.

Some recent regulatory changes that emphasize the role of the Risk Management (RM) in the process of producing financial reporting of credit monitoring are moving in the same direction (see the fifteenth update of the Bank of Italy Circular n. 263 of 27.12.2006). The monitoring of organized activities was mainly "visual and manual" until the progressive introduction of computer technology into business operations. IT is often implemented to manage, control and report credit risk, market risk and other types of core business risk. "However, the IT applications and infrastructure elements are still within the operational risk domain, regardless of their specific purpose. As an example, the failure of a credit risk measurement application is an IT failure and, therefore, a "systems failure" in the sense of operational risk" [3].

On the basis of the above remarks, the aim of this present chapter is to analyse the effects that the enhancement and modernizing of information systems are having on credit portfolio quality, in the light also of the recent regulatory changes that have taken place in the banking sector.

A limitation of actual research concerns the lack of studies that analyse the issue of IT in the process of quality credit risk in small banks, while more surveys that have been conducted refer to the IS in large banks and more recently to smaller banks [4, 5]. A few contributions focus on the implementation of advanced IT solutions in small banks to contribute to loan portfolio management with a view to improving asset quality [6].

The remainder of the chapter is organized as follows: paragraph two outlines the background and literature review, paragraph three the application of the new model to activities of credit risk control and paragraph four discusses the research objective and method and the final paragraph presents evidence and conclusion providing a critical review of alignment between theory and practice.

2 Literature Review

Progress in the technical-scientific field, and in particular in information and communication technologies (ICTs), has generated significant effects throughout the entire entrepreneurial system and, in particular, on the banking information systems that are today totally permeated by them.

The information system, in the sense of a dense and complex network of element whose aim is to support the manager's decision-making process through information inputs [7, 8], if it is analysed in its objective dimension, appears entirely based on the computer component in its hardware and software dimensions. The communicative flow, the number of variables considered to be deserving of attention, the importance attributed to them and the number of stakeholders with which the bank interacts have progressively increased together with an increase in the information flow required by both management in support of the decision-making process and supervisory bodies [9, 10]. The need, increasingly felt by banks to deal with events characterized by unpredictability, the frequency of which is growing, the reduction in the times required for carrying out the different activities and the new rules and procedures imposed by the regulations have rendered obsolete both the traditional decision-making processes often based on values such as trust and knowledge of the counterparty and the traditional organizational structure.

ICT, in its various forms of application, plays an active and decisive role within a bank, thanks, in particular, to the subset of its applications, whose functions are collection, memorization, processing, analysis and recovery of data and information aimed at the rapid dissemination among those involved in the operational activities.

The subjective and objective dimensions of the business information system acquire a decisive role in the current competitive context. Moving in real time, being able to count on prompt and accurate but never redundant information and having available decision-makers with highly professional skills and the ability, on the one hand, to capture weak signals originating in the surrounding environment and, on the other hand, to evaluate appropriately the importance of the information to be subjected to close analysis and interpretation are essential requirements.

Such management requirements imply the need to be able to count on an adequate information system, on an organizational structure that is able to meet fully the new needs, emphasizing the possibilities linked to technical-scientific progress, and on a solid and competent management, supported effectively by the presence of systems based on the most modern computer technologies.

Information procedures become therefore an essential part of the system, their task being to define what has to undergo analysis, the type of data to be recorded, the selection, classification and processing according to which the business reporting is constructed. Computerization presupposes an activity of standardization and therefore a process of measurement, based on the translation into quantitative terms of the phenomenon being analysed. Such an operation leads to the identification of measurements, that is, entities expressed numerically and defined by quantities constructed on the basis of predefined magnitudes that are variable according to the designated objectives.

The activity of standardization and therefore measurement represents, today, a particularly critical aspect in the management of a bank. This is particularly true in the context of the supply and monitoring of credit where the greatest difficulties found lie in the difficulties of the standardization, and therefore of measurement, of variables of a qualitative kind [11].

Banks, especially small and medium sized, today face a trade-off between the need for standardization in compliance with the directives of the national and international supervisory authorities [12] which require increasingly automated, and therefore objective and traceable, processes, and the need to preserve their own particular characteristics and sources of competitive advantage [13].

The exchange and sharing of information (visibility) by actors in the process of credit supply and management becomes fundamental [14, 15], being considered, in the literature, a central element in the achievement of results [14, 16], in guaranteeing transparency in the processes and in the prompt indication of possible anomalies [17].

With respect to the question being examined, it would be interesting to look briefly at the meaning that should be attributed to the concepts of number, datum, magnitude, quantity and measurement, interrelated but not coinciding concepts.

The concept of number has changed over time, from being a constitutive element of that part of reality that is accessible, not to the senses, but to reason, typical of the school of Pythagoras, to being perceived today by modern philosophy of mathematics perspectives a set of signs defined by a given system of axioms. From a spatial-temporal point of view, in addition to the above-mentioned perspectives, we can trace a third according to which number is defined on the basis of the concept of class. Such an approach implies the identification of two dimensions of inquiry: the extensive and intensive dimensions.

With respect to the first dimension, number is definable as "the class of all classes, similar to the given class". From the definition, we deduce the extensive dimension of the phenomenon referable to the enumeration of the members belonging to the class. In the intensive meaning, class is described, on the other hand, on the basis of the characteristics of its members falling therefore outside the concept of number *stricto sensu*.

Number, an important part of the language through which the business economy "speaks", is used by it for the representation of facts and of real trends regarding the life of the company, ascribing to number an instrumental role with respect to a subsequent, necessary activity of analysis and interpretation of the same.

Company representations contain within them a meaning that transcends the mere mathematical expression generally used. Measurement is indeed not limited to the sole activity of enumeration with the relative assignment of numbers to objects on the basis of predefined conventions but implies a subsequent, important activity of interpretation and evaluation of the trends on which the decision-making process is founded.

The quantitative expression of business phenomena enables the scholar to conduct first of all an analysis based on a process of a rational kind, founded on a rigorous and therefore scientific method, and secondly to carry out spatial-temporal comparisons in order to express judgements of past performances and to outline possible trends for future ones.

In business economics, the numbers on the basis of which an appropriate representation of the particular facets of the polyhydric phenomenon of the company is provided, and on which is founded the activity of choice proper to any decision-making process, are denominated data.

The two concepts seem to be interconnected but never coincident, the concept of number being included in that of datum, but the second characterized by a broader application and greater depth.

The concepts of number, quantity and measurement can be analysed in the light of the three dimensions of semiotics: syntactic, semantic and pragmatic.

While the syntactic aspect is present and intrinsic to the concept of number used in the various branches of knowledge, dealing with the "study of syntactic relations between signs, abstracting from the relationships of signs with objects or with interpreters", the semantic and pragmatic aspects, characteristic of contexts in which it is essential not only to attribute a precise meaning between the object of representation and the means used but also to consider the cognitive value assigned to the first, prove to be of little significance for it.

Applying to the notion of number, the concept of magnitude, that is, of unit or index of measurement on the basis of which to express the result of the activity of measurement, the notion of quantity is obtained. The concept of quantity conforms therefore to the numerical representation of a given phenomenon and is characterized by the possibility of applying to it the syntactic and semantic dimension of language. While what has been observed for number is valid for the first dimension, the semantic dimension is ascribable to the link existing between the quantitative expression underlying it and the phenomenon whose representation it is intended to provide. In accounting, language quantities are numerical representations of facts and events expressed using currency as index of measurement.

The last logical category is understood as the final result of the process of measurement. The concept of datum contains all the dimensions of language including pragmatics. The datum appears in fact as a number with which a magnitude is associated, and therefore a quantity, referring to a given, precise phenomenon. The datum proves, therefore, to be the element underlying every process of evaluation. It is with the managerial activity of interpretation that the datum becomes information, and, by means of its stratification, knowledge, which gives rise to decisions which are translated into actions that lead to results.

The Dikar model [18], represented in Fig. 1, has this orientation:

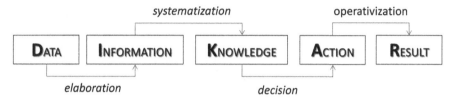

Fig. 1 The Dikar model

Systems of measurement are not generalizable or absolute: they vary in time and space according to the environmental, social and cultural contexts in which they are applied and used.

With respect to the time variable, such systems are changeable to the extent that the object it is intended to represent by means of them appears is variable, as are changeable the means and the techniques used in the same representation; with respect to the spatial variable, the latter differ to the extent that aspects considered important, and therefore worthy of measurement and consequent interpretation, and the tools used for such purposes, appear changeable. The increase in the level of environmental turbulence and the consequent increase in the degree of business complexity have brought about changes both in the aspects considered important in the decision-making process and in the modes of measurement of the performances achieved. The systems of measurement are characterized, furthermore, by the lack of objectivity in an absolute sense being based on activities of measurement carried out by man who, starting from the observation of a given phenomenon, tries to translate the qualitative aspect intrinsic to it into quantitative terms on the basis of certain assumptions. This determines the first limitation that leads to the impossibility of "true and precise" determinations in absolute terms and therefore to not being able to speak of totally objective systems of measurement since "the observer disturbs the observed" [19].

3 Dikar Model and Credit Risk Control

It is said that the ICT structures in banks have very different physiognomies, each one characterized by strong and weak points and considerably dependent on the sourcing model adopted. The sourcing models are differentiated according to the size of the bank; thus, some banking groups preferred to assign the management of information infrastructure to an instrumental company in the perimeter of consolidation large-scale banks or banks belonging to banking groups decided to resort to a so-called mixed model, keeping control of the application portfolio inside and outsourcing the technological management; indeed, the smaller banks have opted for a model of full outsourcing to external services companies [20].

The sample of banks analysed in this work, defined by the Bank of Italy as small-sized banks, is oriented towards a mixed model; this requires them to find the

Fig. 2 Standardization
versus Individualization

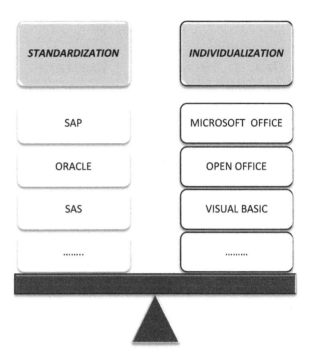

necessary balance between IS standardization, that is, a centralized IS according to consortium logic, and IS individualization, that is, an IS internal to the bank for application portfolio control. We define report standardization as the convergent process of unifying multiple reports [21] and report individualization as the divergent process of adjusting reports to individual preferences [22–24]. The users often supplement standardized IS with individual spreadsheets or develop entire workaround systems (Fig. 2). Unfortunately, these supplements represent several threats to standardize IS, such as data redundancy and limited reuse of existing reports. Consequently, it is important to understand how organizations may balance standardized IS with individually developed supplements [25, 26]. This assumes particular importance in times when governmental organizations continuously introduce new regulatory and supervisory reporting requirements [27].

The main information of a qualitative nature is extracted from centralized score systems (Centralized and Standardized Information System), for example, the Credit Bureau Score of CRIF or of the Risk Central—CR, which are fed by Rating models able to assess the probability of default (PD) by a customer generally over a period of 12 months. Such models use different types of information linked to the socio-economic characteristics of lenders to profession, to geographical location, to available financial assets and wealth, to family status, to external information entered into the databases of the Chambers of Commerce and to other prejudicial events. Finally, the organizational structures responsible for rating assignment supplement the same with other assessment elements, such as, for example, whether

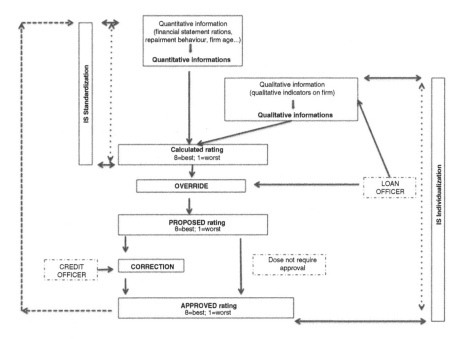

Fig. 3 IS and the rating review process

a business belongs to groups, strategic vision and management quality, the presence of investments in R&S, which feed the bank's internal (Individualized) information system. The integration of quantitative and qualitative information, generated by the centralized IS (IS standardization) and from the bank's internal system (IS individualization), supports the review of the statistical rating and therefore the definition of the customer's final rating (Fig. 3).

As shown by Fig. 3, the periodic use of quantitative and qualitative information generated by the centralized and individualized information system makes possible the continuous refinement of the rating. It is in this phase that there takes place the credit monitoring process which, by means of the constant control of the evolution of the probability of default (PD), makes it possible to highlight any anomalous risk trends and therefore the prompt implementation of politics of mitigation aimed at the reduction of the bank's incurred losses. This process is part of the broader issue of the credit risk control [28–31] and has acquired an important function with the Circ/263 of the Bank of Italy that gives new responsibilities to risk management, including that of performance monitoring credit.

The rating revision rules are differentiated according to type of customers, subdivided into classes, as suggested by the ECB in the operational framework [12], whose aim is to make comparable the models of loan portfolio quality analysis in the various European banking institutions. The framework indicates the criteria of segmentation of customers into more detailed classes of risk with respect to the criteria used in balance sheet practice (in bonis, past due, loans restructured, substandard loans and non-performing loans—npls), and the modes of standardi-zation of data, qualitatively and quantitatively, (Triggers) for the evaluation and monitoring of credit exposures. Thus, the customers are classified into three macro-classes of management (performing, risk cured, in default), depending on the degree of solvency automatically detected by IS standardization; the qualitative information heritage is in fact held by the sector managers (MPLM function), who in turn liaise with the RM for the performance monitoring of credit risk. On the basis of the instructions of Circ/263, the criterion of integration of rating methods adopted by small and smaller banks is the override (discretional modification of the rating itself). The statistical system of rating assignment is not able to process all soft information; the activation of override on the basis of predefined soft informa-tion processed by individualized IS can determine upgrading or downgrading variations in the rating assigned to the debtor by the statistical system: in the first case, the proposals for improvement (upgrading) are subjected to a validation procedure by the RM; vice versa, in the case of downgrading variations the validation is automatic.

With reference to the role of the IS in producing data knowledge, the reporting system of the Credit office provides analytical documentation on meaningful activities. Such disclosures should be as up to date and correct as possible and therefore should not generate inconsistent interpretations. Once the above activities have been completed, the aim is to redesign the data in the IS individualization. In this way, for "every point in time," it can identify the contribution to RM of the operating results in all phases of the process, taking into account deviations, the causes of variations and the impact on the non-performing loans.

3.1 Data and Information in Credit Risk Management

From a strategic point of view, a safe and efficient information system (IS) makes it possible to exploit the opportunities offered by technology to expand and improve products and services offered to customers, to enhance the quality of work pro-cesses, to promote dematerialization of securities and to reduce costs also through virtualization of banking services.

From an operational point of view, an IS enables managers to have information that is detailed, relevant and up to date for taking timely decisions and for the proper implementation of the process of risk management advocated by the new regula-tions. In a context where the banking business is increasingly dependent on new technologies, information security in terms of defence against attacks and continu-ity of service plays an important role in preventing, reducing and controlling operational risk. The IS has, in addition, the task of recording, storing and correctly representing facts and events relevant to the purposes provided by law and by internal and external regulations (compliance). Through an efficient information system, it is possible to speed up the transmission of messages relating to transfers of funds between banks, to implement an efficient flow of data and information between the branches and the central offices, to reprocess and reuse data concerning the various operations many times and for different purposes and to provide customers with an ever wider range of products-computer services, particularly in the area of self-service banking. Today banks require complete and reliable information and an overall integration of different applications, database and documents. In this perspective, a comprehensive and integrated IS able to capture all customer data, risk management and transaction information including trade and foreign exchange is fundamental to the proactive management of loan portfolios in order to minimize losses and earn an acceptable level of return for shareholders [32–34]. In the analysis of the customer, a substantial number of parameters are necessary. Qualitative evaluations, historical and not, such as industry scenarios and a supply chain analysis, are today required to be combined to standard information. It's clear that the presence of an integrated information system able to give a dashboard to monitor in real time with alerting parameters is nowadays a critical aspect for banks. In the analysis of information flows of particular significance is the concept of process visibility factor defined by Balasubramanian and Gupta [35] as the factor that "measures the extent to which process states are visible to specific process stakeholders through process information reporting or recording". The concept of visibility is therefore referable to the possibility of access to, sharing and use of information in real time, relative to a given process on the part of different individuals involved in the decision-making process [36]. On the basis of the paradigm of Information Processing View (IPV), an accurate and transparent management of information would determine a significant reduction in both the level of uncertainty linked to lack of sharing and to information asymmetries [37] and the possibility of errors in carrying out tasks and activities due to different interpretations or the assigning of a different meaning to the same phenomenon [38]. The IPV approach seems particularly interesting if applied to credit management process implemented by the bank in which the standardization of the credit monitoring process requires full sharing, access, analysis of data and information. There is no doubt that banks, on the one hand, are faced with the need for a redefinition of processes that are increasingly based on information technologies and, on the other hand, have to cope with the need to increase their IT budgets. Indeed if visibility requirements can be considered high in the case of the credit decision process, banks seem to establish only low visibility capabilities. An increase in investments dedicated to the strengthening of visibility is necessary today for increasing the performance of the organization as a whole making it possible to increase the speed of throughput and reduce the frequency of errors, thus increasing the objectification and automation of the process. As a result, banks have to prioritize IT investments carefully.

4 Methodology

This chaper starts from the conviction that banks of whatever size must develop information systems and standardized procedures for supporting the manager in operational activities also in the light of the recent regulatory provisions issued by national and international supervisory bodies. This chapter aims to analyse one of the components of the banking risk system: the credit risk.

In credit risk management, it is necessary to coordinate the various control functions, whether first level—line controls—or second level—risk management and compliance—for the purpose of an overall improvement in the quality of the process.

In constructing our theoretical framework, we have to consider the Dikar model (Fig. 4). The model identifies four main phases. The first phase is data elaboration—data that initially are only numbers are elaborated into information. In this phase, the semantic and pragmatic dimensions of the language are added to data.

The 2second phase is systematization. During this phase, the information produced is linked with the system of knowledge of each manager and of the firm as a whole. The third phase is related to the decision-making process and the fourth to the operativization. In the last phase, decisions became actions which produce results.

While the first phase is mainly related to information system stricto sensu, the second, third and fourth are related to the risk management. The last phase, during which results are produced and measured, is related to the system of reporting in its two components internal and external.

Starting from these premises, the main assumption is that an improvement in the quality and quantity of the data processed should increase the level of business information and therefore determine the enhancement of the knowledge system. The enhancement of the knowledge system would create the conditions for improving the decision-making process which should lead to choices and decisions of greater efficiency and therefore produce an improvement in the final results.

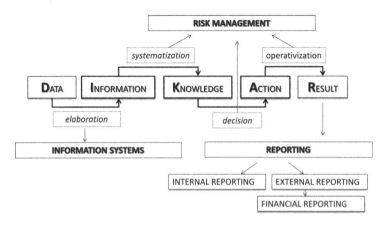

Fig. 4 The theoretical framework

From an operational point of view, the chapter is the second step of a broader research project [39]. The quantitative analysis will be carried out on banks with registered office in the province of Pisa. Such banks can be included in the logical category of small-sized local banks [20] and, operating in the same area, have in common a clientele with the same characteristics. Such an element is fundamental in the study of the npl.

The choice of focusing the analysis on small-sized banks derives from their particular features with respect to peculiarity of the business information system. Small-sized banks today use the full outsourcing approach using external databases to obtain quantitative information. They are significantly affected by the effects of the recent operational changes having a fairly extensive catchment area, but not having at their disposal the economic resources of the large banks.

The subdivision into size classes was made on the basis of the composition of the banking groups in December 2014 and of the total of non-consolidated intermediate funds in December 2008. The "small" banks category includes institutions belonging to groups or independent banks with a total of intermediate funds of between 3.6 and 21.5 billion euros.

The banks analysed are Banca Popolare di Lajatico, Banca di Cascina, Banca di Pisa e Fornacette, Cassa di Risparmio di Volterra and Cassa di Risparmio di San Miniato.

The empirical analysis will be carried out on the financial reporting of the 3-year period 2012–2014. The changes in the systems of controls and the expansion of the data and information processed should have increased the effectiveness of the activity of credit monitoring.

The greater effectiveness of the monitoring activities should have determined changes in the composition of the credit portfolio (Fig. 5).

5 The Impact of Credit Monitoring on Financial Reporting: Evidences

The starting point of our research is to analyse the role of data quality and data management in supporting credit processes to prevent the impairment of asset quality in the balance sheet; the aim is to demonstrate whether it is possible to

Fig. 5 The sample: structure

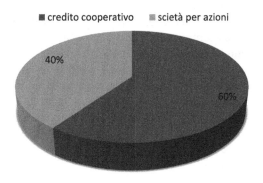

■ credito cooperativo   ■ scietà per azioni

40%

60%

achieve the highest quality of the credit portfolio, exercising control over all the phases involved in this process and, for each of them, to highlight the key variables which indicate a progressive worsening of creditworthiness.

With reference to the first question, the Risk Management (RM) function has undergone a process of regulatory revision that for some scholars [40] represents a driving force for the implementation of effective monitoring of debt positions, for purposes of control of asset quality. The monitoring of credit, in fact, is based on the structuring of the processes that takes into account the models proposed by EBA. The classification of customers includes therefore two positions: "performing loans" and "npls". While using credit, the position of the customer can become an "anomalous" state due to the occurrence of new negative events. Knowledge of these events is linked to the bank's ability to intercept and prepare the tools (including organizational aspects) for monitoring positions systematically, in order to identify "anomalies" responsible for the deterioration in credit quality. The change of state occurs as a consequence of forbearance, applying the technique of override, a tool that is provided by the regulations that allow "modification" of the rating attributed to the debtor according to automated procedures in the context of creditworthiness assessment. This process is carried out by the Monitoring and Problem Loan Management (MPLM) and the RM function on the basis of the mapping of control activities to be carried out within the scope of responsibilities of control for first and second level (the function of RM becomes a second-level function only in the post-crisis period).

Such a kind of innovation is very important; the RM has to assess whether those responsible for the Business Units (BUs) comply with the credit policies, which the bank has defined in the Risk Appetite Framework. Thus, RM identifies some early warning indicators able to represent possible abnormalities compared to the process of monitoring of the first level, which is carried out by MPLM. These indicators refer to the following stages of the process of managing and monitoring credit:

1. Classification of positions;
2. Adequacy of capital amount;
3. Adequacy of the recovery procedure.

The results of the checks are subject to periodic reporting to the business units and to the business structure. In this context, RM checks that the transactions under investigation are classified in accordance with the regulations of EBA and with the rules established by internal regulations, also regarding the time spent in the range.

As seen in Fig. 6, the period 2012–2014 has been characterized by an increase in the percentage of problematic loans. Such a trend seems to be coherent with the ratio of the Asset Quality Review Process. A more objective and austere process in the evaluation of the credit portfolio concomitant with a severe economic and financial crisis seems to have produced, in the banks, a more prudent approach in managing their credit portfolio. A more prudent approach in the asset evaluation seems to be in line with the news rules elaborated by the IASB which will carry in the next year to renew the centrality of the principle of prudence in the preparation of the financial statements (IAS 9).

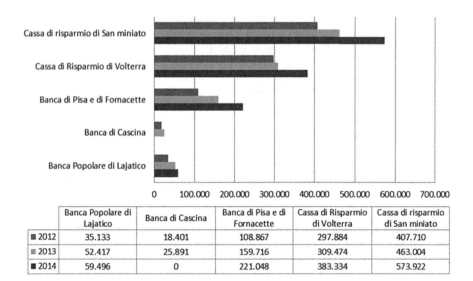

	Banca Popolare di Lajatico	Banca di Cascina	Banca di Pisa e di Fornacette	Cassa di Risparmio di Volterra	Cassa di risparmio di San miniato
■ 2012	35.133	18.401	108.867	297.884	407.710
▪ 2013	52.417	25.891	159.716	309.474	463.004
■ 2014	59.496	0	221.048	383.334	573.922

Fig. 6 The Problematic Loans

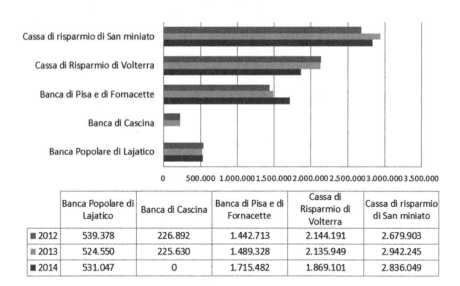

	Banca Popolare di Lajatico	Banca di Cascina	Banca di Pisa e di Fornacette	Cassa di Risparmio di Volterra	Cassa di risparmio di San miniato
■ 2012	539.378	226.892	1.442.713	2.144.191	2.679.903
▪ 2013	524.550	225.630	1.489.328	2.135.949	2.942.245
■ 2014	531.047	0	1.715.482	1.869.101	2.836.049

Fig. 7 The Performing Loans (PL)

Figure 7 highlights an opposite trend for performance loans which, coherently with the previous data, seems to decrease in 2014 except for Banca di Pisa and Fornacette.

Analysing the problematic loans adopting the riskiness buckets classification proposed by the ECB, we notice a sort of deterioration in the composition of the credit portfolio. The credit quality seems to be significantly decreased in 2014 with

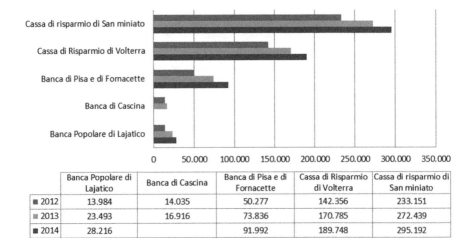

	Banca Popolare di Lajatico	Banca di Cascina	Banca di Pisa e di Fornacette	Cassa di Risparmio di Volterra	Cassa di risparmio di San miniato
■ 2012	13.984	14.035	50.277	142.356	233.151
▨ 2013	23.493	16.916	73.836	170.785	272.439
■ 2014	28.216		91.992	189.748	295.192

Fig. 8 The non-performing loans (NPLs)

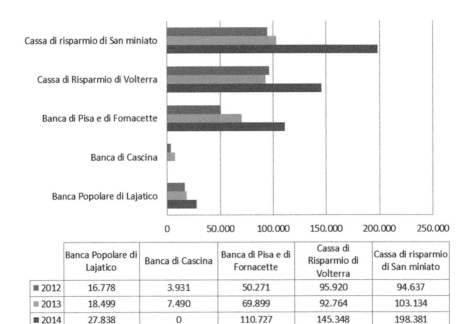

	Banca Popolare di Lajatico	Banca di Cascina	Banca di Pisa e di Fornacette	Cassa di Risparmio di Volterra	Cassa di risparmio di San miniato
■ 2012	16.778	3.931	50.271	95.920	94.637
▨ 2013	18.499	7.490	69.899	92.764	103.134
■ 2014	27.838	0	110.727	145.348	198.381

Fig. 9 Substandard loans

an increase in the percentage of non-performing loans and substandard loans (Figs. 8 and 9). At the same time, the categories of Past Due and Restructured loans have suffered a reduction in 2014 (Figs. 10 and 11).

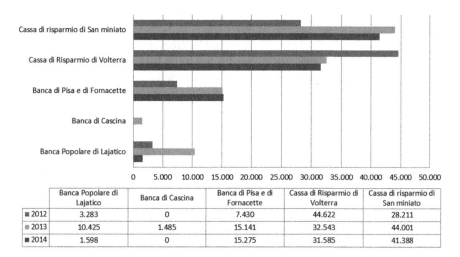

	Banca Popolare di Lajatico	Banca di Cascina	Banca di Pisa e di Fornacette	Cassa di Risparmio di Volterra	Cassa di risparmio di San miniato
■ 2012	3.283	0	7.430	44.622	28.211
■ 2013	10.425	1.485	15.141	32.543	44.001
■ 2014	1.598	0	15.275	31.585	41.388

Fig. 10 The restructured loans

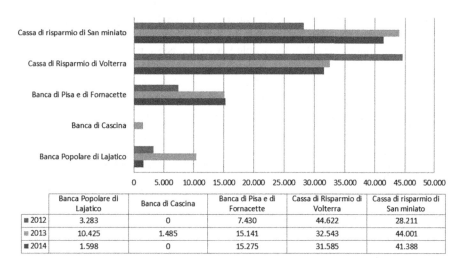

	Banca Popolare di Lajatico	Banca di Cascina	Banca di Pisa e di Fornacette	Cassa di Risparmio di Volterra	Cassa di risparmio di San miniato
■ 2012	3.283	0	7.430	44.622	28.211
■ 2013	10.425	1.485	15.141	32.543	44.001
■ 2014	1.598	0	15.275	31.585	41.388

Fig. 11 The past due loans

Such a trend seems to confirm the success of the policy of the European Banking Authority and of the Bank of Italy in the review of the methodologies and criteria used in the asset evaluation. The 2014 has been the first year in which banks have adopted the new rules. A decrease in the quality of credit seems to be coherent with the main objectives of the rules. Surely, we expect an improvement in the credit portfolio quality, with a reduction of the problematic loans and a better composition of the riskiness buckets, in the coming years. A careful credit position performance monitoring activity will make it possible to identify the downgrading position of lending customers before reaching an irreversible state of insolvency, which feeds the npl entry.

In this direction, the rules contained in Circ/263 (cap. VIII) recognize the important role of data management systems for banking organizations in that the automation of the processes and monitoring of data security will make it possible to meet the growing expectations of rapid and accurate responses. The monitoring system should be based on a reporting system that is capable of measuring the previously identified creditworthiness indicators. The purpose of reporting within IS is to provide analytical documentation on meaningful activities. Such disclosures should be as up to date and correct as possible and therefore should not generate inconsistent interpretations. Once the above activities have been completed, the aim is to redesign the IT system. In this way, for "every point in time", it can identify the contribution to RM of the operating results in all phases of the process, taking into account deviations, the causes of variations and the impact on the npls. The migration of positions in the various riskiness buckets makes visible debtor downgrading and, therefore, the prompt intervention of the MPLM, before the position reaches the irreversible state of npls.

In conclusion, the data provided by the banks analysed seems to show the opening of a virtuous process of change in the banks' portfolio management which accompanying with an increase in the level of business information will determine the enhancement of the whole knowledge system.

References

1. Garzella, S. (2005). *Il sistema d'azienda e la valorizzazione delle "potenzialità inespresse". Una visione strategica per il risanamento*. Torino: Giappichelli.
2. European Central Bank. (2014). *Guideline of the ECB of 25 July 2013 on the statistical reporting requirements of the ECB in the field of quarterly financial accounts (recast)* (Technical report). Frankfurt.
3. IT Governance Institute. (2010). *IT control objectivies for Basel II. The importance of governance and risk management for compliance* (Technical report). USA Printer.
4. Seese, D., Weinhardet, C., & Schlottman, F. (2008). *Handbook on information technology. Finance*. New York: Springer.
5. Gupta, U. G., & Collins, W. (1997). The impact of information systems on the efficiency of banks: An empirical investigation. *Industrial Management and Data Systems, 97*, 10–16.
6. Egloff, D., Leippold, M., & Vannini, P. (2007). A simple model of credit contagion. *Journal of Banking Finance, 31*, 2475–2492.
7. Marchi, L. (2003). *I sistemi informativi aziendali*. Milano: Giuffrè.
8. Mancini, D. (2010). *Il sistema informativo e di controllo relazionale per il governo della rete di relazione collaborative d'azienda*. Milano: Giuffrè.
9. Davenport, T. H. (2014). *Big data at work: Dispelling the myths, uncovering the opportunities*. Boston, MA: Harward Press.
10. Lorino, P. (1995). Le déploiement de la valeur par les processus. *Revue Française de Gestion, 104*, 5–71.
11. Ajah, J., & Inyama, H. C. (2011). Loan fraud detection and IT-based combat strategies. *Journal of Internet Banking and Commerce, 16*, 1–13.

12. European Central Bank. (2013). *Back to banking supervision: Comprehensive assessment* (Technical report). Frankfurt.
13. Porter, M. (2011). *Il vantaggio, competitivo*. Milano: Einaudi.
14. Barratt, M., & Oke, A. (2007). Antecedents of supply chain visibility in retail supply chains: A resource-based theory perspective. *Journal of Operations Management, 25*, 1217–1233.
15. Wang, E. T. G., & Wei, H. L. (2007). Interorganizational governance value creation: Coordinating for information visibility and flexibility in supply chains. *Decision Sciences, 38*, 647–674.
16. Swaminathan, M. J., & Tayur, S. R. (2003). Models for supply chains in e-business. *Management Science, 49*, 1387–1406.
17. Shingo, S. A. (1989). *Study of the Toyota production system from an industrial engineering*. New York: Viewpoint.
18. Venkatraman, N. (1989). The concept of fit in strategy research: Toward verbal and statistical correspondence. *Academy of Management Review, 14*, 423–444.
19. Carnap, R. (1959). *Introduction to semantics and formalization of logic*. Boston, MA: Harvard University Press.
20. Banca d'Italia. (2015). *Relazione annuale* (Technical report). Roma.
21. Haag, S., Cummings, M., & Dawkins, J. (1998). *Management information system for information age*. Boston, MA: McGraw-Hill/Irwin.
22. Baskerville, R. (2011). Individual information systems as a research arena. *European Journal of Information Systems, 20*, 251–254.
23. Beck, U. (2007). Beyond class and nation: Reframing social inequalities in a globalizing world. *British Journal of Sociology, 58*, 679–705.
24. Avital, M., & Te'eni, D. (2009). From generative fit to generative capacity: Exploring an emerging dimension of information systems design and task performance. *Information Systems Journal, 19*, 345–367.
25. Tilson, D., Lytinen, K., & Sørensen, C. (2010). Digital infrastructures: The missing IS research agenda. *Information Systems Research, 21*, 748–759.
26. Yoo, Y. (2013). The tables have turned: How can the information systems field contribute to technology and innovation management research? *Journal of the AIS, 14*, 227–236.
27. Bull, P. (2013). *Statistics for economic and monetary union. Enhancements and new directions 2003* (Tecnichal report). European Central Bank.
28. Altman, E. I., & Saunders, A. (1998). Credit risk measurement: Developments over the last 20 years. *Journal of Banking and Finance, 21*, 1721–1742.
29. Treacy, W. F., & Carey, M. (2000). Credit risk rating systems at large US banks. *Journal of Banking and Finance, 24*, 167–201.
30. Sironi, A., & Marsella, M. (1999). *La misurazione e la gestione del rischio di credito. Modelli Strumenti e politiche*. Roma: Bancaria editrice.
31. Resti, A. (2001). *Misurare e gestire il rischio di credito nelle banche: una guida metodologica*. Roma: Fondo Interbancario di Tutela dei Depositi.
32. Stonebumer, G., Gouguen, A., & Feringa, A. (2002). *Risk management guide for information technology systems* (Technical report). National Institute of Standard Technology.
33. Davenport, T. H., Harris, J., De Long, D. W., & Jacobson, A. L. (2001). Data to knowledge: Building an analytic capability. *California Management Review, 43*, 117–138.
34. Jun, M., & Cai, S. (2001). The key determinants of Internet banking service quality: A content analysis. *International Journal of Bank Marketing, 19*, 276–291.
35. Balasubramanian, S., & Gupta, M. (2005). Structural metrics for goal based business process design and evaluation. *Business Process Management Journal, 11*, 680–694.
36. Graupner, E., Berner, M., Maedche, A., & Jegadeesan, H. (2014). Business intelligence & analytics for processes—A visibility requirements evaluation. In *MKWI Proceedings* (pp. 154–166).
37. Tushman, M. L., & Nadler, D. A. (1978). Information processing as an integrating concept in organizational design. *Academy of Management Review, 3*, 613–624.

38. Karimi, J., Somers, T. M., & Gupta, Y. P. (2004). Impact of environmental uncertainty and task characteristics on user satisfaction with data. *Information Systems Research, 15*, 175–193.
39. Bruno, E., Iacoviello, G., & Lazzini, A. (2015). On the possible tools for the prevention of non-performing loans. A case study of an Italian bank. *Corporate Ownership and Control, 12*, 133–145.
40. Kiff, J., Kisser, M., & Schumacher, L. (2013). *An inspection of the through-the cycle rating methodology* (Working Paper). International Monetary Found.

How to Integrate Languages on Safety: A Participatory Information System to Improve Risk Management

Marco Trizio, Cristiano Occelli, and Alessandra Re

Abstract The chapter presents a participatory method to develop an information system on occupational risk. Sharp-end operators, who constantly deal with unplanned interactions occurring within the socio-technical work system, accumulate a specific experience, centred on risk scenarios rather than on risk factors.

To highlight this experience and benefit from the operators' holistic view on risk, we carried out a descriptive analysis of work activity in three hospital laboratories using an elicitation interview: the "Instructions to the Double". Several multi-factor risk scenarios emerged.

These narrative data were structured into an information system where each work activity is associated with multi-factor risk scenarios. The graphic presentation of work activities and their associated risks provides a common cognitive reference that fosters communication between safety and work domain experts in their different languages, for a more effective and comprehensive risk management.

Keywords Descriptive activity analysis • Participatory risk analysis • Instructions to the Double • Risk management information systems

1 Introduction

In complex organizations, the design of work processes is often split into several team-based engineering flows, where technological, environmental, human and organizational aspects, developed by different organization services, maintain a certain degree of mutual independence [1].

Final adjustments occur at the sharp-end level, where design flows (production or service processes, physical environment, human resources management, quality assurance, etc.) merge to shape the actual work system functioning. We can therefore assume that it is the operators who, carrying out their actions to reach

M. Trizio (✉) • C. Occelli • A. Re
Department of Psychology, University of Torino, Torino, Italy
e-mail: marco.trizio@unito.it; cristiano.occelli@unito.it; alessandra.re@unito.it

© Springer International Publishing AG 2017
K. Corsi et al. (eds.), *Reshaping Accounting and Management Control Systems*,
Lecture Notes in Information Systems and Organisation 20,
DOI 10.1007/978-3-319-49538-5_3

the organizational goals, start experiencing the work context as a socio-technical system.

This assumption has several implications. Facing work conditions that have been implemented without thoroughly checking their interactive complexity [2], the operators need to adapt their performance to cope with unplanned interactions and unexpected constraints, to ensure the achievement of organizational targets [3, 4].

Through their adaptive performance, operators constantly develop micro-organization. As Wenger points out, any organization grows at the intersection of two different sources, i.e. the organization designed by the institution, and the organization emerging from current practices. Their relation should not be seen in terms of congruence but in terms of adjustment through negotiation [5].

Emerging ex post at the operational level, the unplanned interactions can cause discomfort, performance obstacles [6–9] and occupational risks. Each of these outcomes can have negative consequences on operators' health and safety. By way of example, biological risk can result from a synergy of insufficient staff resources, inadequate spaces and poor quality of the available equipment. None of these conditions represents a direct cause per se, but it is the negative interaction between organizational, environmental and technological conditions that causes actual risk scenarios. The mismatch between the normative engineering process, the actual activity and the related risks have been the subject of a rich tradition of field studies, started in Europe more than 30 years ago [10, 11]. Nevertheless, the most common risk analysis techniques rarely point out this kind of risk, which does not surface comparing the occupational health and safety regulations with the risks known to be present on the work processes to be assessed (e.g. manual handling in nursing or chemical risks in clinical analysis laboratories).

This is especially the case when risk analysis is outsourced to external consultants who do not have a direct though informal knowledge of the system to be evaluated.

To highlight the risks caused by unanticipated events and unplanned interactions between the different socio-technical aspects of a work system, we need to perform descriptive analyses of the normal system functioning [12, 13].

2   Different Languages in Risk Analysis and Assessment

While safety experts' analyses mainly focus on nominal work processes and related risk factors, workers' experience is centred on actual work practices and the risk scenarios generated by unplanned interactions and unexpected, but systematically present, constraints and failures.

Therefore, even when apparently referring to the same object, each group speaks a different language. The former, spoken by the health and safety experts, is normative, based on what is expected to be done and on risk factors that are meant to be equally present through the various systems in which the same work processes occur. The latter, spoken by sharp-end operators, is local and systemic, based on what is actually done at the idiographic intersection of the different aspects of a given socio-technical work system.

These languages are both potentially necessary for risk evaluation, but they are still poorly integrated, for cultural and theoretical reasons. The main critical issue concerns the fact that the data necessary to involve operators in risk evaluation are collected according to theoretical models and categories that can create additional mismatch. The operators' perspective is usually addressed with instruments designed to gather perceptions, emotions, motivation and other issues that are certainly relevant for research but do not truly convey a systemic, deeply contextualized experience [14].

Based on these assumptions, our work aimed at developing a procedure to enhance integration of these safety-related languages, first by eliciting workers' knowledge and then by activating an integrated information system for risk analysis and management.

3   Method

3.1   Context

Our study was carried out within a multidisciplinary project that included four University Departments (Information Technology, Psychology, Occupational Medicine, Law), one ICT Company, two small and medium-sized enterprises (SMEs) specialized in designing sensors to monitor chemical and physical risks and three SMEs working on occupational health and safety.

The purpose of the project was threefold: providing a knowledge base of the national regulatory framework related to occupational safety and health in clinical laboratories, installing sensors to monitor both physical environmental conditions and exposure to chemicals in three hospital laboratories, and detecting risks due to non-compliant processes and inadequate working conditions. The expected output was a flow of data towards a Regional Smart Data Platform.

As work psychologists and ergonomists, our specific aim was to carry out a participatory activity analysis to highlight risks embedded in the current working practices, at the intersection between human, technological, environmental and organizational conditions.

Three laboratories of a hospital in Northern Italy were involved in the project: a laboratory that carries out automated as well as high specialized analyses, a pathological anatomy laboratory and a laboratory for toxicological analysis and industrial epidemiology.

In the preliminary phase, the person in charge of each laboratory was informed about the project goals and asked for authorization to interview operators. On this occasion, some introductory interviews were performed to obtain a first description of the work processes, the number of employees and their occupational status.

3.2 Procedure

To support operators to take to reflection what they know in action, we used an elicitation technique. This kind of interview, called "Instructions to the Double" [15], was first developed in Italy in the1970s and then largely shared mainly within the French- and Portuguese-speaking research communities [16–21].

By asking the interviewee "Give me the instructions I need to replace you in your everyday work, so that no one understands that it is not you", the researcher probes the experience of the worker. The researcher uses his/her background knowledge on occupational health and safety (in our case mainly from a psychological and ergonomic point of view) to make the operator focus on work practices relevant for risk analysis.

The first phase of the interview focuses on the organizational structure and the main processes defining the work system. In the second phase, the researcher refers to his knowledge to go beyond what the operators think, feel or perceive, and to reach what they actually know in action, the taken-for-granted part of their work [15].

Supporting the operator saying not only "what" is generally done, but "how" it is actually done, the researcher relaunches what is said to avoid a mere chronological description and takes the cues offered by the interviewee. As an example of relaunching cues, when transmission happens to be interrupted again and again, and eventually the interviewee comes back, the researcher asks: "Are interruptions a main problem in your work?" Usually, the answer is: "A really serious one!" and (s)he goes on describing the sense of responsibility and overload due to interruptions that can have (or actually had) serious effects.

By interacting with each other, the operator and the researcher gradually construct a verbal reformulation of the taken-for-granted knowledge of how the system functions from a socio-technical point of view, making explicit what remains usually unsaid, hidden in the daily routine of the person who is speaking.

In some cases, we also used the Contextual Inquiry as a complementary technique, when we thought it was necessary to further challenge our understanding of the work system, speaking with people during their ongoing work in the physical environment [22].

The two techniques share a set of consistent concepts and principles. Basically, a theoretical assumption, as both claim that positively transforming work practices is derived from an understanding of operators' work and that the best way to understand work is to talk to people in their actual work environment. Furthermore, a procedural assumption: the fact that, when we talk to people about their work in an informal way or in traditional interviews, they tend to speak in abstractions and summaries, giving us a kind of stereotypical model of what anyone in their workplace usually does [15, 23].

Therefore, the technique provides further information about what workers actually do, why they do it that way and their latent needs, giving evidence of their performance adaptation [24].

The procedure was carried out through four phases:

1. Descriptive and participatory analysis of work activity;
2. Risk classification based on a multifactor risk model;
3. Definition of the risk information unit;
4. Qualitative risk assessment based on an activity/risk matrix.

3.3 Descriptive and Participatory Analysis of Work Activity

The aim of this phase was to elicit risks, obstacles to performance and discomfortable situations systematically present in work routines, under ordinary or extraordinary conditions, including emergency situations.

We worked with 11 operators distributed over the three laboratories: three of them supervised the overall activities in each laboratory; the others had a long-term work experience on the processes identified as potentially critical, based on the first exploratory interviews with the management and on a site survey.

Some difficulties arose during the research process. Given an ongoing organizational restructuring, the pathological anatomy laboratory did not authorize interviews with operators. Therefore, our analysis was initially carried out in the other two laboratories, but again, for internal reasons, the automated analysis sector withdrew from the project. In this sector, we could not go deeper in the analysis with further operators, as initially planned.

The results presented are therefore confined to the two organizational units that were totally open to cooperate on the participatory activity analysis: the high-specialized sector for the analysis of metabolic diseases and the toxicology and epidemiologic analysis laboratory.

3.4 Risk Classification Based on a Multifactor Risk Model

The descriptive activity analysis provided many findings about risks and discomforts experienced by the operators in the current work practices, because of the environment, technologies, available resources, organizational rules and procedures. How to structure the collected critical scenarios into a risk classification?

The risk classification proposed by the Italian law (Leg. Decr., no. 81, 2008) is based on analytic risk factors (e.g. chemical, biological, etc.) and lists together structural risks (e.g. electrical systems non-complying with laws and regulations), risks from exposure to toxic substances (e.g. chemical risk) and activity-related risks (e.g. musculoskeletal disorders).

Our analysis was a priori centred on traditional and new risks determined by improper socio-technical work system settings that affect human activity, interacting with current work practices.

How could this analysis converge into a risk management information system that would be meaningful both for safety experts and for the operators as work domain experts?

We referred to a risk classification that was widely used in Italy in the 1970s and is still used in France [25] and Brazil [18]. This classification [26] divides the factors that determine risk in the workplaces into four groups: the first group includes factors that are present both in work and living environments (light, noise, temperature, humidity, aeration); the second group encompasses risk factors typical of work environments (hazardous fumes and gases, toxic chemical substances, ionizing radiations...); the third group consists of one factor only: the dynamic physical work that causes chronic fatigue; the fourth group includes all the other wearing conditions that make the operators physically or mentally tired (monotony, rhythms, uncomfortable postures, anxiety, responsibilities and other organizational aspects).

This classification is accessible to both safety experts and workers as work domain experts. The former can go deeper into each factor (e.g. exposure to chemicals), while the latter can visualize a systemic profile of the risks affecting their organizational unit or each given activity.

As for the fourth group, which essentially packages the organizational risk, on the one hand an inadequate organization can be seen as a cause of risk in itself, and then the problem is delegated to an organization risk management specialist. On the other hand, the organization can be seen as a pervasive aspect that activates all the interactions within the socio-technical system.

By way of example, the very act of patient handling imposes on nurses a physical effort that depends on available workers, time pressure and the quality of available aids. In other words, it depends on organizational preconditions, so that we can argue that what actually determines the physical load is rather the organization than the physical movement in itself [27].

3.5   Definition of the Risk Information Unit

The collected data were transferred manually for qualitative analysis into an electronic datasheet (Excel 2003, Microsoft, USA), firstly drafted during a previous exploratory study carried out in a different hospital [28, 29]. The information sheet (Fig. 1) provides a summary of data collected, and it is structured into four sections related to risk analysis, risk assessment, risk management and monitoring.

The risk analysis section refers to a given activity and includes the localization (where), the operators involved (who), the occurrence frequency (when) and the

Sector: Metabolic deseases			
Analysis under chemical hood	Daily	All (3)	Laboratory

Risk Analysis	Risk evaluation (severity x frequency)			
The biggest problem is the hood. It is not large enough, and sometimes you need to work in couple. Moreover, it is not connected with the outside, it just has filters. Sometimes it smells bad. Furthermore, it's not hermetic, the chemical hoods are different from this one: they have sliding doors and don't allows any spillage. The budget is the problem... Today I said to the maintenance operator: "when it smells bad and I'm forced to open the window, I'll call you". He answered: "we will come immediately". At the moment, the sensor is our nose, and we are not sure that our perception comes early enough. A second problem in working under the hood is at the physical level, as the chair can not be adjusted and it causes static fatigue. Then I take the little stool, my colleague, who is smaller than me, takes a higher stool. Actually we are three of us, and we use three different stools.	Group 1	Group 2 3x3	Group 3	Group 4 1x3
		9		3
	Risk FROM: 2. exposure to chemicals due to non-chemical hood, with possible diffusion in the working environment 4. Inadequate equipment (chair) Risk OF: 2. cancer 4. musculoskeletal disorders			

Risk management	Risk monitoring
Solution: ☐ to be verified X verified ☐ implemented Group 2: chemical hood replacement Group 4: chair replacement	03/08/2015 - report presented to ask for the chemical hood replacement

Fig. 1 Example of a risk information unit

sequence of actions (how) highlighted during the participatory analysis, quoting what the workers said.

In the risk assessment section, the risks pertaining to the given scenario are organized into the risk classification model and assessed as the product of severity (1 indicating discomfort, annoyance; 2 obstacle to performance; 3 occupational risk) and occurrence frequency (1 indicating occasional activities; 2 random but recurring activities; 3 everyday activities). The definition of risks is split into "risk from" (namely a list of the constituent aspects of the work system that contribute to the risk, e.g. exposure to toxic substances) and "risk of" (health and safety consequences, e.g. cancer).

Concerning risk management, the possible solution is indicated as "to be verified", "verified" (by safety experts as for the risk from and by health experts as for the risk of), under way or "implemented" solution. The monitoring section tracks the risk elimination or mitigation process, listing actions undertaken for this purpose and updating the record at any intervention.

Every critical scenario potentially refers to several risks, which are stored in the same sheet, and each activity potentially refers to several risk scenarios, which are stored in several risk sheets.

For the two laboratories where the interviews were authorized, 18 risk information sheets were issued.

3.6   Qualitative Risk Assessment Based on an Activity/Risk Matrix

To integrate the several risk units into an information system, the sheets related to every clinical sector were synthesized into two matrices that show the overall risk profile of the sector.

In the first matrix (Fig. 2), the left column lists the activities that proved to be critical; the horizontal rows show the risks pertaining to each activity, classified into the four-group classification model.

The matrix highlights three types of priorities: (a) activities presenting high severity/probability of harm (calling for immediate intervention; in the example, activities no. 1 and no. 2); (b) activities where several heterogeneous risks are present, representing a cumulative burden on operators (as in activity no. 1); (c) cumulative risk on operators who perform apparently unrelated activities that actually present the same type of risk (in the example, the Group 4, that is organizational risk).

These priorities were summarized into a second quantitative risk matrix (Fig. 3) that, for each sector defined by the product of severity and exposure frequency, shows the number of correspondent activities.

The two matrices allow a comparative view of the different clinical sectors and, being accessible to both the safety and the work domain experts, can foster a cooperative decision-making. To support negotiating priorities, the system allows

Sector: Metabolic Deseases		Group 1	Group 2	Group 3	Group 4	Total per activity
Activities	Risks					
1	Chemical hood analysis		9		3	12
2	Pipetting				9	9
3	Reagents supply chain				6	6
Total per groups			9		18	37

Fig. 2 From the datasheets to the activity/risk matrix

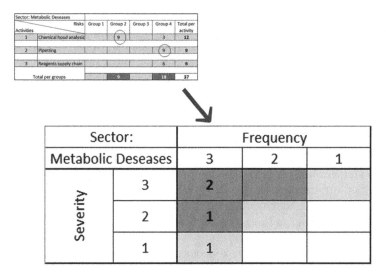

Sector:		Frequency		
Metabolic Deseases		3	2	1
Severity	3	2		
	2	1		
	1	1		

Fig. 3 From the activity/risk matrix to the decision-making matrix

traceability of the overall process, from the final matrix back to the initial risk units and the interventions planned or already implemented.

4 Conclusions

Our purpose of creating an information system on occupational risk was mainly based on two theoretical premises. The first is the socio-technical systems model. In complex systems, unplanned interactions can cause risk scenarios that cannot be detected when each component is taken on its own, with no reference to the other aspects of the work system and to the human activity.

The second theoretical reference is the consolidated research tradition that, especially in Europe, provides evidence of a constant growing experience in the workplaces. We tried to document that this workers' experience, including a holistic and systemic view on risk, has its own language that, in interaction with other languages, can contribute to improve occupational safety, if a consistent information system becomes available.

Our first results seem to support this research direction. The procedure we activated proved to be able to discriminate between clinical units with a lower or a higher risk profile, as the operators confirmed the interview transcription and the consequent elementary risk units and asked to make slight modifications but never questioned the overall risk evaluation.

With reference to the three aforementioned priority criteria, as for the first (high-level occupational risks), three cases were identified: a non-chemical hood used for chemical analyses, with possible dispersion of chemicals and inadequate ventilation controls; highly repeated pipetting potentially causing musculoskeletal disorders; and a container for collection of analysis discharge materials (reagents and blood) which is expected to be airtight, but is not, and could involve a risk of exposure.

Concerning the second criterion (heterogeneous risks in the same activity), our highest risk evaluation relates to one of the sectors that withdrew from the project for internal reasons. The workers highlighted the presence of ground noise, air flow and dust thrown around by rotating fans, open space layout, occupational risk (the non-airtight container) and several fourth group factors, such as inadequate working postures, computers in front of the windows and high time pressure.

As for the third criterion (different activities that are exposed to the same kind of risk and are performed by the same operators), certainly the most shared are the fourth-group organizational risks. In the laboratory where we could perform the deepest study, all the activities were charged by heavy staff shortage, continuous interruptions, overload and focus on multiple dissimilar tasks at once (the "meanwhile" laboratory, they used to say).

Regarding the organizational risk, in one clinical sector the high-specialized and experienced operators reported stress due to the impossibility of meeting the demand by the clinical staff to perform innovative experimental analyses, as they are prevented from buying any extra agent, or standard, by a strict administrative procedure. As Clot suggests [16], a high level of stress is not only due to what the operators do, but to what they would and feel they should do, but are not allowed to.

As a final consideration, it should be pointed out that, when we speak about operators' knowledge and experience, we do not mean that the operators can offer ready-made solutions, as we assume that different languages are coexistent into the system. The four-group risk classification model can support a multidisciplinary risk management through the coordination between polytechnic (1° group), bio-medical (2° and 3° group) and psychosocial (4° group) disciplinary languages. The role of management is essential to transform this coexistence of languages and to make communication, as indicated by Habermas [30], a means for coordinating action.

Within a socio-technical systems approach, this is compulsory, as a physical risk, as in the previous example of patient handling, can call for an organizational solution, and vice versa, continuous interruptions can be addressed with modifications in physical space.

In this view, activating an organizational change means, first of all, changing the power relations within the organization. This could also change the power relations between researchers and the gatekeepers of their studies, giving researchers the possibility to enter the work system, which was not always possible in our research.

As Perrow [2] highlighted, management plays a crucial role in preventing failures—or causing them.

Acknowledgement Project funded in the frame of the ROP ERDF 2007–2013 of Piedmont Region, with the financial support of the Italian Government.

References

1. Davenport, T. H. (2013). *Process innovation: Reengineering work through information technology*. Harvard, IL: Harvard Business Press.
2. Perrow, C. (1984). *Normal accidents. Living with high-risk technologies*. New York: Basic Books.
3. Clot, Y. (2010). *Le travail à coeur. Pour en finir avec les risques psychosociaux*. Paris: La Découverte.
4. De Terssac, G. (1992). *Autonomie dans le travail*. Paris: Presses Universitaire de France.
5. Wenger, E. (1998). *Communities of practice, learning, meaning and identity*. Cambridge: Cambridge University Press.
6. Brown, K. A., & Mitchell, T. R. (1991). A comparison of just-in-time and batch manufacturing: The role of performance obstacles. *Academy of Management Journal, 34*(4), 906–917.
7. Carayon, P., Gürses, A. P., Hundt, A. S., Ayoub, P., & Alvarado, C. J. (2005). Performance obstacles and facilitators of health care providers. In C. Korunka & P. Hoffmann (Eds.), *Change and quality in human service work* (pp. 257–276). Munich: Hampp Publishers.
8. Park, K., & Han, S. W. (2002). Performance obstacles in cellular manufacturing implementation: Empirical investigation. *Human Factors and Ergonomics in Manufacturing and Service Industries, 12*(1), 17–29.
9. Peters, L. H., Chassie, M. B., Lindholm, H. R., O'Connor, E. J., & Kline, C. R. (1982). The joint influence of situational constraints and goal setting on performance and affective outcomes. *Journal of Management, 8*(2), 7–20.
10. Daniellou, F. (2005). The French-speaking ergonomists' approach to work activity: cross-influences of field intervention and conceptual models. *Theoretical Issues in Ergonomics Science, 6*(5), 409–427.
11. Vicente, K. J. (1999). *Cognitive work analysis: Toward safe, productive, and healthy computer-based work*. Mahwah, NJ: CRC Press.
12. Hollnagel, E. (1998). *CREAM: Cognitive reliability and error analysis method*. London: Elsevier.
13. McDonald, N., Corrigan, S., & Ward, M. (2002). *Well-intentioned people in dysfunctional systems*. Keynote paper presented at the Fifth workshop on human error, safety and systems development, Newcastle, Australia.
14. Re, A., Occelli, C., & Micheletti, M. (2008). From action to reflexion: Use of a multi-perspective system representation to support a health care system improvement. In *Activity 2008: Activity analysis for developing work* (p. 72). Helsinky: Pekka Koukka.
15. Oddone, I., Re, A., & Briante, G. (1977). *Esperienza operaia, coscienza di classe e psicologia del lavoro*. Torino: Einaudi. (Tr. fr. *Redécouvrir l'expérience ouvrière*, 1981, Paris: Editions Sociales).
16. Clot, Y. (1999). *La fonction psychologique du travail*. Paris: Presses Universitaire de France.
17. Lacomblez, M., Bellemare, M., Chatigny, C., Delgoulet, C., Re, A., Trudel, L., et al. (2007). Ergonomic analysis of work activity and training: Basic paradigm, evolutions and challenges. In R. Pikaar, E. Konongsveld, & P. Settels (Eds.), *Meeting diversity in ergonomics* (pp. 129–142). London: Elsevier.
18. Muniz, H. P., Brito, J., de Souza, K. R., Athayde, M., & Lacomblez, M. (2013). Ivar Oddone e sua contribuição para o campo da Saúde do Trabalhador no Brasil. *Revista Brasileira de Saúde Ocupacional, 38*(128), 280–291.
19. Scheller, L. (2001). L'élaboration de l'expérience du travail. La méthode des instructions au sosie dans le cadre d'une formation universitaire. *Éducation Permanente, 164*, 161–174.
20. Schwartz, Y. (1988). *Expérience et connaissance du travail*. Paris: Editions Messidor.
21. Teiger, C., & Lacomblez, M. (2013). *(Se) Former pour transformer le travail. Dynamiques de constructions d'une analyse critique du travail*. Laval, QC: Presses de Universitaire de Laval.
22. Bednar, P. A. (2000). Contextual integration of individual and organizational learning perspectives as part of IS analysis. *Informing Science, 3*(3), 145–156.

23. Holtzblatt, K., & Jones, S. (1993). Contextual inquiry: A participatory technique for system design. In D. Schuler & A. Namioka (Eds.), *Participatory design: Principles and practices* (pp. 177–210). Hillsdale, NJ: Lawrence Erlbaum.
24. Wixon, D., Flanders, A., & Beabes, M. A. (1996). Contextual inquiry: Grounding your design in user's work. In *Conference Companion on Human Factors in Computing Systems* (pp. 354–355). Vancouver, BC: ACM.
25. Thébaud-Mony, A., Davezies, P., Vogel, L., & Volkoff, S. (2015). *Les risques du travail. Pour ne pas perdre sa vie à la gagner*. Paris: La Découverte.
26. Oddone, I. (1969). *L'ambiente di lavoro*. Roma: FIOM. (seconda edizione FIM-FIOM-UILM, Roma, 1971; terza edizione INAIL, Roma, 2006).
27. Re, A. (2012). Interdisciplinary research and practice in ergonomics. *Journal of Biological Research, 85*(1), 53–56.
28. Occelli, C. (2011). *Mappe di rischio: Una proposta per l'analisi e la gestione dei rischi in ambito sanitario*. PhD Thesis, Università degli Studi di Torino, Torino.
29. Re, A. (2011). *Miglioriamo la sicurezza. Costruiamo la cassetta degli attrezzi* (Technical report). Torino: ASL TO3.
30. Habermas, J. (1981). *Theorie des kommunikativen Handelns: Handlungsrationalität und gesellschaftliche Rationalisierung*. Frankfurt am Main: Suhrkamp.

Cloud Computing Adoption in Italian SMEs: A Focus on Decision-making and Post-implementation Processes

Adele Caldarelli, Luca Ferri, and Marco Maffei

Abstract Cloud computing is an emerging model in which machines in large data centres can be used to deliver services in a scalable manner. It allows firms to receive the same internal ICT structure with lower costs and a higher degree of flexibility. With this technology come many disadvantages that can have a major impact on the information and services supported by this technology. This chapter pursues two related aims. First, it investigates the decision-making process of implementing cloud computing by highlighting the drivers and ICT requirements of SMEs. Then, it examines the effects following the migration of the ICT system from an in-house data centre to a cloud-based service. We found specific drivers and ICT requirements, suggesting the implementation of cloud computing in SMEs to oversee specific issues. Moreover, our findings show that the advantages arising post-implementation confirm the expectations created by the management during the decision-making process; meanwhile, at least in the short term, no disadvantages arose.

Keywords Cloud computing • Decision-making process • ICT • Post-implementation process

1 Introduction

The persisting crisis within the Italian manufacturing industry reflects the difficulties that domestic enterprises have encountered in adapting to the external changes that have affected the international economic environment over the past 20 years [1]. The country was unprepared for globalisation and the technological changes that increased competitive pressures on a global scale [2]. The main reasons behind such difficulties relate to a lack of innovation within the country in information and communication technology (ICT) [1–4].

A. Caldarelli • L. Ferri (✉) • M. Maffei
University of Naples Federico II, Naples, Italy
e-mail: adele.caldarelli@unina.it; luca.ferri@unina.it; marco.maffei@unina.it

© Springer International Publishing AG 2017
K. Corsi et al. (eds.), *Reshaping Accounting and Management Control Systems*,
Lecture Notes in Information Systems and Organisation 20,
DOI 10.1007/978-3-319-49538-5_4

The dissemination of information systems is usually regarded as a crucial element to guarantee the fast data processing and circulation of information, which in turn favours the creation and maintenance of competitive advantage [4, 5]. Market pressure, cost optimisation and increased productivity appear to be the guidelines that firms adopt to ensure their survival. It seems necessary to adopt an ICT framework that can reduce (fixed and variable) administrative costs and ensure increased productivity while maintaining a flexible structure and enabling a rapid response to market needs [4–7].

According to practitioners, one technology with the potential to solve this problem could be cloud computing [8, 9]. Cloud computing is a distributed computing paradigm that enables access to virtualised resources, including computers, networks, storage, development platforms and applications [10]. These resources can be unilaterally requested, provisioned and configured by the user with minimal interaction with the cloud provider. Furthermore, resources can be rapidly scaled up to meet the user's needs, thus creating the illusion of infinite resources available at any time [11]. Also, resource utilisation can be rapidly measured and controlled by customers because this technology is based on a pay-per-use model [12]. With the support of important industry stakeholders (e.g. Google, Amazon, Microsoft), cloud computing is being widely adopted in different domains. Cloud services such as Google Mail or Dropbox have become everyday useful tools for millions of people. Many firms currently use cloud-based applications (i.e. Salesforce), and small and medium firms are embracing virtual infrastructures offered by cloud service providers (CSP) such as Amazon Web Services (AWS) or Microsoft Azure [13]. The advantages arising from adopting cloud computing are indubitable [14–16]. According to the European Commission (2010) and to Microsoft (2011), this tool could provide many advantages, especially for small and medium enterprises (SMEs). Many authors have broadly identified the strengths associated with the use of cloud computing [13–18], investigating the advantages and disadvantages for firms arising from its adoption. They concluded that cloud computing can be a great opportunity, especially for SMEs; however, these authors identified the advantages and the disadvantages arising from cloud computing without providing any information about the decision-making process that pushes firms to adopt cloud computing and without examining the post-implementation effects to verify whether the expected advantages and disadvantages are confirmed. Therefore, we address these under-investigated issues by pursing the following two aims: (1) investigating the decision-making process of implementing cloud computing by highlighting the drivers and ICT requirements of SMEs and (2) examining the effects of the system 6 months after migration to the ICT system. To reach our aims, we use a multiple case study method. This method allows us to study the information systems in the field, helping us to understand the complexity of the decision-making and implementation process.

We examine three Italian SMEs. Italy is a technologically backward country; indeed, a report published by the Bank of Italy [1, 2] reveals that Italian firms, when compared with their European competitors, show a strong technological gap, and their business is therefore penalised in the competition arena. In this regard, the

Italian government published a 'Digital Agenda' in 2011 encouraging firms to adopt new technologies. According to the document, cloud computing could be a main actor in the Italian technological revolution. Hence, the three Italian SMEs investigated in this chapter could better provide a picture of choosing to implement cloud computing and of the effects following the migration process, which should reveal the benefits.

The remainder of the paper is organised as follows. Section 2 reviews the literature about cloud computing adoption. Section 3 focuses on the research design. Section 4 presents the case studies on three Italian SMEs. Section 5 discusses the results of this study. Section 6 provides concluding remarks.

2 The Extant Literature on Cloud Computing Decision-making and Implementation Processes

The first definition of cloud computing can be found in the document 'Definition of Cloud Computing', which was published by the US National Institute of Information Technology (NIST) [10]. It refers to this technology as 'a network model that allows access to a set of shared information across computing resources (e.g. servers, storage, applications, services) that can be rapidly provided by a provider' [1]. This report also identifies its characteristics, distribution models and architecture, shedding light on the high degree of flexibility, elasticity and cost savings that result from adopting this technology. This view of cloud computing is widely accepted by many authors [8, 14, 15, 19–22]. Indeed, extant literature agrees upon describing cloud computing as a set of technologies that enable, store and process data using hardware and/or software that is distributed and made available virtually on the Internet [23]. Qualified suppliers provide these services to users through a set of technologies and information resources that are available online [24].

The literature on this topic is still limited, and few papers have been published recently. According to Yang and Tate [25], the studies on this topic can be divided into four areas: technology (regarding performance, network, data management), business economics (cost–benefit analysis, market analysis, risks, legal issues), applications (engineering studies) and general studies (non-empirical studies regarding introduction and implementation).

Primitive studies on cloud computing are strictly theoretical. Many authors provided their own definition of cloud computing and highlighted the enormous benefits that this tool could provide to businesses, supporting its adoption [8, 14, 15, 19–22, 26]. The following table compares the definitions of cloud computing found in the literature (Table 1).

According to some authors [19, 20], cloud computing is not a new technology, but instead it is a new use of virtualisation and grid computing. Vouk [22], Plummer et al. [8] and Vaquero et al. [23] do not accept this definition; instead, they define

Table 1 A comparison between different definitions of cloud computing

Definition	Author/s
'Cloud is a pool of virtualised computer resources'.	Boss, Malladi, Quan, Legregni and Hall [20]
'Cloud computing is not a fundamentally new paradigm. It draws on existing technologies and approaches, such as utility computing, software-as-a-service, distributed computing, and centralized data centers. What is new is that cloud computing combines and integrates these approaches'.	Weiss [21]
'A type of parallel and distributed system consisting of a collection of interconnected and virtualized computers that are dynamically provisioned and presented as one or more unified computing resources based on service level agreements established through negotiation between the service provider and consumers'.	Buyya [14]
'Cloud computing embraces cyber-infrastructure and builds on virtualization, distributed computing, grid computing, utility computing, networking, and Web and software services'.	Vouk [22]
'A style of computing where massively scalable IT-related capabilities are provided as a service across the Internet to multiple external customers'.	Plummer, Smith, Bittman, Cearley, Cappuccio and Scott [8]
'A large pool of easily usable and accessible virtualized resources (such as hardware, development platforms and/or services). These resources can be dynamically reconfigured to adjust to a variable load (scale), allowing also for an optimum resource utilization. This pool of resources is typically exploited by a pay-per-use model in which guarantees are offered by the infrastructure pro-vider by means of customized SLAs'.	Vaquero, Rodero-Merino, Caceres and Lindner (2009) [23]
'A model for enabling convenient, on-demand network access to a shared pool of configurable computing resources (e.g. networks, servers, storage, applications, and services) that can be rapidly provisioned and released with minimal management effort or service provider interaction'.	Mell and Grance [10]
'The illusion of infinite computing resources available on demand, the elimination of up-front commitments by cloud users, and the ability to pay for use of computing resources on a short-term basis as needed'.	Armbrust, Fox, Griffith, Joseph, Katz and Konwinski [15]

cloud computing as a new technology. The NIST argue that the difference between cloud computing and other existing technologies is not merely linked to the attribute of virtualisation, but it is primarily about customisation and the possibility of getting 'on-demand' service. Thus, the main difference between cloud comput-ing and other existing technologies is related to its different business model [10]. All of the aforementioned studies provide a theoretical vision of the benefits, costs and risks associated with this tool. Following the increasing level of adoption of the instrument has allowed other authors to empirically demonstrate the benefits, limitations and problems arising from the adoption of cloud computing in enterprises. In 2009, Rosenthal et al. [27] provided a practical approach for cloud computing implementation by empirically analysing the benefits generated by this technology for the 'biomedical informatics (BMI) community'. In the same period, Velte et al. [28] provided a detailed guide to SMEs' and large firms' migration to the cloud computing system using the case study method. This study highlighted firms' motivations for adopting cloud computing and the difficulties they encountered with its implementation. Hosseini et al. [29] conducted a similar study that analysed the risks and rewards of migration to a cloud-based system by interviewing the end users of a firm in the energy sector. The results showed that cloud computing is potentially able to reduce firms' operating costs. More specifically, they found a reduction of 37 % in ICT costs and a reduction of 21 % of maintenance actions. However, the study also highlighted some significant drawbacks, such as loss of customer confidence, loss of control of data, employees' resistance to changing their routines and transfer costs. Sultan [16] conducted a study based on the application of cloud computing in businesses. More specifically, the author identified the organisational and economic benefits generated by the introduction of this tool in an English medium-sized enterprise in the computer industry. The author pointed out that after cloud computing introduction, the costs of the ICT function were reduced by approximately 80 % (it is important to highlight that the employees were reallocated and the previous ICT structure was sold). This study stresses that this instrument is not suitable for all SMEs because the convenience of its usage depends on the size of the ICT structure, the costs the structure has already incurred (and that cannot be eliminated), the security costs and the degree of risk that the firm's management is willing to accept. Based on these studies, other authors have verified the benefits and disadvantages of adopting cloud computing in SMEs [30–35], emerging markets [36, 37], banks [31, 38], the public sector [39–41], the health-care sector [27, 36, 42, 43] and other relevant sectors [35, 44, 45].

In all of the cited cases, cloud computing is regarded as an important solution to corporate networks' problems. That being said, this tool has important drawbacks. Indeed, while providing a number of benefits not achievable with other technologies, it also creates a number of risks that are 'typical' of the outsourcing of ICT function. Therefore, it is necessary to find a proper method of implementation that balances the disadvantages and advantages to determine when the cloud may be an optimal answer to a firm's needs [16, 46].

However, cloud computing has many weaknesses that must be considered before its adoption, many of which have been covered in the literature. For example, the introduction of cloud computing in business contexts requires redesigning and adapting internal control systems due to the existence of potential dangers, especially those related to the loss of data control within the cloud. In a recent document, the NIST argued that cloud computing, as with any emerging technology, is inappropriate for the majority of firms due to 'open issues' [1]. According to several authors (i.e. [47, 48], there are five open issues that present challenges to the efficient implementation of cloud computing. The first is computing performance, as different applications within the cloud may require different levels of performance, which in turn requires increasing costs or decreasing system efficiency. Of course, this issue is not exclusively a cloud computing problem [13, 49, 50]. The second issue is cloud reliability, which relates to the alignment of various factors, such as the hardware and software offered by a provider to employees within firms. A cloud solution depends on many factors in terms of the degree of reliability within an environment [13, 51–54]. Third, economic goals can face challenges due to the openness of cloud computing. While cloud computing offers the opportunity to outsource the ICT function, which can come with economic benefits, it also has many disadvantages. The fourth open issue relates to compliance. Many authors have stated that cloud computing providers are in the best position to enforce compliance rules; this can increase disadvantages for end users [26, 49, 54]. The final issue with cloud computing openness highlighted in the literature relates to information security. Moving data into the cloud means potentially losing control of it, which could create many problems in terms of data security and privacy [13, 15, 49, 51–53, 55–57]. Leaving aside the issues of control and the disadvantages related to the adoption of the instrument, as they are beyond the scope of this work, more in-depth study of what motivates firms to migrate to cloud technology is still required. Specifically, it is important to define advantages as the benefits that a firm should expect to achieve.

The literature identifies five major benefits of cloud computing adoption: reduced costs, increased storage, high automation, flexibility, greater mobility and less focus on ICT function. The most immediate for users is certainly cost reduction. Customers pay for a cloud service that is completely customisable and modelled on the firm's real needs. Thus, it is not yet necessary to support large investments in infrastructure. Related to this, there is another advantage resulting from the adoption of this tool: increased storage. The firm can benefit from external memory that is always available to store its data. Another benefit is high automation. Firms that adopt this tool do not require employees in data centres for data backup and control because these tasks are delegated to the provider. This allows firms to become more flexible. The cloud is customisable depending on the changing needs of the customer. The possibility of changing at every moment, and to obtain economies of scale, is the basis of the competitiveness of the cloud. Accessibility from any location provides greater mobility—customers can access their data at any time and from any location, facilitating multinational firms [14, 15].

The literature identifies a number of disadvantages or problems that may arise following the implementation of cloud computing. Specifically, a disadvantage is defined as the charge (not necessarily financial) that the firm has to bear to use a certain technology. The disadvantages discussed in the literature relate to reliability [13, 51–53], economic objectives [13–15, 58], low level of compliance [26, 49, 57] and difficulties of adaptation, performance and data security [13, 15, 49, 51–53, 55, 57]. Below, the reasons for some authors' misgivings about the use of such technology are given.

The first misgiving regards reliability. Several authors [13, 51–53] highlighted problems related to the capacity of the facilities offered by the provider to ensure stable performance over time.

As regards the economic objectives, the literature is clear that, despite that cloud computing offers the opportunity to outsource ICT, there are numerous disadvantages that must be mitigated, which requires incurring additional costs and reducing the convenience of this tool [13–15, 58, 59]. Another point discussed by several authors concerns the degree of compliance. Indeed, the provider is in a good position to enforce the rules of conformity, and this is a limitation for the firm (or at least it makes the control less effective) [26, 49, 57].

A further critical issue identified by several authors is the level of performance. The performance of a cloud network does not depend only on the model chosen, but also on the state of the network and the software that is used. Often, the use of applications other than those supplied by the provider may cause compatibility issues, lowering performance. However, this kind of problem is common to many technological solutions [13, 49, 50]. One of the most discussed topics is data security. Moving data within the cloud can create problems in terms of the firm's security and privacy [13, 49, 51–53, 55–57].

Despite these disadvantages, several authors stated that cloud computing is a technology that is potentially able to provide a competitive advantage to businesses when it is properly adopted and implemented [49, 51–53]. In the light of this literature, in a context in which the technology is revealed as the most appropriate instrument to ensure the flexibility, efficiency and effectiveness to the ICT function, it appears necessary to examine the reasons that cause firms to adopt (or not adopt) cloud computing.

3 Research Design

In order to achieve our objectives, we opted for a qualitative analysis using the multiple case study method, which allowed us to explore and compare the nature of the decisions between different sectors [60–64]. The multiple case study method has been widely adopted in the ICT field [62, 65–70]. The motivation behind the massive use of this method is certainly conducive to not limiting the research to a single sector, analysing the benefits in several areas and highlighting similarities or differences for end users. Specifically, according to Yin [71, 72], multiple case studies are more appropriate when the aim is to examine contemporary events and when it is not necessary to control behavioural variables. The author points out that this method is appropriate if the goal of the research is to describe the same phenomenon in different moments or to test its replicability. Also, observing multiple cases allows researchers to confirm emerging constructs and propositions [65, 71, 72], making the results more robust and generalisable [73]. According to Benbasat et al. [65], with multiple case study designs, researchers are able to study information systems in the field, understanding the complexity of a particular process, learning the state of the art, generating theories on its practical aspects and enriching their field of study with knowledge contributions.

To enrol cases in the study, we chose Italian SMEs that began using cloud computing within the same period as each other and that operate in different sectors. The decision to select organisations belonging to different sectors is not casual; indeed, it could allow us to shed light on the different motivations firms have for adopting cloud computing, the implementation steps and the advantages and disadvantages of this technology. To prepare for data gathering, to familiarise ourselves with practitioners' perspectives and to identify organisations that have implemented cloud computing in recent years (a very rare phenomenon for Italian SMEs), we interviewed five different cloud provider experts (three ICT consultants and two practitioners) in the fall of 2011. We also used the informal network that our department belongs to as another source to identify potential case study organisations. We approached many contacts during congresses, workshops and seminars where organisations presented their new ICT systems based on cloud computing. Table 2 lists the names of the organisations, their respective sectors, the number of respondents and the number of interviews conducted. We use nicknames for each organisation to protect their privacy.

For each firm, we interviewed the CEO, the head of ICT (or the person in charge of risk management and ICT processes) and, where possible, the end users. The choice of these subjects is not accidental. While the former are persons who directly or indirectly participate in the final decisions, end users are actually affected by the change in the firm. In some cases, it was possible to interview representatives of the provider to which firms have turned in order to verify the effective exchange of information between the various actors involved in the process.

Furthermore, this analysis takes into account both endogenous and exogenous variables, using internal sources (interviews with managers and internal documents that are usually not accessible to the public) and external sources (reports published by the firm, newspaper articles, other firm publications). However, the primary sources of information were the interviews with the CEOs, who were considered to be the decision-makers.

In order to capture more detail and data, the interviews were conducted using a semi-structured questionnaire consisting of nine questions. The goal was to obtain information about firms' preliminary analyses that prompted them to choose a

Table 2 Firms investigated

Enterprise nickname	Sector	Number of internal interviews	Number of external interviews	Total number of interviews
Alfa Home	Household goods	3	0	3
Beta Insurance	Insurance	2	1	3
Omega Tech	Education	3	1	4

cloud-based system as well as to determine the actual advantages and disadvantages arising from its adoption a few months after the system had been fully implemented.

It is worth noting that the questions acted merely as a guideline, as they included a number of key issues to be discussed during the interview rather than represented binding questions to ask respondents. The interviews were recorded and later transcribed for our analysis. Moreover, when the interviews seemed to be incomplete, we asked the respondents for telephonic integrations. In order to avoid individual bias (i.e. the possibility that a single researcher is influenced in some way, falsifying the results of the study), the interviews were conducted by a team of three researchers who defined the key themes for the interviews. At least two members of the group were involved in every interview. The interviewers consulted several internal documents regarding ICT function and any details that might help them to determine the cost of the function, supporting the respondents' answers. Immediately after the interviews, each researcher transcribed the recordings. The researchers organised the interviews chronologically, discussing the transcripts and summarising the data and opinions around the concepts of expected benefits, adoption motivations and the actual benefits from adopting cloud computing.

The questionnaire was based on a theoretical framework derived from the literature. Many authors assume that there are internal and external drivers that explain cloud computing adoption [8, 14, 21, 31, 38]. Internal pressures include cost pressure and increased productivity, whereas external pressure is mainly related to market pressure. These drivers generate different requirements. Cost pressure creates the need to transform fixed costs into variable costs to ensure better flexibility [14]. With reference to productivity requirements, the literature highlights that firms need speed, flexibility, scalability, security, cost-effectiveness and transparency [13, 51–54]. Further, market pressure creates the need to change the business model to consolidate on existing markets [14, 35]. In many cases, after a deep analysis of the firm's ICT needs, management identifies cloud computing as the best solution. However, previous literature analysing the drivers and the ICT requirements to justify the adoption of a new technology does not verify the post-implementation effects. Therefore, we enrich our framework and analyse the implementation steps, paying particular attention to the phases of cloud introduction and its impact on firms. This allows us to investigate whether there are any similarities in cloud computing implementation between firms operating in different sectors. Then, we investigated the effects arising from this technology adoption a few months after its full introduction to understand if this tool can really provide economic advantages to Italian SMEs (Fig. 1).

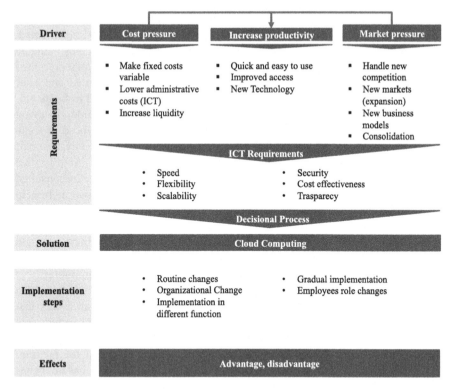

Fig. 1 Framework used to analyse the decision-making process and the post-implementation effects

4 The Multiple Case Study

In this section, we provide evidence on the use of cloud computing in three Italian SMEs.

4.1 Alfa Home

The firm Alfa Home engages in the distribution of household items. Alfa is the largest chain of shops providing products for the home and for wedding registries in Italy, with more than 180 stores in 18 Italian regions.

The constant evolution of the brand and its development created many organisational complications that have caused the widespread loss of efficiency. The main problem with the ICT function was that it was unable to respond quickly to environmental changes, maintaining a good degree of cohesion between the various business functions. These limits reached a peak in 2011 as a result of the financial crisis. In this period, in response to external stress, the management imposed cost rationalisation on the organisation, posing a series of questions to the ICT department. The aim was to combine the communication problems between the different stores (generated by the incompatibility of data, documents and reports) that prevented the firm from obtaining a global vision and reducing costs.

The best solution seemed to be to integrate the stores' software, but in the short term, this generated additional costs (many licences had already been bought, and the servers were old), resistance from staff and other implementation issues typical of change [74, 75]. In addition, the managers, in accordance with the ICT function, looked for a solution that would allow them to integrate the digital e-commerce platform, thus ensuring lower costs, the immediate availability of information, flexibility and scalability. Historically, Alfa has always implemented the latest technology—it was one of the first firms to introduce the Enterprise resource program (ERP) system (based on Microsoft Dynamics) as well as systems for data analysis (Microsoft SQL Server).

> We needed something that would allow management to integrate the already used systems without losing time in employees formation. Our servers were old and we could not concentrate all servers in our headquarters because we would have had to bear huge investments in that historical moment were prohibitive.

The solution to all of these problems was found in cloud computing. The management explained that they implemented cloud computing in 2011 when it became necessary to replace the firm's e-mail platform; they switched to a Microsoft Exchange cloud-based solution. Initially, e-mail was the only function for which it was used. The reasons for outsourcing the mail server included the following: the wish to discontinue managing the servers internally (i.e. on the premise), breaking free from maintenance and disaster recovery problems and the significant increase in space for the mailbox/user. The initial results were positive, and the management began considering total migration to the cloud:

> We have to delete old servers, so we carried out a feasibility study and a cost-benefit analysis. All our tests could be reduced to the most classic of economic problems: "Make or buy".

The initial analysis required the involvement of numerous business functions such as ICT, sales, marketing and finance. Its convenience was immediately apparent, rationalising the business processes (order management of the stores, warehouse management of the stores, etc.). After a lengthy discussion between the CEO and the head of ICT, they decided to optimise the management processes by shifting from the old solutions (the physical servers) to virtual servers in the cloud.

In order to reduce the impact of these decisions, the migration was not performed immediately but instead was done in stages. First, the management addressed the choice of cloud provider. They chose Microsoft Azure, which solved their problems with data storage uniformity and allowed all of the shops in the franchise to benefit from a version of Office by sharing documents on a single platform. Next, a hybrid cloud solution using more than 20 virtual machines in Microsoft Azure

(Infrastructure as a Service) for the definition of highly reliable infrastructure for federation with Microsoft Office 365 was integrated. This farm was based on IaaS, deployed with a Microsoft SharePoint 2013 server farm in hybrid configuration with Microsoft Office 365.

> We have also implemented a farm of more than 15 servers on Microsoft Azure, for the use of our portal community, but also for the federation of the Dominion firm with Office365, along with the replica of the entire structure on Cloud AD (Domain controller, ADFS, DirSync) and as a result of the good results, was introduced the entire platform of Office365, complete with Lync Online, Sharepoint, OneDrive for Business and Yammer.

The CEO emphasised that the adoption required consistent effort on the part of the management. The implementation strategy was designed to avoid or at least minimise the impact of changes on the end users (employees). The idea was that the less the end users saw the change, the less the firm would suffer. Also, for this reason, it was decided that the firm would adopt a platform with graphical user interfaces similar to the previous platform and that it would be integrated with the software already in use. The first implementation was a success, and management has begun using the cloud for more and more functions.

> As explained before, we divided the adoption of the Cloud in steps. In order of time, our last operation is the backup of ERP databases on Cloud, as remote disaster recovery.

The adoption of this technology has led to at least three advantages and three disadvantages. First, the reduced reliance upon machines gave rise to a sharp reduction in maintenance costs and energy usage. Another advantage was the high flexibility that allowed users to easily increase or decrease their resources as needed. Finally, the canon of the cloud represents a certain and tractable cost that can be fully expensed in the year without the need for capitalisation.

> This helps to improve certain business ratios of significant importance for society such as ours.

On the other hand, three disadvantages are attributable to the lack of control of the infrastructure, the strong dependence on the internet to use the services and the higher costs from the monthly fee. Nevertheless, it is possible to quantify the savings resulting from the use of the cloud: the firm spent 30 % less than it did previously.

Concerns about security management were not present:

> I believe that reliability and safety are adequate.

Specifically, the directors felt confident relying on structures (or providers) with proven expertise and authority. The effectiveness of internal security policies contributes to the robustness of the system:

> The Cloud is the future of our firm? I would say it will be absolutely the protagonist in the future, as it is already present.

4.2   Beta Insurance

The Beta Insurance Group is an Italian mutual insurance firm. The success of the enterprise is directly connected to an advanced infrastructure network—in fact, the management stated that they have always adopted expensive ICT solutions but that they were not necessarily at the vanguard. Therefore, the ICT function was seen as something 'extra'—a lot of tools that were necessary for the customers' value creation but only sometimes useful for internal process simplification (management practices, quick searches, etc.). Thus, all of the costs arising from this function were seen as 'a necessary effort' in order to reach the firm's final aims.

However, in 2011, the difficulties of the socio-economic context influenced the firm's growth objectives and its methods to reach these objectives. The management had to choose between a 'pure cost reduction' (cutting expenses) and a strategy to increase market share. The managers' idea was to redesign the strategy, adapting to the environmental changes and moving ahead of competitors. Unfortunately, redesigning a strategy representing one of the keys to success in a context characterised by the objective of 'efficiency' is also important to limit the costs of carrying out internal operations and ICT function. So, in the event of a transfer to new headquarters and with the aim of aligning their infrastructure services to the objectives of growth and innovation dictated by business lines, Beta launched an outsourcing project for its technological infrastructure. The main reason for this was to find greater agility, cost optimisation, service continuity and effectiveness response. Despite the great advantages that emerged in the analysis step, the management was sceptical, so the first implementation included just the creation of a secondary backup site aiming to avoid disaster recovery problems. This project outsourced the data centre and represented an opportunity for a radical technological renewal: the firm has gone from 'homemade' solutions to many services provided by a 'carrier class' provider and aligned to the newest technology. The technology upgrade is guaranteed by the cloud service provider for the entire contractual life (7 years) with the same costs. After the first migration, the management asked the same provider to activate a new primary site, transferring the secondary site to another city:

> When we implement a new technology we always are cautiously. There is always a strong scepticism about what is new and the people are afraid of changes...but when it was necessary to deploy new servers for backups, we said "Why not?" And then we tried.

With this implementation, the management avoided any problems with disaster recovery, but there were still several operational duties inherent in the ICT function (i.e. extending service availability to 24/7, increasing flexibility in relation to the demands of the business lines, introducing a logic of service level agreements [SLA] both internally and externally, constant innovation and openness to mobile services).

In the same year, based on the new strategic lines, the management started to renovate the firm's ICT function. The ICT manager created a study group in order to compare the different technological possibilities offered by the market with the goal of maintaining a defined and predictable ICT budget:

> We needed a service that could be 24×7, which would guarantee at the same time operational simplicity and flexibility.

For each technology, management carried out a cost–benefit analysis and a technological analysis. After a few months, a preliminary report identified the cloud technology as being ideal to satisfy the firm's technological needs. In fact, by using a cloud technology service, availability and assistance were guaranteed 24/7, the system was easy to update (scalability) and use and the new working logic was dedicated to the autonomy and abatement of logistical constraints. The management, after a discussion with the ICT manager, opted to implement cloud computing. As with any new technology, the introduction of cloud computing could have disastrous effects, so the administrators made a plan for its gradual implementation. With the provider's help, the management implemented a cloud-sourcing platform (articulated in the following points):

- Phase of due diligence for detailed definition of the scope.
- Employees have the option to access their own virtual terminal through a thin client.
- Definition of a single fee includes the scope of the growth the firm agreed upon.
- Activation of cloud sourcing, which is integrated and delivered by a carrier-neutral data centre/carrier class located in Italy to manage infrastructure environments (systems, equipment, connectivity and security) and application in the field.
- Maintenance technology and operations via platforms, expertise and operational management procedures that are constantly updated with respect to market standards and best practices.
- Management and optimisation of software licences.
- Service desk for performance monitoring and incident management.
- Management of change requests to the service (change management).
- Government services and verification of SLA for customers.
- Full integration with disaster/recovery service and evolution towards a mode of business continuity.
- Consistency and synergy with side project of virtualising jobs.

In 2012, in the same period of the first implementation, Beta sold its old workstations to the same provider to facilitate the centralized management of the new servers. The adoption of this solution, whose service includes the rental of equipment and user assistance, allowed employees to use their virtual workstations from anywhere via thin clients, eliminating the constraints of physical location and greatly simplifying the ICT assistance services as well as reducing the costs of internal transfers between jobs during reorganisations or individual journeys to zero. Nevertheless, the adoption process encountered many difficulties. The implementation required a redesign of the ICT function governance, reallocating redundant resources to other functions and keeping only a few workers for internal control.

The new platform was implemented in a series of steps. An organisation phase followed the completion of these steps (completed in the last quarter of 2014), finalising the migration. This provided Beta with a solution called 'business continuity in cloud sourcing' (i.e. all of the services are always active in the cloud).

The cloud-sourcing service (complete with directional connectivity, security, systems, equipment, services and application infrastructure) allowed Beta to complete the following:

- Migrate from in-house to total outsourcing without discomfort and with total transparency for the approximately 2500 users managed by ICT services
- Systemically govern and oversee the entire chain of service (directional network, security, systems, basic services and middleware) with a service orientation towards the end user
- Have a single directional connectivity manager, infrastructure services and perimeter security, with clear identification of roles and responsibilities
- Preside over all outsourced services through a single service desk
- Develop a roadmap for standardisation and best practices for adaptation to the existing architecture with a view towards simplification, increased performance and improved security
- Obtain an average annual savings on IT costs and energy costs of more than 20 %
- Guarantee service availability (up to 24/7 and business continuity), greater operational simplicity and speed in obtaining additional resources if required due to the scalability offered in the cloud

Beta achieved substantial cost savings: less need for space enabled by the disposal of the previous data centre allowed it to recover 600 square metres of physical space, now intended for other uses, while at the same reducing energy consumption from the air conditioning system and other utility systems. The switch to cloud computing was made at the end of the useful life of the data centre in-house infrastructures, avoiding the large cost that would be required for their technological renewal.

In addition, beginning in 2015, when the services became fully operational, cloud sourcing enabled new payment methods (i.e. pay-per-use), resulting in 20 % lower costs over 5 years. The cloud also varied the duties of the staff. The service inside was eliminated, as it was deemed to be no longer necessary (due to the standardisation of the equipment and the virtualisation that has transferred many of the operations to the server). The ICT staff was reallocated to different functions (some in internal functions), thus ensuring an increase in productivity via ICT tasks to support the design and development of the principles of governance, which previously were not adequately covered.

In this sense, the firm maximised the effort cloud deployment, obtaining a double benefit: it enjoyed increased productivity and solved a number of problems its previous ICT function had.

For these reasons, in a short time, the firm has begun to use more and more features of the cloud computing platform:

> In scope we experienced some years solutions PaaS / SaaS for human resource management, document management and CRM. Now we are venturing in developing solutions in mobile, collaboration, social, from time to time integrating components with Cloud components in-house, possibly made to services from legacy applications. It is believed that this is the best strategy to pursue innovation, safeguarding the investments made in the past and not exposing the firm to risks of choices monolithic.

There are certainly issues related to security. In this case, the provider guaranteed the possibility of access, security, privacy, backup and anything else required by the regulations in full agreement with the requirements of the monitoring organisations. The choice of provider to ensure information security is crucial (as well as using certifications that attest to the quality of the control process, such as ISO).

4.3 Omega Tech

Omega Tech was founded in 2000. It is focused on two kinds of activities: e-learning and technology services. Since 2006, the firm has been partnered with the world's largest open-source online training platform: modular object-oriented dynamic learning environment (known as Moodle).

The fast expansion of the firm on the market has led, in a short amount of time, to an exponential growth of its ICT needs—the existing structure was not suitable to satisfy the increasing demand. For this reason, in 2011, Moodle's managers began investigating alternate technological solutions that would meet the firm's needs without overburdening it financially. The management was not new to virtualisation experiences. For example, in 2010, they opted for several solutions similar to cloud computing for their secondary functions (i.e. employees' e-mail). The success of this experience persuaded the management to move decisively to cloud computing. The choice of an ideal model initially worried corporate leaders.

> It was about the determination of the right trade-off between the need of privacy and the security of information, that pushed us toward the private cloud and, on the other hand, the need to reduce costs and benefit from economies of scale (public cloud).

Omega managers carried out a deeper analysis on the needs and the characteristics that the ICT structure must have to satisfy all of the firm's needs. Therefore, the management opted to adopt a double solution: a public cloud solution for the less relevant information (e-mail, website, etc.) and a private cloud solution for the most sensitive data (internal data, development data, customer portfolios). This solution saved money while providing a great deal of security for the most sensitive information (that would have been stored in the private data centre). Once the management knew what kind and level of service was needed, they moved to the implementation phase:

> We use public cloud for more standard infrastructure, while we use private cloud for specialised infrastructure. Cloud infrastructure have certainly helped us to get the desired results.

There is a significant difference in the implementation time between the two different services. Indeed, the service provider could activate the public cloud very quickly, with several benefits in terms of optimisation of cost/performance. It gives the possibility to scale vertically with 'pay-as-you-go' models. On the other hand, the private cloud, which is based on specific applications, has a longer activation time because it requires a set of tests. These tests are important in order to ensure quality performance while maintaining an elastic structure, with the possibility of scaling both vertically and horizontally. The difference, in terms of technical and economic performance, was perceived immediately:

> The business processes are improved immediately. With this type of infrastructure we were able to simplify and automate a number of processes by increasing the value of the services provided.

There are many differences between the models. Indeed, the advantages of the private cloud include consolidation of services and the ability to create an ad hoc infrastructure, while the advantages of the public cloud include a higher speed of deployment and flexibility, which are reflected in customers' proactivity, leading to a greater overall availability of infrastructure for end users. The principal business functions to migrate into the cloud were the ICT department, technical support and the sales department. During this time, numerous other implementations that transferred all business functions to the cloud have been performed:

> Actually, the implementations are in constant evolution.

With specific reference to the economic benefits, the management stated that, in the early stages of cloud computing adoption, the costs increased. Indeed, during the implementation phase, the function was duplicated: they preferred to make the new solution functional before deleting those already in use. In addition, some business processes were reviewed and optimised with new multi-purpose software, and the staff, first allocated in the ICT, was moved to other functions to increase productivity.

> In reality, our main intent was not to decrease investment but the ROI maximisation and the improvement of the perceived services quality. At the moment the feedback about our services exposed to the public through consolidation, optimisation and automation of processes is positive.

These objectives have been largely achieved. Eliminating the old server has reduced operating capital, while replacing electrical charges and maintenance with the fees to be paid to the provider increased operating income; thus, there is an improvement in the return on investment. Savings in ICT, without considering the costs of replacing the servers, total about 25 % annually. The savings would be higher if the firm only used the public cloud. Finally, the administrators are confident about questions of security.

Although we were initially sceptical, we have not found security issues in our cloud infrastructures.

5 Discussion

In this section, we discuss the results of our case studies in the light of the previous literature based on our analysis of the case data via our framework. We discuss the key drivers and ICT requirements, the decision-making process in terms of expected advantages and disadvantages, the migration process and the post-implementation effects. However, we should note that the three examined SMEs operate only in Italy and that they have all existed for the same number of years. This is relevant because in many cases, different life cycles of firms may have an effect on their motivations for migration [28].

Referring to key drivers and ICT requirements, all three firms reported their need to increase the dimensions of their ICT structures, reducing the related costs (i.e. storage, maintenance, software, disaster recovery) and increasing flexibility. In two of the cases, cloud computing was used to avoid new ICT investment (Alfa Home, Beta Insurance). This is consistent with Amrbrust et al.'s [15] and Buyya et al.'s [14] statement that this was firms' main motivation to adopt cloud computing. These authors argued that this new technology could help firms to increase flexibility and avoid new investments, providing the required level of service without any empirical results. This allows firms to use expensive technologies at affordable prices [12]. After a deep analysis of the firms' ICT needs, all of the firms identified cloud computing as the best solution. This technical analysis that the management carried out was supported by a cost–benefit analysis of cloud computing implementation.

Referring to the decision-making process, we discuss the expected advantages and disadvantages separately. The expected advantages of the three firms included cost savings (i.e. reduction of investment in software and hardware, employee reduction), scalability, ease of use and flexibility. Despite the great number of subjects interviewed, the expected advantages were the same independent of the interviewees' positions in the firm, their education level and their personal experiences, which are the main variables that influence personal behaviour [76–78]. This supports Buyya et al.'s [14], Armbroust et al.'s [15] and Sultan's [16] claims, all of whom only theoretically discuss the benefits of cloud computing adoption without giving any empirical results. Further, these results are aligned with case studies carried out by many authors [30–35, 79–81] that show the motivations towards cloud computing adoption in different sectors (i.e. banking, oil and gas). Our results show that Italian SMEs, who are not competitive in the international arena, pay particular attention to cost savings.

The main expected disadvantages include the loss of governance of data, the loss of sensitive information, increased control risks and all of the typical disadvantages arising from outsourcing and shared technologies. All of these disadvantages support Weinhardt et al.'s [26], Chow et al.'s [49] and DaSilva et al.'s [54] argument that cloud computing is not a tool for all firms and that its implementation requires a strong level of control to avoid operational problems.

Despite this perceived disadvantage, the three firms chose different migration processes. In two cases (Alfa Home, Beta Insurance), the migration process was defined as having a high degree of complexity and was divided into different steps to ensure a successful implementation, to avoid internal resistance to the change and to avoid potential disadvantages, such as the loss of efficiency [28]. This behaviour is compliant with many authors' findings about secure cloud implementation [35, 44, 45]. What should be noted is that in the third case (Omega Tech), there was full implementation. The company employees were well oriented to the cloud computing implementation, and the management opted for a fast implementation process. The results of the study on this firm show that cloud computing can be rapidly introduced without causing organisational problems if the company's employees are well inclined towards the new technologies.

With reference to the post-implementation effects, what should be noted is that the three firms saw a strong reduction in their ICT investment (hardware and software), completely outsourcing this function to the cloud. More specifically, the SMEs had the following energy savings: 25 % (Omega Tech) and 30 % (Beta Insurance). Also, two of the firms saw a reduction in their general ICT costs of about 22 % (Omega Tech) and 31 % (Alfa Home). This is consistent with Velte et al.'s [28], Hosseini et al.'s [29] and Sultan's [16] findings of similar cost reductions in other European countries and in different kinds of SMEs. Moreover, all of the firms reassigned a portion of their ICT employees to other functions, increasing productivity. For example, Beta Insurance, which needed to enlarge its ICT service, achieved this goal without hiring new personnel. These results are consistent with many other studies carried out by different authors in different countries, highlighting that cloud computing, if implemented properly, can lead to significant cost savings for Italian SMEs [36, 37] and banks [31, 38].

With reference to the post-implementation disadvantages, what should be noted is that 6 months from the first implementation, there were no negative events. The management's fears (i.e. loss of control of data or data leakage) were completely unfounded. All of the interviewees stated that the cloud computing structure was safe and that they had not encountered any problems or disadvantages.

6 Conclusions

In this chapter, we addressed under-investigated issues by pursuing the following two aims: (1) investigating the decision-making process of implementing cloud computing by highlighting three Italian SMEs' driver and ICT requirements and (2) examining the implementation effects 6 months after the firms' migration to their new ICT systems.

We found that each firm had specific drivers and ICT requirements, which suggests that the implementation of cloud computing in SMEs must be done carefully to avoid any issues. Moreover, the advantages arising post-implementation confirm the expectations created by the management during the decision-making process, while at least in the short term, no disadvantages arose. More specifically, the firms needed ICT function reorganisation, cost savings and increased flexibility. After a deep analysis of all of the possible ICT solutions, the management identified cloud computing as the best option. Their analyses showed that cloud computing can be a significantly cheaper alternative to purchasing and maintaining a private system infrastructure. Also, this technology improves operating efficiency, reallocating ICT employees and reducing focus on ICT.

This chapter contributes to the existing literature by providing a clear observation of cloud computing adoption from the decision-making process to the final economic advantage mensuration. We share the same view of many authors [30–35] that cloud computing can be a great opportunity for firms.

This chapter also has practical implications. First, this study is useful for firms in which managers are considering migrating to cloud computing. Thanks to this paper, managers can identify the problems and key drivers to determine whether cloud computing is a good solution for their company. Further, we show how firms decide to implement cloud computing, highlighting the main expected advantages and disadvantages that influenced their final decision. This fills a knowledge gap in the existing literature.

The main limitation of this study is that the cost analysis only focused on system infrastructure costs, so we cannot know the real cost savings or efficiency improvement from reallocating the ICT employees. Also, there are many longer term costs associated with cloud computing (i.e. costs arising from migration to another provider) that we did not take into account. Our post-implementation analysis was only short term. These aspects should be taken into account when analysing the benefits of adoption only a long time after the end of the implementation process.

References

1. Banca d'Italia. *Relazione annuale al Governo*. https://www.bancaditalia.it/UIF/pubblicazioni-uif/relazione-2011.pdf
2. Bugamelli, M., & Pagano, P. (2004). Barriers to investment in ICT. *Applied Economics, 36* (20), 2275–2286.
3. CISCO. (2013). *Netelligent expands line of hosted and managed IT services with Cisco desktop-as-a-service solution*. Cisco systems publications. http://www.cisco.com/c/dam/en/us/solutions/collateral/data-center-virtualization/desktop-virtualization-solutions/netelligent-external-casestudy.pdf
4. Marchi, L., & Mancini, D. (2009). *Gestione informatica dei dati aziendali*. Milano: FrancoAngeli.
5. Quagli, A., Dameri, R. P., & Inghirami, I. E. (2007). *I sistemi informativi gestionali*. Milano: FrancoAngeli.

6. Paoloni, M. (2008). Note introduttive a I nuovi sistemi informativi e le piccole e medie imprese. In F. M. Cesaroni, P. Demartini (Eds.), *A cura di, Ict e informazione economico-finanziaria. Saggi sull'applicazione delle nuove tecnologie nelle grandi e nelle piccole e medie imprese*. Milano: Francoangeli.

7. Potito, L. (2014). Il rischio e l'ambiente. In L. Potito (Ed.), *A cura di, Economia aziendale*. Lavis (TN): Giappichelli editore.

8. Plummer, D. C., Smith, D. M., Bittman, T. J., Cearley, D. W., Cappuccio, D. J., & Scott, D., et al. (2009). *Five refining attributes of public and private cloud computing* (Gartner white paper, 31, 2). http://www.gartner.com/DisplayDocument?doc_cd=67182&ref=g_fromdoc

9. Microsoft. (2010–2011). *Securing Microsoft's cloud infrastructure*. https://cloudsecurityalliance. org/securing-the-MS-Cloud.pdf

10. Mell, P., & Grance, T. (2011). *The NIST definition of cloud computing—Recommendations of the National Institute of Standards and Technology*. NIST Publications. http://csrc.nist.gov/ publications/nistpubs/800-145/SP800-145.pdf

11. Gonzalez-Martínez, J. A., Cano-Parra, R., Bote-Lorenzo, M. L., & Gomez-Sanchez, E. (2015). Cloud computing and education: A state-of-the-art survey. *Computers and Education, 80*(1), 132–151.

12. Ibrahim, S., He, B., & Jin, H. (2011). *Towards pay-as-you-consume cloud computing*. IEEE International Conference on Services Computing, pp. 519–528.

13. Marston, S., Li, Z., Bandyopadhyay, S., Zhang, J., & Ghalsasi, A. (2011). Cloud computing— The business perspective. *Decision Support Systems, 51*(1), 176–189.

14. Buyya, R., Yeo, C. S., & Venugopal, S. (2008). Marked oriented cloud computing: Vision, hype, and realty for delivering IT services as cloud computing utilities. *The 10th IEEE International Conference on High Performance Computing and Communications, 10*(1), 5–13.

15. Armbrust, M., Fox, A., Griffith, R., Joseph, A. D., Katz, R., Konwinski, A., et al. (2010). A view of cloud computing. *Communications of the ACM, 53*(4), 50–58.

16. Buyya, R., Yeo, C. S., Venugopal, S., Broberg, J., & Brandic, I. (2009). Cloud computing and emerging IT platforms: Vision, hype and reality for delivering computing as the 5th utility. *Future Generation Computer Systems, 25*(6), 599–616.

17. Sultan, N. (2011). Reaching for the cloud, how SMEs can manage. *International Journal of Information Management, 31*(3), 272–278.

18. Sultan, N. (2010). Cloud computing for education: A new dawn? *International Journal of Information Management, 30*(1), 109–116.

19. Lee, L. S., & Mautz, R. D., Jr. (2012). Using cloud computing to manage the costs. *The Journal of Corporate Accounting and Finance, 23*(2), 11–16.

20. Boss, G., Malladi, P., Quan, D., Legregni, L., & Hall, H. (2007). *Cloud computing* (IBM white paper).

21. Weiss, A. (2007). Computing in the clouds. *Networker, 11*(4), 16–25.

22. Vouk, M. A. (2008). Cloud computing—Issues, research and implementations. *Journal of Computing and Information Technology, 4*, 235–246.

23. Vaquero, L., Rodero–Merino, L., Caceres, J., & Lindner, M. (2009). A break in the clouds: Towards a cloud definition. *Computer Communication Review, 39*(1), 50–55.

24. Candiotto, R. (2013). *Il sistema informativo aziendale*. Torino: Giappichelli Editore.

25. Limone, M. (2013). *I contratti di Cloud*. www.comparazionedirittocivile.it

26. Yang, H., & Tate, M. (2012). A descriptive literature review and classification of cloud computing research. *Communications of the Association for Information Systems, 31*(1), 35–60.

27. Weinhardt, C., Anandasivam, A., Blau, B., Borrisov, N., Maini, T., Michalk, W., et al. (2009). Cloud computing—A classification, business models and research direction. *Business and Information System Engineering, 1*(5), 391–399.

28. Rosenthal, A., Mork, P., Li, M. H., Stanford, J., Koester, D., & Reynolds, P. (2009). Cloud computing: A new business paradigm for biomedical information sharing. *Journal of Biomedical Informatics, 43*(2), 342–353.

29. Velte, A., Velte, R., & Elsenpeter, R. (2010). *Cloud computing a pratical approach.* New York: McGraw-Hill.
30. Khajeh-Hosseini, A., Greenwood, D., & Sommerville, I. (2010). Cloud migration: A case study of migrating an enterprise IT system to IaaS. In *Proceedings of the IEEE 3rd International Conference on Cloud Computing* (pp. 450–457).
31. Lawler, J., Joseph, A., & Howell-Barber, H. (2012). A case study of determinants of an effective cloud computing strategy. *Review of Information Systems, 16*(3), 145–156.
32. Brender, N., & Markov, I. (2013). Risk perception and risk management in cloud computing: Results from a case study of Swiss firms. *International Journal of Information Management, 33*(5), 726–733.
33. Gupta, P., Seetharaman, A., & Raj, J. R. (2013). The usage and adoption of cloud computing by small and medium businesses. *International Journal of Information Management, 33*(3), 861–864.
34. Mahmood, A. M., Arslan, F., Dandu, J., Udo, G., & Donald, A. N. (2014). Impact of cloud computing adoption on firm stock price—An empirical research. In *Proceedings of the Twentieth Americas Conference on Information Systems, Savannah.*
35. Oliveira, T., Thomas, M., & Espadanal, M. (2014). Assessing the determinants of cloud computing adoption: An analysis of the manufacturing and services sectors. *Information and Management, 51*(5), 497–510.
36. Son, I., Lee, D., Lee, J. N., & Chang, Y. B. (2014). Market perception on cloud computing initiatives in organizations: An extended resource-based view. *Information and Management, 51*(6), 653–669.
37. Kshetri, N. (2013). Privacy and security issues in cloud computing: The role of institutions and institutional evolution. *Telecommunications Policy, 37*(3), 372–386.
38. Subramanian, N., Abdulrahman, M. D., & Zhou, X. (2014). Integration of logistics and cloud computing service providers: Cost and green benefits in the Chinese context. *Transportation Research Part E: Logistics and Transportation Review, 70*(1), 86–98.
39. Choudhary, V., & VithayathIl, J. (2013). The impact of cloud computing: Should the IT department be organized as a cost center or a profit center? *Journal of Management Information Systems, 30*(2), 67–100.
40. Kundra, V. (2011). *Federal cloud computing strategy.* The white house documents. https://www.whitehouse.gov/sites/default/files/omb/assets/egov_docs/federal-cloud-computing-strategy.pdf
41. Singh, S. P., & Veralakshmi, R. S. R. (2012). Cloud computing: A promising economic model for library and information centers. *Journal of Library and Information Technology, 32*(6), 526–532.
42. Mu, E., & Stern, H. A. (2015). The City of Pittsburgh goes to the cloud: A case study of cloud solution strategic selection and deployment. *Journal of Information Technology Teaching Cases, 4*(1), 70–85.
43. Lian, J. W., Yen, D. C., & Wang, Y. T. (2014). An exploratory study to understand the critical factors affecting the Decision to adopt cloud computing in Taiwan hospital. *International Journal of Information Management, 34*(1), 28–36.
44. Sultan, N. (2014). Making use of cloud computing for healthcare provision: Opportunities and challenges. *International Journal of Information Management, 34*, 177–184.
45. Hsu, P. F., Ray, S., & Hsieh, Y. Y. (2012). Examining cloud computing adoption intention, pricing mechanism, and deployment model. *International Journal of Information Management, 34*(4), 474–488.
46. Chong, H. Y., Wong, J. S., & Wang, X. (2014). An explanatory case study on cloud computing applications in the built environment. *Automation in Construction, 44*(2), 152–162.
47. Ashford, W. (2009). Cloud computing more secure than traditional IT, says Google. *Computer Weekly.* http://www.computerweekly.com/Articles/2009/07/21/236982/cloud-computing-more-secure-than-traditional-it-says.htm

48. Doherty, E., Carcary, M., & Conway, G. (2012). *Risk management considerations in cloud computing adoption*. Research by innovation value institute (IVI), 2–7.
49. Badger, L., Grance, T., Patt-Corner, R., & Voas, J. (2011). *Cloud computing synopsis and recommendations* (Special publication 800-146). National Institute of Standards and Technology. http://csrc.nist.gov/publications/drafts/800-146/Draft-NIST-SP800
50. Chow, R. P., Golle, M., Jakobsson, J., Staddon, E., Shi, J., Staddon, R., et al. (2009). Controlling data in the cloud: Outsourcing computation without outsource control. *Proceedings of the 2009 ACM workshop on Cloud Computing Security, 1*, 85–90.
51. Fanning, K., & Centers, D. P. (2012). Platform as a service: Is time to switch. *The Journal of Corporate Accounting and Finance, 23*(5), 21–25.
52. Almulla, S. A., & Yeun, C. Y. (2010). Cloud computing security management. *Proceeding of 2010 Second International Conference on Engineering Systems Management and Its Applications (ICESMA), 1*(1), 1–7.
53. Grobauer, B., Walloshek, T., & Stoker, E. (2011). Understanding cloud computing vulnerabilities. *IEEE Transaction on Computers, 9*(2), 50–57.
54. Fan, C. K., & Chen, T. C. (2012). The risk management strategy of applying cloud computing. *International Journal of Advanced Computer Science and Applications, 3*(9), 18–27.
55. DaSilva, C. M., Trkman, P., Desouza, K., & Lindic, J. (2013). Disruptive technologies: A business model perspective on cloud computing. *Technology Analysis and Strategic Management, 25*(10), 1161–1173.
56. Mangiuc, D. M. (2012). Cloud identity and access management—A model proposal. *Proceedings of the 7th International Conference Accounting and management information systems AMIS 2012, 7*(1), 1014–1027.
57. Mangiuc, D. M. (2012). Delivering security in the cloud. *Proceedings of the 7th International Conference Accounting and management information systems AMIS 2012, 7*(1), 1005–1013.
58. Tiwari, P. K., & Mishra, B. (2012). Cloud computing security issues, challenges and solution. *International Journal of Emerging Technology and Advanced Engineering, 2*(8), 306–310.
59. Ionescu, B., Ionescu, I., Stanciu, A., Mihai, F., & Tudoran, L. (2012). From e-accounting towards cloud accounting in Romania. *Proceedings of the 7th International Conference Accounting and management information systems: AMIS 2012, 7*(1), 983–1004.
60. Enslin, Z. (2012). Cloud computing adoption: Control objectives for information and related technology (cobiT)—Mapped risk and risk mitigating. *African Journal of Business Management, 6*(37), 10185–10194.
61. Ferreira, L. D., & Merchant, K. A. (1992). Field research in management accounting and control: A review and evaluation. *Accounting, Auditing and Accountability Journal, 5*(4), 3–34.
62. Lillis, A. M. (1999). A framework for the analysis of interview data from multiple field research. *Accounting and Finance, 39*(1), 79–105.
63. Gable, G. G. (1994). Integrating case study and survey research methods: An example in information systems. *European Journal of Information Systems, 3*(2), 112–126.
64. Lillis, A. M., & Mundy, J. (2005). Cross-sectional field studies in management accounting research: Closing the gap between surveys and case studies. *Journal of Management Accounting Research, 17*(1), 119–141.
65. Creswell, J. W. (2009). *Research design: Qualitative, quantitative, and mixed methods approaches* (3rd ed.). Thousand Oaks, CA: Sage.
66. Benbasat, I., Goldstein, D. K., & Mead, M. (1987). The case study research strategy in studies of information systems. *MIS Quarterly, 11*, 369–386.
67. Lee, A. S. (1989). A scientific methodology for MIS case studies. *MIS Quarterly, 13*(1), 32–50.
68. Lee, A. S. (1991). Integrating positivist and interpretive approaches to organizational research. *Organization Science, 2*(4), 342–365.
69. Smith, N. C. (1990). The case study: A useful research method for information management. *Journal of Information Technology, 5*, 123–133.

70. Mumford, E., Hirschheim, R., Fitzgerald, G., & Wood-Harper, T. (1985). *Research methods in information systems*. Amsterdam: North-Holland.
71. Mumford, E. (1991). Information systems research—Leaking craft or visionary vehicle? In H.-E. Nissen, H. K. Klein, & R. Hirschheim (Eds.), *Information systems research: Contemporary approaches & emergent traditions* (pp. 21–26). Amsterdam: Elsevier Science Publishers B.V.
72. Yin, R. K. (1981). The case study crisis: Some answers. *Administrative Science Quarterly, 26* (1), 58–65.
73. Eisenhardt, K. M., & Graebner, M. E. (2007). Theory building from cases: Opportunities and challenges. *Academy of Management Journal, 50*(1), 25–32.
74. Yin, R. K. (1984). *Case study research: Design and methods*. Beverly Hills, CA: Sage.
75. Santos, F., Eisenhardt, M., & Kathleen, M. (2004). Multiple case research. In Lewis-Beck, M., Bryman, A., & Liao, T. (Eds.), *Encyclopedia of research methods for the social sciences*. Sage Publications.
76. Martinez, M. (2004). *Organizzazione, informazioni e tecnologie*. Bologna: Il mulino.
77. Rossignoli, C. (2004). *Coordinamento e cambiamento—Tecnologie e processi interorganizzativi*. Milano: FrancoAngeli.
78. Slovic, P. (1987). Perception of risk. *Science, 236*(4799), 280–295.
79. Slovic, P. (2000). *The perception of risk*. London: Earthscan.
80. Rohrmann, B. (1995). Technological risks—Perception, evaluation, communication. In R. E. Melchers & M. G. Stewart (Eds.), *Integrated risk assessment new directions* (pp. 7–12). Rotterdam: Balkema.
81. Carroll, M., Merwe, A., & Kotze, P. (2011). Secure cloud computing: Benefits, risks and controls. *IEEE Information security in South Africa, 1*, 1–9.

Legislation-Aware Cloud Computing: An Overview

Beniamino Di Martino, Giuseppina Cretella, and Antonio Esposito

Abstract During the recent few years, Cloud Computing has gained a strategic importance in the development of the ICT sector. Cloud Services have been adopted by companies, public administrations, and private customers to store and process data. As the requirements in terms of information reliability, accessibility, and availability increase, so do the requirements related to confidentiality and security of sensitive and classified data (e-mail, medical records, etc.). These are therefore translated into legal requirements constraints. When data are used by a Cloud application, security and confidentiality issues may arise due to the geographical distribution of the Cloud Providers' data center. Indeed, it is a very common practice for a Cloud Provider to have its registered office in a country, while the several data centers it controls are located in different continents of the world. This business strategy, clearly aimed at maximizing profit by reducing expenses (especially in terms of taxes), is in contrast to the variegated national laws, which may provide specific requirements and security measures for the treatment of different kinds of data. This chapter presents an overview of the current initiatives concerning the legislation awareness in Cloud Computing and reports the main aspects to take into account to approach such a topic.

Keywords Cloud Computing • Law awareness • Law compliance

1 Introduction

Recently, Cloud Computing has gained relevant shares in the IT market and has consequently imposed itself in all the industrial sectors which rely on information technologies to effectively deliver their services. The massive use of Internet and the widespread distribution of mobile devices, which provide a cheap and continuous access to online resources to companies, professionals, public administrations,

B. Di Martino • G. Cretella • A. Esposito (✉)
Department of Industrial and Information Engineering, Second University of Naples, Aversa, Italy
e-mail: beniamino.dimartino@unina2.it; giuseppina.cretella@unina2.it; antonio.esposito@unina2.it

© Springer International Publishing AG 2017   77
K. Corsi et al. (eds.), *Reshaping Accounting and Management Control Systems*,
Lecture Notes in Information Systems and Organisation 20,
DOI 10.1007/978-3-319-49538-5_5

and consumers, have strongly contributed to the development and adoption of Cloud Computing. Also, the volume of data exchanged has dramatically increased, thus amplifying the issues connected to their management. Cloud Computing provides the means to build online service which guarantees access to scalable, always available and transparent services and resources, without the need for customers to own such resources or know their exact location. This is why in both legal-economic and sociological literature, the concept of Access Culture [1] is used to describe a situation in which it is not important to own a resource, but it is fundamental to always be able to access it. Since such resources are offered by third parties, it is necessary that providers guarantee the continuous availability and reliability of their services. In order to enforce the respect of Service Level Agreements (SLAs) and the safe and secure management of the data exchanged between users and service providers, it is necessary to emanate efficient and rigorous laws which regulate access to both services and data. In the last years, particular attention has been devoted to standardization efforts, which aim at defining shared formalisms for the description of Cloud Services [2, 3] and the measurement of their performances. The indexes and parameters used to evaluate a service's performances have also to take into consideration their safety, security, and privacy levels. However, maintaining the desired levels of protection of data and privacy required by current legislation in a Cloud Computing infrastructure is a serious challenge, as is meeting the restrictions on cross-border data transfer [4], because of the geographically distributed nature of the Cloud.

The remainder of this chapter is organized as follows: Sect. 2 reports the main issues in data sharing and privacy involved with Cloud Computing applications; Sect. 3 describes projects and initiatives carried out to define standards for law representation and tagging; Sect. 4 presents few hints on an ontology-based approach which exploits semantics to ensure law alignment among Cloud Services; Sect. 5 reports some conclusion regarding the current issues and some consideration on possible future works.

2   Legislation Awareness and Data Privacy

As we have already stated in the introduction, with the steady diffusion of mobile applications the volume of data processed has increased, and the urge to define means to control and manage them has grown accordingly. When applications rely on Cloud Computing Services, the need to provide a strong legislation to protect customers' data arises. As Cloud Services process users' data on machines that the users do not own or operate themselves, **privacy issues** often arise. Probably, privacy represents the main concern users express on the adoption of Cloud Computing, since many customers fear for the disclosure of private and sensitive data. Unless technological mechanisms to allay users' concerns are introduced, this may prove fatal to many different types of Cloud Services. One typical scenario in which Cloud users express most of their concerns regards the actual possibility for providers to use their data for purposes of which they may not be aware. For instance, a Cloud Provider could use the data exchanged with the user for marketing purposes, without asking for her consent. Therefore, there is an increasing awareness for the need for design for privacy from both companies and governmental organizations. While local laws for data management already exist, expressing precise rules for the exchanging, treatment, and storage of sensitive data within the national boundaries, there are still problems regarding their actual application. As already stated before, the resources offered by Cloud can be provided by servers which may be scattered throughout the world: so, it could be difficult to determine the exact legislation to apply in each situation. Furthermore, if the data are migrated from a data center to another, and such centers reside in different countries, then the legislation could vary and data management should adapt accordingly. This is not an easy task, since it requires a complete knowledge of the legislations of the involved countries, and mechanisms to ensure compliance to such legislation each time data leave a center to move elsewhere.

The privacy challenge for software engineers is to design Cloud Services in such a way as to decrease privacy risk and to ensure legal compliance. Laws placing geographical and other restrictions on the collection, processing, and transfer of personally identifiable and sensitive information limit usage of Cloud Services as currently designed. For example, a UK business storing data about individual customers with the prominent Cloud Service Provider Salesforce.com could find itself in breach of UK data protection law. Customers may be able to sue enterprises if their privacy rights are violated, and in any case the enterprises may face damage to their reputation. There have been a number of high-profile privacy breaches in the news recently. It is also important to allay users' fears about the usage of Cloud Services. Concerns arise when it is not clear to individuals why their personal information is requested or how it will be used or passed on to other parties: this lack of control leads to suspicion and ultimately distrust. There are also security-related concerns about whether the personal data in the cloud will be adequately protected.

3 An Overview of Existing Initiatives and Frameworks

Several sectors are becoming interested in the adoption of Cloud Computing technologies and some of them need to face with regulation compliance issues to exploit the benefit of Cloud Computing because in spite of obvious benefits, the issue of regulatory compliances by Cloud Computing can seriously impede its utilization. In particular, the healthcare industry challenges are continuing to grow in the areas of regularity compliance for protecting patient privacy. The challenge looms large as the healthcare sector is under heavy pressure due to regulatory compliance mainly for protecting the privacy of PHI (protected health information). Godbole and Lamb in [5] discuss the adoption of cloud-based application architectures in the healthcare sector and its implication. Khan and Bai in [6] propose an approach that enables Cloud Computing clients to verify health regulatory compliance claimed by Cloud Computing providers. In their approach, clients of Cloud Computing could check automatically how the Cloud Provider meets the regulatory compliance for their health records. The approach is based on three processes: (1) mechanisms to represent health regulations in machine-processable form; (2) collection of service-specific compliance-related real-time data from cloud servers; and (3) automatic reasoning about the compliances between the machine-processable regulations and the collected data from servers. However, this approach lacks an automatic technique to collect and represent regulations in a machine-processable form. This can be achieved by exploiting a plethora of standards for law representation. In fact at European level, many initiatives have been carried out to define standards for law representation and tagging:

- **Metalex** [7], which has also been used as an input for the CEN workshop on an Open XML interchange format for legal and legislative resources, which officially started on July 7, 2006. The objective of the Workshop is to develop a **CEN Workshop Agreement** (CWA) on an Open XML interchange format for legal and legislative resources. Several European initiatives are currently collaborating to improve the MetaLex standard in order to retain compliance among the different formats used throughout Europe. Among these, the most relevant ones are represented by LexDania, CHLexML, NormeInRete, and Formex. The **MetaLex** standard has been developed within the **EPOWER** project, with the objective to introduce ICT technologies to support citizens and governments in accessing and managing the growing volume of legal information produced by national, international, European, and local authorities. The standard is based on an XML-based formalism for the markup of legal documents, and it provides a generic and easily extensible base for the complete representation of legal documents and constraints. The current version of the standard, going under the name of CEN MetaLex, can be considered as an interchange format between other, more jurisdiction-specific XML standards. MetaLex is independent of the specific juridical systems and of the languages in which the laws are expressed, and it can be integrated with the XML schemas used by other frameworks, operating at national and international levels. Together with the European initiatives presented in Sect. 3, MetaLex also provides compliance with the **Akoma-Ntoso** standard, which has been realized within the *Strengthening Parliaments' Information Systems in Africa* project.
- The **SDU BWB** [8] standard is an XML-based format used to encode the laws currently stored in the Dutch **Basiswettwenbestand** (BWB) database. The original standard was published by **SDU** and is currently maintained by the Dutch government.
- **LexDania** [9] is a project initiated by the Danish Ministry of Science, Technology and Innovation with the purpose of defining a standard for the creation and interchange of legislative documentation. The project has developed a complex structure for the definition of XML schemas: core elements and types have been defined and organized in a multilayered architecture and are used as building

blocks for the definition, creation, and maintenance of new documents types and applications.

- **CHLexML** [10] is a Swiss standard, based on XML, for the representation of legal texts, with particular attention to multilingual issues, which represent a hot topic for the Swiss Confederation. The project, started in 1998 and directed by the *Coordination Office for the Electronic Publication of Legal Data Federal Office of Justice* (COPIUR), aimed at harmonizing federal, cantonal, and even private sector legal documentation, by employing information technologies in the legislative field to elaborate uniform norms and standards.

- The **E-LAW** [11] project, born in Austria, aims at a complete reform of legal text production, which include documents like government bills, committee reports, legal enactments of the *Nationalrat*, and decisions of the *Bundesrat*. As in other initiatives, XML represents the foundation stone for the creation of a uniform electronic production chain for legal documents. However, in the E-LAW project XML represents only a storage and interchange format, while more classical software and formats (like Word) are to be used during production of the legal texts.

- The **NormeInRete** [12] project can be considered as a precursor for the definition of standards for tagging documents with legislation information. Also, the project aimed at providing instruments to automate the tagging and guarantee interoperability among public administrations adhering to the project.

  The standard produced within the project consists in an XML schema which can be used to represent and describe approved laws, thus enabling users to mark up their documents and data with information relative to the applicable norms. The project has been developed in three steps, which reflected the necessity to uniform the semantics and nomenclature used in laws and to provide a machine-readable standard for their representation. In particular, the three steps can be resumed in:

  - Issues of circulars for the standardization of names used to address legal documents.
  - Production of a standard, based on XML, for the digital representation of laws and norms, in order to support the markup of documents and data.
  - Design and implementation of a federated website, in which public administrations can add and retrieve law defined through the approved standard.

In order to ease the adoption of the NormeInRete standards, a set of tools for editing and textual analysis able to adapt existing and new documents to these standards and to provide specific functionality for drawing (drafting) the enactment of legislation have been developed. XMLeges family tools have been developed by ITTIG [13] (Institute of Legal Information Theory and Techniques) in order to create a unique point of access to legal documents in a distributed environment and a system of permanent links between legal materials, able to guide users toward the participating authorities websites. This application suite for legal drafting includes:

- *xmLeges Linker* that can be used to implement automatic legislative document hyperlinking by identifying the regulatory references in a text and describing them using the standard URN-NIR.
- *xmLeges Marker* that is able to convert a legislative text into a XML-NIR file. Automatic detection and tagging of the documents formal structure provides a fast and safe conversion of the text in a specific XML standard, simplifying the burden of a manual conversion.
- *xmLeges Classifier* that is a tool for the automatic classification of legislative text paragraphs into provision types (e.g., Duty, Permission, Sanction, Abrogation, etc.). It is able to implement the Provision Model provided by the NormeInRete XML standard. It is implemented by a multiclass SVM machine learning technique.
- *xmLegesExtractor* whose purpose is to select relevant text fragments corresponding to specific semantic roles that are relevant for the different types of provisions. xmLegesExtractor is realized as a suite of Natural Language Processing tools for the automatic analysis of Italian texts, specialized to cope with the specific stylistic conventions of the legal parlance.

Finally, *xmLeges Editor* integrates all the previous modules into a visual tool. By using this tool, it is possible to produce documents according to NIR DTD (XMLSchema), URN, and Metadata legislative standards. The environment has the aspect of a common text editor; it doesn't require any technical knowledge about standards, since it hides all the xml details to the final user. This editor uses a set of grids to aid the user in drafting documents but is expressly designed for the Italian languages; thus, it does not support other than Italian language.

- **Akoma-Ntoso** [14] project aimed at providing concepts, formats, and tools for the development of IT support to parliamentary activities for countries in sub-Saharan Africa. The project Akoma-Ntoso started indeed from an internationalization and a complete reengineering of the XML of Normeinrete, which represent its backbone.

The Akoma-Ntoso standard can be applied to the entire legislative chain, from law proposal to the final approval of the legislative decree, also including the reports of commissions, chambers, magistrates, and so on. Having a unique pattern to follow in the entire proposal-approval chain allows users to efficiently and effectively query a native XML database, in order to retrieve all information available on a specific legislation: which parliamentary acts have altered a certain regulation, when such changes have been enacted, and who has proposed an amendment to a law and when.

Together with the development of a set of interconnected standards for the machine-readable representation of laws and actors, the project also aims at defining supporting languages and guidelines for their use, making it possible to accurately describe, produce, store, and manage judicial, parliamentary, and legislative documents.

The standard is based on the following elements:

- A common model for the representation of documents, based on XML for the definition of their structure and syntax.
- A shared model for the exchange of documents, based on the similarities which characterize the different legislative processes, despite the influence of languages and cultural and historical backgrounds. In particular, such a model focuses on resolving issues like:

  1. The creation of documents using a single shared tool, regardless of its nature.
  2. Provide a graphical representation of the document using again a unique shared tool, always independent of nature, language, etc.
  3. Guarantee accessibility to the documents, intended as the possibility to navigate and explore them through references, in a fashion similar to text hyperlinks.

- A shared scheme for data representation, which has to be explicitly supported by the documents adhering to the standard.
- A shared scheme for the representation of references ontologies and metadata. Metadata provide auxiliary information which enriches the documents, such as the publication date, or the name the last modifier. However, in order to correctly interpret them, ontologies are used to add semantics to the documents.
- A common scheme for quotations and cross-references: the entire set of parliamentary, legislative, and judiciary documents can be seen as a network in which each document is connected to another by means of expressions in natural language. The adoption of a common convention for the names and references, among common reference mechanisms, as proposed by Akoma Ntoso, improves documents' accessibility and navigability.

The Italian Senate, from 2013, has already begun to mark the bills in Akoma-Ntoso, and tests are in course within the initiative OpenParlamento.

4 A Semantic-Based Approach

In the previous sections, we have briefly introduced some of the main attempts to provide a homogeneous description of legislative documents and some initiatives aimed to propose tools to automatically check the compliance of Cloud Services to regulations. Apart from Akoma-Ntoso, which was born to support African governments, the described formalisms have been developed in European countries. Other initiatives have been carried out worldwide: in the USA both the government [15] and private organizations (**Legal-RDF** [16]) have contributed to define formalisms for laws description; in Australia the government has financed the project **EnAct** [17], which involves Tasmania, Canada, some federal states of the USA, and New Zealand; in Japan several initiatives are being carried out by academia [18], legal experts [19, 20], and government [21].

Most of the cited approaches have a few elements in common:

- The use of XML for the definition of schemas to support some or all the activities connected to the production, storage, and transmission of legal documents.
- The exploitation of semantic-web technologies (RDF, OWL) to enrich the annotated documents and provide useful semantics.

Using XML and semantic-web technologies, it is indeed possible to develop a methodology for the description of Cloud Services and their composition [22]: so, we think it is feasible to leverage the existing frameworks and technologies to annotate Cloud Services with legal information and support users in choosing the ones satisfying their requirements.

Figure 1 reports a schematic representation of a possible framework architecture which associates law definitions to Cloud Services' representations. This schema includes three semantic databases in which are stored three different kinds of information:

- The *Cloud Services Database* will include information about the functionalities and the service levels of the Cloud Providers offer, in particular, this database's

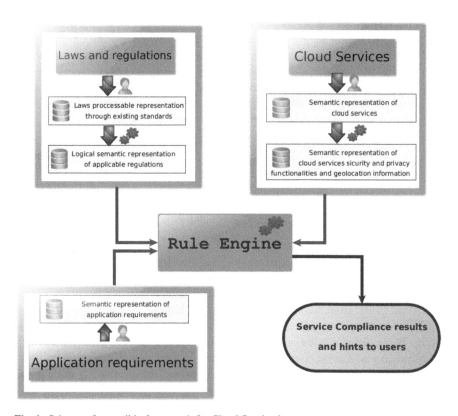

Fig. 1 Schema of a possible framework for Cloud Service law awareness

own information regarding the geographic areas in which the infrastructures running them are located and the functionality offered in terms of security and privacy by the services. This database will be obtained by processing existing semantic Cloud Services representations and deriving from them the information that is relevant to perform the compliance checking. Figure 2 provides a draft ontology that includes a set of concepts that might be useful to formalize the

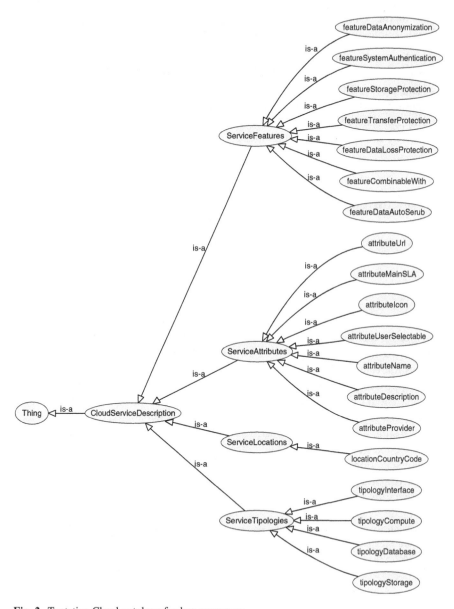

Fig. 2 Tentative Cloud ontology for law awareness

service description. These concepts include the service location, service features such as data anonymization, data loss protection, transfer protection, and so on.

- The *Laws and Regulations Database* will include the formalization in logical predicates of the law prescriptions. This information will be obtained by processing the representation of regulations performed by existing standards such as the ones reported in Sect. 3.
- The *Application Requirements Database* will include a processable representation of the application requirements in terms of kind of data the application handles and kind of treatment that will be performed on the data.

The law and regulations database contains all the annotated law and supplies inferences rules to the engine that running these rules on the assertions that represent the description of the Cloud Service is able to determine if the service is compliant with the law of interest. In particular, the engine takes into account the more appropriate regulations and laws by discerning based on the information provided by the application requirements.

5   Conclusion

Cloud Computing represents a revolution in Information Technology (IT) that offers various benefits to computing users. However, Cloud Computing usage is generally associated with security and compliance issues such as laws, regulations, data privacy, data protection, and contractual agreements. While most of the Cloud Providers can guarantee some measurable nonfunctional performance metrics, e.g., service availability or throughput, there is a lack of adequate mechanisms for guaranteeing that the provider is compliant with the actual legislation in terms of security, trust, and privacy. This lack represents an obstacle for moving most business relevant applications into the Cloud.

The approach proposed in [6] is valid, but it is limited to the healthcare field. The approach should be extended to all areas (such as juridical, statistical, etc.) and should allow the user to define the requirements of his/her application, for instance by specifying whether the application is related to legal data, medical data, or sensitive data. Moreover, given the plethora of existing frameworks developed for law representation and tagging, it would be worthwhile to investigate how and if it's possible to extract useful information from these representations to perform automatic checking of law compliance.

Acknowledgments This research has been supported by the European Community's Seventh Framework Programme (FP7/2007–2013) under grant agreement n 256910 (mOSAIC Project), by PRIST 2009, Fruizione assistita e context aware di siti archeologici complessi mediante dispositivi mobili, and CoSSMic (Collaborating Smart Solar-powered Micro-grids—FP7-SMARTCITIES-2013).

References

1. Valtysson, B. (2010). Access culture: Web 2.0 and cultural participation. *International Journal of Cultural Policy, 16*(2), 200–214.
2. Oasis topology and orchestration specification for cloud applications (tosca) tc. https://www.oasis-open.org/committees/tc_home.php?wg_abbrev=tosca
3. Davis, D., & Pilz, G. (2012). Cloud infrastructure management interface (cimi) model and rest interface over http.
4. Pearson, S. (2009). Taking account of privacy when designing cloud computing services. In *Proceedings of the 2009 ICSE Workshop on Software Engineering Challenges of Cloud Computing* (pp. 44–52). IEEE Computer Society.
5. Godbole, N. S., & Lamb, J. (2013). *The triple challenge for the healthcare industry: Sustainability, privacy, and cloud-centric regulatory compliance.* 10th International Conference and Expo on Emerging Technologies for a Smarter World (CEWIT 2013), pp. 1–6, IEEE.
6. Khan, K. M., & Bai, Y. (2013). *Automatic verification of health regulatory compliance in cloud computing.* 2013 I.E. 15th International Conference on e-Health Networking, Applications & Services (Healthcom), pp. 719–721, IEEE.
7. Boer, A., Winkels, R., & Vitali, F. (2008). *Metalex xml and the legal knowledge interchange format.* Berlin: Springer.
8. World encyclopedia of law—sdu-bwb. http://lawin.org/sdu-bwb/
9. Tucker, H. (2004). Lex dania-white paper. *A system of XML schemas for Danish legislative documentation.*
10. Association e-justice.ch—chlexml. http://www.svri.ch/de/CHLexML.html
11. Schefbeck, P. A. E. (2006). *The e-law project in Austria.*
12. Francesconi, E. (2006). Norme in rete project: Standards and tools for italian legislation. *International Journal of Legal Information, 34*, 358.
13. Institute of legal information theory and techniques. www.ittig.cnr.it/
14. Vitali, F., & Zeni, F. (2007). Towards a country-independent data format: The akoma ntoso experience. In *Proceedings of the V legislative XML workshop* (pp. 67–86). Florence, Italy: European Press Academic Publishing.
15. Gullickson, K. (2008). *Drafting legislation using xml in the us house of representatives.* World e-Parliament Conference, pp. 25–26.
16. McClure, J. (2006). Legal-rdf vocabularies, requirements & design rationale. In *Proceedings of the V Legislative XML Workshop* (pp. 149–159).
17. Arnold-Moore, T., Clemes, J., & Tadd, M. (2000). Connected to the law: Tasmanian legislation using enact. *Journal of Information, Law and Technology, 1*, 00–1.
18. Ogawa, Y., Inagaki, S., & Toyama, K. (2008). Automatic consolidation of Japanese statutes based on formalization of amendment sentences. In Y. Ogawa, S. Inagaki, & K. Toyama (Eds.), *New frontiers in artificial intelligence* (pp. 363–376). Berlin: Springer.
19. Maeda, M. (2003). *Workbook hosei shitsumu* (Rev. ed.). Gyosei, Tokyo.
20. Ogawa, Y., Yamada, M., Kato, R., & Toyama, K. (2011). Design and compilation of syntactically tagged corpus of Japanese statutory sentences. In Y. Ogawa, M. Yamada, R. Kato, & K. Toyama (Eds.), *New frontiers in artificial intelligence* (pp. 141–152). Berlin: Springer.
21. Ministry of internal affairs and communications, horei data teikyo system. http://law.e-gov.go.jp/cgi-bin/idxsearch.cgi
22. Di Martino, B., Esposito, A., & Cretella, G. (2015). Semantic representation of cloud patterns and services with automated reasoning to support cloud application portability. *IEEE Transactions on Cloud Computing, PP*(99), 1–1.

The Impact of Cloud Infrastructure on Business Value: A Qualitative Analysis

Roberto Candiotto and Silvia Gandini

Although this work is the result of a common will, every
paragraph has been written by a single author, particularly:
– 1st and 2nd sections by Roberto Candiotto.
– 3rd and 4th sections by Silvia Gandini.

Abstract The interpretation of organizations like dynamic entities imposes some fundamental challenges for today's managers. Firms have not derived value simply by linking IT to their business processes: they have learned how to benefit from IT by developing a competency in creating and evolving an IT architecture, able to identify and implement the organization's strategic objectives. Cloud computing represents a possible answer to companies' needs of flexibility, giving them the chance to implement new services more quickly than the past and without expensive capital investments. The aim of this work is to analyze the impact of cloud (in short, from now on the term "Cloud" will be used as "Cloud Computing") on value creation opportunities for companies that decide to migrate their IT infrastructure toward the *on-demand* model. The assumption that similar choices, from a technological point of view, can imply various value expectations has been attested through the cross-analysis of two companies that both chose public cloud, but starting from deeply different motivations.

Keywords Cloud computing • IT infrastructure • IT value • IT management • IT business impact

R. Candiotto (✉) • S. Gandini
Dipartimento di Studi per l'Economia e l'Impresa, Università del Piemonte Orientale, Vercelli, Italy
e-mail: roberto.candiotto@uniupo.it; silvia.gandini@uniupo.it

© Springer International Publishing AG 2017   89
K. Corsi et al. (eds.), *Reshaping Accounting and Management Control Systems*,
Lecture Notes in Information Systems and Organisation 20,
DOI 10.1007/978-3-319-49538-5_6

1   Introduction

Cloud computing can be defined as a set of technologies, typically in the shape of a service offered to a client by a provider, which enable to store, to file away, and to process data items, thanks to the use of hardware and software resources, distributed and shared online.[1] The vision of computing as a service focuses on the linkage between business processes and IT services so that the first can be seamlessly automated using the second; service computing has led to the development of software for millions to consume, rather than to run on their individual computers [1]. To deliver this vision, many computing paradigms have been proposed over the last few years,[2] but cloud represents an extension of them wherein the capabilities of business applications are exposed as sophisticated services that can be accessed over a network.

The study of cloud can be particularly interesting not only for its multidisciplinary character, determined by the involvement of different disciplines in data collection, data processing, and data storage operations, and for the use of *Information and Communication Technologies* (ICT) [2], but also for its transversality toward different organizational research themes, typical features of studies about information systems' organization. Many researchers focused their attention on this phenomenon, considering its potential to transform large parts of the IT industry [2, 3], and identifying its most relevant features such as the prevalence of economic variables [4] and of organizational implications and goals [5, 6] over purely technological aspects. But very few works have concretely analyzed what potentialities can emerge from the combination of the global availability of cloud infrastructure at a low cost and companies' capability to create business value [7]. When cloud is conceived as a public service, it can be interpreted as a virtual space where the infrastructure is provisioned for an open use by the general public, resources are shared, and dynamically allocated, according to customers' real needs and basing on a usage model focused on "pay as you grow."

Hence, it's reasonable to think that cloud could be used to optimize, transform, and create companies' value chain, basing on its capability to improve the following aspects:

- *Cost flexibility*, because cloud services can help an organization reduce fixed IT costs (software licenses, servers, and networking equipment) by enabling a shift from capital expenses (capex) to operational expenses (opex);
- *Business scalability*, since cloud enables a company to benefit from economies of scale by allowing for rapid provisioning of resources without scale limitations;

---

[1]http://www.nist.gov/

[2]Here are some paradigms promising to deliver IT as a service: web, data center, service-oriented architecture, grid computing, P2P computing, market-oriented computing.

– *Market adaptability*, because cloud in turn facilitates rapid innovation and helps speed time to market by enabling businesses to rapidly adjust processes, products, and services to meet changing needs.

Moreover, in order to evaluate the maturity and the adoption of technologies and applications, and to understand how they are potentially relevant to solving real business problems and exploiting new opportunities, the *Hype Cycle* model is often used.[3]

Actually cloud is still interpreted as a phase of the *commodization* process of IT investments,[4] but really this technology is looking for a specific identity over the ICT market and could represent a strategic evolution step in the use of the Internet.

In the light of previous considerations, this work is aimed to analyze if cloud services can have a positive impact not only on companies' IT costs but also over their capability to improve business value through innovation. To answer this question, it's been assumed that the adoption of similar cloud services can be influenced by multiple motivations, leading implementation projects to have different degrees of strategic impact.

The assumption has been tested through a qualitative cross-analysis of two companies that both implemented a cloud infrastructure. The analysis has regarded the projects' phases and characteristics (assessment of actual criticalities, provider selection, role of the IT management), and the improvements expected/already perceived from the new context, leading to find some analogies but also substantial differences in companies' behavior.

2   Research Project Description

Analyzed companies:

1. Multinational of the fashion sector (company A)
2. Consortium for the *Waste of Electric and Electronic Equipment*—WEEE disposal (company B)

   Research methodology: qualitative cross-analysis through direct interviews [8]
   Period: June–October 2014
   Interviewed person:

---

[3]Basing on this model, each hype cycle drills down into the five key phases of a technology's life cycle: the evolution starts from a breakthrough moment (*Technology Trigger*), goes through a period of extreme excitement (*Peak of Inflated Expectations*), then of disillusionment (*Trough of Disillusionment*), and can finally arrive to a true understanding of the technology's applicability, risks, and benefits (*Slope of Enlightenment*), before the rapid growth phase of adoption begins (*Plateau of Productivity*). Cfr.: http://www.gartner.com/

[4]According to Gartner, in 2014 cloud was at the end of the third phase (*Trough of Disillusionment*).

- Global IT Coordinator (company A)
- IT manager (company B)

  Goals:

- What are the main differences between analyzed companies about strategy, organization, and IT architecture.
- What are the reasons underlying the migration of the IT infrastructure to cloud.
- How cloud projects were structured and realized.
- What is the projects' strategic impact.

2.1 Analyzed Companies

Company A is a multinational of the fashion sector structured in the following business units: (1) *BU Italy*, which covers Italy market and is also the operative headquarter; (2) *BU International Business*, which manages commercial relations with distributors in 100 countries worldwide; (3) *BU France*, which covers France and Benelux markets; (4) *BU Deutschland*, which covers Germany and Austria markets; and (5) *BU North America*, which covers USA market and was founded in 2012 as a start-up.

The IT management of the group is composed of local IT manager (except for BU North America) and, at a central level, of a *Global IT Coordinator* who is responsible for the company's IT investments and for the monitoring of BU behavior about the use of IT. Strategy and cultural values are deeply oriented to internationalization, and the main goal is to develop the brand worldwide but respecting local markets' peculiarities through excellent industrial design, specialized know-how, and a global strategic approach.

The technical architecture is managed at local level and coordinated at central level, and each BU is provided with the following applications:

- *ERP*, which supports financial and distribution operations and is locally deployed at BU level;
- *PLM*, which supports the processes underlying the collections' design and the product development and is implemented at central level;
- *BI*, whcih supports the processes underlying the corporate reporting and is implemented at both central and BU levels;
- *Local enterprise applications*, integrated with the ERP and managed at local level (sales force automation, retail, and B2B).

In 2012, the incorporation of BU North America as a start-up required a way to rationalize the IT investment for the new reality. Management decided to provide the BU with the same set of applications of others, but externalizing the IT infrastructure and deciding at first for an outsourcing solution. However, after a careful evaluation of the main international provider over the market, in January 2014 the infrastructure of the North America area migrated to a public cloud. As of now, assessment of actual criticalities has been done for all other BUs, in order to migrate the whole infrastructure of the group.

Company B is a consortium for the WEEE disposal that operates on the Italian market and is composed of appliances, consumer electronics, and computer equipment producers. The main activities involve (1) the recall from some certified collection points, (2) the transportation to selected treatment plants, and (3) the recycling and the retrieval of materials.

A *WEEE Coordination Centre* is responsible for the control of all national consortium, in order to assure high service levels, to correct behaviors, and to protect municipalities that decide to equip collection points for their citizens. In the last few years, a substantial decrease of disposal requirements has characterized the WEEE market, implying a need for major flexibility in the consortium production processes. Efficiency and business continuity are therefore the main critical success factors to respect national regulations and manage irregular workloads at the same time.

The IT manager is responsible for the technical architecture, which is provided with a production system, an ERP system, and a service for market information collection. Up to 2010, the IT infrastructure has been managed in hosting with some problems related to server maintenance, power availability, and long provisioning time. For these matters, IT direction decided to migrate the whole infrastructure to a public cloud.

2.2 Projects' Analysis

A clear comprehension of how a company IT services can be similar to available cloud services and the ability to implement cloud in the most coherent way allow us to reduce risks related to migration projects and so to obtain a major value from investments. Cloud implementation requires a wide-ranging strategy and new responsibilities for the IT management, in order to realize a structured governance system and to assure alignment between the cloud and the company's strategy. From a technical point of view, since the IT management could lose control and vision over the IT architecture it is necessary to develop the capacity to orchestrate internal and external services and to evaluate the trade-off between the costs and benefits of the migration. Another important aspect of public cloud projects is data sharing outside the company limits so that management have to know all controls and security policies of provider's offering.

In the light of previous consideration, cloud projects have been analyzed considering the following aspects: (a) *strategic goals and resources assessment*, (b) *provider selection*, and (c) *impact on IT costs*.

(a) *Strategic goals and resources assessment*

   The great availability of cloud services and the large number of provider on the cloud market imply the necessity to consider carefully a cloud migration. IT management should create integration between IT investments and business. For this matter, it is important to structure migration projects starting from an assessment of actual resources, to analyze criticalities and needs, and to understand what kind of benefits cloud could generate.

In this section, interviews have been structured as follows:

– What are the main motivations for the migration to cloud?
– How this passage can support strategic goals?
– Who has/have the responsibility to decide for IT investments?
– Was the assessment of pre-cloud situation a formalized process?
– Has the assessment required external competencies?
– What criticalities/opportunities of improvement arose from the assessment?
– How cloud can solve criticalities and support opportunities?

(b) *Provider selection*

Before implementing cloud services, companies should evaluate the amount and typology of the data they want to externalize. This kind of analysis is important to understand not only the project's feasibility but also the economic and organizational consequences of an eventual loss of data. The *Italian Data Protection Authority*[5] suggests companies to test providers' reliability considering the following aspects: (1) references and guarantees offered to preserve the confidentiality and security of data; (2) measures adopted to assure business continuity; (3) quality of services and degree of responsibility if problems occur; (4) location, in order to understand if there is a normative gap; and (5) characteristics of the contractual terms.

In this section, interviews have been structured as follows:

– What are the main assessment benchmark used to evaluate providers?
– How the reliability of selected provider was tested?
– Does the selected provider give information about the location of externalized data?
– Are the contractual terms clear and comprehensible?

(c) *Impact on IT costs*

In the last few years, companies' continuous expansion to meet business goals has in some cases led to a congestion of their data center. Under this perspective, cloud represents a solution for a more "ecological" way to manage data center, giving companies the possibility to (1) take advantage of shared and dynamic infrastructures; (2) reduce the number of servers in-house; (3) automatize a lot of maintenance activities; and (4) cut maintenance, license, upgrading, storage, security, and energy costs.

In this section, interviews have been structured as follows:

– What are the cost elements to consider in the migration project?

---

[5]http://www.garanteprivacy.it

– How can pre-cloud and cloud costs be compared?
– What kinds of cost benefits have already been obtained and what are expected?
– Could the cost benefits have a strategic impact?

3 Results of the Analysis

3.1 Strategic Goals and Resources Assessment

In the case of company A, strategy is oriented to develop the brand worldwide and to improve the international development but respecting local markets' peculiarities. Moreover, the introduction of the Global IT Coordinator has allowed to better promote organizational changes besides all the BUs and to assure alignment between IT choices and business goals for all the reference markets.

Cloud migration started in 2014 for the BU North America in order to provide it with a flexible and scalable infrastructure. The success of this project led the IT management to evaluate the same choice for all the other BUs. In this case, the main purpose was an improvement in flexibility and efficiency of the actual infrastructure at economic conditions, to free resources for the following more strategic IT investments: (a) the strengthening of the Business Intelligence system, to increase the value of available data; (b) the development of a new Product Lifecycle Management and 3D system, to reduce time to market; and (c) the introduction of new Global Supply Chain functionalities, to increase customer satisfaction and to reduce the working capital at the same time.

Assessment has been realized in different sessions. For the BU North America, the preliminary analysis was focused on a comparison between all the possible options (*on premise*, *cloud*, and *hosting*) to understand strength and weaknesses of each of them. For the European BU, the analysis was based on a double perspective and regarded:

1. The actual *application portfolio*, to evaluate what are the most critical applications that have a direct impact on the company's business;
2. The *system catalogue*, to discover infrastructural problems of single BU and to make a general evaluation of the whole company's IT infrastructure.

The results of this last analysis were then shared with local IT departments, in order to define a general plan of action and to compare strengths and weaknesses of the possible options (upgrading of actual infrastructure or migration to cloud). Both for BU North America and for European BU, the assessment and the implementation plans have been structured in a standardized way and followed by a cloud broker, which previously was the company's IT consultant.

In the case of company B, strategy is oriented to manage the WEEE in an excellent and efficient way, because performances are controlled and monitored

Strategy	COMPANY A	COMPANY B
	International development	Process efficiency
Organizational complexity	High (5 business units WW)	Low
Motivations of the change		
- Obsolete IT infrastructure	●	●
- Problems about systems security	●	●
Expected benefits from the change		
- improved business continuity	●	●
- increased infrastructure scalability	●	●
- Improved corporate image (more innovation for investitors)	●	
- IT investments reduction	More resources for the future strategic development of applicaton portfolio	More resources for an eventual infrastructure development
Responsibility of IT investments	Centralized unit Strategic Functions (Global IT Coordinator)	IT Direction
Structured process for the assessment of actual resources	●	
Involment of external actors in the change process	Cloud broker (previous IT consultant), from assessment activities	System integrator (applications provider), after the infrastructure migration

Fig. 1 Strategic goals and resources assessment: a comparison of results

by the Coordination Center, but they are also strictly related to the workloads trend. In this context, it is necessary to dispose of a solid and secure IT infrastructure, able to assure business continuity and to avoid penalties. Moreover, the same infrastructure must be scalable because workloads could exceed production capacity. The passage to a cloud infrastructure was determined by previous considerations and also by some problems related to server maintenance, power availability, and provisioning time for additional resources. In fact, when compared with the upgrading of existing infrastructure in hosting cloud represents the only solution able to assure a rapid scalability. The assessment process was not formalized and did not involve external competencies, but it was very useful to understand the most important criticalities of the pre-cloud situation. Cloud migration required a collaboration between the company's IT management and an external system integrator, but only in the last phases of the process (Fig. 1).

Hence, the analysis realized for the area *strategic goals and resources assessment* has allowed to make the following considerations:

- Motivations at the base of cloud adoption are firstly economic.
- When strategy is more oriented to market development, the passage to cloud could represent an input for innovation, leaving to the IT management major resources for applications' strategic improvement.
- Complex organization requires a structured assessment process, supported by external specialists.

– Complex projects require a greater involvement of the cloud broker since the assessment activities, to assure a major alignment between IT systems and business.

3.2 Provider Selection

In order to accomplish to the *Italian Data Protection Authority* guidelines, companies decided to focus on international players, although they had different motivations and goals. For company A, the choice was imposed by the desire to improve corporate reputation worldwide, while company B related the success of provider to its capacity to assure a high degree of business continuity.

Anyway, in both cases the selection was deeply influenced by what the most important consulting companies said about the major cloud player on the market and it was realized considering strengths and weaknesses of two different offerings: (1) Amazon, for its positioning as a leader, and (2) Microsoft, for its development and worldwide recognized capabilities.

In the case of company A, the analysis was realized with the support of the external specialist, leading to the following considerations:

– Although Amazon Web Services enjoy a high reputation on the cloud market, they are too much standardized and not subject to discounts or special prices.
– Windows Azure is a quite recent solution, but, if compared with Amazon, it presents a greater economic flexibility and a major interoperability with existing applications.

In the case of company B, the analysis was realized independently by the IT manager, leading to the following considerations:

– The Amazon Web Services are numerous, growing (giving the possibility to improve economies of scale for all users), and characterized by high degrees of scalability and transparency;
– Windows Azure is quite recent and has a scarce experience in the management of those clients whose main needs are related to a rapid scalability.

Fig. 2 shows how in general providers can be evaluated based on three fundamental aspects: (1) *contractual characteristics*, to understand if it possible to obtain discounts or special prices; (2) *development and innovation degree*, as an index of acquired experience; and (3) *reputation over international markets*, as a measure of reliability and potential development.

Basing on the above said considerations, company A decided to migrate the IT infrastructure to the cloud of Microsoft, for its reputation and for the consequent possibility to better support the strategic value of the project. Instead, company B chose the cloud of Amazon, privileging so the provider with a major experience in the infrastructural field.

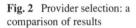

Fig. 2 Provider selection: a comparison of results

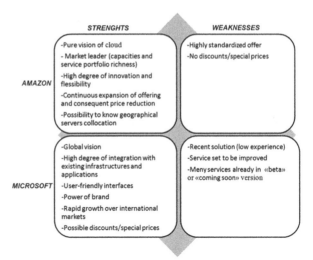

Hence, it is possible to say that the companies characterized by a global vision, whose strategy is mainly oriented to technological innovation and to the enforcement of the brand, tend to select provider for their international reputation, in order to legitimate organizational changes also for external stakeholders. Instead, companies whose strategy is more oriented to internal efficiency tend to select provider with a pure and standardized infrastructural offering.

3.3   Impact on IT Costs

In the case of company A, the economic evaluation started from the BU North America through a perspective comparison between on-premise and externalized solutions. Although the necessity to consider at the first year some capex related to the implementation of the set of applications, cloud remained however the most convenient solution.

The analysis for the European BU has been realized comparing the costs of infrastructural options for *to-be* situation (new on-premise or cloud) with those of *as-is* situation (old on premise). Only for cloud option, it was necessary to introduce at the first year some capex related to the migration of existing applications on the new virtualized infrastructure. Moreover, in the BU Italy it was decided to consider a hybrid cloud, in order to exploit a quite recent internal infrastructure for the *Production Data Management* system. This is the only case of minor convenience for cloud (but only for the first year because of the migration costs).

In the case of company B, evaluation was done comparing costs related to the upgrading of existing infrastructure in hosting, as noticed in the assessment phase,

		ANALIZED SCENARIOS		
		Hosting	**On premise**	**Cloud**
COMPANY A	**ANAM**	€ 97.517	€ 159.385	€ 54.112
	AFRA		€ 81.000	€ 56.250
	AGER		€ 79.750	€ 50.000
	AITA		€ 78.000	€ 104.000
COMPANY B		€ 13.298		€ 8.066

	COMPANY A				COMPANY B
	ANAM	**AFRA**	**AGER**	**AITA**	
Hosting	€ 97.517				€ 13.298
On premise	€ 159.385	€ 81.000	€ 79.750	€ 78.000	
Cloud	€ 54.112	€ 56.250	€ 50.000	€ 104.000	€ 8.066
	34% of on premise	69% of on premise	63% of on premise	133% of on premise	
	55% of hosting				61% of hosting

Fig. 3 Impact on IT costs: a comparison of results

with those of the passage in cloud. Also in this case, and only for cloud, it was necessary to consider some migration costs.

The analysis shows how, for both companies, cloud represents in general the most convenient solution among considered options (Fig. 3).

The saving ranks around:

- 55 % in the case IT infrastructure is directly realized in cloud, as for the BU North America, giving the advantage to cut capex and free resources for future business expansions through a rapid provisioning;
- 46 % (on average) in the case of a migration, with the possibility to dispose of major resources for a future strategic development of applications (company A) or for infrastructural expansions (company B).

4 Consideration About the Value of Cloud and Conclusions

Although today cloud is recognized as one of the most important technologies, a few companies use it to implement new business models and improve their capability to create innovation. A careful analysis of companies' value propositions and value chains at the same time is necessary to make a judgment about the impact of cloud projects on business value.

Enterprises can apply cloud to generate additional revenue streams by *enhancing*, *extending*, or *inventing* new customer value propositions. And cloud can be used to improve, transform, and create new organization and industry value chains (Fig. 4).

Fig. 4 The changing level
of cloud (IBM realized this
model basing on the classic
Venkatraman model about
the changing level of Ict.)

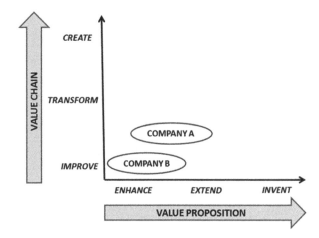

With regard to *value proposition*:

– As for company B, organizations can use cloud to improve current products and services to retain current and attract new customers, garnering incremental revenue (*enhance*).
– As for company A, cloud can support the creation of new products and services or the use of new channels to attract existing or adjacent customer segments to generate significant new revenues (*extend*);
– Companies can use cloud to create a new "need" and own a new market, attracting new customer segments and generating entirely new revenue streams (*invent*).

With regard to *value chain*:

– For both the analyzed companies, cloud adoption can help an organization maintain its place in an existing value chain through increased efficiency and an improved ability to partner, source, and collaborate (*improve*).
– By assisting in developing new operating capabilities, cloud can help a company change its role within its industry (as for the international expansion of company A) or enter a different industry (*transform*).
– Organizations can use cloud to build a new industry value chain or disintermediate an existing one, radically changing industry economics (*create*)

In conclusion, it is possible to say that similar projects, under a technical point of view, can lead companies to use cloud to incrementally enhance their customer value proposition while improving organizational efficiency or to significantly extend customer value propositions, resulting in new revenue streams. The rapid scalability of economic resources allows companies to focus on their business rather than on the supporting IT infrastructure. And this is true: more companies operate in a competitive environment and have market-oriented strategies, as this work has confirmed even if for only two cases.

References

1. Buyya, R., et al. (2009). Cloud computing and emerging IT platforms: Vision, hype, and reality for delivering computing as the 5th utility. *Future Generation Computer Systems, 25*, 599–616.
2. Avison, D. A., & Pies-Heje, J. (1995). *Research in Information Systems: A handbook for research students and their supervisors*. Oxford: Elsevier Butterworth-Heinemann.
3. Leavitt, N. (2009). Is cloud computing really ready for prime time? *Computer, 42*(1), 15–20.
4. Chellappa, R. K., & Gupta, A. (2002). Managing computing resources in active intranets. *International Journal of Network Management, 12*(2), 117–128.
5. Ahronovitz, M., et al. (2010). A white paper produced by the Cloud Computing Use Case Discussion Group. Cloud Computing Use Cases, 10.
6. Aymerich, F., Fenu, G., & Surcis, S. (2008). An approach to a Cloud Computing network. In *Proceedings of the 1st International Conference on the Applications of Digital Information and Web Technologies*.
7. Lacity, M. C., et al. (2010). A review of the IT outsourcing empirical literature and future research directions. *Journal of Information Technology, 25*, 395–433.
8. Yin, R. K. (2009). *Case study research*. Thousand Oaks, CA: Sage.

Security SLAs for Cloud Services: Hadoop Case Study

Massimo Ficco and Massimiliano Rak

Abstract Cloud paradigm is currently one of the most remunerative segments of Information Technology. It has gained the interest of a very large number of corporates and organizations. However, despite the promising features, security is the major concern for businesses that want to shift their services to the cloud. On the other hand, business critical systems must be certified against a set of security controls to be compliant to security standards, as well as to mitigate potential security incidents. Therefore, cloud service providers must employ adequate security measures that conform to security controls expected by the information systems they host; moreover, they should be able to grant the correct application of such controls to their customers. Security service level agreements (SLAs) are a way to face such issues, through the definition of contracts among cloud service providers and customers that clearly state the security grants applied to the offered cloud services. This chapter illustrates a case study that describes how it is possible to implement such security SLAs on a concrete cloud service, which offers Apache Hadoop services over public cloud providers. The chapter outlines how to write and assess security SLAs on such services.

Keywords Cloud security • Service level agreement • Security controls

1 Introduction

Cloud computing is nowadays a largely adopted technology for providing any kind of services. Its success is due to the on-demand self-service, which enables user to acquire cloud service and resources according to a pay-by-use business model. In general, cloud service providers (CSPs) offer guarantees in terms of service availability and performance during a time period of hours and days. The provisioning contracts regulate the cost that customers have to pay for provided services and

M. Ficco (✉) • M. Rak
Department of Industrial and Information Engineering, Università degli Studi della Campania
"Luigi Vanvitelli", Via Roma 29, 81031, Aversa, CE, Italy
e-mail: massimo.ficco@unina2.it; massimiliano.rak@unina2.it

© Springer International Publishing AG 2017   103
K. Corsi et al. (eds.), *Reshaping Accounting and Management Control Systems*,
Lecture Notes in Information Systems and Organisation 20,
DOI 10.1007/978-3-319-49538-5_7

resources. On the other hand, due to their openness to the Internet, cloud services are prone to cyber attacks, which aim at violating security and privacy of the targeted enterprise systems. Several works proposed in the literature present models and mechanisms for monitoring and assuring service privacy and security guarantees in the cloud computing context [1, 2]. In particular, several works explore SLAs for security and analyze security metrics in new paradigms like cloud computing [3, 4]. By incorporating security parameters in the SLA could improve the quality of the service being offered. This objective has profound implications in the security solution to be implemented and delivered. Moreover, it the last years, many security standards and requirement frameworks have been developed in order to address risks to enterprise systems and critical data. On the other hand, most of these efforts are essentially exercises in reporting on compliance and defining security program resources to face evolving attacks that must be addressed.

The *security controls* are guidelines to identify and prioritize security actions, which are effective against cyber threats, with a strong emphasis on "what works," i.e., tools, processes, architectures, and services that have been used and demonstrated real-world effectiveness. However, the available standards leave the process of security controls selection to the organizations. Moreover, the type of security controls to be applied depend on the asset to be protected and are identified on the basis of a risk analysis, which provides a set of significant risks and data to assist in the treatment of these risks.

In this chapter, we propose a method for security controls selection for a cloud-based service. In particular, we consider an Apache Hadoop service as case study. Apache Hadoop is an open-source software framework for distributed storage and distributed processing of very large datasets on cloud. We preset model to manage the SLA life cycle, which can be used to cover the semantic gap among CSC security requirements and security controls offered by CSPs, as well as adopted to compare the services offered by different CSPs. Moreover, we perform an asset evaluation to determine the most critical security controls to be implemented to protect the provided cloud service.

The rest of the chapter is organized as follows: Sect. 2 introduces the system model, as well as the definition of the problem we are focusing on. Section 3 presents the related work in the field of security controls applications. Section 4 introduces the adopted security SLA model, whereas Sect. 5 describes the risk assessment model to be used by the cloud customers. Section 6 illustrates the proposed approach on the Hadoop case study. Section 7 presents a short summary and future work.

2 Problem Definition

Cloud computing paradigm involves many use cases (see [5] for an overview), each of them implying different types of security issues and different ways of involving security and SLAs. Existing standards [6–8] offer a clear classification of the main

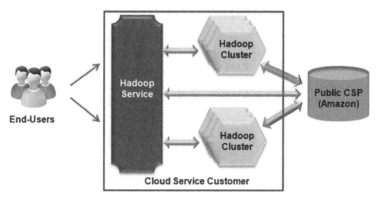

Fig. 1 The system model

concepts associated with cloud computing and of the roles that parties may assume in cloud scenarios.

In this chapter, we assume the common scenario, in which a cloud customer (CSC) wants to know the security grants offered by a public CSP, such as Amazon, in order to decide whether to acquire cloud resources, which will be used to provide a service (in our case study a Hadoop service) to its end users. Figure 1 depicts the scenario we are focusing on.

Therefore, this study focuses on the typical security issues related to the services offered by the CSP to the CSC: *How can the CSC rely on CSP services? How reliable is the offering?* In order to well outline the issues, few considerations are useful: the CSC is not a big cloud service provider, whose reliability is (ideally) granted by its dimension and relevance in the market. The CSC is a cloud service reseller that focuses on a specialized market with well-identified needs, differently from big CSPs, like Amazon, which has no interest in offering services *customized* for a specific audience. The CSC, on the other hand, has the need to evaluate the security risks associated with the usage of the cloud service, especially in case of management of critical data. In such a context, he needs detailed information about the security offered by the CSP, which often is not granted by big CSPs. Thus, we focus on the adoption of security SLAs as a way: (1) to allow CSC to be able to make a concrete risk assessment of adoption of cloud services and (2) to enable CSCs to add value to their services in a well-defined market niche. In order to obtain such a result, we propose that the CSP offers a security SLA able to represent, in a transparent manner, the security grants offered by the cloud provided to its CSCs. Moreover, we propose simple risk model that enables the CSC to compare the security SLA offered by the CSP in order to evaluate the cloud service that best fits his security needs.

3 Related Work

The main problem in adopting security controls is the lack of a clear representation in the cloud computing context, which makes it difficult to connect organizational certification efforts to the services offered by CSPs. In this direction [9] proposes a compliance vocabulary, which creates a set of security SLA terms that are derived from security controls in governance documents, including the NISTSP800-53 [2], the Common Criteria Part 2 [3], the DISA Secure Application Security Technical Implementation Guide (STIG), and the Cloud Security Alliance Cloud Control Matrix (CCM) [10]. Existing services would rely on the compliance vocabulary to represent the controls it must satisfy and embed the corresponding terms in its SLA. In [11], authors propose a methodology to evaluate the information security controls. They rank the controls quantitatively in accordance with given criteria. Peláez [12] describes how to measure the effectiveness of security controls. In particular, a qualitative risk assessment method is adopted. It assigns a huge amount of metrics to each security control in order to measure its quality.

4 Security SLAs and Security Controls

The main goal of security SLAs is to represent the security level offered by the cloud service in a clear way, in order to cover the gap between the CSC, which focuses on his own requirements, and the CSP, which focuses on the security mechanisms he is able to implement [2].

In order to characterize the security in a service, Lindskog [13] defines four dimensions, including type of protection service (e.g., confidentiality), protection level (e.g., number of assets that must be encrypted), adaptiveness (i.e., the ability of a service to change protection levels at run-time), and protection level specification (i.e., the security policy). Bernsmed et al. [14] develop a framework that supports the security SLA management in federated clouds. In this work, we adopt the security model proposed in the SPECS project [15]. Such an SLA model is founded on an SLA life cycle, based on all the up-to-date standards, which includes five main phases: negotiation, implementation, monitoring, and remediation.

In order to cover the semantic gap among CSCs and CSPs, the SPECS SLA model adopts the concept of security controls. Security controls can be physical, technical, or administrative [16]. Each category of controls can be further classified by using either preventive or detective approaches. Preventive controls attempt to avoid the occurrence of unwanted events. They inhibit the use of unauthorized computing resources. Detective controls attempt to identify unwanted events after they have occurred. Examples of detective controls include audit trails, intrusion detection methods, and checksums. Other types of controls are usually described as deterrent, corrective, and recovery, which do not belong to either preventive or detective categories. Deterrent controls are used to discourage malicious users from intentionally violating information security policies or procedures. These are usually constraints that make it difficult to perform unauthorized activities or influence a potential intruder to not violate security. Corrective controls remedy the circumstances that allowed the unauthorized activity. They could result in changes to existing physical, technical, and administrative controls. Recovery controls restore lost computing resources or capabilities caused by a security violation. Deterrent, corrective, and recovery controls are considered to be special cases within the major categories of physical, technical, and administrative controls. For example, deterrence is a form of prevention because it induces dissuasive effect to the intruder. Corrective controls can be assimilated to technical controls, when antivirus removes a malware, or with administrative controls, when backup procedures enable restoring critical data. Finally, recovery controls can be considered as administrative controls when they implement disaster recovery and contingency plans.

The SPECS SLA model reports, for each service covered by SLA, the security controls that the CSP offers on top of it, as represented in Fig. 2. The model assumes that security is expressed in terms of (1) cloud resources, i.e., the description of the resources obtained by the cloud customer, (2) security capabilities, i.e., set of security controls granted on the cloud resources, (3) security metrics, which are the measurable (and externally verifiable) part of the security offered on the cloud service, and (4) service level objectives (SLOs), expressed as thresholds on security metrics, which represent the concrete grants offered to CSCs. Such model is built in order to be perfectly compatible with the WS-Agreement standard, and SPECS offers a WSAG extension to represent the model in a machine readable format.

According to the above model, CSP can build up a security SLA associated with its own service. In particular, the SLA implementation requires:

- A description of the cloud service
- The identification of the implemented security controls
- The identification of the security metrics that can be granted
- The formalization of the security SLA

The inclusion of the security controls in the SLA favors a comparison of offered service and shifts some certification burden to the CSP-based contractual SLA terms. Finally, on the basis of a risk assessment, the CSC can choose which CSP best meets their strict compliance requirements.

5 Security Risk Assessment

As presented in [17], a security model has to be considered three interconnected dimensions: *asset* is anything that has value to the organization; *threat* can inflict damage to assets of an organization; and *security control* is a management, operational, or technical mechanism, which allows defining assets against threats. It is clear that the main property of an asset is its importance for the organization.

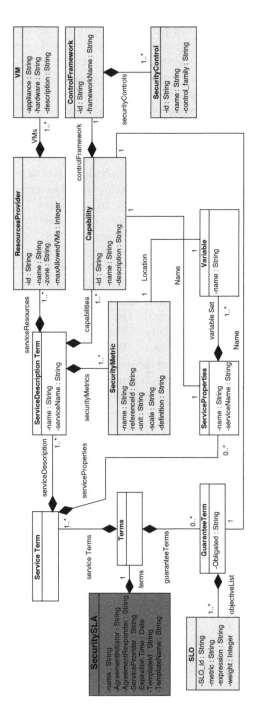

Fig. 2 SPECS SLA model

Therefore, in order to identify which CSP offers the service that best meets his requirements, an analysis of potential risks for the asset should be performed by the CSC. In particular, a risk evaluation matrix should be implemented. As Table 1 shows, the matrix represents the likelihood and consequences of each threat, which are used to compute the risk values.

Then, for each identified threat should be verified which kinds of security controls are offered by the considered CSPs. Such security controls represent mitigation means for the analyzed threat. Thus, on the basis of the level of risk the CSC accepts for the asset, it is necessary to select the CSP.

Definitely, providing security control compliance services can be economically advantageous for CSPs to attract CSCs with strict compliance requirements. Therefore, for each category of CSC, CSPs should choose the security controls to be implemented on the basis of CSC needs, considering also the costs (in terms of money), difficulty of implementation, and time consumption of maintenance that the CSC should waste to implement on its own the same security controls. This analysis would allow identifying the more appropriate security mechanisms to be implemented in comparison to their cost and the level of risk the CSC accepts. Additional security mechanisms can be contracted with the CSC in the security SLA.

6 Security Control Assessment

According to the proposed approach, in order to identify the security level to be offered to CSCs through an SLA, a CSP has to determine which, and how many, controls have to be implemented to protect the hosted service. In the context of this work, we assume that the only applied security controls are those implemented by a basic Hadoop cluster. We adopted NIST SP 800-53r4 guidelines to determine the implemented security controls. According to the NIST structure, the security controls are organized into 18 families, such as access control, security assessment

Table 1 Evaluation matrix with risks likelihood and consequences

	Insignificant	Minor	Moderate	Major	Catastrophic
Rare	Acceptable	Acceptable	Acceptable	**Acceptable**	**To be evaluated**
Unlikely	Acceptable	Acceptable	Acceptable	**To be evaluated**	**To be evaluated**
Possible	Acceptable	Acceptable	**To be evaluated**	**To be evaluated**	**To be evaluated**
Likely	Acceptable	**To be evaluated**	**To be evaluated**	**To be evaluated**	**To be evaluated**
Certain	**To be evaluated**	**To be evaluated**	**To be evaluated**	**To be evaluated**	**To be evaluated**

Table 2 Access controls for Apache Hadoop cluster

Name	Control	How	
Access Control Policy and Procedures	The organization develops and documents: (1) An access control policy that addresses purpose, scope, roles, responsibilities, management commitment, coordination among organizational entities, and compliance; and (2) Procedures to facilitate the implementation of the access control policy and associated access controls	The purpose of introducing a policy of access control is to increase the security with respect to external attacks, to ensure the functionality and integrity of our system The roles within the system are admin and users. The access control is assigned to the admin	Yes
Account Management	The organization: (a) Identifies and selects the types of information system accounts; assigns account managers for system accounts; establishes conditions for group and role membership (b) Assigns managers for information system accounts (c) Establishes conditions for group and role membership (d) Monitors the use of information system accounts	The types of accounts available in the system are admin who creates and manages accounts and users who are all users who use the system The account manager is an admin account Ubuntu All the users belong to the group user, which will have limited Hadoop permissions Monitor access to the cluster via the log files *auth.log* content in *var/log/* and the performed operations through the Hadoop log files	No
Access Enforcement	The system enforces approved authorizations for logical access to information and system resources in accordance with applicable access control policies	Only via SSH	Yes
Unsuccessful Login Attempts	The system enforces a limit of consecutive invalid login attempts by an user during a defined time period	Login takes place without the use of a password, with no limit on failed attempts	No

and authorization, personnel security, identification and authentication, system and communications protection, incident response, system and information integrity, etc. Each family contains a set of security controls related to the general security topic of the family. They can involve aspects of supervision, policy, oversight, manual processes, actions by individuals, and mechanisms. Tables 2, 3, and 4 list tree security control families and some related security controls applied to the considered case study. For each security control is described the name, a description of the control, how to apply it, and if it is already implemented by the Hadoop cluster. For example, as reported in Table 3, Hadoop does not support any security control to protect against Denial of Service (DoS) attacks [18–20], which could

Table 3 System and communications protection for Apache Hadoop cluster

Name	Control	How	
Denial of Service Protection	The system protects against or limits the effects of Denial of Service, by employing some protection mechanism.	Using Secure Copy for the initial handshake will have problems of denial of service because an attacker could send a lot of files and then to consume system resources; No protection mechanism is provided.	No
Cryptographic Protection	The information system implements cryptography policies in accordance with applicable federal laws, directives, policies, regulations, and standards.	There is no encryption on the data stored on the distributed file system. The only encryption in the system is the encryption key that can be RSA or DSA.	No

Table 4 System and information integrity controls for Apache Hadoop cluster

Name	Control	How	
System and Information Integrity Policy and Procedures	The organization: (a) Defines system and information integrity policies; (b) Defines procedures to facilitate the implementation of the identified policies.	To recover data from a damaged Data Node, a client implements a checksum on the file HDFS, which compute a checksum for each Tile and stores it in a separate hidden file. When a client retrieves file, it verifies that the data received from each Data Node match the checksum. Otherwise, the client can choose to retrieve that block from another Data Node that has a replica of that block.	Yes
Malicious Code Protection	The organization: (a) Employs malicious code protection mechanisms at information system entry and exit points to detect and eradicate malicious code; (b) Addresses the receipt of false positives during malicious code detection, and the resulting potential impact on the availability of the system.	The system does not provide mechanisms to protect from malicious code if not one already present on the Linux below.	No

exhaust cloud resources used to run the CSC's services, whereas in Table 1 it is shown that the Hadoop framework provides mechanisms to manage the access control policies. Therefore, on the basis of hypothetical security requirements of the market niche to be covered, the CSP has to assess which controls have already been implemented by the hosted service, as well as identify which should be added to satisfy CSC's security requirements. Then, for each identified control, it has to define the possible metrics to evaluate the control, as well as provide the assessment tool for supporting the CSC audit (monitoring). For example, in order to protect against the DoS attacks, CSP could deploy a prevention mechanism, such as mOSAIC-IDS [21], SNORT [22], and OSSEC [23], which are intrusion detection system to detect anomalous activities against the Hadoop cluster [24, 25]. Security metrics used to perform measurements of the correct delivery of the security capability during system operation could be *"false_positives,"* *"true_positives,"* *"detection_latency,"* etc.

However, the process of security control assessment has to take into account the changes to the system and its operating environment, or the changes outside CSP direct control, which may introduce new security vulnerabilities, and may require a new assessment of some or all security controls. Moreover, new security controls could be added in order to cover possible new market niches.

7 Conclusions

Security is a key issue that inhibits many businesses and government organizations from moving to the cloud. For an organization to have cloud-based services with certification guarantees means increased service efficiency and reputation.

In this chapter, we propose an approach to perform the security assessment of the cloud services offered by CSPs. The results of this assessment are used in determining the overall security offered to the CSC, identifying residual vulnerabilities in the system, providing credible and meaningful inputs to the cloud security administrators, as well as enabling little CSPs to add value to their services in a well-defined market niche, by using security SLA able to describe the security offered on top of their services. On the basis of an accurate risk assessment of required cloud services, a CSC can compare the security SLAs offered by different CSPs in order to evaluate the cloud service that best fits his security requirements.

Acknowledgment This research is partially supported by the European Community's Seventh Framework Programme (FP7/2007–2013) under Grant Agreements no. 610795 (SPECS), as well as the POFESR Campania 2007/2013, Asse 2, 00 2.2, "Bando Sportello dell'Innovazione, Azione 3 e 4, Progetti di trasferimento Tecnologico Cooperativi e di Prima Industrializzazione per le Imprese Innovative ad Alto Potenziale" project ITINERE (ID 06-05-070138).

References

1. Ficco, M. (2013). Security event correlation approach for cloud computing. *Journal of High Performance Computing and Networking, 7*(3), 173–185.

2. Cicotti, G., Coppolino, L., D'Antonio, S., & Romano, L. (2015). Runtime model checking for SLA compliance monitoring and QoS prediction. *Journal of Wireless Mobile Networks, Ubiquitous Computing, and Dependable Applications (JoWUA), 6*(2), 4–20.

3. Ficco, M., & Rak, M. (2012). Intrusion tolerance as a service: A SLA-based solution. *Proceedings of the 2nd International Conference on Cloud Computing and Services Science (CLOSER)* (pp. 375–384).

4. Ficco, M., & Rak, M. (2012). Intrusion tolerance in cloud applications: The mOSAIC approach. *Proceedings of the 6th International Conference on Complex, Intelligent, and Software Intensive Systems (CISIS 2012)* (pp. 170–176).

5. Cloud Computing Use Cases (2010, July). White Paper, ver. 4.

6. ISO/IEC 17789:2014, Information technology—Cloud computing—Reference architecture. Retrieved from http://www.iso.org/iso/catalogue_detail?csnumber=60545

7. NIST. (2013, April). Special Publication (SP) 800-53, Revision 4.

8. Common criteria (Part 2) for IT security evaluation V3.1. (2012, September). Retrieved from https://www.google.it/?gws_rd=ssl#q=Common+criteria+(Part+2)+for+IT+Security+Evaluation+V3.1

9. Hale, M. L., & Gamble, R. (2013). Building a compliance vocabulary to embed security controls in cloud SLAs. *Proceedings of the IEEE 9th World Congress on Services* (pp. 118–125).

10. CSA. (2012). *Cloud controls matrix.* Retrieved from https://cloudsecurityalliance.org/research/ccm/#_overview

11. Lv, J.-J., Zhou, Y.-S., & Wang, Y.-Z. (2011). A multi-criteria evaluation method of information security controls. *Proceedings of the 4th International Conference on Computational Sciences and Optimization* (pp. 190–194).

12. Peláez, M. H. (2010, April). *Measuring effectiveness in information security controls.* SANS Institute InfoSec Reading Room. Retrieved from https://www.google.it/?gws_rd=ssl#q=Measuring+Effectiveness+in+Information+Security+Controls

13. Lindskog, S. (2005). *Modeling and tuning security from a quality of service perspective.* Ph.D., Department of Computer Science and Engineering, Chalmers University of Technology Goteborg, Sweden.

14. Bernsmed, K., Jaatun, M., Meland, P., & Undheim, A. (2011). Security SLAs for federated cloud services. *Proceedings of the International Conference on Availability, Reliabilty and Security.*

15. SPECS project, Secure provisioning of cloud services based on SLA management. Retrieved from http://www.specs-project.eu/

16. Tipton, H. F. (2003). *Access control principles and objectives.* Retrieved from https://www.cccure.org/Documents/HISM/003-006.html

17. Breier, J., & Hudec, L. (2013, September). On selecting critical security controls. *Proceedings of the 8th International Conference on Availability, Reliability and Security (ARES)* (pp. 582–588).

18. Ficco, M., & Rak, M. (2016). Economic denial of sustainability mitigation in cloud computing. *Organizational Innovation and Change, 13,* 229–238.

19. Ficco, M., & Rak, M. (2015). Stealthy denial of service strategy in cloud computing. *IEEE Transactions on Cloud Computing, 3*(1), 80–94.

20. Ficco, M., & Rak, M. (2012). Intrusion tolerance of stealth DoS attacks to web services. In *Information Security and Privacy* (LNCS, Vol. 376, pp. 579–584).

21. Ficco, M., Venticinque, S., & Di Martino, B. (2012). mOSAIC-based intrusion detection framework for cloud computing. In R. Meersman, H. Panetto, T. Dillon, S. Rinderle-Ma, P. Dadam, X. Zhou, et al. (Eds.), *On the move to meaningful internet systems: OTM 2012* (LNCS, Vol. 7566, pp. 628–644).

22. OSSEC, an open source host-based intrusion detection system. Retrieved from http://www.ossec.net/

23. SNORT, an open source network-based intrusion detection system. Retrieved from https://www.snort.org/

24. Ficco, M., Rak, M., & Di Martino, B. (2012, November). An intrusion detection framework for supporting SLA assessment in cloud computing. *Proceedings of the 4th International Conference on Computational Aspects of Social Networks (CASoN 2012)* (pp. 244–249).
25. Esposito, C., & Ficco, M. (2016). Recent developments on security and reliability in large-scale data processing with MapReduce. *International Journal of Data Warehousing and Mining, 12*(1), 49–68.

Exploring Sentiment on Financial Market Through Social Media Stream Analysis

Francesco Bellini and Nicola Fiore

Abstract The aim of this chapter is to present the prototype developed in the TrendMiner project in the financial domain. TrendMiner is a Research & Development project co-funded by the European Commission under the 7th Framework Programme contract nr. FP7-ICT-287863. We developed a web-based prototype summarising the media stream in terms of its likely impact on a selected financial asset from economic and political-economic perspectives. The platform is able to gather the events occurring along the social media timeline and to build a tailored visualisation/summarisation of these data with price movements of a given stock or index. The results of the prototype have been evaluated and summarised in this chapter, and three examples are used as proof of concepts for validating the prototype outcomes against the known market behaviours and the existing literature. The TrendMiner financial use case prototype shows its ability to play as another decision support tool besides the consolidated market forecast techniques such as technical and fundamental analysis.

Keywords Finance • News • Tweets • Social media • Stock • Markets • Sentiment • Corporate

1 Introduction

One of the most important research streams in finance is to understand the determinants of stock market dynamics. According to the theory of efficient financial markets [1], stock prices accurately reflect the whole public information available at all times. Hence, the stock prices adjust according to the new information almost instantaneously, so no extra returns can be achieved by trading on that. Fama and other later authors then asserted that the stock price moves at the time of information release and neither before nor after is possible to have extra returns.

F. Bellini (✉) • N. Fiore
Eurokleis, Via Romeo Romei, 27, Rome, RM 00136, Italy
e-mail: francesco.bellini@eurokleis.com; nicola.fiore@eurokleis.com

© Springer International Publishing AG 2017
K. Corsi et al. (eds.), *Reshaping Accounting and Management Control Systems*,
Lecture Notes in Information Systems and Organisation 20,
DOI 10.1007/978-3-319-49538-5_8

Subsequent studies suggest that the content of the news could influence the way people behave. Some of these works [2–4] have shown that positive and negative emotions affect in a different way individual cognition and behaviour, since "bad" news have more impact than "good" ones and bad information is processed more thoroughly than good. According to Tetlock et al. [5, 6], the fraction of negative words in firm-specific news stories forecasts low firm earnings, and firms' stock prices underreact to the information embedded in negative words. The findings suggested that linguistic media content captures otherwise hard-to-quantify aspects of firms' fundamentals, which investors quickly incorporate in stock prices. Schumaker and Chen [7] show that adding textual features of news can improve the forecasting accuracy of a stock prediction system.

Compared to the traditional press, Internet is a communication channel that broadcasts news much faster and enables the exchange of information at approximately zero cost. Bagnoli, Beneish and Watts [8] find that whisper forecasts (unofficial forecasts of earnings per share that circulate among traders and investors) are, on average, more accurate than First Call forecasts and constitute better proxies for market expectations of earnings than the First Call forecasts. Recent studies [9, 10] have been further concentrated in web search data showing that search volumes of stock names reveal investor attention and interest, and high search volumes thus predict higher stock prices in the short term and price reversals in the long term.

Social media feeds are becoming an important source of data to extract streams of information that could influence the investor behaviour. In the past 5 years, new contributions have shown that the information extracted from social network such as LiveJournal [11], Facebook [12] and Twitter [13] may be correlated with stock indices like the Dow Jones Industrial Average and further used to predict stock market fluctuations. This can be achieved through mood indicators resulting from the analysis of text supplied by social media and expressed in a time series format.

This chapter summarises the achievements of the TrendMiner project in the context of its financial use case (the other one was on politics) that actually started from the recognition of these early attempts. In order to contribute to this specific research field, the TrendMiner financial use case aimed at investigating any link or relationship between financial market and investors' sentiment derived from text mining. As a proof of concept, three different examples are analysed which are discussed in the following paragraphs.

2 TrendMiner Architecture and Components

TrendMiner provides a platform for cross-lingual text mining and summarisation of large-scale stream media. The platform was developed through an interdisciplinary approach, combining deep linguistic methods from text processing, knowledge-based reasoning from web science, machine learning, economics/finance and political science.

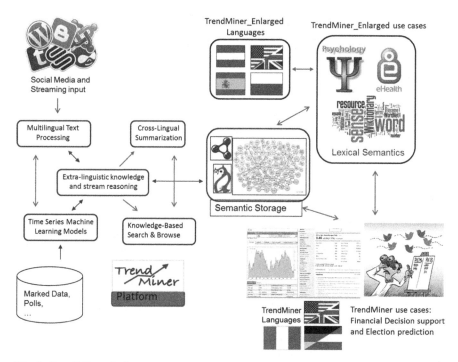

Fig. 1 TrendMiner platform

The platform covers all the phases of the social media stream processing life cycle: large-scale data collection, multilingual information extraction and entity linking, sentiment extraction, trend detection and summarization and visualisation (Fig. 1).

The high-level representation of the architecture identifies the major functional blocks of the system covering all the phases of the social media data processing chain: data collection, deployment of different analysis and transformations and summarisation and visualisation.

The data collection is supported by two complementary components that are responsible for monitoring different social media sources. The processing services are classified into two groups depending on their usage in the processing life cycle. The first group performs the resources pre-processing (metadata extraction) regardless of any context of usage, namely entities detection, language identification and geo-location detection. The results produced by these components are stored in the data repository and serve as a base for subsequent data searching and browsing. The second group of services computes collective analytical information based on user-defined context and resources selection. Finally, a presentation layer service provides an abstraction over the actual data prior to its presentation to the financial (and also political) analyst (end user).

3   Processing of Information in the Financial Domain

The process for analysing information within the financial domain considers the following phases:

- Data Collection
- Computation of polarity, annotation and sentiment
- User interface and examples of market investigations

3.1   Data Collection

Data collection was implemented with reference to the information coming from Twitter accounts, news and financial markets. The activities described in the following paragraphs have been carried out in order to isolate a consistent number of meaningful resources needed for the use case implementation.

Tweets Selection and Collection   In the first stage of TrendMiner, we drove the tweets collection through specific keywords. The keywords were manually extracted from news that generated "rumours" during an observed period. Keywords allow to build a detailed sample of tweets that isolates the comments on observed companies, persons and products.

In the final version, we reversed the approach: instead of collecting the tweets that match certain keywords, we collect all the tweets originated from selected financial sources, and in the second stage we carry out the search for specific keywords. In this way, we do not restrict the collection only to the topics related to some rumours, but we collect whatever is generating interest in the financial domain and we build a dataset to be further investigated afterwards.

The identification of sources has been a time-consuming task and was carried out by following the approach below:

- Worldwide search on Twitter accounts accessed by people who share ideas on investments and global economy;
- Identification, within each account, of a list of users focused on specific issues of economics and finance. A preference was given for the Twitters acquisition. Our search was aimed to expand as much as possible the number of users who share investment ideas, and for this objective we visited each account individually;
- In the financial domain, English is the language primarily accessed worldwide, so the majority of the selected lists use this language. However, some lists in German and in Italian language were selected too.

By using the above-described approach, more than 3000 users were identified; more than 2000 of these are individual users and about 1000 are users operating within news providers. We started to collect the Tweets selected as above since

October 2013 and we synchronised our collection with the data warehouse of the TrendMiner platform. The dataset is now around 3 GB with more than 2.5 million of tweets representing a good starting point for our investigations. A key point for future development will be its maintenance and improvement.

In order to perform the collection of Tweets, we used the APIs provided by Twitter that allows to search within the timeline according to the keywords provided. A python routine was implemented by using these APIs. The routine creates the connection, performs the authentication and runs the search on the Twitter timeline. The routine was scheduled twice a day for the same period of collection described. During this period, the keyword list has been daily refined according to the trending topics in order to refine the selection of Tweets that will concur to the sentiment definition.

News Collection and Analysis The news documents are collected from selected sources that are supposed to provide "price-sensitive" news. The information has been crawled according to the sources identified by the financial research team and to a specific crawling strategy.

Financial Instruments Data Collection In order to combine sentiment and market prices, we have designed and implemented a structure to collect market data with the following features:

- Sentiment can be correlated not only with equity prices but also with currencies, bonds, common funds, exchange trade funds (ETF), etc. This means that the data structure shall allow the detection of each kind of prices that we generalised through the Financial Instrument (FI) concept. In this way, we can access prices and volumes (if any) of any type of market data.
- The structure is flexible in terms of time period and allows to investigate the links between sentiment and market data on monthly, weekly, daily and infra-daily basis.

The prototype focuses only on stock prices and stock indices gathered daily; however, more refined investigations could be conducted in the future.

3.2 Computation of Polarity, Annotation and Sentiment

The following step is the evaluation of entity polarity [14, 15] using the sentiment data for a specific single day. The polarity is the sentiment associated with the entity referring to the keywords list and can be positive, very positive, negative and very negative. We give a score to each word depending on the category of polarity it belongs to and increase/decrease the polarity strength when a word is preceded by a modifier, i.e.: not good $= -1$; good $= +1$; very good $= +2$. For this purpose we developed a tool that reads shorts notices associated with actual values of companies listed at the MIB (stock exchange in Milano) and, using a heuristic combining repeated word in the context of an increase or a decrease of the values, we generated an opinionated lexicon for the Italian language (in the financial domain). This lexicon has been merged with a "classical" computational lexicon of Italian, and it was being manually checked against longer texts, also in different domains.

On the polarity data, we also consulted the list of words deemed to be positive or negative, as they are defined in the subjectivity lexicon of Loughran and McDonald Financial Sentiment Dictionaries [16]. This is for the English text, but we also provided for Italian translation. We are currently implementing a sentence level polarity computation for Italian newspapers and porting the strategy to Tweets.

The output of the collection is a list of *json* arrays containing the Tweets. This format is processed in a pipeline approach by a series of language processing tools (Gorrell et al. [17], Preotiuc et al. [18]) to provide tokenisation, language detection, annotation and sentiment analysis. The processed data are then aggregated over a time period (Samangooei et al. [19]) to produce features suitable for describing movements in a time series, e.g. word frequencies or aggregate sentiment relating to a given person, party or company.

4   User Interface and Examples of Market Investigations

The TrendMiner user interface allows to show time-based sentiment and activity on a particular topic of interest and compares them visually with the time series of a financial instrument (price, index, etc.). Since the user interface has been designed at a prototype level and permits only to show few changes in sentiment over time, we can display daily values for max 1 month. If we go over a longer period, then we have to deal with weekly readings. In addition, the interface in the research programme has been designed and implemented to be unique for all the TrendMiner use cases that cope with finance, politics and health. For this reason, it does not include sophisticated features and quantitative tools specific for the financial domain. It allows to investigate financial markets and investor sentiment at the "explorative" level, but this permits in any case to get very interesting results. The following figures show how the user interface works according to the available components (Fig. 2).

4.1   Social-Economy

As a first example, we choose to investigate a social-economy situation creating a specific track in the system (with the parameters shown in Fig. 3) to which corresponds the entity distribution shown in Fig. 4.

As a first result, we can see that entities like Draghi, Yellen, growth, Europe and USA are more mentioned than topics like jobless, unemployment, deflation and recovery. We see also that Draghi and Yellen are mentioned when they approach

TrendMiner Project

Fig. 2 Cockpit for track management

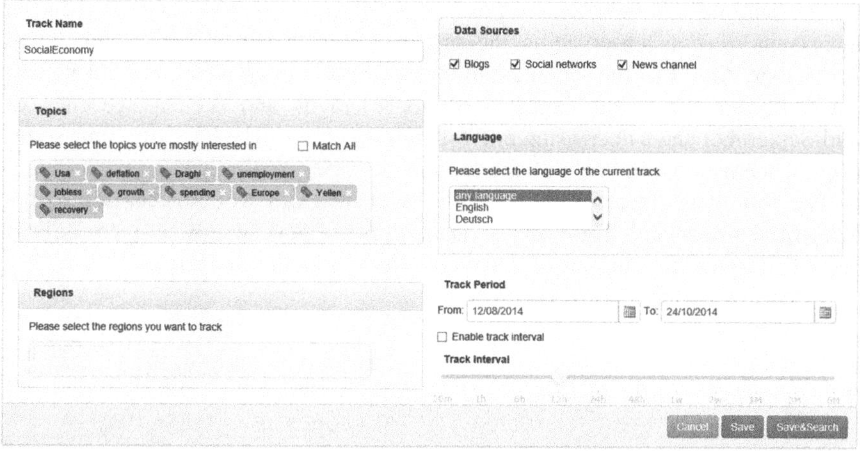

Fig. 3 Track set-up

their periodic speech, and, apart from these events, the interest of the financial community is less evident. Instead, the topic growth is evident over all the observed period, and this applies to the topic Europe that is more evident than USA.

We also tried more topics like austerity, claims, households and others, but their influence is low if compared with the above terms, and we experienced that lower activities have low impact over the sentiment readings. This first screening is important in order to establish which terms should be monitored over the time (they could be the topics with more weight on the sentiment changes) and which terms should be discarded instead.

Mentions of the entities for subperiods

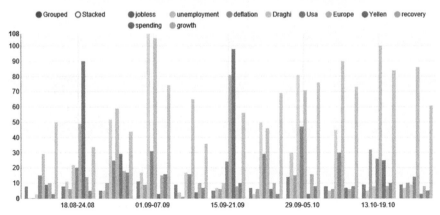

Fig. 4 Number of entities for each topic

The sentiment is then reported in Fig. 5. Here the average value is 0.24; an increasing trend is observed in the first period with a peak in the middle of September. After that the sentiment drops. A possible interpretation of this pattern could be an increasing expectation from Draghi and Yellen speeches of mid-September and a decreasing interest after this event. The FTSE100 time series (Fig. 6) seems to be in line with the sentiment.

The following figures show how the user interface works according to the available components. The cockpits in Figs. 7 and 8 show how a query is built according to topics, data source, locations, language and time period.

4.2 Initial Public Offering (IPO)

As a second example, we investigated the IPO of Alibaba Group that took place on 19th September 2014. The entities chart of Fig. 9 shows a high interest around the IPO date. We compared Alibaba vs some peers, in order to see if some discontinuity happens in the period. As can be seen, when the listing is over all the peers seem to have the same mood (as it is logic), and this is an important result in terms of reliability of our dataset.

The sentiment chart (Fig. 10) shows an average value of 0.47 that is higher than the average of the social-economy case. On the other hand, the trend seems the opposite to the one of the stock price, meaning that sentiment roughly increases when stock price decreases.

The stock price (Fig. 11) decreases immediately after the listing date and increases at the end of the observed period. During the days close to the listing date, activities are driven by Alibaba's topic while the sentiment strongly decreases

Average sentiment of the track divided by subperiods

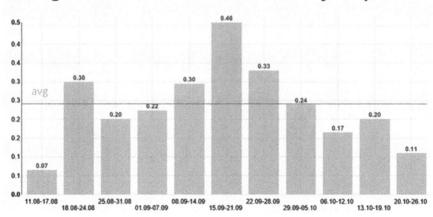

Fig. 5 Sentiment pattern

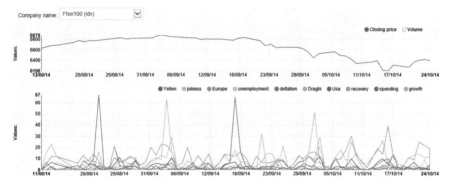

Fig. 6 Topics activity and FTSE100 time series

the day after the listing. This behaviour may be expected as the attention of investors typically drops right after an important event (Simon [20]).

4.3 New Product Announcement

As a third example we analysed the Apple stocks around the date of the iPhone 6 announcement. The topics have been chosen by selecting the terms most related to this stock (Fig. 12). It shows the weights of each entity during the selected period and that iPhone 6 is the one most relevant. Figures 13 and 14 show sentiment, activity and stock price.

Order: by Group   ☑

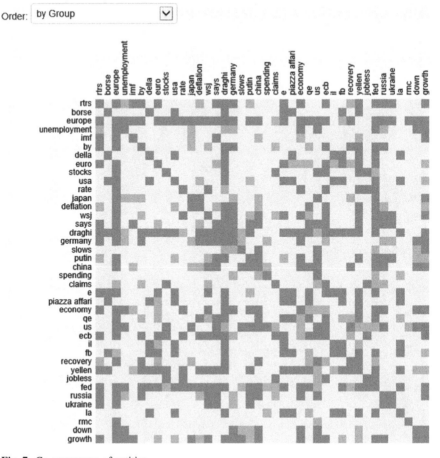

Fig. 7 Co-occurrence of entities

The chart of activity combined with the stock price shows a peak in the activity around the 8th September 2014. This corresponds, on one hand to a negative change in sentiment, while on the other hand to a positive reverse in the stock price. This is an interesting configuration to be examined in order to decide for a long position on the stock. The same also happens from the third to the fourth week, even if the peaks and the increase of stock price are less evident.

This trend can be explained by the fact that the iPhone 6 announcement was seen by the market as the most significant driver of the stock price for a long time. A reduction of the sentiment at the same time of the peak in activity is considered by some traders/investors as an acceptable behaviour. This may happen (Simon [20]) because a greater amount of information is exchanged among the actors when a new product (the iPhone 6) is expected to drive the future stock price. In general, during this phase, expectation and activity increase around the new factor and decrease

Fig. 8 Topics, word cloud and source indications

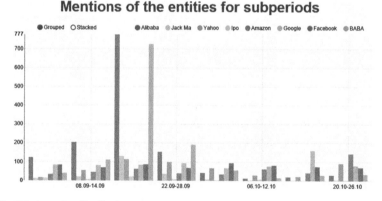

Fig. 9 Alibaba entity distribution

when more details are known and the decision investment has been taken. Another theory, which leads to the same conclusion, considers the investor sentiment as a contrarian indicator (Thorp [21]) that foresees a bullish market when the sentiment reaches low values and vice versa.

Of course, this is not a unique strategy for a long position in the stock. Strategies for short positions could be also detected. As a result, the trader/investor can base his strategy not only considering the market price but also with the information provided by the text mining.

Average sentiment of the track divided by subperiods

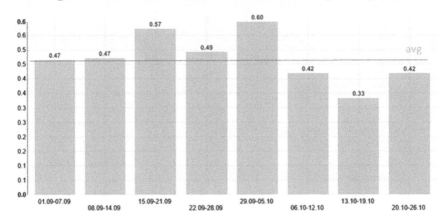

Fig. 10 Alibaba sentiment pattern

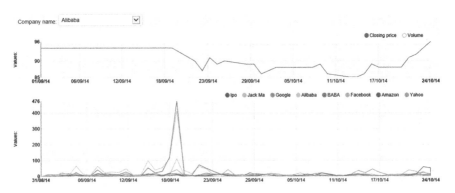

Fig. 11 Alibaba activity and stock exchange price

5 Conclusions and Future Developments

From the three examples analysed, we can draw the following considerations.

Sentiment can be considered as an additional source of information to drive investment decisions. This can be used together with the consolidated tools of technical analysis. However, at this stage quantitative approaches for the computation of the sentiment are still missing. It is not yet clear whether the absolute value of a sentiment can be associated with a bullish or to a bearish market. Contrarian strategy is one of the most used in the market and helps to discover situations in which extremely bullish or extremely bearish configurations happen in order to decide to go long or short in investment. Actually, these configurations are

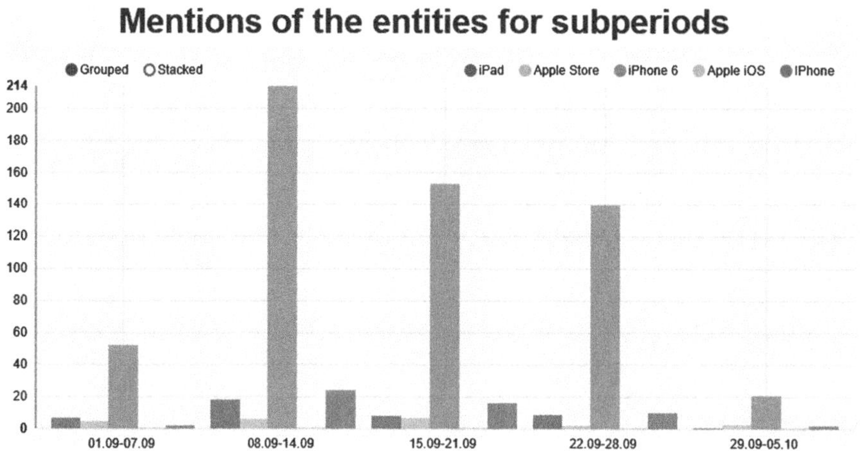

Mentions of the entities for subperiods

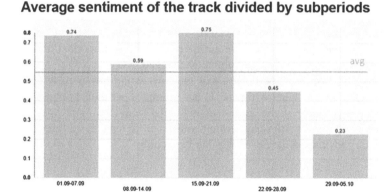

Fig. 12 Number of entity mentions in a period

Average sentiment of the track divided by subperiods

Fig. 13 Sentiment of the track

investigated through mathematical and statistical tools, but a second source value coming from moods and opinions could be of great influence.

Of course, either the visual links or the quantitative readings will lead in any case to subjective valuations for investments, because the decision of which amount the sentiment must change in order to shift from a bullish configuration to a bearish one is very subjective. This stresses the concept that a decision support system is the most valuable aid for investment choices.

Given these considerations, our examples of market investigations assess some important points:

- The validity of underlying dataset. All the examples, although not similar in the content, have found feedback and compliance in the system. This means that this dataset must be maintained and improved.

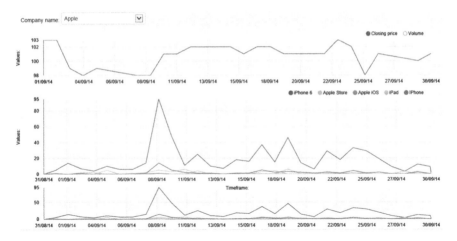

Fig. 14 Stock market and Twitter data in the time frame

- Some topics must be identified and observed during the time. This helps to find out average values and quantitative changes in sentiment. These topics must be started and investigated on financial instruments with a consistent "volume" of moods around them, which are primarily the most important indices, and secondly the stocks with high volume exchanged.
- An investigation must be done about the forecasting power of the sentiment when quantitative values will arise. In our examples, we used daily prices but we need to investigate if the sentiment indicator would be more appropriate to forecast weekly or infra-day market values or if long daily time series are necessary to analyse the next infra-day behaviour.

References

1. Fama, E. F. (1970). Efficient capital markets: A review of theory and empirical work. *Journal of Finance, 25*(2), 383–417.
2. Baumeister, R. F., Bratslavsky, E., Finkenauer, C., & Vohs, K. D. (2001). Bad is stronger than good. *Review of General Psychology, 5*, 323–370.
3. Fiske, S. T., & Taylor, S. E. (1991). *Social cognition*. New York: McGraw-Hill.
4. Brief, A. P., & Motowidlo, S. J. (1986). Prosocial organizational behaviors. *Academy of Management Review, 11*, 710–725.
5. Tetlcok, P. C., Saar-Tsechansky, M., & Mackassy, S. (2008). More than words: Quantifying language to measure firms' fundamentals. *The Journal of Finance, 63*(3), 1437–1467.
6. Tetlock, P. C. (2007). Giving content to investor sentiment: The role of media in the stock market. *The Journal of Finance, 62*(3), 1139–1168.
7. Schumaker, R. P., & Chen, H. (2009). Textual analysis of stock market prediction using breaking financial news. *ACM, 27*(2), 1–19.
8. Bagnoli, M., Beneish, M. D., & Watts, S. G. (1999). Whisper forecasts of quarterly earnings per share. *Journal of Accounting and Economics, 28*(1), 27–50.

9. Da, Z., Engelberand, J., & Gao, P. (2011). In search of attention. *Journal of Finance, 66,* 1461–1499.
10. Preis, T., Moat, H. S., & Stanley, H. E. (2013). Quantifying trading behavior in financial markets using Google trends. *Nature UK Scientific Reports, 3,* 1684.
11. Gilbert, E., & Karahalios, K. (2010). *Widespread worry and the stock market.* International AAAI Conference on Weblogs and Social Media.
12. Karabulut, Y. (2011). *Can Facebook predict stock market activity?* National Bureau of Economic Research, Behavioral Finance Meeting, Standford, CA.
13. Bollen, J., Mao, H., & Zeng, X. (2011). Twitter mood predict the stock market. *Journal of Computational Science, 2*(1), 1–8.
14. Godbole, N., Srinivasaiah, M., & Skiena, S. (2007). *Large-scale sentiment analysis for news and blogs.* ICWSM.
15. Zhang, W., & Skiena, S. (2010). *Trading strategies to exploit blog and news sentiment.* Fourth International Conference on Weblogs and Social Media (ICWSM).
16. Loughran, T., & McDonald, B. (2011). When is a liability not a liability? Textual analysis, dictionaries, and 10-Ks. *Journal of Finance, 66*(1), 35–65.
17. Gorrell, G., Petrak, J., Bontcheva, K. Emerson, G., & Declerck, T. TrendMiner D2.3.2 Multilingual resources and evaluation of knowledge modelling—v2.
18. Preotiuc-Pietro, D. Samangooei, S., Varga, A., Gelling, D., Cohn, T., & Niranjan, M. (2014). TrendMiner D3.3.1 Tools for mining non-stationary data—v2 Clustering models for discovery of regional and demographic variation—v2.
19. Samangooei, S., Preotiuc-Pietro, D., Jing, L., Niranjan, M., Gibbins, N., & Cohn, T. Trendminer D3.1.1 Regression models of trends in streaming data.
20. Simon, H. A. (1955). A behavioral model of rational choice. *Quarterly Journal of Economics, 69,* 99–118.
21. Thorp W. A. (2004, September/October). CFA Using investor sentiment as a contrarian indicator. CI Features.

The Integration of Management Control Systems Through Digital Platforms: A Case Study

Katia Corsi, Daniela Mancini, and Giuseppina Piscitelli

Abstract This study investigates the contribution of digital platforms to management control systems. They are hardware/software solutions able to connect people in a "social" and safe environment and to provide tools useful to create, organise, search and share documents, information, ideas, calendars and so on. Several studies have investigated the organisational implications of such platforms, but prior studies have provided little attention to their implications on management control systems (MCSs). In order to conduct the study, we examined the case of an Italian subsidiary of a European group, working in bathroom ceramic sector. We describe the introduction of a digital platform to support communication flows inside the organisation, and we illustrate how this platform has become more important as a device to support management control processes. The implementation of the digital platform affects each components of management control system and contributes to increase the level of integration among those components. The paper aims to contribute both to academia, filling the gap in studies regarding the relationship between MCSs and ICTs, and to practitioners, highlighting how a digital platform could be implemented to support management control processes.

Keywords Management control systems • Digital platforms • Information sharing • Integration • Microsoft SharePoint

1 Introduction

Companies are constantly involved in searching new forms of activities' coordination in order to improve the levels of efficiency and effectiveness of operational processes, to guide operations towards objectives and to align employees' activities

K. Corsi (✉)
University of Sassari, Sassari, Italy
e-mail: Kcorsi@uniss.it

D. Mancini • G. Piscitelli
Parthenope University of Naples, Naples, Italy
e-mail: daniela.mancini@uniparthenope.it; pina.piscitelli@uniparthenope.it

© Springer International Publishing AG 2017   131
K. Corsi et al. (eds.), *Reshaping Accounting and Management Control Systems*,
Lecture Notes in Information Systems and Organisation 20,
DOI 10.1007/978-3-319-49538-5_9

to organisation's goals. Management control systems are a set of controls and organisational mechanisms that companies use to realise that alignment [1].

Information and communication technologies (ICTs) offer useful solutions to improve coordination of activities and processes. In the last decades, the spread of the Internet and the development of ICT have provided new digital solutions useful to share ideas, information and documents, to manage complex projects and to find people and their personal details [2–7]. In general terms, these platforms can be defined as "shared, unbounded, heterogeneous, open, and evolving socio-technical systems comprising an installed base of diverse information technology capabilities and their user, operations, and design communities" ([8]: 748).

Digital platforms are "generative" technological tools that typically include the following components:

1. A tool to share contents, with other employees, across the organisation
2. A tool to organise information and document sharing, activities and communication flows among people and teams
3. A tool to search information and people
4. A tool to analyse data from multiple sources, visualising them in a graphic way

It is known that ICTs do not produce any relevant effect on value creation if it is considered as an isolating system [9]: what is important is the way in which ICTs interact with other systems as information system, activity systems and human resource management, etc. [10]. From an organisational point of view, studies highlight that ICT adoption can generate a better coordination among offices, a more efficient sharing of information and a greater increase of productivity [11, 12].

In this field of research, studies regarding digital platforms are essentially focused on organisational issues [2, 5–7, 13–15], while little investigation is upon their implementation for control's aims and their implications on management control systems (MCSs).

In this research, we explore the effects of digital platforms on MCSs in order to highlight if and how they help companies to better organise their MCSs package. Through the literature review and the analysis of a case study, we intend to highlight:

1. If a digital platform, primarily implemented to improve information sharing among organisational units, is also useful to support MCS
2. How a digital platform affects each component of MCSs:

   (a) Organisational control, in terms of a wider and timelier sharing of values and culture
   (b) Administrative control and information procedures, in terms of their reconfiguration, transparency and compliance
   (c) Cybernetic control, in terms of enhancing behaviour alignment, integration of models, activities and tools

3. How a digital platform affects the MCS as a whole, especially in terms of coordination and integration of its components

Our study contributes to the existing literature on the relationship between ICT and MCS in two ways. First, it expands the studies on the use of ICT by providing evidence on the use of digital platforms. Second, it expands the studies on MCS by considering a recent technological tool usually employed for information sharing. The research, finally, contributes to enrich the theoretical debate about the relationship between MCSs and ICTs and to highlight new capabilities of digital platform. From the empirical point of view, the paper describes a possible application of a digital platform in support of management control, with a specific focus on the integration of control system mechanisms and components.

The paper is structured as follows: in the second section, we review the literature concerning the implications of ICT adoption on MCS and the digital platform potentialities; in the third section, the research methodology is presented, while in the fourth section, the case study is described and commented; in the last section, we discuss the main findings, highlighting the limits of the research and suggesting further directions for future research.

2 Literature Review

MCSs include a number of devices (accounting models, hardware/software devices, organisational structure, policies and decision support systems) that companies use to align employees' behaviour to organisation's goals and strategies [1, 16–18], influencing the employees' behaviours and measuring corporate performance [19–21]. These systems are usually studied, analysing separately the following aspects: strategic control, relational control, organisational control, management control, risk control, internal control system over financial reporting and compliance control [22–27]. Other studies assert that the MCSs come from the systematic coordination of several mechanisms [1, 26]:

- Cultural control systems based on value, beliefs and social norms (organisational or clan control)
- Cybernetic controls that act on results through the definition of objectives, their measurement and the distribution of reward and compensation (management control)
- Administrative control systems that include control mechanisms able to monitor employee behaviour defining governance rules, organisational structure and policies and procedures [28]
- Compliance control systems that include a mix of mechanisms able to assure transparency and compliance with law, regulation and internal standards.

The academic debate on the relationship between MCSs and ICTs highlights the existence of a bidirectional link [29], which means that the implementation of an ICT tool may affect MCSs, stimulating changes in their components and, conversely, MCS assets and characteristics may influence ICT's implementation and use.

Usually scholars analyse separately each component of MCS and different ICT tools [29, 30]. For the first aspect, studies consider management accounting systems [31], performance measurement systems [32], balanced scorecard scheme, activity-based costing, etc. For the second aspect, scholars consider office automation tools or integrated tools for management and control function as ERP systems, BI systems, Internal Auditing Suite, CRM and SCM software and so on.

Regarding to the influence of ICTs on MCSs, in recent years, particular attention has been addressed to ERP. They are integrated technology solutions used by companies to support operational processes that have relevant organisational, managerial and accounting implications [33, 34]. Examining ERP's impacts, some studies show that ERP's characteristics (as integration, standardisation, centralisation, etc.) provide a lot of accounting and forward-looking information [35–37]. Other studies also highlight the positive impact of ERPs on management accounting practices, in terms of data collection: they show ERP's support to MCSs as an integrated database which, through a centralised data repository, could allow each user a direct access to the available information [38, 39].

ICT also influences the information quality and the effectiveness of decision-making processes. Scholars explore how ICT acts on the relationship between cost and effectiveness of information processes: ICT improves the accuracy of information and the timeliness of information process [40]. Particularly, ERP systems have the ability to support long-term decisions in a more timely way, even if detecting this impact is not always easy [41].

Another important area of research investigates the relation between ICT and the organisation, with particular regard to management accountants' role [1, 35, 42] and administrative processes. Studies highlight that ICT activates a hybridisation of management accountant professionals: management accountants experience an enlargement of their responsibilities and competencies, while simultaneously, non-accountants assume familiarity with numbers and indicators and problem-solving responsibilities, formerly considered the domain of the accounting department [35, 43–45].

Recently some studies examine how ICT actuates the dematerialisation of administrative and managerial processes and how it generates changes in organisational procedures [46, 47].

Literature concerning ICT and MCS also investigates integration and disintegration of information systems [41]. It examines the level of integration that companies reach through different kinds of ICT products and identify three steps of integration [48]:

- Data integration, which refers to the fact that "data are stored and maintained in one place only" ([29]: 43)
- Hardware/software integration, which concerns "network connectivity" and the communication among computers
- Information integration, which concerns "the interchange of information between different departments"

The first two levels affect ICTs, while the latter concerns MCSs. Studies analyse integration inside different components of MCSs in terms of data, information flows or procedure consistency [1, 26], while few studies examine how ICTs support integration between MCS components looking to MCSs as a whole.

As highlighted above, studies are essentially concentrated on ICT traditional solutions, disregarding new solutions as digital platforms.

Scholars analysed digital platform in different decisional contexts, sectors and functions [2, 6, 7, 14, 15, 49]. These studies examined, especially through case studies, how and why they can improve communication within groups [13], facilitate creativity [5], stimulate the generation of knowledge [2] and dematerialise processes [50], but only few (to the best of our knowledge) consider the possible impact on management control system.

These studies show that the new solutions, compared with the traditional ones, have a different approach to manage the complexity. From modular systems that allow flexibility through the composition of the various modules (mixing and matching strategy) [51, 52], they switch to generative systems, which allow a better flexibility, arising from the continuous interaction of several employees that can create new output without entering any input in the original system [53].

Digital platforms underline a sociotechnical process and not only a technological one [8], which allows to communicate, store and process all types of information and also to prepare a structure of information not fully defined. These platforms are based on the concept of "generativity" because "they are never fully complete, that they have many uses yet to be conceived of, and that the public and ordinary organizational members can be trusted to invent and share good uses" ([54]: 43). This concept, therefore, is not separable from socialisation's concept, based on variously coordinated interactions among different persons. Some authors [3], in fact, discern in digital platforms three types of structure of social interactions, such as information sharing, collaboration and collective action.

In this viewpoint, digital platforms present broad potentialities, in terms of organisational integration: this allows us to conjecture the relationship between digital platforms and MCSs, which includes the cybernetic perspective (the most traditional), but also the administrative and cultural ones.

Digital platforms could easily support an interactive management of inside and outside company's workflow, incentivising not only information integration but also integration in procedural, administrative, documental, interpersonal and cultural field [55].

Digital platforms are relevant tools of communication because they offer the opportunity for interacting with several subjects and establishing close relationships able to contribute to the creation of organisational knowledge and organisational memory [56, 57]. ICT supports the acquisition process of knowledge in big enterprises more than in small and medium enterprises, because of the several difficulties in information sharing among individuals and groups [58, 59]. In big enterprises, the digital platforms are considered as a tool, which can compensate traditional problems associated with ERPs (such as centralised control, administrative orientation, over-standardisation of communication, loss of social interaction among users, etc.) [60, 61].

In literature, some contributions (certainly still few) analyse new digital solutions focusing essentially on the concept of organisational integration and control, as a form of coordination. Particularly some scholars [8] distinguish "digitising" as technical process from "digitalisation", as sociotechnical process of applying techniques to a broader social and institutional context. These authors show that new technologies, at the same time, strengthen and weaken the ability of organisations to exercise control. The new technologies, through the digitisation of processes, allow to increase the control points and generate more "granularity", which leads to the paradox of control between centralisation and decentralisation.

Other authors [3], in analysing the digital platforms in virtual communities, focus on the role of social interactions as forms of control/coordination. They identify three different structures of social interactions (as mentioned above), not necessarily all present in every digital platform. These interactions are related to the three traditional forms of control/coordination (market, hierarchy and clan) [62]:

- In the sharing of information, the platform supports the diffusion of codified information among all the users; there is a form of external control without formal rule or governance mechanism, since each user performs similar tasks independently, pursuing its objectives (market).
- In the collaboration, the platform generates common interests and values among users through the dissemination of information codified or abstract, and it aims to create a relationship of trust among users who are still free to pursue their goals: in this context control/coordination is still horizontal although adjusted so formal and hierarchical (hierarchy).
- In the collective action, the platform should support the negotiation of objectives and create a spirit of loyalty between the groups, in order to generate high congruence between the objectives of the members. There is an environment in which prevail trust and shared values between the users (clan): in this context, the control/coordination is based on "mutual adjustments", although formal and hierarchical control can exist.

3 Methodology and Research Design

In order to fill the literature gap, this research highlights if and how digital platforms affect MCSs, as relevant systems of governance, using a qualitative case study methodology [63, 64].

From a methodological viewpoint, the case examined represents an exploratory case, in which the empirical evidence has the helping function to formulate a theory, which will be tested in future research. Particularly, this type of case study aims to highlight what happens in the presence of a given phenomenon, which is the implementation of a digital platform. According to the literature on methodology research, the exploratory case study (compared to the descriptive and explanatory

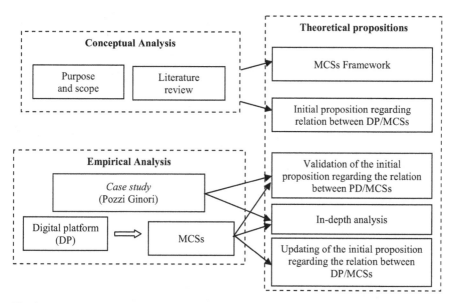

Fig. 1 Research design

ones) is appropriate when it is quite difficult to draw on empirical evidence of previous literature [65].

In order to ensure the necessary methodological rigour, we represent the research design followed in this work in Fig 1.

The case study concerns the description of a digital platform developed with Microsoft SharePoint suite and its utilisation by an Italian subsidiary of a European group (Sanitec) working in bathroom ceramic sector. We analyse the structure and the functioning of the platform, examine the main reasons of its implementation and describe the most relevant business processes supported. In order to deeply understand the case study, we used multiple information sources:

- Semi-structured interviews to key users of the digital platform aiming to understand the effective use and application environment of the platform. We interview two key users: the general director of the factory and the head of purchasing department. The interviews, of about half and an hour, were tape-recorded and transcribed.
- Analysis of project documents and reports produced by the headquarter work team in the first phase of the implementation, including presentations to explain the philosophy and objectives of the project;
- Deep observation of the platform's functioning and of the user's interaction.

The case examined is particularly useful to investigate the implication of a digital platform on MCSs for many reasons. The platform was implemented 3 years ago, after a long period (1 year) of presentations and discussions in meetings between company's project team and function team of each subsidiary. The international nature of the group and the centralised organisational structure made seriously important the need of collaborative tools in order to support communication and coordination. This need was emphasised by the growth strategy followed by the group. It was based on acquisitions of local and famous companies and brands all over European countries with a consequent proliferation of languages, information systems, procedures and so on.

4 Case Study Description

The case study concerns the description of a digital platform realised through Microsoft SharePoint suite and its utilisation by an Italian subsidiary of a European group (Sanitec). The group operates in several European countries (Italy, German, England, France and so on) through specific plants and brands for each country. The Italian company is a wholly owned subsidiary acquired in 1994. It operates with one of the most famous and ancient ceramic brand, in a productive plant located in Gaeta. The subsidiary has a functional structure where purchasing and production activities, human resource and industrial control take place and report to the headquarter. Administration and commercial functions are located in another Italian subsidiary, while ICT, planning and control are located, respectively, in Poland and Finland. Table 1 shows companies' results and performance realised in 2014.

The collaboration platform is regularly used by 2 years. It is organised as a website and structured in the following sections:

- An intranet area where employees can find information and documents of general interest
- Several thematic sections, with reserved access to different departments of the group, where documents, reports, projects, managerial processes and their related administrative and information flows are shared

The project starts with the creation of an intranet of the group called "Insider" (Fig. 2), accessible from each person of the company, even in the factory. Through

Table 1 The financial performance of the examined company (millions of euro)	Group	2014
	Net sales	701.8
	Operating profit	67.9
	Net profit	42.5
	Average number of employees	6149
	Italian subsidiary	**2014**
	Net sales	45.517
	Operating profit	−4.171
	Net profit	−8.446
	Average number of employees	424

Fig. 2 Insider home page

Insider it is possible to collect and share information regarding several aspects of the group or business unit. The intranet is a multilingual interactive environment; it is articulated in three main sections:

1. Sanitec: this section is divided into three different subsections called About us, People and Market Information. They provide information about the company, such as details on governance model and people, financial performance, social and political situation and competitive positioning in Europe and in the global market. In this area, it is possible to find information on the change of top management, figures on financial results, on ICT products and innovation, on purchasing market dynamic and on new rules and laws.
2. Resources: this section is divided into three different subsections called Organisation, Processes and Policies providing information about human resource organisation and management, operating processes and company's policies, i.e. organisational structure; job opportunities among the group; interviews to managers; social events, like travels and sport activities reserved to the employees; directives and open management letters; and standard document models like greeting card.
3. Cooperation: this is a section with restricted access used to deliver specific services to the employees such as travels and meeting arrangements (Travel and Meetings), to manage operating process workflows (Workgroup) and to share certain documents and information about the subsidiaries (My local site) such as headed papers, company's standard forms and greeting card with company's brand.

Insider helps the company to improve and easy manage institutional communication and helps people to know each other, to improve and intensify information exchange. Before the implementation of the digital platform, information sharing was very poor among the group and limited to the communication of organisational changes. According to the interviewers, in the first stage, the tool helps employees to intensify communication and interaction among the company and the subsidiaries, in terms of quantity and frequency of information exchange. Despite this, the platform was not able to overcome the inter-functional barriers.

> Before the implementation of the platform the purchasing function had only an annual meeting to define and share strategic vision and objectives. After the implementation of the digital platform, we have continuous contacts; we use the platform for both an instant exchange of information and a periodical brainstorming. Now information about problems and the solutions adopted by the other purchasing functions are recorded and shared through the platform, this helps to improve processes. Also the culture is changed, we are more collaborative and prompt to help each other, despite the fact that each purchasing function compete with the other among the group. While at the subsidiary level, I think that we have reached a low level of collaboration because the purchasing function and the production function are low integrated. (The Chief Purchasing Officer)

In this sense some utilities are particularly useful, such as (a) the "search" function, through which it is possible, for example, to collect information on colleagues, on function activities and on new projects; (b) the tool to comment every news and article; and (c) the tool for instant messaging.

During the interviews, we deeply analysed and observed these tools and contents and their usage. In order to reach the aims of this research, we have conducted a deep investigation on the following subsections: Services and Utilities, Investment Demand and Operations.

The subsection "Services and Utilities" is in "Shortcuts" section, and it is an interactive space where the company manages two very important services for each subsidiary:

1. The travel service, i.e. arrangements of business travels and transfers for managers and top managers
2. The EDP support service, i.e. computer services aiming to remove malfunctioning of information system, hardware and software tools and security system assistance (maintenance, security interventions, etc.)

Before the implementation of the digital platform, each subsidiary had an office dedicated to travels and overnight stay arrangements on the bases of managers' requests. Each activity of the process was managed manually, and several information and communication channels were used contextually (e-mail, fax, internal mail, etc.). In order to rationalise travel expenses, the process has been centralised to the headquarter and managed by the digital platform. It is used to:

1. Collect the starting request for the transfer using an online form, where managers provided travel details.
2. Deliver the service proposal containing different travel solutions.
3. Manage the approval process of the transfer.
4. Give some additional information for a pleasant business trip like weather forecast, tourist information, news and details on strikes, etc.

According to the purchasing manager, this new way to manage the travel service helps each subsidiary to rationalise the number of suppliers and to reduce administrative costs of the process and business trip costs.

The EDP service is an interactive area that the Group EDP Department, located in Poland, uses to:

- Solve problems concerning hardware and software devices. Each employee located in the subsidiaries can fill a form starting a request for intervention (ticket) including the detailed description of the malfunction. The request is numbered and automatically classified, according to the level of priority. Every information regarding the problem is managed through the platform and automatically replicated via e-mail until the problem is solved, and these information are also recorded in order to have a repository of the history of each malfunction.
- Communicate some update and news regarding the information systems, the call conference system and maintenance interventions.
- Measure automatically and communicate the EDP performance for the support service in terms of timeliness, punctuality and quality of the process. Periodically, in this section, online satisfaction questionnaires are delivered.

The second examined subsection, "Investment Demand", is in workgroup space, a restricted area, which contains the following subsections:

- Investment demand: it is an area reserved to the head of the factory and used to manage high-cost investment.
- Intelligence: it is an area reserved to the marketing and commercial function.
- Information management: it is an area where the ICT function communicate with the other ones providing information on IT organisational structure (name and details of ICT employees, job descriptions, scheduled holidays, etc.), on planned activities (IT audit plan, SAP migration calendar, work in progress, etc.) and on documents and internal policy (disaster recovery plans, security policy, etc.).
- Operations: it is an area reserved to the operational functions, in particular production, purchasing and logistic.

The Investment Demand area (see Fig. 3) is an interactive area used by the head of the factory to manage the approval process of relevant investments. Before the implementation of the digital platform, the information flow management was very complicated: the whole documentation used for the request and the approval of investments for customer projects were managed with paper documents and sent via e-mail after a scanning.

The Investment Demand area is able to:

- Support the manager to submit his request to the top management of the group, filling a standardised form containing some detailed information to proper classify the type of the investment.

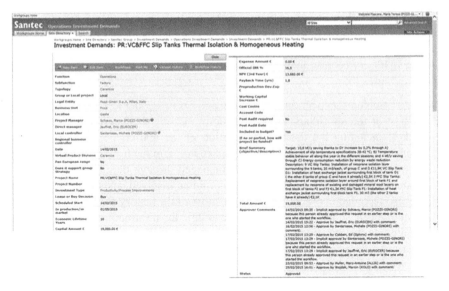

Fig. 3 Investment demand area

- Upload some financial details in order to promote the project credibility as performance indicators (NPV, net present value; WCI, working capital increase; payback period).
- Share some attached information like the business case, the investment evaluation, technical details and so on.
- Automatically identify the approval chain, on the bases of the amount of the investment and other additional information provided with the initial request submission.
- Monitor and manage each approval phase and the whole approval process.

  Before the implementation of the digital platform, the investment process approval was very complicated because we have to prepare a paper dossier, scan it in order to have an electronic version, and send to the headquarter. Now, the management of the process is better than the past because it is paperless; the control of the process remained the same in term of activities, but now it is easier and really effective. (General Director of the factory)

- Stimulate the share of knowledge, giving the possibility, to the head of the factory, to examine the database of the investment dossiers of each subsidiary of the group, to learn technical solution and to investigate measures and methodologies of evaluation adopted in other approved investment projects.

  There is also a time of information sharing, in fact I can access to every approved dossier, I can see all the documentation attached to the investment request, and I can see also the technical documentation. These is very useful, anyway it also depends on the accuracy and on the level of detail of investments requests. (General Director of the factory)

Fig. 4 Suppliers' approval process

The third subsection, "Operation", is the most developed area inside the "Workgroup" section; it includes some contents useful to manage purchasing function (Fig. 4):

- Suppliers' evaluation (which has not yet been completely implemented).
- Suppliers' approval.
- Global purchasing.

The first area is a module that the company is implementing; it supports the suppliers' evaluation process. Before the implementation of the digital platform, the suppliers' evaluation took place one time in a year, and it concerned only the main suppliers identified on the bases of two dimensions:

- The amount of purchases.
- The financial situation measured considering, financial solidity and vendor rating indicators such as timeliness of delivery, prices, payment conditions and distance.

With the implementation of the digital platform, the company introduces a different evaluation system called OTIF: every 3 weeks the digital platform automatically elaborates data, coming from the ERP system, regarding suppliers' performance, measured by the timeliness of the delivery (on time, into a reasonable interval, out of time).

The second area is an interactive environment where the purchasing function manages suppliers' approval process, from the identification of the supplier portfolio, through the vendor rating procedure until the supplier approval. The supplier approval area makes the purchasing function able to manage: 1) the request form through which an organisational unit asks for the creation of a new code and a new supplier, 2) the authorisation process where the approval chain is automatically identified considering the category of materials, 3) the final communication of the successful or unsuccessful end of the process. The purchasing process is long and complex, and the digital platform helps managers to monitor each step of the process and to calculate automatically performance indicators using an interface with the ERP system. The users are able to:

1. Search, select and read identification data of suppliers, employing research keys such as website, country, product categories or destination of goods and services (raw materials, marketing services and so on).
2. Monitor the duration of the suppliers' approval process and the sequence of the activities.

The third area, called "Global Purchasing," contains information and data elaboration regarding the following processes:

1. Data market: elaboration of data related to specific sectors, these reports are produced by the employees and free uploaded and shared on the platform.
2. Lead buyer category is a specific space where buyers can share some information on their work, for example, report on specific kind of materials and goods.
3. Local report package: in this area, the company manages globally data entry of each subsidiaries, used for performance measurement.

In the local report package are uploaded budgets and performance information of purchasing activity in terms of negotiation carried out, numbers of item included, starting and final price and type of transactions (cost out or cost saving) for each category of materials. The company uses an ERP system to manage and follow each purchasing transaction and uses the digital platform as an interface to decentralise the data entry, to collect information on performance, which are automatically elaborated for the entire group according to different dimensions (material, geographical area, etc.). These information are useful to discuss results, premium and benefits with top management using a shared system, while in the past each manager had his personal statistics. In order to collect information useful for the reporting system, a calendar of deadline for uploading each information is shared by the headquarter.

According to the head of the purchasing function, the collaborative platform is very useful for several reasons:

• It creates more frequent occasion to discuss work problems and projects also between people working in different countries and subsidiaries.
• It makes easier the use of benchmark of performance and comparisons between different administrative and business models.
• It helps the organisation to standardise processes and procedures and to speak really the same language.
• It facilitates best practice sharing and makes more transparent the benefits coming from innovation in operational processes, in administration ones and in technical solutions.

Table 2 The main impacts of the digital platform on MCS components

Impacts	Intranet insider	Travel service	EDP service	Investment demand	Purchasing
Cultural control					
Sharing of values, believes, social norms	Increased				
Management of institutional communication	Increased				
Human relation	Increased			Increased	Increased
Collaboration among different functions					
Collaboration among the same function in different subsidiaries				Increased	Increased
Cybernetic control					
Performance measurement	Shared		Shared and automatic	Shared and standardised	Shared Automatic and detailed
Performance benchmark				Facilitated	Facilitated
Distribution of the rewards and compensation					Shared
Reporting system			Timely in elaboration and sharing	Standardised and timely in elaboration and sharing	Standardised and timely in elaboration and sharing
Data collection			Scheduled	More simple and homogenous and accurate	Scheduled and homogenous
Administrative control					
Homogeneity of documents	Increased	Increased	Increased	Increased	Increased
Data collection along each administrative process		Automated and timely	Automated and timely and detailed	Automated and timely and accurate	Automated and timely and accurate
Governance rules	Timely shared and updated				
Identification of people involved in each process				Automated and fixed	Automated and simple
Organisational structure	Plain and simple				

(continued)

Table 2 (continued)

Impacts	Intranet insider	Travel service	EDP service	Investment demand	Purchasing
Procedures	Timely shared and updated	Timely shared and updated	Timely shared and updated	Timely shared and updated	Timely shared and updated
Efficiency of administrative processes		Increased	Increased	Increased	Increased
Compliance control					
Authorisation system				Automated, transparent and interactive	Automated, transparent and interactive
Transparency of administrative processes (people involved, document needed and activity performance)		Increased	Increased	Increased	Increased
Monitoring of the progress of processes (phases concluded, phases in progress, time spent)		Increased	Increased	Increased	Increased

- It induces a cultural change and makes people more open-minded and collaborative.

Considering the MCS theoretical framework adopted in this work and the empirical evidence emerging from the case study, Table 2 summarises the impacts of the implementation of the digital platform on the sections/functions examined in Pozzi Ginori.

5 Discussion and Conclusion

The paper analyses the relationship between MCSs and digital platform in a manufacturing company.

Control system is a package of organisational mechanisms used to guide companies towards their goals. These systems usually are studied, analysing separately the following components: cybernetic, cultural and administrative and compliance. Usually automation provides tools (e.g. ERP or BI) able to manage individually these different subsystems. Preview studies do not consider digital platforms as a tool for management control, but are focused on DPs' implications on information and knowledge sharing. Secondly, literature examines ICT as a tool able to improve data, hardware/software and information integration, with little attention to its role in improving coherence between components of management control systems.

In the case examined, the objective of the implementation of digital platform was to encourage a more fluid communication and a more open shared information, realised with the intranet. The results obtained exceeded those expected; in fact the platform has become an integrated environment, a unique place where the company and its subsidiaries manage coherently each dimension of MCS.

The digital platform makes the company able to manage, for example, each step of the administrative process for supplier's approval, and to monitor automatically the involved employees and the time consumed, consistently with compliance and administrative perspectives of control system. The digital platform provided also some instruments able to elaborate information in order to help managers in decision-making, and it is also able to match information for management control and monitoring of objectives. Moreover the digital platform helps the company to spread different culture and values than the past, it makes more easy the collaboration and the exchange of information, it makes more transparent the benchmark between business units, and it gives to the managers a positive meaning of control environment where good results must be imitated, while bad results can find collaborative solutions.

For the company, the implementation of the digital platform has represented an opportunity to activate several changes in internal processes. In particular:

- A more effective realisation of the integration of control and management processes, administrative procedures, information flows and management accounting processes.
- A more transparent and compliant information flow.
- A higher level of integration between different control mechanisms, based on results, behaviours and culture.

The case study shows that a digital platform is able to support simultaneously most part of MCS components. In other words, this ICT tool gives to the company the opportunity to reach a higher level of integration. This integration is based on the convergence of different control subsystems in the same ICT platform and not only on data integration, hardware/software and information integration, because of the fact that the digital platform contains tools:

- To share information and manage information flows from an office to another, tracing every action and defining people, time and deadline for the execution of the activities. In this way, the system helps the examined subsidiary in its compliance and transparency purposes.
- To publish and share ideas, objectives and information in a well-defined community, in order to create a control mechanism based on cultural and soft variables.
- To manage the budgeting process, the variance analysis and the reward system, offering tools able to automatically match objectives and results formalised on a dashboard.

- To organise and manage digital documents and dossiers in order to improve efficiency in administrative processes.

According to the literature, this work confirms that digital platforms are useful to improve communication, knowledge and information sharing among organisational units and project teams. It also demonstrates original implications of these platforms related to MCSs. They can represent a relevant opportunity to improve simultaneously each component of the control systems and to reach a higher level of integration. The research also highlights some critical success factors in using these platforms for management control aims, in particular the capacity of employees to respect the deadline for the uploading of data and to share detailed information and, finally, their perception of benefits coming from platform.

The previous considerations are limited to the case study examined. Many are possible directions for future research; in particular it would be interesting to extend the research to a greater number of case studies comparing different kinds of organisations and sectors and types of digital platforms.

References

1. Malmi, T., & Brown, D. A. (2008). Management control systems as a package—Opportunities, challenges and research directions. *Management Accounting Research, 19*, 287–300.
2. Cremona, L., Lin, T., & Ravarini, A. (2014). *The role of digital platform in interfirm collaborations*. VIII Mediterranean Conference on Information Systems.
3. Spagnoletti, P., Resca, A., & Lee, G. (2015). A design theory for digital platforms supporting online communities: A multiple case study. *Journal of Information Technology, 30*, 364–380.
4. Overbeek, S., van Middendorp, S., & Rijsenbrij, D. (2005). The digital workspace, in the financial sector. *IT Management Select, 11*, 38–51.
5. Agrifoglio, R., & Metallo, C. (2011). Virtual environment and collaborative work: The role of relation quality in facilitating individual creativity. In A. D'Atri et al. (Eds.), *Information technology and innovation trends in organizations*. Berlin: Springer.
6. Capriglione, A., Casalino, N., & Draoli, M. (2011). Relational networks for the open innovation in the Italian Public Administration. In A. D'Atri et al. (Eds.), *Information technology and innovation trends in organizations*. Berlin: Springer.
7. Alvino, F., Agrifoglio, R., Metallo, C., & Lepore, L. (2011). Learning and knowledge sharing in virtual communities of practices: A case study. In A. D'Atri et al. (Eds.), *Information technology and innovation trends in organizations*. Berlin: Springer.
8. Tilson, D. (2010). Digital infrastructures: The missing IS research agenda. *Information Systems Research, 21*(4), 748–759.
9. Baskerville, R., & Meyers, M. (2002). Information systems as a reference discipline. *MIS Quarterly, 26*, 1–14.
10. Beynon-Davies, P. (2009). Formated technology and informated action: The nature of information technology. *International Journal of Information Systems, 29*, 272–282.
11. Noble, F. (1995). Implementation strategies for office systems. *Journal of Strategic Information Systems, 4*, 239–253.
12. Law, D., & Gorla, N. (2006). Exploring factors underlying effective office information systems. *Information and Management, 31*, 25–35.
13. Mansou, O. (2009). Group intelligence: A distributed cognition perspective. In *Intelligent Networking and Collaborative Systems, INCOS '09* (pp. 247–250).

14. Iacoviello, G., & Lazzini, A. (2013). IS to support project management: Implication for managerial accounting. In D. Mancini, E. Vaassen, & P. Dameri (Eds.), *Accounting information systems for decision making*. Berlin: Springer.
15. Mancini, D., & Ferruzzi, T. (2014, November 21–22). *Using collaboration platforms for management control processes: New opportunities for integration*. Paper presented at ITAIS 2014, Genova.
16. Brunetti, G. (1979). *Il controllo di gestione in condizioni ambientali perturbate*. Milano: F. Angeli.
17. Merchant, K. A. (1985). *Control in business organization*. Boston, MA: Pitman.
18. Marchi, L., Marasca, S., & Riccaboni, A. (2013). *Il controllo di gestione*. Arezzo: Knowita.
19. Otley, D. T. (1994). Management control in contemporary organizations: Towards a wider framework. *Management Accounting Research, 5*(3–4), 289–299.
20. Anthony, R. N., & Govindarajan, V. (2004). *Management control systems*. New York: McGraw-Hill.
21. Mancini, D. (2010). *Le condizioni di efficacia del sistema di controllo aziendale. Qualità e sicurezza del sistema di controllo*. Torino: G. Giappichelli.
22. Bergamin, B. M. (1991). *Programmazione e controllo in un'ottica strategica*. Torino: UTET.
23. Paolini, A. (1993). *Il controllo strategico. Uno schema di analisi*. Milano: Giuffré.
24. Mancini, D. (1999). *L'azienda nella rete di imprese, la prospettiva del controllo relazionale*. Milano: Giuffrè.
25. Corsi, K. (2003). *Il controllo organizzativo. Una prospettiva transazionale*. Milano: Giuffrè.
26. D'Onza, G. (2008). *Il sistema di controllo interno nella prospettiva di risk management*. Milano: Giuffrè.
27. Lamboglia, R. (2012). *La componente immateriale e organizzativa del sistema di controllo aziendale*. Milano: Giuffrè.
28. Corsi, K. (2008). *Il sistema di controllo amministrativo-contabile. Prospettive e dinamiche evolutive alla luce degli IAS/IFRS*. Milano: Giuffrè.
29. Rom, A., & Rohde, C. (2007). Management accounting and integrated information systems: A literature review. *International Journal of Accounting Information Systems, 8*, 40–68.
30. Grabski, S. V., Leech, S. A., & Schmidt, P. J. (2011). A review of ERP research: A future agenda for accounting informations systems. *Journal of Information System, 25*(1), 37–78.
31. Chiucchi, M. S., Gatti, M., & Marasca, S. (2012). The relationship between management accounting systems and ERP systems in a medium-sized firm: A bidirectional perspective. *Managemet Control*.
32. Silvi, R., Bartolini, M., Raffoni, A., & Visani, F. (2012). Business performance analytics: Level of adoption and support provided to performance measurement systems. *Management Control*.
33. Amigoni, F., & Beretta, S. (a cura di). (1998). *Information Technology e creazione di valore. Analisi del fenomeno SAP*. Egea, Milano.
34. Corsi, K., Rizzo, D., & Trucco, S. (2012). Integrated-multi-layered information systems in engineer-to-order multinational business processes: Managerial, accounting and organizational aspects. In D. Mancini, E. Vassen, & R. P. Dameri (Eds.), *Accounting information systems for decision making*. Berlin: Springer.
35. Scapens, R. W., & Jazayeri, M. (2003). ERP systems and management accounting change: Opportunities or impact? A research note. *European Accounting Review, 12*, 201–233.
36. Stratman, J. F. (2007). Realizing benefits from enterprise resource planning: Does strategic focus matter. *Production and Operations Management, 16*(2), 203–216.
37. AlSudairi, M. A. T. (2013). Analysis and exploration of critical success factors of ERP implementation: A brief review. *International Journal of Computer Applications, 69*(8), 44–52.
38. Hakkinen, L., & Hilmola, O. (2008). Life after ERP implementation: Long term development of user perceptions of system success in an after-sales environment. *Journal of Enterprise Information Management, 21*(3), 285–309.

39. Chapman, C. S., & Kihn, L. (2009). Information system integration, enabling control and performance. *Accounting, Organizations and Society, 34*(2), 151–169.
40. Marchi, L. (2003). *Il sistema informativo aziendale*. Milano: Giuffrè.
41. Dechow, N., & Mouritsen, J. (2005). Enterprise resource planning systems management control and the quest for integration. *Accounting, Organizations and Society, 30*(7/8), 691–733.
42. Granlund, M., & Malmi, T. (2002). Moderate impact of ERPs on management accounting: A lag or permanent outcome? *Management Accounting Research, 13*, 299–321.
43. Burns, J., & Baldvinsdottir, G. (1999, April). *Hybrid accountants: Where do they belong and what (are they expected) to do?* Paper presented at the conference on management accounting change—A European perspective, Manchester.
44. Caglio, A. (2003). Enterprise resource planning systems and accountants: Towards hybridization? *European Accounting Review, 12*, 123–153.
45. Burns, J., & Baldvinsdottir, G. (2005). An institutional perspective of accountants' new roles—The interplay of contradictions and praxis. *European Accounting Review, 14*(4), 725–757.
46. Korkman, O., Storbacka, K., & Harald, B. (2010). Practices markets: Value co-creation in e-invoicing. *Australasian Marketing Journal, 18*(4), 236–247.
47. Salmon, M., & Harald, B. (2010). E-invoicing in Europa: Now and the future. *Journal of Payment Strategy and Systems, 4*(4), 371–380.
48. Boot, P., Matolesy, Z., & Wieder, B. (2000). *Integrated information systems (ERP systems) and accounting practice—The Australian experience*. 3rd European Conference on Accounting Information Systems, Munich, Germany.
49. Martin, K., & Todorov, O. (2010). How will digital platforms be harnessed in 2010, and how will they change the way people interact with brands? *Journal of Interactive Advertising, 10* (2), 61–66.
50. Resca, A., Za, S., & Spagnoletti, P. (2013). Digital platforms as sources for organizational and strategic transformation: A case study of the midblue project. *Journal of Theoretical and Applied Electronic Commerce Research, 8*(2), 71–84.
51. Garud, R., & Kumaraswamy, A. (2005). Vicious and virtuous circles in the management of knowledge: The case of Infosys Technologies. *MIS Quarterly, 29*(1), 9–33.
52. Sanchez, R., & Mahoney, J. T. (1996). Modularity, flexibility, and knowledge management in product and organization design. *Strategic Management Journal, 17*, 63–76.
53. Zittrain, J. (2006). The generative internet. *Harvard Law Review, 119*, 1975–2040.
54. Zittrain, J. (2008). *The future of the internet*. New Haven, CT: Yale University Press.
55. Yoo, Y. (2013). The tables have turned: How can the information systems field contribute to technology and innovation management research? *Journal of the Association for Information Systems, 14*(5), 227–236.
56. Huber, G. P. (1991). Organizational learning: The contributing processes and the literatures. *Organization Science, 2*(1), 88–115.
57. Crossan, M., Lane, H., & White, R. (1999). An organizational learning framework: From intuition to institution. *Academy of Management Review, 24*(3), 522–537.
58. Hsiao, D. W., Trappey, A. J. C., Ma, L., & Ho, P. S. (2009). An integrated platform of collaborative project management and silicon intellectual property management for IC design industry. *Information Science, 179*, 2576–2900.
59. Lopez-Nicola, C., & Soto-Acosta, P. (2010). Analyzing ICT adoption and use effects on knowledge creation: An empirical investigation in SMEs. *International Journal Information Management, 30*, 521–528.
60. Aloini, D., Dulmin, R., Minimmo, V., & Spagnesi, A. (2014). *Benefits and barriers of social/collaborative ERP systems: A staff of the art and research agenda*. Paper presented at ITAIS 2014—Genoa.
61. Grabot, B., Mayere, A., Lauroua, F., & Houe, R. (2014). ERP 2.0, what for and how? *Computers in Industry, 65*, 976–1000.

62. Ouchi, W. G. (1980). Markets, bureaucracies, and clans. *Administrative Science Quarterly, 25*, 129–141.
63. Eisenhardt, K. M. (1989). Building theories from case study research. *Academy of Management Review, 14*, 532–550.
64. Yin, R. (1994). *Case study research. Design and methods*. London: Sage.
65. Kuhn, T. S. (1970). *The structure of scientific revolutions*. Chicago: Chicago University Press.

AIS and Reporting in the Port Community Systems: An Italian Case Study in the Landlord Port Model

Assunta Di Vaio and Luisa Varriale

Abstract The aim of this chapter is to analyze the role of Accounting Information Systems (AIS) in the information management when in the relationships system, characterizing the port communities (PCs), an information technology platform has been adopted, such as the Port Community System (PCS). More specifically, drawing upon the existing literature on the architecture of PCS for the information flows management among the port users, this chapter aims to investigate the nature and role of reporting to support the decision-making of Port Authorities (PAs) in the landlord port model.

In order to achieve our goal, we have conducted a literature review on the Port Community Systems (PCSs) and AIS in PCSs. Using the case study methodology, we have also conducted some semi-structured interviews with port users and Port Authority (PA) in an Italian seaport. The analysis conducted outlines a strong need to get more detailed reporting on goods. In this way, the PCSs, which include the functions of AIS, can help to improve the information basis for PAs in the future developmental decisions of seaports.

Keywords Port community systems • Information management • AIS • Reporting

1 Introduction

Over the last decades, the port organizational models have been of interest due to significant changes. First, very interesting phenomena concerning the increase of the efficiency of the infrastructures and the effectiveness of the port facilities have been observed. In order to obtain these targets, the port reforms have led to the development of four port models, like service ports, tool ports, landlord ports, and private ports. The landlord port is the most widespread organizational form characterized by the separation between public (e.g., PA) and private (e.g., concessionaires) [1–6]. Therefore, the control, coordination, and promotion activities by the

A. Di Vaio (✉) • L. Varriale
Parthenope University, Naples, Italy
e-mail: susy.divaio@uniparthenope.it; luisa.varriale@uniparthenope.it

© Springer International Publishing AG 2017
K. Corsi et al. (eds.), *Reshaping Accounting and Management Control Systems*,
Lecture Notes in Information Systems and Organisation 20,
DOI 10.1007/978-3-319-49538-5_10

PA have required that the information on traffic flows managed by concessionaires and other port users would be readily available and easily accessible for PA. In this direction, the adoption of PCS became relevant in the competition among seaports.

Drawing from these studies, this manuscript aims to investigate the role of AIS in the information management when in the relationships system, characterizing the PCs, an information technology platform has been adopted, like the PCS. Hence, considering the main contributions and results of previous studies on the architecture of PCSs for the information flows management among the port users, in this chapter we analyze the nature and role of reporting to support the decision-making process of PAs in the landlord port model. We have conducted a literature review on the PCSs and on the contribution of AIS in PCSs. Using the case study methodology, we have also conducted some semi-structured interviews with port users and PAs in an Italian seaport.

The chapter is structured as follows: Sections 2 and 3 focus on the analysis of PCS in the seaports literature. Section 4 evidences the role of AIS in the PCS. Sections 5 and 6 outline the methodology adopted and the description of the case study. Finally, in the last section we present a brief discussion on the results of the interviews and some final considerations.

2 Port Community System (PCS)

In the last decades, due to the numerous changes occurring in the world, such as the high competitiveness of markets and the increasing innovativeness of the supply and demand, the seaports have to face many challenges adopting the international regulations about the organizational and managerial models and information technologies (IT) in the decision-making process. The seaports need to manage specific criticisms related to the evolution of the international trade and container throughput, the introduction of ultra-large container vessels, the deep changes of customers' demand, and the development of IT, addressing the same seaports to assume a strategic position as "hub ports" [7].

Regarding the growing role of IT in the seaports, we observe that these organizations perceive an increasing need to adopt IT tools to support all their processes, in particular, the requirements related to containerized and passengers traffic. Thanks to the technology, seaport users are able to manage data and information with real time about cargo and passenger flows and availability of port facilities, and also IT makes ships and terminals to work together assuming a collaborative orientation as parts of an integrated office infrastructure [8]. In this direction, seaports can effectively and efficiently carry out customs control adopting IT tools [9]. Thus, in the seaports which implement IT, all the actors involved, that is, port administration, terminal operators, truckers, customs, freight forwarders, carriers, ship agents, and other organization, are electronically linked by the IT systems, improving the information and data sharing within the port community [8].

In order to facilitate the communication process and the development of the inter-organizational relationships among the actors in the port community, the port community systems (PCSs) have been introduced.

Different contributions in the literature provide interesting and variegated definitions of PCSs concept focusing their attention on role, functions, or their network nature. For instance, Srour and colleagues [3, 10] have defined PCSs as "holistic, geographically bounded information hubs in global supply chains that primarily serve the interest of a heterogeneous collective of port related companies." In this definition, the heterogeneous companies mainly concern the terminal operators, carriers (ocean, road, and rail), freight forwarders, enforcement agencies (i.e., customs), port authorities, various lobby groups (including workers' unions, environmentalists, and other policy makers), and also other shareholders of maritime transportation [10, 11]. Furthermore, PCSs have been defined as "networks which link up the port with all the companies that use it" [12]. Instead, according to the European Port Community Systems Association [13] have conceptualized PCS as an electronic platform that permits to connect the multiple systems operated by a variety of organizations that make up a seaport community explaining the integration of each organization to the port community system [12, 14].

PCS permits "an easy, fast, and efficient information exchange," that is, Electronic Data Interchange (EDI) ([15]: 1]; the customs declarations; the electronic management of all information about the handling operations in import and export; the traceability of the traffic flows along supply chain; the reporting and statistics; and so on [15]. In addition, PCS facilitates both collaboration and integration, allowing both members of the community to immediately access relevant data and to interact and control data improving the quality of the same data among the stakeholders, and also preventing the replication of the same [16]. Likewise, Carlan and colleagues ([17]: 1) define PCS as "an electronic platform which connects the multiple communication systems of each of its members." This definition is based on the main tasks attributed to PCS which consist in improving the port operations efficiency, and increasing the competitiveness along the supply chain, which requires the cooperation between private and public stakeholders.

Therefore, PCSs promote the fast and safe exchange of information between both private and public organizations with the specific goal to improve the competitiveness of seaports [17, 18]. From this point of view, all the involved organizations have to efficiently and effectively collaborate creating the critical prerequisites able to optimize all the logistic processes using a single data submission [9].

The main function recognized for PCSs consists in making the users to manage the service requests and directly upload their information into the port's information system. Indeed, PCSs significantly reduce paperwork, can improve data quality, allow integrating data among different stakeholders, and support the port management for operations. In this perspective, although a crucial role has been recognized for PCSs in increasing the competitive power of the port, numerous companies still show strong resistances to adopt them [10, 14]. Otherwise, the seaports tend to invest increasing resources in infrastructure and improve their operation systems, including port community systems, which are "computer networks which link up the port with all the companies that use it, including hauliers, rail companies, shipping lines, feeder ports, shippers and customs officers" [14].

Regarding the architectures of the inter-organizational relationship systems for the information and data sharing in the port community, the authors [10] have distinguished four different architectural types: bilateral, private hub, central orchestration hub, and modular distributed plug and play architecture.

The first architectural type of PCSs, bilateral, concerns one-to-one connections in which two partners are strongly linked sharing and integrating their data and information and services requests, mostly using easy communication channels and technological tools, such as phone and fax. Otherwise, also adopting Electronic Data Interchange (EDI), the integration between the two partners easily occurs without the need of intermediaries. The second and third architectural types of PCSs, private hub and central orchestration hub, allow connecting to many partners with minimal linkages, requiring only one connection point or more than one connection point. In fact, two different typologies of hubs perform: in the private hub only one party owns the same hub and all the connections (generally large), whereas in the central orchestration hubs the parties perform and are interconnected in a kind of network. In detail, the private hub consists in a one-to-many type, instead the central orchestration hubs are considered many-to-many. The fourth and last architectural type of PCSs, modular distributed plug and play architecture, concerns hubs in which parties are connected not permanently and mainly considering their plug and connect capabilities; indeed, they tend to connect and share information and data only when they need to interact to quickly conduct businesses and it is not possible to standardize the information and data sharing and communication process.

In summary, in all the architectural types of PCSs, independently of their definition, many ports tend to consider as main means of communication the EDI because of the high costs for the initial investments and the historical evolution of dislocation [19]. As a consequence, small ports face more difficulties to implement EDI as outlined in some empirical studies in the literature [10, 15, 20–22].

Four stages have been identified in designing and implementing of PCS [21]: project initiation, systems analysis and design, implementation and adoption, and maintenance and growth. In fact, the process begins with the correct and clear identification of the need for an information system, and then it continues analyzing the business setting and the goal to achieve, including the design of the architecture and the following selection of the communication language.

As already evidenced, PCSs are generally based on EDI technology. EDI has been widely recognized as a system in which data and information about commercial or administrative transactions are transferred from computer to computer on the basis of an agreed standard [19]. Thanks to EDI technology, the information within an organization is managed by computers but for transferring and sharing between organizations, papers, forms, or printouts are not necessary; easily all the data transfer occurs between the organizations' databases [22–24].

Some authors have grouped the benefits of EDI into three main categories ([24]: 74): "direct benefits, such as paper savings, avoiding repetitive administrative procedures, or reducing administrative personnel; indirect benefits, such as avoiding errors, faster payments/improved cash flow; and finally, strategic benefits, such as increasing business relationships with companies using EDI or improving customer loyalty."

3 The Adoption and Evolution of PCSs in Seaports

The prevalent literature focused on PCSs outlines that these systems are implemented by a few but important seaports in different countries all over the world (e.g., Germany, France, UK, Spain, Belgium, China, USA, Netherlands, South Korea, and Singapore) [7, 10, 17].

Some scholars have systematically reviewed the main contributions of the literature from 1994 to 2015 on the adoption of PSCs by seaports, evidencing that they had been primarily based on the costs and benefits of the PCSs [17]. Also, the results of this systematic review have evidenced that there are many studies with descriptive nature, i.e., Tijan and Sasa [25], Donselaar and Kolkman [26], and so on, based on the case studies or benchmarking analysis methodology, whereas only few studies are focused on the identification of performance indicators (see Duran and Cordova [27]).

Moreover, the literature shows that the first ports that have adopted the Port Community platforms (PCp) are in Germany (Hamburg and Bremen), France (Le Havre), the UK (Felixstowe), and Singapore. Among these different seaports, Portnet in the seaport of Singapore is the most investigated PCS platform in the previous research because of its organizational model and peculiarities; in fact, this platform has high levels of development, allowing the representative port community system and the PSA's terminal operating system (CITOS) and custom declaration system (TradeXchange) of Singapore government to be strictly connected [7].

Furthermore, other ports have adopted the port community platforms, such as the ports of Los Angeles and Long Beach (USA) which have adopted eModal; the ports of Amsterdam and Rotterdam (Netherlands) which have, respectively, implemented before Portnet and then Portbase; the port of Hong Kong (China) which is a public port (service port) implemented before the Tradelink and then OnePort [7, 17].

The slow development of these systems could be justified considering the high costs of the investment [17] and also other variables, like training and education; instead, the size of the ports does not seem really crucial in affecting the choice to adopt the PCSs [7]. These results have been clearly shown in the study on the Cyprus by Forward [28].

The presence of more advanced technical infrastructures in the seaports significantly facilitates the adoption of PCSs because the employees are more comfortable and able to use the platforms, especially because of their increasing experience and exclusive knowledge about PCSs. Otherwise, most studies have evidenced that trust becomes more and more relevant when the reliability of the system tends to decrease [7]. In this direction, the cost is recognized less important than the benefits of the system, specifically the reliability of the same system.

4 The Role of AIS in the PCSs

The adoption of technology provides information and data to the port users with real time regarding the status of cargo, paperwork, and availability of port facilities, allowing ships and terminals to work together toward an integrated system [8].

Traditionally, port users utilized paper-based methods, such as sending fax or handing in documents directly for the delivery of cargo. Also, port users used to send the documents via e-mail thanks to the Internet channel. Every time the information and data have to be typed again in the port's information systems requiring more time and making more mistakes [7].

In this scenario, the adoption of technology by port users provides interesting and relevant advantages in the port community, especially considering the integrated information technologies useful for the Accounting Information Systems (AIS).

The port community deals with a large amount of information, both internal and external, which tends to make more complex the decision-making process [29]. As already outlined, the application of new accessible and integrated information technologies useful for Accounting Information Systems (AIS) can significantly facilitate the information and data collecting and management.

Thus, thanks to AIS in the PCSs, port users, especially PAs, can benefit of a faster and clearer information and data management process, not easily in terms of quantitative information but especially in terms of significant qualitative knowledge. That is, the players in the port community are able to get relevant factors and knowledge with details about the accounting and financial areas and, consequently, the value of the ports. In sum, the AIS can let the data and information "speak for themselves" among all the users, supporting their decision-making process, and the system does not easily integrate these elements. Besides, because of the characteristics of the landlord port model in which the activities are carried out by PAs through the concessionaires agreement to private operators, reporting becomes very relevant assuming a crucial role for the PAs.

Hence, IT may support the actors in rapidly sharing and managing information and data in the real time, and also it may help the accounting activities and controlling function. The implementation of an integrated information system, rather than the use of spreadsheets, allows firms to produce higher quality information becoming more rapid and efficient. Most theoretical and empirical studies show the positive effects of IT on the firms' performance and evidence its key role to support management accounting activities and to facilitate exchange of information among firms [30].

Compared to the AIS in the port community, the PCSs provide a broader function consisting in controlling and reporting activities of all the actors of the port community depending on the infrastructural model of the same platform. Thus, PCSs do not easily improve the coordination and collaboration for transferring goods and their information and data among all the involved stakeholders. In this direction, the combination between AIS and PCS might create positive conditions able to improve the relationships between the Port Authority and all the users in the port community also making more effective and efficient the different port organizational models, that is, service port, tool port, landlord port, and private port models [8].

On the other hand, previous studies focused on PCSs have paid their attention to the private and public partnerships between the port stakeholders [31], or they have mainly investigated the collective work achieved by the port community or the adoption process [32].

This study is focused on the private and public partnership, that is, the landlord model, in order to investigate the main effects provided by the PCSs integrated to the AIS, especially considering their main role in supporting the control and reporting activities.

5 Methodology

The authors adopt a case study methodology investigating one port experience in Italy, the Port of Livorno. We have chosen Livorno because it has been one of the first ports which implemented a PCS, called Tuscan Port Community System (TPCS). The system is started in 2010, and it has been oriented mainly to manage goods in the logistic supply chain.

This is an explorative study conducted through semi-structured interviews with key actors in the investigated sector through face-to-face meetings. In detail, we gathered information and data during our interviews with the key actors, managers, in the port of Livorno.

5.1 Case Study Description

In 2011/2012, thanks to the financial support by the European project, named MOS4MOS, the port of Livorno (Italy) implemented the Tuscan Port Community System (TPCS), a platform based on web service structure. It falls within the services of general interest regulated by the Ministerial Decree on 14th November, 1994. Therefore, it is a information support to the public authorities, and, at the same time, the TPCS represents a "centralized data."

TPCS enables ocean carriers and the shipping agents to obtain information about goods; in this way, it is possible to complete the poster for the leaving goods (called MMP) and incoming goods (called MMA). The data management is fully automated; in this phase, the players involved can act only in case of error messages. The freight forwarders can submit the customs declaration by TPCS and the electronic boarding requests. The terminal concessionaires can plan the boarding thanks to TPCS; indeed, the data on the loads management by TPCS can be transferred on management software of the concessionaires. The road carriers can control on TPCS the condition of the goods at the terminal and to carry it away. Finally, the PCS permits to public authorities, and, in particular, the PA to monitor, control, and supervise the port activity chain in real time, both incoming and outgoing.

In summary, TPCS responds to all the innovative systems of communication between traders and Control Authorities (e-Customs, customs, and paperless controls). It permits the exchange and display of data among the port users (e.g., ocean carriers, freight forwarders, terminal, customs, institutions of public control, and road carriers). Thanks to the TPCS, the brokers, the terminal concessionaires, the importers, and the exporters can easily communicate; in fact, they can interact overcoming any hierarchical barriers and finally simplifying and improving their work with the development of the port traffic.

The PA supplies a free website, hardware, and a specific line allowing the operators to interact. This system does not require any staff to support the process; there is a control room managed by the PA. The security of data is guaranteed from different archiving and recovery systems. The member of the port community can access by the login (username and password). The platform is composed of two of fifteen prototypes proposed: the former, "T2L Electron Intra-Community Flight Formalities," refers to the international transit and the codes to be used for completing the documents certifying the Community status of goods not shipped under Community transit; the latter, "paperless Customs control," is related to the so-called process of dematerialization of customs controls.

TPCS is composed by four functional areas: import, export, national and community cabotage (CNC), and customs single window (SUD).

Regarding the first area (import), TPCS manages the ship voyages and the goods arriving at Livorno port. In addition, it provides information about the further embarking of goods for the final destinations. The platform allows to manage the applications related to the management of the MMA (i.e., poster of incoming goods). This phase related to import is mainly based on management of the document called "A3" by the players involved in the process. Fig. 1 evidences the phases of process; in detail, it is possible to observe: the custom forwarder draws up the MMA and sends it to AIDA, that is, a software application that processes the data. Then, the MMA processed is transferred to customs forwarder in a condition entitled "not clearable" by the A3. Later the custom forwarder sends the A3 to

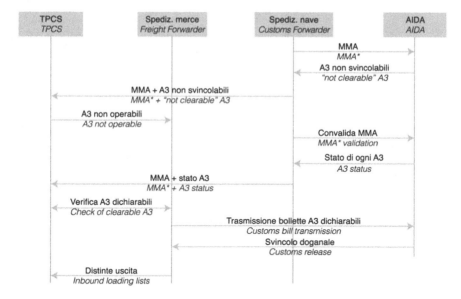

Fig. 1 Import phase (Source: http://www.tpcs.eu)

TPCS. In the second phase, the freight forwarder accesses A3 by TPCS, even if the A3 is still not working (called A3 not operable), but this operation permits freight forwarder to fill the statements of outcome. At the same time, the custom forwarder obtains by AIDA the result for each A3 that can be with or without "customs release." The custom forwarder verifies the A3 status by PCS, and he sends the customs bills to AIDA. Finally, obtaining the customs release the custom forwarder sends to TPCS the inbound loading lists.

Concerning the export area, TPCS manages ship voyages and leaving goods. It is possible to check the condition of MMP (i.e., poster for the leaving goods) by the software.

Fig. 2. shows that in the export phase the port users involved are more than those included in the import phase. More in detail, in this phase there are also the terminal and the agency. The first step of the process evidences the role of the agency that deals with the ship's data entry by the TPCS. In this relationship, both players agree on some profiles on the operation of incoming goods by ships (i.e., ship name, voyage, estimated time of arrival—ETA—closing time—CT—and so on). In the same phase, the agency indicates the custom forwarder that can download the file in order to create the MMP.

The terminal validates the ship's data entry. Then, the freight forwarder sends outbound loading lists to TPCS within the closing time.

After these steps, the customer forwarder download by TPCS the data to create the MMP. The platform manages the D, E, F, S, X, N data flow according to the customs regulations. Furthermore, the MMP is sent to AIDA for the processing. The data process by AIDA is called IRISP, and the customs forwarder sends IRISP

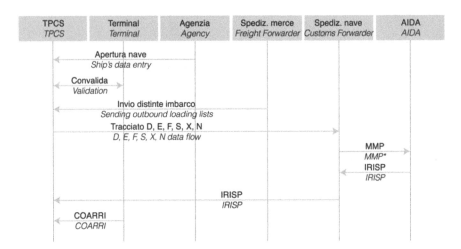

Fig. 2 Export phase (Source: http://www.tpcs.eu)

to TPCS. Finally, the terminal concessionaire sends to TPCS the report on goods embarked entitled COARRI.

In both phases (import and export), the relationships among the players for the data management are developed by the platform.

Regarding the national and community cabotage (CNC) the MOS4MOS project aimed to create a seaport network in order to track the goods "house to house." The software application concerns also goods without customs implications. The main players involved in CNC are: agency, customs forwarder, freight forwarder, terminal concessionaire and the other Member State port community system. CNC provides the following supporting activities: the transfer of data between systems for the exchange of T2L; the data management and the creation of the MMA and MMP; and finally, the transformation of T2L data in XML messages and PDF documentation, that can be transferred to other Member State port community system. Also, in this case the relationship among the players is managed by the platform.

Finally, concerning "customs single window" (SUD), it enables port users to submit documents at a single location and/or single entity. Such documents are typically customs declarations, applications for import/export permits, and other supporting documents such as certificates of origin and trading invoices. The main scope of the local government and public authorities involved is to increase the efficiency through time and cost savings for users in their dealings with government authorities. Thanks to the digitization of the process, the SUD permits to require and control certifications and authorizations via computer.

6 Concluding Remarks

This study contributes to the existing literature on PCSs by investigating the structure of the PCSs in a landlord port model characterized by the PA like a player with tasks of coordination and control of the information on traffic flows managed by the port users.

The descriptive analysis shows that the PCS represents the main coordination mechanism in the relationships among the port users. The data information management on the traceability of the goods would seem to meet the objectives of PA and other users of the seaport. Indeed, the reduction of papers and of time along the port supply chain, the easy access to the PCS, and the ability to access the system at any time and from anywhere are the main benefits obtained thanks to the PCS.

The case study described evidences an architecture of the inter-organizational relationships system for the information and data sharing characterized by central orchestration hub. That is a system that permits to connect to many port users with minimal linkages.

Regarding the main tools of the AIS, like the external reporting, we observed that the reports produced by the system present information processed related to the traceability of the goods. We observed that the reports produced by the "national and community cabotage" area of the PCS are intended to other Member State port community system.

In the relationship between PA and port users involved in the import and export processes, the PCS analysis does not clearly evidence the transfer of the information processed by PCS to PA. According to the results of the interviews, the managers of PA can access the system to provide the reports on the goods information flows. This means that the production of the reports could not respect a specific time schedule. Finally, the reports do not include financial and qualitative information about the goods. The information is obtained by the manifests; it is processed by clearing sensitive data and transferred as a statistic base to the departments of the PA. In the AIS, the financial information is relevant above all in the decision-making of top management.

In summary, these results seem in line with the study on PCS mainly with the results of study of [7] in which the authors have verified the relationship between the adoption of PCS and the port organization size. Indeed, the adoption and the development of the PCS are linked to the intention to use by top management, in our case the PA in accordance with the customs.

This study presents some limitations, because of its explorative nature; in fact, we consider only one case study in which exclusively one single partner, that is, PA, has been analyzed, and also we do not clearly describe the technical details and related benefits derived from the adoption of specific AIS and reporting tools.

In order to know in depth and clearly the causes that limit the possible development of the benefits of AIS using PCS, in the future we aim to extend the analysis to the accounting managers of the organizations (port users and PA) involved in the processes described in this case study.

Acknowledgements The authors are grateful to the operators interviewed for their precious contribution to the case study investigated. A special thanks to Dr. Paolo Scarpellini, project manager of TPCS at Livorno PA, for his help to a better understanding of the use of the digital platform in the relationships system described in this manuscript. Besides, thanks are reserved to Dr. Serena Rocco for supporting our study through some interviews conducted during her graduation thesis. Any errors are entirely attributed to the authors.

References

1. Goss, R. (1990). Economic policies and seaports: The diversity of port policies. *Maritime Policy and Management, 17*(3), 221–234.
2. Baird, A. (1995). Privatisation of trust ports in the United Kingdom: Review and analysis of the first sales. *Transport Policy, 2*(2), 35–143.
3. Liu, Z. (1995). Owner and productive efficiency: The experience of British ports. In J. McConville & J. Sheldrake (Eds.), *Transport in transition: Aspects of British and European experience* (pp. 163–182). Aldershot: Avebury.
4. De Monie, G. (1996). Privatisation of port structures, in ports for Europe: Europe's maritime future. In L. Bekemans & S. Beckwith (Eds.), *In a changing environment* (pp. 267–298). Brussels: European Interuniversity Press.
5. Baudelaire, J. (1997). Some thoughts about port privatisation. In A. M. Goulielmos (Ed.), *Essays in honour and in memory of late professor emeritus of maritime economics Dr Basil Metaxas* (pp. 255–260).
6. Di Vaio, A., Medda, F. R., & Trujillo, L. (2011). An analysis of the efficiency of Italian cruise terminals. *International Journal of Transport Economics, 38*(1), 29–46.
7. Keceli, Y., Choi, H. R., Cha, Y. S., & Aydogdu, Y. V. (2008). *A study on adoption of port community systems according to organization size*. Third 2008 International Conference on Convergence and Hybrid Information Technology (pp. 493–501).
8. World Bank. (2007). *Port Reform Tool Kit—Module 2—The evolution of ports in a competitive world*, 2nd ed.
9. Long, A. (2009). Port community systems. *World Customs Journal, 3*(1), 63–72.
10. Srour, F. J., van Oosterhout, M., van Baalen, P., & Zuidwijk, R. (2008). *Port community system implementation: Lessons learned from international scan*. Transportation Research Board 87th Annual Meeting, Washington, DC.
11. Aydogdu, Y. V., & Aksoy, S. (2015). A study on quantitative benefits of port community systems. *Maritime Policy and Management, 42*(1), 1–10. doi:10.1080/03088839.2013.825053.
12. Rodon, J., & Ramis-Pujol, J. (2006). *Exploring the intricacies of integrating with a port community system*. 19th Bled eConference eValues, Bled, Slovenia.
13. EPCSA, European Port Community Systems Association. (2011). *The role of Port Community Systems in the development of the Single Window*. White Paper.
14. Keceli, Y. (2011). A proposed innovation strategy for Turkish port administration policy via information technology. *Maritime Policy and Management, 38*(2), 151–167. doi:10.1080/03088839.2011.556676.
15. Srour, F. J., & Ruoff, K. (2004). *Transportation XML: Building a framework for the next paradigm of web services and federated databases*. The TRB 83rd Annual Meeting Proceedings, Washington, DC.
16. Hoffer, A., George, J. F., & Valacich, J. S. (2005). *Modern systems analysis and design*. Upper saddle River, NJ: Pearson Education.
17. Carlan, V., Christa, S., & Thierry V. (2015). *Port Community Systems costs and benefits: from competition to collaboration within the supply chain, 1–27*. Paper presented at WCTRS-SIG2 (11–12/5/2015), Antwerp.

18. Tsamboulas, D., Moraiti, P., & Lekka, A. M. (2012). Port Perform Implementation Evaluation for Port Community System Implementation. *Journal of Transportation Research Board, 2273*, 29–37.
19. Iacovou, C. L., Benbasat, I., & Dexter, A. S. (1995). Electronic data interchange and small organizations: Adoption and impact of technology. *MISQ Quarterly, 19*(4), 465–485.
20. Muller, G. (1999). *Intermodal freight transportation*. Washington, DC: Eno Foundation.
21. Peterson, D. M. (2003). Power to the BPEL: A technology for web services. *Business Communications Review, 33*(6), 54.
22. van Heck, E., & Ribbers P. M. (1999). The Adoption and Impact of EDI in Dutch SME's. *Proceedings of the 32nd Hawaii International Conference on System Sciences, Hawaii.*
23. Vincent, S. (2003). Making EDI work in India, Article 4: Port Community Systems and EDI in the future, Exim India.
24. Jimenez-Martinez, J., & Polo-Redondo, Y. (2004). The influence of EDI adoption over its perceived benefits. *Technovation, 24*(1), 73–79.
25. Tijan, E., & Sasa, A. (2014). *Seaport cluster information systems—A foundation for Port Community Systems' architecture*. Information and Communication Technology, Electronics and Microelectronics (MIPRO), 37th International Convention on. IEEE.
26. Donselaar, P. W.-V., & Kolkman, J. (2010). Societal costs and benefits of cooperation between port authorities. *Maritime Policy and Management, 37*(3), 271–284.
27. Duran, C., & Cordova, F. (2012). Conceptual analysis for the strategic and operational knowledge management of a port community. *Informatica Economica, 16*(2), 35–44.
28. Forward, K. (2003). *Recent developments in port information technology*. London: Digital ship Ltd.
29. Fernandèz-Alles, M. D. L. L., & Valle-Cabrera, R. (2006). Reconciling institutional theory with organizational theories; How neoinstitutionalism resolves five paradoxes. *Journal of Organizational Change Management, 19*(4), 503–517.
30. Rom, A., & Rohde, C. (2007). Management accounting and integrated information systems: A literature review. *International Journal of Accounting Information Systems, 8*(1), 40–68.
31. Bagchi, P. K., & Paik, S. K. (2001). The role of public-private partnership in port information systems development. *International Journal of Public Sector Management, 14*(6), 482–499.
32. Rodon, J., & Ramis-Pujol, J. (2006). Exploring the intricacies of integrating with a port community system. *BLED 2006 Proceedings* (Paper no. 9, 1–15). Accessed May 27, 2015, from http://aisel.aisnet.org/bled2006/9

Building Effective SMA Systems Taking Advantage of Information Technology

Iacopo Ennio Inghirami

Abstract Strategic management accounting (SMA) is a set of valuable tools to manage a company at its best. However, it is expensive and complex to implement. After a first part of theoretical introduction about the SMA framework, this paper will attempt to assess the possible contribution from the information technologies (IT) in this field both theoretically and empirically. The second part describes a medium-size company and its experiences in implementing a SMA system. We will describe the Nespoli Group, which comprehends 45 medium-size firms localized all-over Europe and the issues linked to the management of such a differentiated multinational ensemble of entities. In the third part, we will propose a new approach to the use of information technology in SMA systems. For this purpose we will evaluate in depth a particular indicator, the service level agreement (SLA), to understand how IT can effectively improve SMA systems. Several final considerations conclude the paper.

Keywords Accounting information systems • Strategic management accounting • Business intelligence • ERP systems • Simulation • Modelling

1 Introduction

Most textbooks of management accounting define the discipline in terms of its decision-making role. It is generally stated that since managerial functions involve using information for better planning and control, management accounting principles are very important for effective and successful management at all levels. In this paper, we will review the role of strategic management accounting (SMA) that claims to be the future of management accounting discipline.

The purpose of the paper is to analyse the definition and the use of the SMA in a medium-sized company: the Nespoli Group Spa. The Nespoli Group is a worldwide

I.E. Inghirami (✉)
University of Milano-Bicocca, Milan, Italy
e-mail: iacopo.inghirami@unimib.it

© Springer International Publishing AG 2017
K. Corsi et al. (eds.), *Reshaping Accounting and Management Control Systems*,
Lecture Notes in Information Systems and Organisation 20,
DOI 10.1007/978-3-319-49538-5_11

167

family-owned Italian company, mainly operating in the "Tools for painting" market.

The Nespoli Group's established position on domestic and international markets increases the interest on the analysis of the company's performance measurement models. In particular, the Nespoli Group started a pilot project regarding service level agreement. We have found some interesting aspects in this project, in particular a relevant contribution from information technologies.

Moreover, we will explore new approaches for the use of information technology. In particular, we would like to propose some thoughts on increased exploitation of the potential of information systems.

2 Mutual Relations Between Accounting Information Systems and Strategic Management Accounting

2.1 Accounting Information Systems and Strategic Management Accounting: Some Definitions

The definition of accounting information system (AIS) depends on the definition of accounting itself. It is possible to distinguish between the two kinds of accounting: financial accounting and management accounting. Financial accounting is defined as:

> The art of recording, classifying, and summarizing in a significant manner and in terms of money, transactions and events which are, in part at least, of financial character, and interpreting the results thereof [1],

Likewise, management accounting is defined as:

> The process of identification, measurement, accumulation, analysis, preparation, interpretation and communication of information used by management to plan, evaluate and control within an entity and to assure appropriate use of and accountability for its resources. Management accounting also comprises the preparation of financial reports for non-management groups such as shareholders, creditors, regulatory agencies and tax authorities [2].

The aim of financial accounting (FA) is to gather and summarize financial data to prepare financial reports, such as a balance sheet and income statement, for the organization's management, investors, lenders, suppliers, tax authorities and other stakeholders. FA main recipients are external users, and financial reports must follow precise layouts and rules. In fact, FA must accomplish national and international principles, such as the generally accepted accounting principles (GAAP) or their equivalent in each different country. The focus of FA is to exhaustively represent all the events that occurred by means of reports produced every month, quarter and year.

The theories and the reference models adopted by FA have been defined from a long time and will not change in the future. Hence, FA systems are stable and do not evolve, particularly when comparing this field with other management topics. Once the organization has introduced and implemented a system, FA can run for several years with very little or no changes at all, unless there is a change in external requirements such as new rules, principles or laws.

While FA is oriented towards the request of external users, management accounting (MA) focuses on the needs of managers. In literature, it is possible to find several conceptual models that may be useful in providing information to managers.

These well-known and well-defined models are designed for planning activities and, after the execution of the activities themselves, to control the obtained results and to report discrepancies, if any. Garrison et al. present this non-exhaustive list of reference models [3]:

- Cost classification
- Job-order costing
- Process costing
- Cost behaviour
- Cost-volume-profit relationship
- Variable costing
- Activity-based costing
- Profit planning (budgeting)
- Capital budgeting
- Advanced reporting

In the mid-1980s major complaints versus MA emerged in the literature [4]. In fact, although MA is considered essential for informed management activity, MA itself seems to have some flaws, particularly arising from its roots in cost accounting, as it is possible to observe in the above-reported list. As a matter of fact, traditional MA approach considers cost classification and analysis, cost-volume-profit models, profit planning (budgeting), capital budgeting and advanced reporting.

Researchers [5, 6] argued that:

1. MA had not evolved over the past decades.
2. MA is too focused on costs.
3. MA is not very useful for managers, because it is not focused on strategy and on market opportunities.

Manager risks to undertake incorrect decisions based on inadequate and obsolete management accounting data. The lack of attention to clients, competition and performance, together with a poor or even non-existing strategic approach, could lead to incapacity to cope with the new highly competitive environment [7].

Strategic management accounting (SMA hereafter) is a promising and well-acquainted evolution of management accounting [8]. SMA tries to address all the above-mentioned criticisms levelled against management accounting. SMA was initially proposed by Simmonds at the beginning of the 1980s [9], and it was not taken seriously until the late 1980s. Simmonds argues that SMA greatly differs

Table 1 Traditional management accounting versus strategic management accounting

	Traditional MA	Strategic MA
1	Historical	Prospective
2	Single entity	Relative
3	Introspective	Outward looking
4	Manufacturing focus	Competitive focus
5	Existing activities	Possibilities
6	Reactive	Proactive
7	Programmed	Un-programmed
8	Data oriented	Information oriented
9	Based on existing systems	Unconstrained by existing systems
10	Built on conventions	Ignores conventions

from MA because of its focus on the comparison of the business with its competitors. Langfield-Smith affirms that there is no agreed definition of SMA in literature [7]. However, Wilson declares that MA differs from SMA in several aspects (see Table 1) [10].

An interesting definition of SMA has been proposed by Bromwich [11], who argues that SMA is:

> The provision and analysis of financial information on the firm's product markets and competitors' costs and cost structures and the monitoring of the enterprise's strategies and those of its competitors in these markets over a number of periods.

Ma and Tayles argue that SMA finally bridged the gap that existed between MA and strategic management [12]. SMA moved MA from monetary issues to a more multidimensional approach. It is not simply a new orientation, which is aimed towards strategy; it is a radically different way of rethinking MA around strategic concepts [8]. In fact, according to Lord [13], the functions commonly associated with SMA are:

1. To collect information related to competitors
2. To use accounting for strategic decisions
3. To cut costs on the basis of strategic decisions
4. And to gain competitive advantage through it

2.2 Strategic Management Accounting: An Empirical Perspective

A straightforward characteristic of the SMA literature is the paucity of empirical research [14]. Actually, most of the literatures regarding SMA were at conceptual level and with a prominent academic emphasis. The main concern is that SMA adoption cannot be measured directly: it is in fact necessary to investigate the adoption of those techniques that can be reconnected to the SMA concept. This is an alternative way to define SMA.

While researching the link between SMA and strategy, Cinquini and Tenucci [15] proposed to define the ensemble of techniques that companies really implement instead of trying to measure the implementation of SMA itself. Cinquini and Tenucci measured the adoption of one or more of the following techniques:

1. Activity-based costing/management (ABC/M)
2. Attribute costing
3. Benchmarking
4. Competitive position monitoring
5. Competitor cost assessment
6. Competitor performance appraisal on public financial statements
7. Customer accounting
8. Integrated performance management systems
9. Life cycle costing
10. Quality costing
11. Strategic costing
12. Strategic pricing
13. Target costing
14. Value chain costing

Actually, organizations hardly understand the meaning of SMA concept; hence, it is easier to ask them if they currently implement some of the above-mentioned techniques and then evaluate if they are de facto applying a SMA approach. Several researchers followed this course: Guilding et al. [16] created a report based on the survey of 12 SMA practices in different countries and concluded that the extent of diffusion was not uniform in New Zealand, the UK and the USA. Fowzia [14] measured the implementation of 14 SMA techniques and in this way measured business strategy and strategic effectiveness of manufacturing organizations in Bangladesh.

2.3 Strategic Management Accounting and Information Technology

The mentioned literature has essentially academic roots and does not consider actual implementations of the SMA systems. This means that on the one hand the researchers did not consider the implementation aspects and, on the other hand, they do not assess the potential related to information technology.

As regards the first aspect, we must note that to implement SMA systems is extremely expensive. In fact, it is not sufficient to adopt an online transaction processing (OLTP) system, but you also need to implement an online analytical

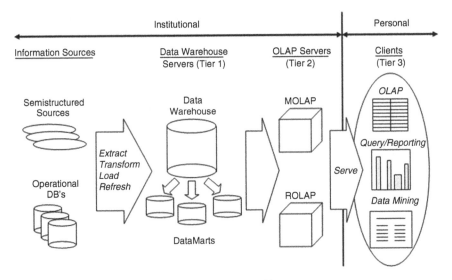

Fig. 1 Strategic management accounting: traditional architecture

processing (OLAP) system. Traditional SMA architecture is based on a three-layer structure (see Fig. 1).

The first tier is a database server that is a relational database system, and it is devoted to data warehouse (DW) support. The second tier is an OLAP server that is typically implemented using either (1) a relational OLAP (ROLAP) model, that is, an extended relational DBMS that maps operations on multidimensional data to standard relational operations, or (2) a multidimensional OLAP (MOLAP) model [17]. The third tier is a front-end client layer, which contains query and reporting tools, analysis tools and/or data mining tools to support the end users.

This architecture has been developed in the last years and is quite functional, but it is heavy and expensive. The major drawbacks are related not only to the sophistication of the scheme itself but also to complexity and cost of the required equipment, both hardware and software. Even relatively small projects, such as pilot projects, may often result to be difficult to implement, expensive and prone to failures. However, it should be stressed that a robust IT architecture is the only one capable to collect and process information necessary for the implementation of an SMA. In fact, neither an OLTP system nor an OLAP system can support by themselves the needs of a SMA system.

Recent studies suggest that it is possible to delete a level, i.e. you can use three-tier architecture taking advantage of IMT (in-memory technology)-based software [18] (Fig. 2).

IMT boosts the software of the end users and thus enables them to create their own hypercubes directly in seconds with intuitive and easy-to-use tools. In this way, IT professionals can focus on pure data issues, and end users can "play" alone with the cleaned and corrected data sets following their thoughts and intuitions.

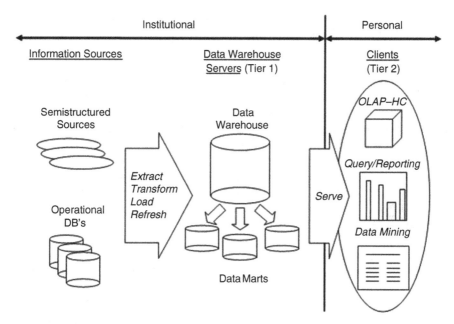

Fig. 2 Strategic management accounting: IMT-based architecture

The second aspect is even more intriguing: is it possible to envisage new perspectives in SMA systems arising from the potential offered by current computer technology? SMA theory is based on the evaluation of static indexes. Computers are used as calculators even if employed in complex models. Instead, in many cases it would be useful to adopt models that describe a process, rather than a static situation. In this case we can take full advantage of both the calculation power of the computers and their ability to handle large volumes of data.

We will present a case to prove this assertion, that is, a case in which it was built a model that describes a process. This system is then employed to perform simulations.

3 Methodology

The methodology used is the case study research approach, following the methods recommended in the literature. The decision to analyse a single case study [19] may be useful for giving a detailed outline of the grounds and distinctive features of the development and subsequent implementation of the internal reporting model represented by the SMA.

The case study approach [20] is interesting since it may offer the option of constructing theories and generalizations based on the study of a single operational case [21–23]. In the case examined, the benefits of such an approach can be seen in the ability to illustrate the factors that drove the company to adopt a SMA system and the consequences within the planning and control function.

We were searching for an empirical case to deeply investigate the implementation of a SMA system. The selected company was interested in developing a SMA system; hence, we followed systematically the implementation of the new system.

The research carried out feature aspects of a qualitative and quantitative nature: the data examined are based on interviews and the company's economic and financial documentation made available to the public on the company's website and on internal reporting documents. The period analysed concerns the period from 2011 to 2014. The interviews were conducted with the headquarter CFO and those responsible for management control: the questions were designed to explain the various stages of the SMA's implementation to illustrate the progress achieved and the benefits in terms of company results achieved.

The interview as opposed to the questionnaire approach offers greater flexibility even if the results were characterized by a certain degree of subjectivity due to the difficulties of interpreting the answers. However, this was useful for understanding the competitive context in which the company operates and the particular features of the sector to which it belongs.

The contribution of the paper to the literature is motivated by the lack of surveys about the SMA implementation. The major limitation of this research is that results are related to the analysis of a single case study. This study cannot lead to general conclusions, and it will be necessary to conduct a comparative study between the observed company and other companies. Thus, this study represents a starting point for further research in the application of SMA concepts.

4 Strategic Management Accounting in Action: The Nespoli Group Case

4.1 Presentation of the Nespoli Group

The Nespoli Group was founded in North Italy right after the Second World War. At the end of the 1940s, Oreste and Bruno Nespoli started what was called "Pennellificio Nespoli" (the Nespoli Brush factory). Initially the company was made of a few artisans working with clear and simple rules: serious work and customer satisfaction.

The company grew steadily, and at the end of the 1970s, it passed from being a small business to becoming an industrial-sized complex. At the end of the 1990s, Nespoli Group started a series of acquisitions in the Paint Tools sector throughout Europe (see Table 2).

The first strategic acquisitions have been made in Spain, France and Germany. Together with the acquisition of Franpin Group, it acquired ZFI (Zhongshan

Table 2 Nespoli Group acquisition history

Year	Country	Company
1996	Spain	Rulo Pluma s.a.
1999	France	Roulor s.a., Monitor s.a., Le Herisson s.a.
2001	Germany	Schabert GmbH
2004	France	Franpin Group
2005	Germany	Friess GmbH
2006	France	Milbox s.a.
2008	France	Mancret
	Italy	Gubra s.r.l.
	Germany	Techno
	Italy	Gaia s.r.l.
	Italy	Italideal—Cia s.r.l.
2009	Italy	Grand Chic s.rl.
2010	Spain	Castor
	Italy	Pippo brand
	Italy	Eurostile
2011	Germany	Noelle Group

Franpin Industries) its China-based factory. Later on, Nespoli Group decided to diversify its offer and made further acquisitions in the sector of Aerosol Paint Spray with the acquisition of Italideal and CIA in Torino (Italy).

In addition, Metal Tools become part of Nespoli Group business with the acquisition of Milbox in France in 2006 and of Techno in Germany in 2008. Nespoli Group entered in the business of Wood and Leather Treatment through the acquisition of Gubra and Grand Chic (Italy).

In 2010, it was added as another business unit for Cleaning Tools, driven by the acquisition in Italy of the well-known Pippo and Eurostile brands. Today the Nespoli Group, led by Luigi and Alessandro Nespoli, is the first European group in the market segment of "Tools for painting", in terms of sales figures, production volumes and market size. Entering in UK, Poland, China, Russia and Turkey markets, the Group had a turnover approaching 350 million euros with over 2000 employees. The Nespoli Group owns several renowned brands such as Nespoli, Roulor, Franpin, Rulo Pluma, Friess, Techno, Pippo and Coronet, and it manufactures tools for several "private labels".

4.2 The Implementation of Nespoli Group's SMA System: Architectural and Theoretical Aspects

In recent years, Nespoli Group started a relevant project with the aim to provide top management and business analysts with reporting information and key indicators that are common across the entire group and that could be analysed in a consistent way with various levels of details.

Dr. Bosisio, the Nespoli Group Chief Information Manager (CIO), declared that DataManager is the powerful and flexible tool utilized for getting deeper into business information, empowering business analysts with OLAP technology. As we said earlier, SMA should be fed by various sources of data; however, the principal source remains a sound and well-running ERP system. Here a problem arises, because the various companies that compose the Nespoli Group are actually running diverse ERP systems, such as legacy systems (IBM AS400), SAP, Oracle and MS Dynamics. Therefore, (1) in the long term, the Group has to choose a single ERP system, and all the companies have to gradually switch to it; (2) in the short term, it is necessary to create a system that can receive data from several sources, clean it and consolidate it.

The Common Nespoli Group's ERP

Dr. Bosisio stated that several considerations forced top management to progressively adopt a unique ERP system throughout the Group:

1. To unify processes and data of all the legal entities
2. To cope with the obsolescence of hardware and connectivity
3. To deal with the increasing number of malfunctions and difficulties in finding spare parts
4. To replace non-updateable software
5. To fight decreasing performance
6. To counteract decreasing security

During 2012, the Group has started a major project for an ERP common to all the companies of the Group itself. A "steering committee" expressly created for this task (1) has defined the specific characteristics that the new software should possess, (2) has performed a software selection and (3) has chosen the hardware architecture and the related organizational aspects.

The steering committee has stated that all the companies of the Nespoli Group have to move towards the implementation of Microsoft Dynamics NAV ERP system in external data centres. This system will unify the bookkeeping and the fiscal accounting of each legal entity composing the Group. Moreover, the steering committee decided to perform a "pilot" implementation in Noelle Group, Nespoli Deutschland and Coronet Germany, treating them as "model company" and considering from the beginning the needs of all the Group's companies. The project started in September 2012 for Noelle Group, in January 2014 for Nespoli Deutschland and in June 2014 for Coronet Germany.

The Nespoli Group's SMA System

Waiting to have a unique ERP system in all the Group's companies that will ease the data gathering phase, it was necessary to predispose a sound SMA system to support top management's activities. For this purpose, it has been developed a proprietary system called DataManager, basically a data warehouse. This system gathers fiscal and managerial data from every company's transactional system.

DataManager extracts final data by means of appropriate interfaces from those transactional systems. Utilizing listed processes and documented rules, it consolidates the gathered data, and it arranges data sets that can be analysed from final users. This final data allows managers to prepare budgets and forecasts regarding sales, purchases, stock and manufacturing.

The outcome of the Nespoli Group's SMA system consists in several managerial reports regarding cost classification, job-order costing, process costing, activity-based costing, profit planning and budgeting and advanced reporting. In particular, managers can access SMA via an Excel interface and directly analyse information. In fact, it is possible to modify reports and dynamically choose legal entities, time periods, etc. freely picking the desired dimensions of analysis. A non-exhaustive list comprehends:

- Business unit analysis
- Market channel analysis
- Customer chain analysis
- Trend analysis
- Stock analysis—expiring/obsolete product, consumption spread, ABC analysis, Stock Health Evaluation

4.3 The Implementation of Nespoli Group's SMA System: The Service Level Agreement Pilot Project

In the last 10 years, the Nespoli Group is grown exponentially through acquisitions in Italy and abroad. In a first step, the model of development has been to acquire new companies, leaving the dedicated local management of the acquired companies. The dual advantage was to maintain business continuity and to have a simplification of the chain of command; the disadvantage was the maintenance of an identity of the acquired companies that was not merged into the "Nespoli vision", as stated by Dr. Ripamonti (Group Planning & Control).

In recent years, the size and complexity of the Group have become such as to require a change in the Group's vision; hence, it was created a headquarter structure with the goal to:

- Steer the group as a single entity.
- Act as a chain of transmission between strategies identified by the ownership and Group companies.
- Develop the business unit that represents the main product lines (Paint Tools, Metal Tools, etc.) by focusing on the needs of customers.

The Group's strategy continues to be a growth strategy, walking in two directions:

(a) *Markets*: strength in markets already served and further geographic expansion into new high-growth markets such as Turkey, Russia and China
(b) *Business*: diversification in products for household cleaning, spray paints, in specific products for the construction industry (Metal Tools) and in products dedicated to the care of the wood and leather

Dr. Scribani, the Nespoli Group Chief Value Officer (CVO), explained the growth path for products: firstly, these are complementary products; secondly, they are often purchased from the same "buyer"; and thirdly, they fall into the Nespoli Group "mission". Similarly, the growth path in the new markets is aimed:

1. To exploit the competitive advantages already acquired in the markets currently occupied. It is possible to adopt a "copy and paste" strategy.
2. To exploit the high rates of growth in emerging countries.
3. To follow Nespoli Group main customers in their international expansion.

In order to develop this vision, the Group has started to implement IT tools that allow setting up basic information on the subject of strategic planning and control. Furthermore, the Group has chosen to implement a "pilot project" to test the real potential of the system itself. This project consists in a system capable to evaluate the "service level agreement".

The Service Level Agreement Concept

A service level agreement (SLA) is a document describing the level of service expected by a customer from a supplier, laying out the metrics by which that service is measured, and the remedies or penalties, if any, should the agreed-upon levels not be achieved.

In the field of organized large-scale retail trade (OLSRT), there is a high level of attention to the quality and the level of service. In particular, customers (i.e. large retail stores or large retail groups) require that the rate of delivery on time of ordered products is greater than percentages of 95 %.

Delays and bad deliveries create revenue loss to the customer itself, which charges substantial penalties to its suppliers for this reason. Usually these penalties are planned in the supply agreement, and therefore both the supplier and the customer are aware of them.

The problem arises at the time of accounting. In fact, while the penalty is born in a certain period, the related accounting can take place several months away. Not only it is often impossible to trace the events that led to the penalty, but also it is very difficult to account the penalty itself. In other words, an accounting period, which ended positively, could later prove to be a negative period.

To avoid this problem, it is necessary to monitor continuously orders and shipments. The daily collection of information for each order, for each shipment and for each customer, indicating the level of service and the causes that have led to any stock-outs (delays by suppliers or production), allows a better control of the supply chain.

Nespoli Deutschland Jan-May 2014 *Navision Transactional System*	SLA % on Amount	Amount Ordered	Lost Turnover	Outstanding Amount
January 2014	97,0%	1.566.647	47.348	-
Complete	100,0%	47.401	-	-
Partial	99,2%	188.482	1.546	-
Partial and Close	96,6%	1.330.764	45.802	-
February 2014	97,4%	4.300.646	109.077	2.196
Complete	100,0%	6.847	-	-
Partial	99,3%	1.013.400	4.879	2.196
Partial and Close	96,8%	3.280.399	104.198	-
March 2014	97,1%	6.825.555	196.597	1.665
Complete	100,0%	75.676	-	-
Partial	98,7%	2.823.248	35.650	1.665
Partial and Close	95,9%	3.926.632	160.947	-
April 2014	96,1%	6.481.729	253.691	1.597
Complete	99,8%	38.766	64	-
Partial	99,7%	1.923.253	3.234	1.597
Partial and Close	94,5%	4.519.711	250.393	-
May 2014	94,1%	7.485.149	364.816	77.597
Complete	100,0%	36.830	-	-
Partial	95,3%	3.384.737	81.930	77.597
Partial and Close	93,0%	4.063.582	282.886	-
Grand Total	96,0%	26.659.726	971.529	83.055

Fig. 3 The SLA report

Service level agreement (SLA) key measures are integrated into a supply chain scorecard (see Fig. 3) that is consistently measured across the organization allowing benchmarking inside the Group. The main KPI analysed in SLA report are:

- Forecast accuracy
- Stock levels
- Internal/external supplier delivery performance
- Transport provider measurements
- Warehouse operation measurements
- Order fill rate
- Product availability or stock-out rate
- Days sales outstanding
- Customer delivery transport measurements
- Customer order outstanding analysis

In addition to the above-mentioned tactical aspects, the model developed to measure SMA allows several strategic thoughts. As a matter of fact, it is possible to evaluate the convenience to operate on a particular market. After loading all the information related to logistics and production, you can simulate the production levels achievable and then decide whether it is possible or not to meet the demands of a potential market.

It is important to underline the complexity of the model: in fact it requires (1) a thorough understanding of the processes, (2) the availability of information related to logistics and production and (3) the availability of adequate computer facilities and databases.

5 Evaluation of the Nespoli Group's SMA System and Conclusions

Several considerations can be done about the Nespoli Group's experience. However, it is important to stress that what we described is only the initial part of a long and challenging process. The final goal is to implement a rich set of procedures not only aimed to support the management, but that will also evaluate the Group's performance.

The Nespoli Group is a multinational, multilingual ensemble of companies, formed over a quite long time. The definition of a common SMA is the first effort to implement a common management background. A relevant aspect has been the definition of a common timing for data collection and subsequent elaboration of reports and documents. The SMA system homogenizes the data, the process to create reports and reports themselves. Moreover, the system acts as communication media within the Group, and it replaces all other means of communication.

Even if the SMA system was born according to the needs of the Group's headquarter, the implementation of the system in all the companies eased dramatically the management of each company of the Group itself. While preserving the autonomy of each legal entity, the adoption of SMA eases the coordination within the Group. The SMA facilitates the vertical integration between legal entities' management and Nespoli Group's management. In this way, it is ensured an effective coordination, and both local entities' and Group's strategies can be reached.

In this respect, the Nespoli Group's experience is highly positive. Against a relevant investment in terms of structures and management empowerment, the Group has acquired an invaluable tool that turned to be irreplaceable to manage each legal entity composing the Group and the Group itself.

Finally, this model allows Nespoli Group's management to keep checking whether it is possible or not to meet the demands of a particular market and then decide whether to continue or to leave the market itself.

References

1. Singh Wahla, R. (2011). AICPA Committee on Terminology. Accounting Terminology Bulletin, 1, Review and Résumé.
2. CIMA. (2005). *The Chartered Institute of Management Accountants: CIMA official terminology*. Elsevier Science.
3. Garrison, R. H., Noreen, E. W., & Brewer, P. C. (2010). *Managerial accounting* (13th ed.). New York: McGraw-Hill.
4. Johnson, H. T., & Kaplan, R. S. (1987). *Relevance lost: The rise and fall of management accounting*. Boston, MA: Harvard Business School Press.
5. Cooper, R. (1996). The changing practice of management accounting. *Management Accounting, 74*(3), 26.
6. Parker, L. D. Reinventing the management accountant. Transcript of CIMA 2002, Glasgow University. http://www.cimaglobal.com/Documents
7. Langfield-Smith, K. (2008). Strategic management accounting: How far have we come in 25 years? *Accounting, Auditing and Accountability Journal, 21*, 204–228.
8. Shah, H., Malik, A., & Malik, S. M. (2011). Strategic management accounting—A messiah for management accounting? *Australian Journal of Business and Management Research, 4*, 01–07.
9. Simmonds, K. (1981). Strategic management accounting. *Management Accounting, 59*, 26–29.
10. Wilson, R. M. S. (1995). Strategic management accounting. In D. Ashton, T. Hopper, & R. Scapens (Eds.), *Issues in management accounting* (pp. 159–190). London: Prentice-Hall Europe.
11. Bromwich, M. (1990). The case for strategic management accounting: The role of accounting information for strategy in competitive markets. *Accounting, Organizations and Society, 15*, 27–46.
12. Ma, Y., & Tayles, M. (2009). On the emergence of strategic management accounting: An institutional perspective. *Accounting and Business Research, 39*, 473–495.
13. Lord, R. (1996). Strategic management accounting: The emperor's new clothes? *Management Accounting Research, 7*, 347–366.
14. Fowzia, R. (2011). Strategic management accounting techniques: Relationship with business strategy and strategic effectiveness of manufacturing organizations in Bangladesh. *World Journal of Management, 3*, 54–69.
15. Cinquini, L., & Tenucci, A. (2010). Strategic management accounting and business strategy: A loose coupling? *Journal of Accounting and Organizational Change, 6*, 228–259.
16. Guilding, C., Cravens, K. S., & Tayles, M. (2000). An international comparison of strategic management accounting practices. *Management Accounting Research, 11*, 113–135.
17. Turban, E., Sharda, R., & Delen, D. (2011). *Decision support systems and intelligent systems* (9th ed.). Saddle River, NJ: Prentice Hall.
18. Inghirami, I. E. (2014). Reshaping strategic management accounting systems. In G. Phillips-Wren, S. Carlsson, A. Respicio, & P. Brezillon (a cura di), *DSS 2.0—Supporting decision making with new technologies* (pp. 495–506). Amsterdam: IOS Press BV.
19. Dyer, W., & Wilkins, A. (1991). Better stories, not better constructs, to generate better theory. A rejoinder to Eisenhardt. *The Academy of Management Review, 16*(3), 613–619.
20. Ryan, B., Scapens, R., & Theobald, M. (2002). *Research method and methodology in finance and accounting*. London: Thomson.
21. Mintzberg, H. (1979). An emerging strategy of direct research. *Administrative Science Quarterly, 24*(4), 582–589.
22. Yin, R. J. (1981). The case study crisis: Some answers. *Administrative Science Quarterly, 26*, 58–65.
23. Eisenhardt, K. M. (1989). Building theories from case study research. *The Academy of Management Review, 14*(4), 532–550.

Accounting Information System and Organizational Change: An Analysis in "First Mover" Public Universities

Elisa Bonollo, Simone Lazzini, and Mara Zuccardi Merli

Abstract This chapter aims to investigate the role of accounting information system in supporting the adoption of accrual accounting in public universities and its main effects on the organization. The study is focused on Italian public universities, with a specific reference to the accounting management of research projects. The treatment of the research projects is particularly interesting because of their relevance in the university budget and their effects on the whole organization (e.g. on the delegation system). Therefore, the configuration of the new accounting information system of universities is not a mere technical problem but involves organizational changes. The research is based on a comparative case study of two Italian public universities (Universities of Genoa and Pisa) relating to the role of the accounting information system in supporting the research project accounting and in affecting their organization (in terms of competences and responsibilities).

Keywords Accounting information system • Public organizations • University

1 Introduction

Since the 1990s, Italian public organizations have been interested in a modernization process to overcome the traditional bureaucratic model [1–3]. This process was legislation driven and focused (in Italy as well as in other countries) on public financial management reforms, so much so that some international scholars coined the term "New Public Financial Management" [4–6]. In Italy, these reforms also led to the adoption of new accounting systems (i.e. accrual accounting, cost accounting, etc.) with the aim to better satisfy the stakeholder information needs, improve the level of efficiency and empower the staff to use public resources.

E. Bonollo (✉) • M. Zuccardi Merli
Department of Economics and Business Studies, University of Genoa, Genoa, Italy
e-mail: bonollo@economia.unige.it; zuccardi@economia.unige.it

S. Lazzini
Department of Economics and Management, University of Pisa, Pisa, Italy
e-mail: simone.lazzini@unipi.it

© Springer International Publishing AG 2017
K. Corsi et al. (eds.), *Reshaping Accounting and Management Control Systems*,
Lecture Notes in Information Systems and Organisation 20,
DOI 10.1007/978-3-319-49538-5_12

183

In recent years, these changes have also involved Italian public universities, initially with academic studies focused on the criticalities of the traditional public accounting, then with empirical research describing the state of the art or the experiences of first adopter universities and, finally, with legislative initiatives addressed to all public universities [7–11].

More specifically, Law no. 240 of 2010, Legislative Decree no. 18 of 2012 and Ministerial Decree no. 19 of 2014 changed the accounting information system of public universities, which passed from the traditional cash- and commitment-based accounting system to accrual accounting with an annual "authorizing" budget. As a consequence of this reform, the universities have to adopt a single economic and investment budget rather than having separated and independent budgets prepared by the central administration and by each individual peripheral units (departments, centres of excellence, etc.). Thus, the main consequent innovation consists of a complete redesign of the accounting information system.

In this context, the chapter aims to investigate how the information system supports the use of the accrual accounting and affects the organization of the university, with specific reference to the accounting management of research projects.

The treatment of research projects is interesting because of their relevance in the university budget (in terms of revenues, costs and investments) and the impact of their management on the whole organization (in terms of competences, responsibilities, etc.). Therefore, the configuration of the accounting information system [12] is not only a technical problem but involves the whole management of the university [13].

The method of analysis used is a comparative case study [14–16] in order to provide a picture of the main elements characterizing the configuration of the accounting information system of the universities, with particular reference to the IT procedures and organizational changes for the management of research projects. More specifically, in our research the Universities of Genoa and Pisa are analysed and compared. This choice is due to the fact that these Universities have introduced the accrual accounting system earlier than requested by law and have already highlighted criticalities in connection with this change. The sources of data were internal documents and semi-structured interviews. More specifically, in both Universities we examined documents such as university accounting rules and accounting manuals, guides and training documents prepared by the accounting software provider, university organizational charts and organizational deliberations of the university general manager. The semi-structured interviews were conducted in both Universities face-to-face with members of the accounting unit of the central administration. Each interview lasts about 1 h and was conducted twice, in June 2014 and then in June 2015 (with the same persons).

The chapter is structured as follows. It starts with a literature review on the accrual accounting in the public sector and an analysis of the renewal of the public university accounting information system. Secondly, the chapter presents peculiarities and organizational changes related to the accounting management of research projects. Finally, the comparative case of the Universities of Genoa and Pisa is described and discussed.

2   Accrual Accounting in the Public Sector and Organizational Change: A Literature Review

The Italian university system has recently been going through a process of change that has involved also its accounting information system [8]. The main laws and government interventions of this process of change are depicted in Table 1.

Since the 1990s, Italian public universities have been able to choose their accounting information system, and their central administration and peripheral units have produced their own budgets and annual reports. It was very difficult both to conduct unitary policy through the accounting documents (for internal

Table 1 Main laws and government interventions on Italian public universities

Normative reference	Main topics	Effects
Law 68/1989	University reform	Organizational, financial, accounting autonomy
Law 537/1993	Financing evaluation	New financing system Institution of the National Commission for the Evaluation of the Italian University System Institution of a University Evaluation Commission in each university
Leg. Decree 29/1993 Leg. Decree 286/1999	Control system	Introduction of an internal control system (only for the activities supporting research and teaching)
Law 43/2005 (art. 1-ter)	Programming evaluation	Adoption of a 3-year plan (according to ministerial direction) Ministerial ex post performance measurement regarding all university activities (with impacts on future financial resources)
Ministerial Decree 14/11/2006	Accounting	Introduction of an Information System on Public Organizations' Operations (SIOPE)
Ministerial Decree 01/03/2007	Accounting	Adoption of a common reclassification scheme of annual report
Law 1/2009	Financing	Introduction of a percentage of State financial resources distributed according to performance obtained by each university
Law 15/2009 Leg. Decree 150/2009	Programming evaluation	Adoption of a 3-year performance plan, an annual performance report, a system of performance measurement and evaluation (only for the activities supporting research and teaching)
Law 240/2010	University reform	Organizational changes Accounting changes
Leg. Decree 18/2012 Ministerial Decree 19/2014	Accounting	Introduction of ministerial accounting standards Adoption of mandatory budget and annual report schemes

stakeholders) and to have a unitary photo of the results of universities (for external stakeholders) [17]. This need to satisfy information requirements of internal and external stakeholders and the need to make public managers accountable for a proper use of resources have required that lawmaker introduces changes in the accounting information system. These changes are within a wider reform process that also concerns other public organizations and that, with different timing, aims to introduce accrual and cost accounting systems with or in replacement of the traditional public accounting [18, 19]. This reform process, as already said, is the so-called "New Public Financial Management" widely investigated by Italian and international scholars [1–6].

Actually, the traditional cash- and commitment-based accounting system had already been criticized in the 1950s [20, 21], but it has been in the 1990s, with the "New Public Financial Management", that many authors suggested again that lawmaker should innovate the accounting information system of public organizations. According to these authors, the traditional public accounting system did not provide the necessary information for an effective management of resources and for the control of results [2, 22–24]. That is why the adoption of accrual and cost accounting was proposed [4, 25, 26].

Some authors pointed out that the benefits of accrual accounting would be associated with the contemporary adoption of the cost accounting system [2, 27, 28]. Other authors also associated the introduction of accrual accounting with a greater focus on the management of assets, the availability of comprehensive information on liabilities and the improvement of transparency and accountability towards external stakeholders [23, 29, 30].

We should also point out that some studies have highlighted criticalities regarding the replacement of the traditional public accounting system with accrual accounting [29, 31]. Just think of the challenge of valuating the starting capital and the operating capital, particularly in connection with assets with a cultural or historical value, art and museums [32–35], the risk of a poor control of expenditure [18], the difficulty of interpreting the result for the year [36–38] and the need to define uniform accounting standards [39, 40].

The main pros and cons of the adoption of the accrual accounting in public organizations are summarized in Table 2.

The accounting system change does not just impact on technical aspects, but reveals its effects on the whole management, also and above all on the organization. Indeed, the accounting information system is not a mere technical tool and is not neutral. It is at the same time the result of a progressive accumulation and stratification of experiences, procedures, processes and information needs and the factor that affects the future development of the organization, as possible element of cultural change or, on the contrary, possible factor that causes inertia and resistance to change [29, 41–43].

Innovations of accounting information systems are often considered as essential in the process of organizational change. In recent decades, scholars of the so-called "alternative" perspectives of accounting highlight the interdependence between accounting information systems and human behaviours [44], although with

Table 2 Accrual accounting in public organizations

Main Pros	Main references
Providing information for an effective management of policies and resources and for the control of results	Anessi Pessina (2000), Anessi Pessina and Steccolini (2007), Anselmi (1995), Borgonovi (1995), Hood (1991, 1995) and Olson et al. (1998)
Providing more accurate information on the economic dimension of management	Anselmi (1995), Anthony (2000), Borgonovi (2002), Paulsson (2006) and Sicilia and Steccolini (2011)
Greater focus on the management of assets, availability of comprehensive information on liabilities and improvement of transparency and accountability towards external stakeholders	Anselmi (1995), Buccoliero et al. (2005), Pezzani (2005) and Steccolini (2004)
Compliance with rules, norms and values (often imposed from outside)	Covaleski and Dirsmith (1988), Covaleski et al. (2003), Meyer and Rowan (1977) and Steccolini (2009)
Providing a mean of power for influencing actors' behaviours	Baxter and Chua (2003) and Hopwood (1994)
Providing a mean of power for enhancing positions of specific stakeholders	Odgen (1997) and Pinch et al. (1989)
Main Cons	
Difficulty of valuating the starting capital and the operating capital, particularly in connection with assets with a cultural or historical value, art and museums	Barton (2000), Carnegie and Wolnizer (1999), Christiaens and De Wielemaker (2003) and Micallef and Peirson (2008)
Risk of a poor control of expenditure	Catturi et al. (2004)
Difficulty of interpreting the annual result	Garlatti and Pezzani (2000), Guthrie (1998) and Mautz (1981)
Need to define uniform accounting standards to ensure both the comparability in space and time and the reliability of annual report	Agasisti and Catalano (2009) and Borgonovi (2004)

different theoretical assumptions, methods and aims, according to the "critical" or "interpretative" perspectives.

Scholars of the "critical perspective" emphasize the critique of the status quo and the emancipation towards a better society. They are focused on the mutual influence between power relations and accounting information systems. Their belief is that accounting information systems play an important role in maintaining existing structures of power and that the accounting rules are the result of particular forms of domination (e.g. the accounting standards represent a compromise between stakeholders and power holders). In this context, some authors propose to take an active role and help to change the existing accounting information systems in order to improve the functioning of society [45–48].

The "interpretative perspective" argues that a same stimulus (regulatory requirement or new available technology) can lead to a different reconfiguration of the accounting information system, as expression of the organizational interdependence. This organizational interdependence, in turn, depends on specific dominant culture, available distinctive expertise and existing formal and informal power relations.

There are several approaches of the "interpretative perspective". The main ones are the new-institutional, *Foucault*'s and *Latour*'s approaches. The new-institutional approach focuses on the role of the accounting information systems in supporting the change in organizational culture and in obtaining legitimization, consensus and visibility for the organization itself [49, 50]. According to this approach, the adoption of an accounting information system, in this case the accrual accounting, is influenced by the will more to conform to rules, norms and values (often imposed from outside) than to consider its efficiency and effectiveness on management [51, 52]. According to scholars of *Foucault's* approach, accounting practices are instruments of power, able to influence and guide the behaviour of individuals in formalized organizational contexts, such as those of public organizations [41, 53, 54]. *Latour*'s approach argues that accounting is used by some stakeholders to strengthen their positions through a targeted use of the information obtained precisely through the accounting information system [55, 56].

The main contributions of "alternative" perspectives are summarized in Table 3.

In short, the "alternative perspective" to mainstream accounting rejects the assumption of objectivity of the accounting information system and underlines, even if with different approaches, the impact on the organization, people and environment (issues that can be found, however, also in traditional studies of *Economia Aziendale*).

Table 3 Main contributions of "alternative" perspectives to mainstream accounting

Alternative perspectives	Main references
Critical perspective	
Mutual influence between accounting information system and power relations	Broadbent et al. (2001) and Laughlin (1987)
Active role of accounting researchers in order to help changes in society	Lemman and Tinker (1987) and Tinker et al. (1982)
Interpretative perspective	
New institutional approach	
Accounting information system as an instrument of organizational change and of legitimization	Covaleski and Dirsmith (1988), Covaleski et al. (2003), Meyer and Rowan (1997) and Steccolini (2009)
Foucault's approach	
Accounting information system as an instrument of power and guide for actors' behaviours	Baxter and Chua (2003), Burchell et al. (1980) and Hopwood (1994)
Latour's approach	
Accounting information system as an instrument used by some stakeholders to strengthen their positions	Ogden (1997) and Pinch et al. (1989)

Table 4 University documents in budget and reporting phases

Budget phase (within $31/12/n - 1$)	Reporting phase (within $30/04/n + 1$)
Consolidated 3-year budget	Consolidated annual report
• Economic budget	• Statement of assets and liabilities
• Investment budget	• Income statement
Consolidated annual budget	• Accompanying notes
• Economic budget	• Cash flow statement
• Investment budget	• Report on operations
"Chart of expenses classified by missions and programmes"	• SIOPE[a] statements
Consolidated traditional public accounting budget	• "Chart of expenses classified by missions and programmes"
	• Board of auditors' report
	Consolidated traditional public accounting report
	Consolidated financial statements
	• Statement of assets and liabilities
	• Income statement
	• Accompanying notes

[a]*SIOPE Sistema informativo sulle operazioni degli enti pubblici* [Information System on Public Organizations' Operations]

3   The New Accounting Information System of Italian Public Universities

In order to adapt the accounting information system of universities to the information needs of internal and external stakeholders, Italian lawmaker introduced accrual and cost accounting systems and the documents specified in Table 4 (Law 240/2010, Legislative Decree 18/2012 and Ministerial Decree 19/2014). The deadline for universities to switch to the new accounting information system was 1 January 2015.

The main innovations can be summarized in the following points:

- Universities are required to adopt accrual accounting, unlike in the past, when they could adopt the accounting information system they preferred. The non-coexistence between cash- and commitment-based accounting and accrual accounting has been established to prevent the risk of generating confusion in decision-making process. According to several authors, public managers could receive inconsistent information from the joint presence of the two accounting systems and end up by basing their decisions on the traditional public accounting system [28, 37, 57].
- Cost accounting must be mandatorily used in order to provide information for the decision-making process and to make public managers accountable in terms of use of public resources, investments and so on [8].
- The consolidated 3-year budget must be prepared to ensure the economic and financial sustainability of the medium-term activities of the university.

- The consolidated annual budget, consisting of the economic and investment budgets, becomes an authorizing document, thus avoiding the reduction of control on available resources.
- The consolidated annual budget (as well as the consolidated annual report) is a single "consolidated" document, which means that it is referred to the university as a whole, including both the central administration and any peripheral unit such as departments, centres of excellence, libraries, etc. [58, 59].
- The consolidated traditional public accounting budget and report must be prepared and accompanied by a reclassification of expenses by missions and programmes (connected with the COFOG code), in order to consolidate and monitor public organizations' accounts.
- The consolidated financial statements must be prepared in compliance with the ministerial accounting standards; the consolidation area includes university, university foundations, subsidiaries and other organizations where the university has the majority of votes in the shareholders' meeting or the power to appoint the majority of the members of the boards of directors.
- General accounting standards, the Statement of Assets and Liabilities, the Income Statement and the Cash Flow Statement, valuation criteria for annual report items and criteria for the preparation of the first Statement of Assets and Liabilities have been introduced by Ministerial Decree.

Clearly, the lawmaker wished to ensure the required attention for the economic aspect of management (accrual accounting), the control of the resources used compared to those planned (consolidated annual authorizing budget), the consolidation of accounts of all public organizations at national level (reclassification of expenses by missions and programmes) and the comparability over time and space (general accounting standards and consolidated annual report schemes set forth by Ministerial Decree).

Although several studies have been published on the accounting information system of Italian public universities since the approval of Law 240/2010, most of them have focused on an analysis of the contents of the reform [17, 60, 61], on the implementation stage of the new accounting information system [11, 60] and on existing best practices [8]. There is a lack of studies investigating how these accounting innovations impact on operations and organization. The next sections of our work will analyse in depth one of these issues, connected to the accounting management of research projects.

4 The Accounting Management of Research Projects

The introduction of accrual accounting in universities has been only a part of a thorough reconfiguration of the relationships between the central administration and peripheral units and has become one of the most complex situations universities had to face over the last few years.

At present, departments and other peripheral units (e.g. centres of excellence) are no longer independent as to accounting. The former budgeting and financial reporting documents have been unified at university level.

Therefore, the accounting information system of the universities had to be configured for the need to pass from the traditional public accounting to accrual accounting and to support the new competencies of peripheral units within the framework of the new accounting information system.

The main point is to define which economic and financial flows each unit can record autonomously and how they are interconnected at central level. To this purpose, it is essential for the accounting information system to reflect the delegation system, where powers are conferred upon units, and the reconciliation processes.

The choice of a more or less extended delegation between the central administration and peripheral units involves the management of universities, for example as regards payment of suppliers, treasury control, contract management, utility cost allocation and particularly the management of research projects.

Under this perspective, the accounting management of research projects takes on a crucial role due to the importance of research within the university and to the complexity of their accounting. The management of research projects entails the need to allocate tasks between the department that carries out the research activity and the central administration that has to report said activity in the consolidated financial statements and therefore determine its accrual in each financial year.

The accounting information system of universities is mainly dealt with in Ministerial Decree 19/2014, which imposes how to prepare the consolidated annual report.

The legislation identifies specific accounting standards for universities and refers, for any specific item not dealt with in the Ministerial Decree, to civil law provisions and the accounting practices defined by the *Organismo Italiano di Contabilità (OIC)*, the Italian commission for accounting. We can, therefore, acknowledge how the lawmaker elected to intervene selectively on the preparation of the annual report by specifying only the criteria concerning those items that, being peculiar of universities, could not have been easily dealt with in the civil law or in the accounting standards established by the OIC.

Article 4 (letter g) of the Decree indicates annual report valuation criteria for the research projects. More specifically, the lawmaker highlighted how the valuation of accrued income or deferred income in the university takes on a peculiar significance in connection with the accrual of income derived from ongoing projects and research funded or co-funded by third parties.

The lawmaker identifies two types of research projects: "competitive" research projects and "commissioned" research or research deriving from "technological transfer". The first type of project is usually accessed by taking part in competitive selection procedures that are generally proposed by international or national public institutions (European Union, Italian Ministry of University and Research, etc.) or by public or private foundations that have an interest in specific fields of research.

The second type of project consists of research activities commissioned to departments by external entities, called "outsourced research projects".

Projects that start and finish within the same financial year are assessed on the basis of the cost criterion, where annual report items are valued based on cost. This cost "should be intended as the whole expense borne to procure a given good or service, including those that can be directly or indirectly allocated for the reasonably allocable portion" (article 2, Ministerial Decree 19/2014). Therefore, for annual research projects, valuation is quite easy because all the costs incurred for the implementation of the project accrue during that year and are allocated to it based on the pertinence between the costs and the revenues [19].

As regards multi-year research projects, each university can choose a valuation based on the cost criterion or as a function of the progress of works. We also point out that, once made, this choice will be univocal. This means that the choice will concern all the research projects of that university, subject to the condition that the Accompanying Notes will specify the method used and criteria adopted.

The valuation of multi-year research projects requires the identification of the portion of costs and revenues to be allocated to the year considered as distinguished from the portion that must be transferred to future years.

Between the two options above mentioned (cost criterion and work in progress criterion), the legislator seems to prefer the former solution. In detail, the adoption of the cost criterion consists in the determination of the portion to be allocated to the year considered by assuming that the revenue to be allocated corresponds to the costs incurred during the year and, consequently, proceeding by booking a deferred income (if revenue amount is higher than the cost incurred for the implementation of the project) or accrued income (in the opposite case).

This accounting method has two important consequences: firstly, this approach implies the income neutrality of the research projects during their implementation period. The revenues allocated during the various years always correspond with the costs of those years, so no impact is expected on the annual result. Any margin will emerge only during the closing year and usually in "outsourced research projects". The second consequence regards the accrued income or deferred income that has originated from the progression of costs during the years (*cost-to-cost method*) rather than in connection with the time relevance of the economic component to the year, as traditionally happens.

Consequently, the accounting management of research projects first of all requires the definition of specific competencies between the departments or other peripheral units where the research activities are carried out and the central administration that takes care to reflect them in the consolidated annual report. Then the configuration of the accounting information system must ensure the allocation of the cost items to the different research projects, their subdivision by peripheral units and, finally, the determination of the portion of revenues to be allocated to the year considered and the closing of accounts at the end of the year [8].

5 The Comparative Case Study of the Universities of Genoa and Pisa

The comparative case study considers the Universities of Genoa and Pisa that have introduced the accounting innovations of the last university reform earlier than required by law. Consequently, they have already faced criticalities that other Italian public universities will now have to overcome. Moreover, they are comparable, as they have similar sizes in terms of students and employees and therefore supposedly the same management complexity.

The University of Genoa has adopted accrual and cost accounting since January 2013, whereas the University of Pisa has started the process of transition to accrual accounting at the end of 2012.

Both Universities use the *Cineca*'s U-GOV application platform that, as we will say, has affected the organizational aspect of the management. U-GOV is an application platform for the introduction of an integrated accrual and cost accounting system. In this regard, we should point out that the charts of accounts for accrual accounting and cost accounting are distinct but, obviously, interconnected. More specifically, the U-GOV system uses the chart of accounts for cost accounting to enter the provisions of the consolidated annual authorizing budget. Subsequently, when management operations are carried out, these provisions will be checked for budget availability in order to proceed with cost accounting and/or accrual accounting bookings.

As regards the accounting management of research project, the U-GOV system allows to:

- Manage research project master data with a taxonomy previously defined at central level.
- Connect the research project with organizational units, human resources and funders involved.
- Book and report on the acquisition and use of financial resources connected with the costs and revenues of the research project.

In order to describe the accounting management of research projects and its organizational impacts, the following phases will be summarized:

- Configuration of the "project form".
- Management of research projects during the year.
- Closing of the year.

The *configuration of the "project form"* has been managed centrally during the start-up phase of the U-GOV system. Specifically at the Genoa University, the organizational unit *Support for Research* of the central administration has worked with peripheral units for the identification of types and names of existing and potential research projects. Then this central unit has defined the taxonomy of projects, developed at three levels (classes, macro-typologies, typologies). The other information has been defined by the *Cineca*'s U-GOV staff and the personnel of the accounting unit of the central administration. The University of Pisa has assigned the configuration of the "project form" to a dedicated staff at central level.

The *configuration of the "project form"* has also required the specification of sub-forms that will collect information in the initial phase of research projects, such as:

- Cost/revenue statement forms and activity statement forms with lists of cost/revenue items and activities to be booked and/or reported.
- Typology and master data of funders.
- Financing schemes according to the types of reporting requested.

Therefore, potential connections between projects, cost and revenue items for accrual and cost accounting, activities to be carried out, funders and reporting criteria are already created during the configuration phase. Moreover during this phase, both Universities decided to assess research projects by reporting their value (at the year end) with the *cost-to-cost method*.

The *management of research projects* during the year involves peripheral units in both Universities. At Genoa University, these peripheral units can enter the data of the research project proposals and label them as "draft". Then when there is the signature of an agreement, convention, resolution, ministerial decree, etc., the peripheral units confirm the data and label them as "final". We should however outline that peripheral units often fit the data only when the research projects have the "final" status to avoid loading and then erasing research projects remained only fine words.

The "draft" phase does not exist in the University of Pisa.

The information to be entered creates the actual connections between the research projects and:

- The organizational structure, by entering the organizational units involved in the research project.
- The human resources, by entering the names of the university employees involved, their roles and their commitment in terms of work time.
- External funders, by entering their names and cash contributions.
- The accrual and cost accounting system, through the project codes, the financial resources available, the project start and end dates, the project typology, the financial scheme and finally the cost/revenue statement form adopted.

The transition to accrual accounting has also led to a redesign of activities and responsibilities between the central administration and peripheral units. Fig. 1 shows the procedures between the old and the current accounting information system for both Universities.

In the past, with the traditional public accounting, the accounting management of research projects involved mainly peripheral units that dealt with the approval of their budgets, the phases of revenues and expenditure, the closing of accounts and the preparation of their annual reports. The central administration intervened only for the construction of the traditional consolidated public accounting report of the whole university [62].

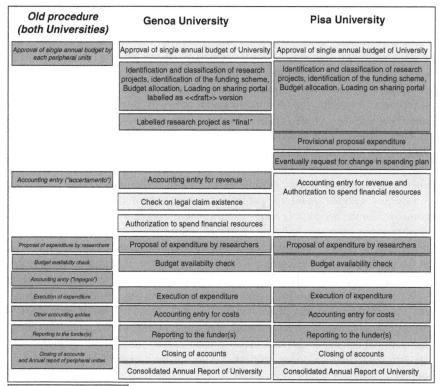

Old procedure (both Universities)	Genoa University	Pisa University
Approval of single annual budget by each peripheral units	Approval of single annual budget of University	Approval of single annual budget of University
	Identification and classification of research projects, identification of the funding scheme, Budget allocation, Loading on sharing portal labelled as <<draft>> version	Identification and classification of research projects, identification of the funding scheme, Budget allocation, Loading on sharing portal
	Labelled research project as "final"	
		Provisional proposal expenditure
		Eventually request for change in spending plan
Accounting entry ("accertamento")	Accounting entry for revenue	Accounting entry for revenue and Authorization to spend financial resources
	Check on legal claim existence	
	Authorization to spend financial resources	
Proposal of expenditure by researchers	Proposal of expenditure by researchers	Proposal of expenditure by researchers
Budget availability check	Budget availabilty check	Budget availability check
Accounting entry ("Impegno")		
Execution of expenditure	Execution of expenditure	Execution of expenditure
Other accounting entries	Accounting entry for costs	Accounting entry for costs
Reporting to the funder(s)	Reporting to the funder(s)	Reporting to the funder(s)
Closing of accounts and Annual report of peripheral unites	Closing of accounts	Closing of accounts
	Consolidated Annual Report of University	Consolidated Annual Report of University

Central Administration
Peripheral unit

Fig. 1 Old and new procedures at Universities of Genoa and Pisa

At present, we should point out a process of centralization that is not so much the operational management of the research projects (that still depends on peripheral units), but their accounting management and, therefore, the information management.

This could mean changes in actors' behaviours and decision-making process. Indeed, the central administration has much more updated information than in the past and could use it in order to play a proactive role in collecting money for research projects, for example, during the year the central administration could support those peripheral units showing more difficulties in collecting money for their research activities.

In detail, when the research project has reached the "final" stage, according to the so-called "pro-forma invoice" or the outgoing invoice or another legal claim, the revenue is booked in the accrual and cost accounting by the peripheral unit at Genoa University and by central administration at the University of Pisa. In all cases, the U-GOV system requires that the period of accrual of the revenue be defined; it is a particularly significant piece of information because, at the year end, in adjusting entries, the IT procedure will automatically connect the non-accrued revenue portion to the following period.

At the same time, in the Genoa University the central administration checks on the mere existence (not on the legal regularity) of the documents under which bookkeeping entry of the revenue was carried out. If the check has been completed successfully, the central administration authorizes the peripheral unit to use financial resources, regardless of the time of actual payment of the amount due for the research project. This phase is carried out manually and has led to the creation of a new organizational unit called *Authorization for budget and support for accrual accounting*, within the organizational area *Resources and Accounting* of the central administration. Differently Pisa has preferred to act directly on individual skills, without constituting a specific organizational unit to authorize to spend.

In the past with the traditional public accounting, the authorization to spend was automatic after the accounting entry "*accertamento*", booked at the peripheral level and without any information flow towards the central administration. At present, as already said, in both Universities, even if in different ways, the central administration has the opportunity to know the type and amount of research projects at the same time they begin and therefore has the potential to monitor the ongoing ability of the peripheral units to attract financial resources and their possibility to spend money for research projects. Up to now, the central administration of both Universities seems not to exploit this possibility. Perhaps technical software modifications, organizational changes of "*Gelmini* reform" and new legal requirements (e.g. electronic invoice) have requested a lot of time and efforts without any room for changes in actors' behaviours.

During the research project, the researchers can make proposals for spending in connection with their work. Following these requests, the peripheral unit checks the budget availability for the research project and then, if the outcome is positive, the relative amount is reduced and subsequently the bookkeeping entries in accrual and cost accounting are made. In the U-GOV system, the availability of the budget can be checked through an analytical control (on the budget availability of the individual cost item used for the booking) or a synthetic control (on the resources globally available during the year for the research project). For reasons connected with the management flexibility in conducting research projects, the Universities use this availability check synthetically on the global budget availability of the project.

The check of budget availability and the following bookkeeping entries are carried out in the peripheral units. More specifically, in the current organizational configuration, at the peripheral level, there are an *Administrative Secretary* (in charge of whole administrative management) and several heads of organizational units including the *Support for Research Unit*. Nowadays in both Universities, uniform procedures have not yet established so that there is not a clear distinction between the above-mentioned roles in relation to the management of research projects.

At the *year end*, in both Universities the *cost-to-cost procedure* will be managed centrally and will be started by booking depreciation in cost accounts, so that the cost for the use of fixed assets allocated to the research project will be considered in the said calculation. Only afterwards will the *cost-to-cost method* be applied on each typology of research project. It is the U-GOV system itself that automatically, in the cost accounting, adjusts revenues to the annual costs. Then in accrual accounting the procedure is made up of the determination of depreciation and the determination of the "project balances" and the *cost-to-cost method* will be applied. The U-GOV system will automatically generate the deferred income item, if revenues exceed costs. On the contrary, if revenues are lower than costs, an accrued income item will be activated manually by the user who allocates the accrued portion to the year.

In short, the transition from traditional public accounting to accrual accounting with the single annual authorizing budget and the adoption of the U-GOV application have led to organizational changes. In Genoa at the central level, within the organizational area *Resources and Accounting*, there is a new organizational unit authorizing peripheral units to use the financial resources of the budget and supporting them with the accrual accounting. Pisa has preferred to act directly on individual skills, without constituting an *ad hoc* unit. Furthermore, at peripheral level, in both Universities the accounting management of research projects is carried out by the *Administrative Secretary* and/or the head of *Support for Research Unit*. We should highlight a centralization not for operational management but for the accounting management and, therefore, relating to information flows.

6   Discussion

From the organizational point of view, Universities of Genoa and Pisa have passed from a situation in which the peripheral units had their own budgets and their annual reports to a situation in which the budget and the annual report are under the responsibility of the central administration. Consequently, the Universities of Genoa and Pisa had to reconfigure all the accounting procedures that operate simultaneously at the central and peripheral level. The configuration of their IT applications is essentially oriented to an integrated management of research projects. This integration spans over three different but interconnected planes:

- A first plane concerns technical-accounting integration, which takes form in the chart of accounts that links cost accounting entries to accrual accounting entries.
- A second plane regards integration at the level of attributions between central administration and peripheral units. The accounting information system breaks down the research project booking process into subprocesses that are attributed to different entities. For example, we point out how peripheral units mainly operate on booking entries during the year, while the central administration has taken upon itself the budgeting phase, the closing of accounts and the reporting of research projects in the consolidated annual report.
- The third integration plane concerns the decision-making process. The management of research projects implies integration between the decision-making

processes that link peripheral units and central administration. In this way, the accounting information system operates as a carrier for the decision-making process. Indeed, the accounting treatment of research projects is fed by a decision-making process of the peripheral units and this process, in its turn, will trigger the decision-making process of the central administration. This integration plane seem to be at an early stage, because technical and organizational changes have requested a lot of time and efforts, but in the future also actors' behaviours and decision-making process will be certainly deeply affected by accounting information system changes.

As regards criticalities, our investigation showed how, for technical-accounting aspects, including the most significant, the new accounting information system requires manual actions from the operators. The definition of accrued income, for instance, requires the operators to identify the portion of revenues accrued during the year, to be booked with the integration entry. This not only involves a quite large amount of work but also exposes to the risk of errors and inaccuracies.

7 Conclusions

The outcome of our research activities shows how accounting management of research projects, and more generally the transition from traditional public accounting to accrual accounting, is not a mere technical accounting problem but definitely becomes a managerial issue as it impacts on the organization and (potentially) on decision-making process.

The accounting management of research project needs an organizational reconfiguration that clearly conveys the differences between competencies and responsibilities in the peripheral units where the research project activities are developed and the central administration that has the task of reporting those activities in the annual report.

For all these reasons, the accounting information system is important both as an instrument closely connected with operational processes of the public organizations and for its prescriptive value, as it affects the definition of accounting procedures, responsibilities and organizational tasks. Indeed, the analysis conducted shows how the role of the accounting information system in support of research projects is not a neutral item. Indeed, accounting information system has restrictions and boundaries that affect accounting procedures and organization.

Further research perspectives may concern an extension of the cases examined to understand whether other Italian public universities made different choices in terms of accounting procedures and organizational change. Another possible extension of the research may investigate the impact of the new accounting information system on accountability and decision-making processes in the medium term.

References

1. Anselmi, L. (2003). *Percorsi aziendali per le pubbliche amministrazioni*. Torino: Giappichelli.
2. Borgonovi, E. (2002). *Principi e sistemi aziendali per le pubbliche amministrazioni*. Milano: Egea.
3. Mussari, R. (2005). Public sector financial reform in Italy. In J. Guthrie, C. Humphrey, L. R. Jones, & O. Olson (Eds.), *International public financial management reform: Progress, contradictions and challenges*. Greenwich: InformationAge Press.
4. Olson, O., Guthrie, J., & Humphrey, C. (1998). International experiences with 'new' public financial management (NPFM) reforms: New word? Small word? Better word? In O. Olson, J. Guthrie, & C. Humphrey (Eds.), *Global warning: Debating international developments in new public financial management*. Oslo: Capelen Akademisk Forlag As.
5. Lapsley, I. (1999). Accounting and the new public management: Instruments of substantive efficiency or a rationalising modernity? *Financial Accountability and Management, 15*, 201–207.
6. Guthrie, J., Olson, O., & Humphrey, C. (1999). Debating developments in new public financial management: The limits of global theorizing and some new ways forward. *Financial Accountability and Management, 15*, 209–228.
7. Agasisti, T., Arnaboldi, M., & Catalano, G. (2008). Reforming financial accounts in the public sector: The case of Universities. *Irish Accounting Review, 15*, 1–29.
8. Azzone, G., Campedelli, B., & Varasio, E. (Eds.). (2011). *Il sistema di programmazione e controllo negli atenei*. Bologna: Il Mulino.
9. Catalano, G., & Tomasi, M. (Eds.). (2010). *Esperienze di contabilità economico-patrimoniale nelle università*. Bologna: Il Mulino.
10. Cantele, S., Martini, M., & Campedelli, B. (2013). Factors affecting the development of management control systems in Universities. *Economia Aziendale Online, 4*, 167–183.
11. Paolini, A., & Soverchia, M. (2013). Le università statali italiane verso la contabilità economico-patrimoniale ed il controllo di gestione. *Management Control, 3*, 77–98.
12. Marchi, L. (2003). *I sistemi informativi aziendali*. Milano: Giuffrè.
13. Mancini, D., Vaassen, E. H. J., & Dameri, P. R. (2013). Trends in accounting information systems. In D. Mancini, E. H. J. Vaassen, & P. R. Dameri (Eds.), *Accounting information system for decision making*. London: Springer.
14. Ferraris Franceschi, R. (2006). Elementi di criticità negli studi di economia aziendale. La sfida della ricerca qualitativa. *Rivista Italiana di Ragioneria e di Economia Aziendale, 106*, 250–258.
15. Cooper, D. J., & Morgan, W. (2008). Case study research in accounting. *Accounting Horizons, 22*, 159–178.
16. Yin, R. K. (2003). *Case study research: Design and method*. Beverly, CA: Sage Publishing.
17. Agasisti, T., & Catalano, G. (2013). Innovation in the Italian public higher education system: Introducing accrual accounting. *Public Money and Management, 33*, 92–94.
18. Catturi, G., Grossi, G., & Riccaboni, A. (2004). Evoluzione storica e prospettive della contabilità negli Atenei italiani. *Annali di Storia delle Università Italiane, 8*, 1–14.
19. Sostero, U. (1998). *Il postulato della competenza economica nel bilancio d'esercizio*. Milano: Giuffrè.
20. Cassandro, E. (1979). *Le gestioni erogatrici pubbliche*. Torino: Utet.
21. Zappa, G., & Marcantonio, A. (1954). *Ragioneria applicata alle aziende pubbliche*. Milano: Giuffrè.
22. Anselmi, L. (1995). *Il processo di trasformazione della pubblica amministrazione*. Torino: Giappichelli.
23. Pezzani, F. (2005). L'evoluzione dei sistemi di contabilità pubblica. *Azienda Pubblica, 4*, 561–565.
24. Anessi Pessina, E. (2000). *La contabilità delle aziende pubbliche*. Milano: Egea.
25. Hood, C. (1991). A public management for all seasons. *Public Administration, 69*, 3–19.

26. Hood, C. (1995). The new public management in the 1980s: Variations on a theme. *Accounting, Organizations and Society, 20*, 93–109.
27. Paulsson, G. (2006). Accrual accounting in the public sector: Experiences from the central government in Sweden. *Financial Accountability and Management, 22*, 47–62.
28. Anthony, R. N. (2000). The fatal defect in the federal accounting system. *Public Budgeting and Finance, 20*, 1–10.
29. Steccolini, I. (2004). *Accountability e sistemi informativi negli enti locali*. Torino: Giappichelli.
30. Buccoliero, L., De Nardi, F., Nasi, G., & Steccolini, I. (2005). L'implementazione della contabilità economico-patrimoniale negli enti locali italiani: I risultati di un'indagine empirica. *Azienda Pubblica, 4*, 591–614.
31. Hyndman, N., & Connolly, C. (2011). Accruals accounting in the public sector: A road not always taken. *Management Accounting Research, 22*, 36–45.
32. Barton, A. D. (2000). Accounting for public heritage facilities—Assets or liabilities of the governments? *Accounting, Auditing and Accountability Journal, 13*, 219–235.
33. Carnegie, G., & Wolnizer, P. (1999). Unravelling the rhetoric about the financial reporting of public collection as assets: A response to Micallef and Peirson. *Australian Accounting Review, 9*, 16–21.
34. Christiaens, J., & De Wielemaker, E. (2003). Financial accounting reform in Flemish universities: An empirical study of the implementation. *Financial Accountability and Management, 19*, 185–204.
35. Micallef, F., & Peirson, G. (2008). Financial reporting of cultural, heritage, scientific and community collections. *Australian Accounting Review, 7*, 31–37.
36. Garlatti, A., & Pezzani, F. (2000). *I sistemi di programmazione e controllo negli enti locali*. Milano: Etas.
37. Guthrie, J. (1998). Application of accrual accounting in the Australian public sector: Rhetoric or reality? *Financial Accountability and Management, 14*, 3–19.
38. Mautz, R. K. (1981). Financial reporting: Should government emulate business? *Journal of Accountancy, 152*, 53–60.
39. Agasisti, T., & Catalano, G. (2009). Una proposta di principi contabili per il settore universitario. In G. Catalano (Ed.), *La contabilità economico-patrimoniale nelle università-aspetti metodologici e principi contabili*. Bologna: Il Mulino.
40. Borgonovi, E. (2004). Principi contabili: Anche nell'amministrazione pubblica? *Azienda Pubblica, 2*, 173–178.
41. Baxter, J., & Chua, W. F. (2003). Alternative management accounting research: Whence and whither. *Accounting, Organization and Society, 28*, 97–126.
42. Hopwood, A. G. (1987). The archaeology of accounting systems. *Accounting, Organizations and Society, 12*, 201–234.
43. Hopwood, A. G. (1990). Accounting and the domain of the public-some observations on current developments. In J. Guthrie, L. Parker, & D. Shand (Eds.), *The public sector—Contemporary readings in accounting and auditing*. Marrickville: Harcourt Brace Jovanovich.
44. Young, J., & Preston, A. (1996). Commentaries: Are accounting researchers under the tyranny of single theory perspectives? *Accounting, Auditing and Accountability Journal, 9*, 107–111.
45. Broadbent, J., Jacobs, K., & Laughlin, R. (2001). Organizational resistance strategies to unwanted accounting and finance changes. *Accounting, Auditing and Accountability Journal, 14*, 565–586.
46. Laughlin, R. (1987). Accounting systems in organizational context: A case for critical theory. *Accounting, Organizations and Society, 12*, 479–502.
47. Lehman, C., & Tinker, T. (1987). The 'real' cultural significance of accounts. *Accounting, Organizations and Society, 12*, 503–522.
48. Tinker, A. M., Merino, B., & Neimark, M. D. (1982). The normative origins of positive theories: Ideology and accounting thought. *Accounting, Organizations and Society, 7*, 167–200.

49. Covaleski, M. A., & Dirsmith, N. W. (1988). An institutional perspective on the rise, social transformation and fall of a university budget category. *Administrative Science Quarterly, 33*, 562–587.
50. Covaleski, M. A., Dirsmith, N. W., & Samuel, S. (2003). Changes in the institutional environment and the institutions of governance: Extending the contributions of transaction cost economics within the management control literature. *Accounting, Organization and Society, 28*, 417–441.
51. Meyer, J., & Rowan, B. (1977). Institutionalized organizations: Formal structure as myth and ceremony. *American Journal of Sociology, 83*, 340–363.
52. Steccolini, I. (2009). *Cambiamento e innovazione nei sistemi contabili pubblici*. Milano: Egea.
53. Burchell, S., Clubb, C., Hopwood, A. G., Hughes, J., & Nahapiet, J. (1980). The roles of accounting in organizations and society. *Accounting, Organizations and Society, 5*, 5–27.
54. Hoopwood, A. G., & Miller, P. (Eds.). (1994). *Accounting as social and institutional practice*. Cambridge: Cambridge University Press.
55. Ogden, S. G. (1997). Accounting, Transforming frameworks of accountability: The case of water privatization. *Accounting, Organization and Society, 20*, 193–218.
56. Pinch, T., Mulkay, M., & Ashmore, M. (1989). Clinical budgeting: Experimentation in the social science: A drama in five acts. *Accounting, Organization and Society, 14*, 271–301.
57. Anessi Pessina, E., & Steccolini, I. (2007). *I sistemi contabili degli Enti locali: Stato dell'arte e prospettive di riforma*. Milano: Egea.
58. Coran, G., & Sostero, U. (2007). I sistemi contabili universitari come strumenti per il monitoraggio dell'economicità: Un'evoluzione possibile? In A. Cugini (Ed.), *La misurazione della performance negli Atenei*. Milano: Franco Angeli.
59. Salvatore, C. (2012). *Il cambiamento della governance delle Università italiane come strumento di corretto governo* (Quaderni monografici 9). Roma: Rirea.
60. Cantele, S. (2012). *Contabilità, budget e controllo economico nelle Università*. Roma: Rirea.
61. Mussari, R., & Sostero, U. (2014). Il processo di cambiamento del sistema contabile nelle università: Aspettative, difficoltà e contraddizioni. *Azienda Pubblica, 2*, 125–147.
62. Bonollo, E., Lazzini, S., & Zuccardi Merli, M. (2016). Innovations in accounting information system in the public sector. Evidences from Italian public universities. In D. Mancini, R. P. Dameri, & E. Bonollo (Eds.), *Strengthening information and control systems. The synergy between information technology and accounting models*. London: Springer.

A Performance Management System to Improve Student Success in Italian Public Universities: Conditions and Critical Factors of an IT System

Lucia Giovanelli, Federico Rotondo, and Ludovico Marinò

Abstract Didactic performance plays a central role in the survival and success of public universities especially because of the present and future effects on the public financing system of Italian universities. It also contributes to the goal of quality assurance in higher education, which is pursued by a new frame that is set by the state. The aim of this paper is to design a performance management system to improve student success. It also aims to highlight the conditions and features that an IT system should have in order to effectively serve its purpose. The level of analysis is the degree course of a department of an Italian public university, which is responsible for the organization, planning and results of didactics. Three specific moments during the student's career are considered: precollege and entrance phase, degree course duration and final phase and postcollege outcomes.

Keywords Universities • Performance management • Student success • Information system

1 Introduction and Objectives

In management literature, performance evaluation systems have been proposed as fundamental tools to improve rationality in the decision-making process as well as organizational mechanisms to align an individual behaviour to a firm objective and, consequently, to improve strategic and operational management [1].

Performance management has also been gaining momentum in the public sector. This follows new managerial paths of reform, mainly in the Western countries,

L. Giovanelli • L. Marinò
Department of Economics and Management, University of Sassari, Sassari, Italy
e-mail: giovanel@uniss.it; lmarino@uniss.it

F. Rotondo (✉)
Department of Humanities and Social Sciences, University of Sassari, Sassari, Italy
e-mail: frotondo@uniss.it

K. Corsi et al. (eds.), *Reshaping Accounting and Management Control Systems*,
Lecture Notes in Information Systems and Organisation 20,
DOI 10.1007/978-3-319-49538-5_13

which have broadened the responsibilities of public managers and have emphasized the concepts of efficiency, effectiveness and long-term economic performance [2].

In Italy, in the early 1990s, while the public sector in general was undergoing a profound reform, which was inspired by New Public Management (NPM), public universities delayed the introduction of managerial practices and tools [3]. This was most likely due to the large organization, management and accounting changes that were introduced during the 1980s (DPR 382/1980; DPR 371/1982). Such changes conditioned the acceptance of a new process of change. Consequently, the innovations that were inspired by NPM were barely implemented by Italian public universities. Furthermore, the principle of autonomy, which was established by Law no. 537/1993, was not accompanied by an adequate assumption of responsibility [4]. The public finance problems of Italy, as well as the general financial crisis, determined budget-cutting policies and a season of deep changes in the governance, organization, management and accounting of universities, started with Law no. 240/2010 [5]. Performance-based principles and reward systems in resource allocation, competitive mechanisms among public universities and a new accounting model were introduced [6].

In order to survive and succeed, Italian public universities must develop advanced information systems at all levels (central administration, departments and degree courses). This will improve decision-making qualities and, consequently, performances that are related to their activities (research, didactics, services for students and transfer of technology to the local territory). In particular, didactic performance plays a central role due to the effects it has had and will have in the future on the public financing system of universities (Decree no. 893/2014).

The aim of this paper is to design a performance management system to improve student success that is the degree of attainment within the regular duration of the degree course. It also aims to highlight the conditions and peculiarities that an IT system should have in order to effectively serve its purpose. This paper is theoretical but with an explorative nature, as the proposed system is built on a literature review and on what the Italian law requires, and is currently being tested in a bachelor's degree course of an Italian university. The level of analysis is the degree course of a department of an Italian public university, which is responsible for the organization, planning and results of didactics. The complex concept of student success [7] is investigated at three specific moments in time: the precollege and entrance phase, duration of degree course and final phase and postcollege outcomes. The rationale behind the model is that student success must be planned in advance and operationalized into concrete actions and indicators. It must also be evaluated along a student's career through a continuous monitoring system and must rely on a sound and complete IT system.

This paper is organized as follows. Section 2 presents a literature review on performance management in the public sector and in public universities. Meanwhile, Sect. 3 outlines the Italian situation, with a particular focus on the evolution of legislation on university and didactic evaluations. In Sect. 4, a performance management system that improves didactic outcomes is proposed, as well as an assessment of the characteristics that an IT system should have in order to make it properly work. Finally, Sect. 5 is devoted to discussion and conclusion.

2 Performance Management Systems in the Public Sector and in Public Universities

Over the last 25 years, performance measurement systems have been one of the main tools that have been introduced by the reforms of Western countries, following the principles of New Public Management (NPM) [8]. Since the 1980s, the attention that has been paid to the development of result-based management mechanisms has increased. This has led some scholars to label the current era as that of the "audit society" [9].

However, the accountability purpose of a performance measurement system, which is to inform citizens and funders on resource use, has often prevailed over its primary purpose of giving public managers and policy-makers timely and useful information to improve service outcome [10]. Furthermore, in the public sector, performance management, which is the concrete use of performance information in decision-making, has been barely achieved. This is due to some critical factors, which have been highlighted in literature. The first problem is that the adoption of a performance measurement system has usually been seen as a fulfilment of the law. This issue is related to the poor managerial culture, which has traditionally affected the public sector. This can be seen, for instance, by the common underestimation of developing accompanying mechanisms to enhance performance management. In fact, while major efforts have been made to collect and report data by public administrations, much more commitment is required to link long-term strategic objectives to short-term activities. Although environmental variables unavoidably have an impact on public sector performance [11], literature agrees on the fact that supportive leadership, completeness of a management cycle and organizational culture are key elements to promote performance information use [12].

Furthermore, some authors argue that the public sector's uniqueness sometimes imposes upon the success of performance management. The concept of performance itself, with reference to public services, seems to be rather controversial. On the contrary, the approach that is used to develop performance management systems in the public context has often assumed that outputs can be easily measured and counted [13] through a narrow range of indicators. This has given rise to unintended consequences [14] and, in the worst cases, to what has been defined as a "performance paradox" [15].

Additionally, since the early 1990s, public universities have been subjected to an increasing emphasis on management by objectives that are developed following a sort of goal-directed and institutional approach. They strictly adhere to an instrumental and technically rational paradigm, which leads to a lack of coupling between goals and performance indicators. Modell contrasts such an approach in his study on the development of performance measurement by the government in order to control the university sector in Sweden [16]. He highlights the need for performance measurement systems that are more tailored to objectives, targets and standards, as well as being capable of providing information to a broad range of constituencies.

Following a macro perspective, scholarly attention has mainly focused on the implementation of performance evaluations in the public sector. However, the subject of their outcome has almost never been evaluated [17]. In particular, at different stages of the reforms of public universities, several concerns regarding the potentially negative effects of performance measurement for the quality of teaching and student success have risen on an international level. In addition, the student perspective has often been disregarded by academic research on performance measurement. Actually, among the multiple perspectives under which didactic performance can be evaluated, the degree attainment within the regular duration of a university course by a student is obviously the main outcome of the didactic activity. This perspective has never been more important, considering the complex social, political and cultural issues of modern society and the current financial crisis. Furthermore, the decision level of the units that are directly involved in the organization, planning and monitoring of student careers, such as university departments and degree courses, has also been disregarded.

The construct of student success is very complex. This is because, over time, multiple definitions have been proposed, for example, considering degree attainment as the definitive measure of success [18]. Traditional measures of student success are included in the category of academic achievement, such as scores on entry exams, college grades and credits that are earned in academic years or terms. These represent progress towards a degree. Otherwise, the category of postgraduation achievement comprises graduate school admission test scores, professional school enrolment and postcollege employment rates and income. To evaluate success, student satisfaction with his/her learning experience must also be taken into account [19], as well as the plurality of outcomes that are related to the benefits for individuals and society [20].

In the array of measures of student success that are explored in literature, there is wide agreement on the multidimensional nature of the concept, as well as on the different meaning it has in relation to at least three specific moments in time. These moments are during the precollege and entrance phase, along the degree course duration and in the final and postcollege phase. Finally, some external variables that are conducive to good student outcomes, such as parental encouragement, support of friends, finances, economic trends and workforce development needs, are typically beyond the direct control of organizations [21]. Consequently, student engagement, which has a considerable impact on didactic performance as it is conducive to student success, can be greatly influenced by universities and their didactic structures [22]. In fact, decision-makers at department and degree course level can reasonably affect the behaviour of students and create fruitful institutional conditions. Student behaviours include the time and effort that students put into their studies and the interaction with faculty and peers. Meanwhile, institutional conditions include didactic resources, educational polices, programmes and structural features [7].

3 Introducing Performance Budgeting in Italian Public Universities: Lights and Shadows

Recent reforms of the Italian university sector have aimed at improving performance, which is evaluated from the double perspective of educational quality improvement and efficiency in service delivery. This is achieved through the gradual introduction of a quasi-market framework [23] and giving increased autonomy to universities [24].

In particular, since the 1990s, several acts have changed the resource allocation model from the state to universities in order to abandon an incremental financing system that is based on historical expenditure and supply.

Nevertheless, in Italy, the evolution towards performance budgeting financing models followed a rough path. In fact, the frequency and speed of the changes, which affected the ministerial parameters that were used to allocate the share of rewards of the state funding (Fondo di funzionamento ordinario or FFO) in the last 15 years, did not let universities align their behaviours to the incentives that were set by the financing system. In other words, the retroactive effects of the models led to a sort of "schizophrenia" in university and department decision-making. Initially, Law no. 537/1993 considerably increased the degree of financial autonomy of universities, giving them the possibility of managing resources from the state without a purpose bond. This promoted the transition to a lump sum budget model [25]. Furthermore, in order to remedy the situation of lack of balance, which was provoked by the use of historical expenditure as the main resource allocation principle, FFO was shared in a basic share (linked to historical expenditure) and a (even smaller) share to restore equilibrium (8 % of FFO in 1999).

In the second phase, which started with the Ministerial Decree no. 146/2004, a performance budgeting model was introduced for the first time. DM no. 146 set new criteria for the "restoring equilibrium share". This is now based on educational demand (full-time equivalent students, for 30 %), educational results (number of university credits—CFU—earned by current students, for 30 %), research results (30 %) and specific incentives (as they were not identified, this 10 % was spread on the other shares). In this phase, for the allocation of reward shares (66.6 %), didactic performance seems to prevail over research performance. This means that university competition is mainly influenced by attractiveness (number of full-time students regularly enrolled) and educational quality (CFU earned and annual number of graduated students).

The third phase started with Law no. 1/2009. From 2009 (with a retroactive effect), this established the allocation of a reward share (no less than 7 % of FFO) on the basis of two variables. These were (a) educational supply quality and educational results and (b) research quality. Under this framework, resources were allocated for 34 % and 66 %, respectively, in relation to didactic and research performance. Prior incentives were changed and competition became dramatically oriented towards research quality. With regard to didactic performance, the model was simplified, passing from the original five to two weighted indicators: A1, the number of "active" students (at least five CFU earned) shared and weighted for each category, and A2—CFU earned/CFU expected ratio (DM no. 71/2012).

Nevertheless, as soon as universities began to assimilate the model, it was changed by DM no. 893/2014, following the principles of Law no. 240/2010. It introduced a demand-driven mechanism in resource allocation. In relation to the basic share of the FFO (for about 20 %), this entered into force in 2015. However, by 2019, it is going to become the only criterion for the whole basic share of the FFO. Under the new framework, didactic performance plays a key role and is measured with just two essential indicators. These are the number of current students and the standard cost per student for each university. A current student is defined as a "student enrolled within the regular duration of the degree course" (art. 1, c. 1., DM no. 893/2014), irrespective of the number of CFU earned. Meanwhile, the standard cost is an economic measure that defines an efficiency target in service delivery. In theory, it shows how much it should cost a university to educate a student within the expected time and considering the different socio-economic and structural contexts. In brief, the product of standard cost for the number of current students, in relation to the National standard cost, determines a portion of the basic share (20 % in the FFO 2014) that is given to each university, without any consideration of qualitative didactic performance. This is in line with the basic hypothesis of quasi-market theory. This argues that the free choice of service users rewards the best performers, drives supply towards higher levels of need satisfaction, increases efficiency and improves resource allocation in the market [26].

The Law no. 240/2010 also established the introduction of an accreditation system for university departments and degree courses, based on specific indicators defined in advance by a National agency (Agenzia nazionale di valutazione del sistema universitario e della ricerca, or ANVUR). The following Decree no. 19/2012 disciplined the implementation of the system of self-evaluation, periodic evaluation and accreditation (autovalutazione, valutazione periodica e accreditamento, or AVA), started in the academic year 2012/2013. Table 1 summarizes all the different laws and reforms about the financial system and the overall evaluation criteria set for public universities.

The new financing model has strongly impacted universities, as it tends to reward those with a high number of current students and penalize those with a low level of attractiveness. Otherwise, the propensity to increase the number of enrolled students seems to depend not only on service quality but also on context variables, which remarkably affect the demand characteristics. Thus, the hypothesis that the choice of users rewards the best producers is mostly unrealistic. This is because information asymmetry and other factors that influence demand should be considered. The choice of a certain university, for instance, is largely conditioned by context variables such as quality of life and services of the city in which the university is located, rather than income, logistical reasons and prestige. The evaluation of didactic quality shows the traditional ambiguity of relational services. Evidently, the number of enrolled—or graduated—students, the number of CFU earned or that of out-of-course students (those who have not completed the degree course within its regular duration) may also depend on the ease of graduating in

Table 1 Reforms, laws and interventions in the Italian public universities

Act	Topic
Law no. 537, 24 December 1993	Financial autonomy of public universities
Ministerial Decree no. 146, 28 July 2004	New evaluation model (and financing system) for public universities
Law no. 1, 9 January 2009	Merit and quality of research activity and university system
Law no. 240, 30 December 2010	Organization and recruitment in public universities, quality and efficiency of the university system
Legislative Decree no. 19, 27 January 2012	Efficiency, reward system and accreditation system of public universities
Ministerial Decree no. 71, 16 April 2012	State funding (FFO) allocation for 2012
Ministerial Decree no. 827, 15 October 2013	Triennial planning of public universities 2013–2015
Ministerial Decree no. 104, 14 February 2014	Indicators and parameters for university monitoring and evaluation 2013–2015
Ministerial Decree no. 893, 9 December 2014	Standard cost for current students
Ministerial Decree no. 335, 8 June 2015	State funding (FFO) allocation for 2015

countries where the educational qualification has the same legal force. Parameters that are used by the financing system drive the behaviour of service deliverers. This is because they naturally try to draw as many resources as possible, sometimes creating distortive effects on service quality or incentives to overproduction. On the other hand, it is certainly simpler to achieve a better performance in a favourable environment and vice versa. Demand quality in the entrance phase, which is related to socio-economic factors, also has an impact on didactic performance.

Financing mechanisms that are based on rewards tend to increase the gap between the best performers, which will gather extra resources, and the worst performer, whose funds will be progressively cut. Although this is an intended consequence of such a competitive model, in cases where a university is strongly affected by territoriality or socio-economic handicaps, resource cut increases unfairness between universities.

4 A Performance Management System to Improve Didactic Performance of a Bachelor Degree Course

A bachelor degree course, which usually lasts three academic years in Italian universities, is considered. The rationales behind the model are that the improvement of didactic performance in an organization derives from student success [7] and that the latter should be planned in advance and explained in terms of strategic goals and operational results, which are measured by appropriate indicators. In addition, specific actors must be appointed as responsible for achieving such goals through a set of actions that are taken at scheduled times. During the whole educational cycle, a continuous monitoring of student activities, as well as a report that relies on an information system that includes all of the useful performance information, should be developed. For this purpose, a performance management system is a powerful tool that can be used to increase rationality in decision-making at a degree course level.

The functioning and effectiveness of such a system are strongly related to the characteristics of the information system. The operational complexity of an organization and the multitude of information that is gathered from the outside to depict the context in which the educational offer will be delivered need advanced systems of data storage and integration. In fact, a balanced planning and control system [27], including a plurality of objectives for each phase of the didactic path (precollege and entrance phase, degree course duration and entrance in the job world), must rely on a double-purpose information system. Not only should it be useful to collect and archive internal and external data, but also, it should select and aggregate the data to inform decisions [28]. It can be defined as a "strategic intelligence system" that is able to continuously store data, regardless of the time of the decision-making [29, 30].

After defining the strategic goals, they must be translated into strategic and operational actions that are to be entrusted to a specific responsible actor and performed within a scheduled time. The responsible actor, scheduled time, actors involved and indicators to be reported and evaluated must be clearly defined for each operational phase (Table 2).

For example, in the following section, a mapping of strategic goals, actions and indicators of student success for each key phase of a university student's career is shown. The law that is related to each indicator (reference), as well as its impact (low–medium–high) on the financing system of universities, is also shown.

4.1 Phase A: The Precollege Phase and Entrance to Academic Year "t"

The central purpose of this phase is to protect a student's interest and support him/her in making the right choice. In this regards, the actions to be taken should not be oriented towards increasing attraction rate (more enrolled students in a certain degree course). Instead, they should be oriented towards enrolling students who are really motivated to that specific course and have the right basic skills.

During this phase, a wrong degree choice compromises a student's whole educational path and often leads to student failure. It is also the main reason for the presence of "accidental students" that express an improper demand. In turn, this

Table 2 The information system to monitor and evaluate didactic performance

Phases	Strategic goals	Indicators	Operational objectives	Strategic/ operational action	For each action					Standard parameter	Relationship with the financing system
					Actor responsible	Time	Actors involved	Indicator	Expected result		
Phase A				1							
Phase B				1.1							
				1.2							
				2.							
...				...							

significantly worsens a degree course's performance, as it negatively impacts on abandonment rates and inactive students.

The information system supports decision-making by giving useful information about the context in order to frame the potential characteristics of students and prefigure enrolment policies that foster their future performance. The collection of such external data is crucial. This can be done through simple questionnaires that are submitted during student orientation programmes. They should permit a full mapping of the student in terms of educational provenience, place of residence, part-time or full-time status, score average, attitude and so on.

Strategic Goals

1. Attracting high-quality and motivated students
2. Enhancing the consistency between enrolment alternatives and student status (part time or full time)
3. Improving the quality of students entering university (Table 3)

Some strategic actions that need to be taken in order to achieve the strategic goals are shown below. Such actions, in turn, are translated into operational actions that specific actors must take in due times. These are measured through a set of indicators (for space reasons operational actions are not reported). Indicators that are used at this moment do not have a direct impact on financing. Nonetheless, attracting high-quality and motivated students consequently leads to good results along all of student careers, thus increasing the number of graduated students and their entrance into the work force.

Strategic Action 1
Orientation policies and programmes for the entrance phase, in collaboration with high schools of selected territories, which are aimed at attracting motivated and skilled students for a certain degree course.

Strategic Action 2
Communication plan of the degree course.

Table 3 Indicators for strategic reporting and evaluation

Code	Indicator	Measurement	Impact on the financing system
A1	High-quality students rate	Enrolled students with high school final score >90/Total enrolled students ratio	Low
A2	High-quality students rate	Students passing mathematics entrance exam/ Total enrolled students ratio	Low
A3	High-quality students rate	Students passing Italian entrance exam/Total enrolled students ratio	Low
A4	Working students rate	Students enrolled as part-time students/Total enrolled students ratio	Medium
A5	Improving entrance quality rate	Students recovering from entrance exam failure (mathematics or Italian) before degree course beginning/Students who failed entrance exam	Low

4.2 Phase B: The Educational Path (Duration of the Degree Course)

4.2.1 Phase B.1: The First Year of the Degree Course

The first year is probably the most delicate phase of a student's career, as he/she has to get used to a new way of living and studying. During this phase, student behaviour must be monitored and continuously supported, especially in the case of problems. Above all, during the first months of the first year, a student may feel confused or just realize that he/she has made the wrong choice of degree course or university studies. In the worst case, he/she may decide to leave university.

For this reason, it is essential to guide and go after him/her, to understand his/her problems and help him/her to cope with them. Expected results include a reduction in the abandonment rate between first and second year and an increase in the average number of university credits that are earned by a student.

Strategic Goals

1. Increasing the rate of enrolment to second year (equal to reducing the abandonment rate)
2. Increasing the number of university credits that are earned in relation to expected credits (those shown in the degree course plan)
3. Increasing the average number of university credits that are earned by a student (Table 4)

Strategic Action 1
Monitoring freshmen career and evaluating the critical factors at the end of terms.

Strategic Action 2
Reviewing teaching programmes and coordinating professors and lecturers.

4.2.2 Phase B.2: The Second and Third Year of the Degree Course

During this phase, it is important for decision-makers to be informed about the study delay of the students who enrolled 1 and 2 years before. A critical factor of an information system is the timeliness in taking note of passed exams, which can be fostered by leaving the hardcopy archive in favour of online systems. Data stored in this way should be promptly made available by the information system for reporting selected indicators in order to evaluate a student's career and take specific action to remove any hindrances.

Strategic Goals

1. Increasing the average number of university credits that are earned by a second- and third-year student
2. Increasing the monitoring activity of teachings

Table 4 Indicators for strategic reporting and evaluation

Code	Indicator	Measurement	Impact on the financing system
B1.1	Study continuation and abandonment rate	Students enrolled to the second year of the same degree course/Students enrolled in the previous year $\times 100$	High
B1.2	Student productivity rate	Number of students enrolled to the second year of the same degree course with at least 40 CFU/Students enrolled in the previous year ratio[a]	High
B1.3	Student productivity rate	Number of students enrolled to the second year of the same degree course with at least 12 CFU/Students enrolled in the previous year ratio[b]	High
B1.4	Inactivity rate	Number of students earning no CFU in the first year/Students enrolled in the first year ratio[c]	High

[a]This coincides with the 1.Ia.1 indicator of the Ministerial Decree on triennial planning 2013–2015 (DD.MM. no. 827/2013 and 104/2014). The last Ministerial Decree on resource allocation (FFO) for 2015 (D.M. no. 335/2015) establishes the new limit of 20 CFU that are earned in 2014 by students that enrolled in the academic year 2013/2014
[b]This coincides with the 1.Ia.2 indicator of the Ministerial Decree on triennial planning 2013–2015 (DD.MM. no. 827/2013 and 104/2014)
[c]This indicator previously contributed to the weighting factor that was used to allocate the share of FFO related to didactic among Italian universities

Table 5 Indicators for strategic reporting and evaluation

Code	Indicator	Measurement	Impact on the financing system
B2.1	Rate of student productivity	Variation of university credits that are earned on average by a student, compared to the previous year	High
B2.2	Rate of monitored teachings	Number of teachings evaluated by students/Total number of teachings	Low
B2.3	Student satisfaction rate	Satisfaction level about teachings compared to standard parameters	Low
B2.4	Rate of internationality	Number of enrolled students who took part in mobility programmes/Total enrolled students[a]	Medium

[a]With reference to the Ministerial Decree on triennial planning 2013–2015 (DD.MM. no. 827/2013 and 104/2014) the indicator 1IIe.2 is "number of students going abroad in mobility"

3. Promoting participation in international exchange and mobility programmes
4. Increasing the number of internships (Table 5)

Strategic Action 1
Monitoring student careers and also making evaluations term by term in order to promote participation in international mobility programmes.

Table 6 Indicators for strategic reporting and evaluation

Code	Indicator	Measurement	Impact on the financing system
B3.1	Rate of graduates in due time	Annual percentage of graduates in the expected time	Medium
B3.2	Student satisfaction rate	Satisfaction level of students who are about to graduate	Low

4.2.3 Phase B.3: The Second Term of the Third Year of the Degree Course

In the second term of the third year, students must be oriented towards the successful completion of their degree courses (acquisition of all university credits and graduation in due time).

Strategic Goals

1. Increasing the annual percentage of graduates in due time
2. Increasing the satisfaction level of students who are about to graduate (Table 6)

Strategic Action 1
Monitoring students to enhance the frequency and outcome of remaining exams and assigning degree thesis with a didactic weight that corresponds to the university credits that are set for the degree course.

4.3 Phase C: Post-degree Phase and Entrance into the Job World

After graduating students must be supported in their choice of the next best path. It is important to encourage the best students to continue their study with a master's degree or a first-level master. However, attention has also got to be paid to help a student choose the best way in relation to his/her own needs and peculiarities. Otherwise, those who decide to not continue the studies should be oriented towards a post-degree internship experience in order to promote their entrance into the work force.

In this phase, the information system must include a multitude of external data on the labour market. The main critical factor is the cost of gathering such information. This can be effectively reduced by taking operational actions that are aimed at involving the firms and companies of the territory.

Strategic Goals

1. Increasing the annual percentage of graduates with a post-degree internship

Table 7 Indicators for strategic reporting and evaluation

Code	Indicator	Measurement	Impact on the financing system
C1	Internship rate	Number of graduates with a post-degree internship, within a year from their degree/ Total graduates in the same year ratio	Low
C2	Employment rate within a year	Number of graduates employed within a year from their degree/Total graduates in the same year ratio[a]	Medium
C3	Employment rate within 3 years	Number of graduates employed within 3 years from their degree/Total graduates in the same year ratio	Low
C4	Internal master's degree attraction rate	Number of graduates enrolling in a master's degree of the same department/Total graduates in the same year ratio[b]	High
C5	External master's degree attraction rate	Number of graduates enrolling in a master's degree of another department or university/ Total graduates in the same year ratio[c]	High

[a]This coincides with the A4 indicator of the Ministerial Decree on triennial planning
[b]It is important to distinguish between internal and external master's degrees
[c]This is a rate of student departure

2. Increasing the percentage of graduates who find a job within a year from their degree (Table 7)

Strategic Action 1
Updating data and linking graduate registry to the business world.

Strategic Action 2
Organizing events aimed at promoting demand–supply matching and training students to enter into the work force.

The balanced set of the above-mentioned indicators is useful to express, control and evaluate the achievement of didactic performance objectives. In summary, two simple indicators can show the performance improvement of a didactic structure. The rate of graduates in due time (number of graduates of an academic year/total enrolled students of 2 years before ratio) expresses the output of the educational process. It is also a measure of efficiency and internal effectiveness. This is because it accounts for the ability of a didactic organization to graduate students within the time expected for a degree course. On the other hand, the student employment rate within 1 and 3 years from their degree is an extraordinary measure of external effectiveness of the degree course. This is because it expresses the real outcome of the educational process.

5 Conclusion

For university management, the development of advanced information systems to cope with the increased competition and progressive lack of resources is challenging. Competing and succeeding in such a complex environment seems to be related to the improvement of the decision-making quality, followed by performances that are related to university activity. Since the 1990s, several reforms have changed the resource allocation model from the state to universities in order to abandon a financing system based on historical expenditure and supply, in favour of reward systems, which are based on didactic and research performance. Following Law no. 240/2010, the recent DM no. 893/2014 introduced a demand-driven mechanism in resource allocation. In particular, didactic performance is extremely important due to the effects it has on the public financing system of universities and the goal of quality assurance in higher education that are set by the state.

Starting with the complex concept of student success, this paper was aimed to design a performance management system to improve didactic performance. It also aimed to highlight the conditions and peculiarities that a university IT system must have in order to be effective. Considering the key role it has on didactic organization, planning and outcomes, the degree course was viewed as a privileged decision-making level. Meanwhile, a bachelor's degree course was chosen as the time interval over which the system is to be implemented. In fact, degree course policy can reasonably affect the behaviour of students and create fruitful institutional conditions to foster student engagement. Furthermore, the multidimensional nature of didactic success led to the identification of three specific moments of a student's career to be separately evaluated: precollege and entrance phase, degree course duration and final phase and postcollege outcomes.

For each moment in time, a set of strategic goals, which are then translated into strategic and operational actions and finally measured by performance indicators, were identified. Responsible and involved actors, as well as the scheduled times, were also identified. The rationales behind the model are that improving didactic performance derives from student success and that this can be rationally planned in advance and explained in terms of strategic goals, operational results and indicators. A key point of this study is the importance of a sound and complete IT system. The multitude of internal and external information that needs to be gathered to monitor a student's career along its different phases requires advanced systems of data storage and integration. The possibility of selecting and aggregating archived data to inform decisions at the right time marks the evolution towards a "strategic intelligence system". This is a significant difference for university didactic performance. The proposed system is currently being tested in a bachelor's degree course of a department of an Italian university. Future research avenues are related to the results of the biennial test and include the refinement of the model and its extension to other degree courses.

References

1. Flamholtz, G. E. (1996). *Effective management control: Theory and practice.* Boston, MA: Kluwer Academic Publishers.
2. Pollitt, C., & Bouckaert, G. (2002). In E. Ongaro (Ed.), *La Riforma del Management Pubblico.* Milan: Egea.
3. Busetti, S., & Dente, B. (2014). Focus on the finger, overlook the Moon: The introduction of performance management in the administration of Italian universities. *Journal of Higher Education Policy and Management, 36*(2), 225–237.
4. Palumbo, R. (1999). *L'Università nella sua Dimensione Economico-Aziendale.* Turin: Giappichelli.
5. Agasisti, T., & Catalano, G. (2013). Debate: Innovation in the Italian public higher education system: Introducing accrual accounting. *Public Money and Management, 33*(2), 92–94.
6. Giovanelli, L., Rotondo, F., & Caffù, S. (2014). *Implementing accrual accounting in Italian universities: Critical aspects of an information system.* Paper presented at XI itAIS Conference, Genoa.
7. Kuh, G. D., Kinzie, J., Buckley, J. A., Bridges, B. K., & Hayek, J. C. (2006). *What matters to student success: A review of the literature.* Commissioned Report for the National Symposium on Postsecondary Student Success: Spearheading a Dialog on Student Success.
8. Walsh, K. (1995). *Public services and market mechanisms. Competition, contracting and the new public management.* London: MacMillan Press.
9. Power, M. (2000). The audit society-second thoughts. *International Journal of Auditing, 4,* 111–119.
10. Hatry, H. P. (2002). Performance measurement: Fashions and fallacies. *Public Performance and Management Review, 25,* 352–358.
11. Andrews, R., Boyne, G. A., & Enticott, G. (2006). Performance failure in the public sector. *Public Management Review, 8,* 273–296.
12. Dull, M. (2009). Results-model reform leadership: Questions of credible commitment. *Journal of Public Administration Research and Theory, 19,* 255–284.
13. Broadbent, J. (2007). If you can't measure it, how can you manage it? Management and governance in higher educational institutions. *Public Money and Management, 27,* 193–198.
14. Heath, G., & Radcliffe, J. (2007). Performance measurement and the english ambulance service. *Public Money and Management, 27,* 223–228.
15. Van Thiel, S., & Leeuw, F. L. (2002). The performance paradox in the public sector. *Public Performance and Management Review, 25*(3), 267–281.
16. Modell, S. (2003). Goals versus institutions: The development of performance measurement in the Swedish university sector. *Management Accounting Research, 14,* 333–359.
17. Andersen, S. C. (2008). The impact of public management reforms on student performance in Danish schools. *Public Administration, 86,* 541–558.
18. Venezia, A., Callan, P. M., Finney, J. E., Kirst, M. W., & Usdan, M. D. (2005). *The governance divide: A report on a four-state study on improving college readiness and success.* San Jose, CA: The Institute for Educational Leadership, the National Center for Public Policy and Higher Education, and the Stanford Institute for Higher Education Research.
19. Strauss, L. C., & Volkwein, J. F. (2002). Comparing student performance and growth in 2- and 4-year institutions. *Research in Higher Education, 43*(2), 133–161.
20. Pascarella, E. T., & Terenzini, P. T. (2005). *How college affects students: A third decade of research.* San Francisco, CA: Jossey-Bass.
21. Pascarella, E. T., Pierson, C. T., Wolniak, G. C., & Terenzini, P. T. (2004). First generation college students: Additional evidence on college experiences and outcomes. *The Journal of Higher Education, 75*(3), 249–284.
22. Pike, G. R., & Kuh, G. D. (2005). A typology of student engagement for American colleges and universities. *Research in Higher Education, 46*(2), 185–209.
23. Le Grand, J. (1991). Quasi-markets and social policy. *The Economic Journal, 101,* 1256–1267.

24. Maran, L. (2009). *Economia e Management dell'Università. La Governance Interna tra Efficienza e Legittimazione*. Milan: Franco Angeli.
25. Agasisti, T., & Catalano, G. (2006). Il Finanziamento Pubblico delle Università Con Modelli Formula-Based: Aspetti Metodologici ed Esperienze Applicative in Alcuni Paesi Europei. In G. Brosio & G. Muraro (Eds.), *Il Finanziamento del Settore Pubblico*. Milan: Franco Angeli.
26. Le Grand, J. (2011). Quasi-market versus state provision of public service: Some ethical considerations. *Public Reason, 3*(2), 80–89.
27. Kaplan, R. S., & Norton, D. P. (1992, January–February). The balanced scorecard: Measures that drive performance. *Harvard Business Review*, 71–79.
28. Culasso, F. (2004). *Information Technology e Controllo di Strategico*. Milan: Giuffrè.
29. Marchi, L., & Mancini, D. (2009). *Gestione Informatica dei Dati Aziendali*. Milan: Franco Angeli.
30. Galeotti, M. (2009). Strategic Intelligence: il Sistema delle Informazioni e delle Analisi per la Gestione Strategica. Paper presented at the Conference: "Predictive Enterprise". *Rome.*

Intelligent Systems in Health Care: A Socio-Technical View

Andreea-Roxanna Obreja, Penny Ross, and Peter Bednar

Abstract This chapter reflects on the relationship between various stakeholders in the health-care industry and intelligent medical systems. It takes into consideration the potential impact that intelligent systems have on health care. The aim of the chapter is to emphasise a set of decisive factors for the successful deployment of intelligent systems in health care including the individual needs of patients and medical staff. The motivation for this study was the publicity and investment that intelligent agents like Watson have benefitted from since the outset of their trial deployments in health-care organisations, which have preceded doctors' feedback. In this chapter, we discuss some incentives to use intelligent medical systems and the ethical considerations. Potential roles of intelligent systems in health care are explored from a socio-technical perspective. Additionally, potential decision-makers and their responsibilities in assessing the medical personnel's attitude towards the intelligent systems before their final deployment are discussed. The conclusion outlines limitations of both human clinicians and intelligent agents and how they can work together to overcome them.

Keywords Intelligent systems • Socio-technical analysis • Systems practice • Organisational change • Work-related learning • Intelligent agents • Health-care systems

1 Introduction

Expert medical systems have been around for decades. One of the first examples is MYCIN, developed by Shortlife in 1976 at Stanford University, representing the first research effort able to solve complex real-world problems and provide clinical assistance [1]. The recent advances in Artificial Intelligence have brought about a new generation of expert systems, empowered with cognitive capabilities such as

A.-R. Obreja (✉) • P. Ross • P. Bednar
School of Computing, University of Portsmouth, Portsmouth, UK

Department of Informatics, Lund University, Lund, Sweden
e-mail: andreea-roxana.obreja@port.ac.uk; penny.ross@port.ac.uk; peter.bednar@port.ac.uk

© Springer International Publishing AG 2017
K. Corsi et al. (eds.), *Reshaping Accounting and Management Control Systems*,
Lecture Notes in Information Systems and Organisation 20,
DOI 10.1007/978-3-319-49538-5_14

machine learning, reasoning and decision-making. They include off-the-shelf applications such as IBM's Watson, HP's Autonomy and Palantir but also their precursors, a set of in-house-built intelligent decision support systems using scorecards and dashboards to improve clinical outcomes.

Principles of Soft Systems Thinking, ETHICS and AIM have been used for the purpose of the analysis of human–computer interaction in this chapter which include analysing the health-care industry from a systemic point of view and focusing on the people system rather than the IS technology they use to do their jobs ([2], pp. 18–19; [3], pp. 3–5). To avoid confusion between the notion of system in IT (sum of technology and applications) and the one in Systems Thinking (people and technology), intelligent systems such as Watson will be referred to as intelligent agents. A clinical decision support system (CDSS) incorporates established clinical knowledge which is constantly updated with patient information in order to improve the patient care standards and includes a knowledge base software to integrate patient information with the knowledge base and a user interface for the clinician to interact with the system. The intelligent agent is a large-scale CDSS which is intended to deal with expert knowledge only and is able to process both structured and unstructured data ([4], p. 5; [5], p. 504).

Research   The initial aim of the chapter was to outline the considerations that various decision-makers have been taken into account and others that have been ignored before allocating resources for the implementation of intelligent medical agents. Given the limited academic works specifically targeting intelligent agents and the lack of feedback available from medical staff who have used them in real-world practice to comment on their effectiveness, the scope of the chapter was amended to a balanced account of the consequences of adopting intelligent agents in health-care organisations affecting the medical staff's day-to-day job. The pre-adoption considerations advised in this chapter are based on the previous deployments of CDSS as outlined in academic publications, the initial feedback of users who participated in testing the intelligent agents at work and case studies with advertising character sponsored by intelligent agents' software vendors. Caution needs to be employed in using results from these case studies by constantly comparing the outcomes they present with academic conclusions based on the adoption of CDSS.

The motivation of the authors was the publicity and investment that intelligent agents like Watson have benefitted from since the beginning of their trial deployments in health-care organisations. The feedback that has surfaced so far seems more concerned with the potential technical capabilities of these agents rather than the impression they have made on clinical personnel [6]. This chapter does not present itself as a comprehensive review of all the consequences associated with the adoption of intelligent agents. This chapter researches the stakeholders with decisional powers in the adoption process and their involvement in a technology-assisted medical process. It also aims to outline some examples that should be considered before the final deployment of intelligent agents in order to ensure a smooth integration of the technology in the daily jobs of both doctors and administrative staff in health care.

Thus, this chapter is structured as follows. The first section sets up the context used to briefly review intelligent medical agents from a socio-technical point of view. The second section provides a brief account of how expert systems have evolved into intelligent agents. The third section introduces a systemic view of the health-care industry and starts analysing the people system around it by considering the administrative decision-makers. The stakeholders' views are discussed in Sect. 4. In Sect. 5, the ethical aspects are reflected upon. Finally, conclusive remarks are presented in Sect. 6.

2   Considering Intelligent Systems

An expert system is defined as "a piece of software which uses databases of expert knowledge to offer advice or make decisions in areas such as medical diagnosis" (Oxford Dictionary). There are two key aspects connected to the technology behind expert systems: they are built to simulate the judgement and cognitive processes of the human brain and they are processing expert knowledge and experience from a particular field ([7], pp. 4–12). Both these aspects point to the human element's decisive role in creating the expert system: the data that is fed into the system, regardless of whether it is development data or the knowledge that medical staff has gathered over the years.

The technology behind expert medical systems was first pioneered in the early 1960s using programs that performed statistical analysis. The Dendral (1961) project and the software it produced represents the first use of Artificial Intelligence in biomedical research and was developed by Joshua Lederberg (geneticist) and chemistry professor Carl Djerassi. The 1970s brought a wave of IT systems performing diagnoses and making therapy recommendations which included PIP, CASNET, INTERNIST, CADUCEUS and PUFF [1].

Liebowitz ([8], pp. 32-1, 32-2) predicted that the stand-alone systems named above would evolve into fully integrated information systems that would also connect to hospital database systems and medical devices (e.g. EMRs, ECG and EEG, CT and MRI). The predicted evolution started to materialise after 2010 through advanced systems employing technologies such as machine learning, natural language processing and speech recognition brought about by the advances in Artificial Intelligence. Examples of systems already on the market and adopted by medical bodies include IBM Watson, HP Autonomy and Palantir. The recent support that expert medical systems have received both from technology companies and medical bodies is partly justified by the increased use of technology in health care and diverse stakeholder demands.

Health care has recently been under scrutiny after a series of failures to achieve its targets ([9], pp. 1–4), both at a scalable level (deadlines, budget, patient waiting time) and at a less quantifiable one—"quality of care".

In their attempt to become value-based organisations, medical bodies are struggling to maximise their services' value, achieving best outcomes at lowest costs, and at the same time working towards patient-centred systems organised to meet their patients' needs [10]. Patients start being seen as customers and technology as a catalyst to improve their satisfaction with the service they receive. In an environment with a decreasing number of experts and increased demands and pressure, expert medical systems are often seen as strong arguments in favour of a technology-assisted health care.

The promoted advances in cognitive computing and artificial intelligence together with the pressure put on human capabilities have paved the way for what has been advertised by software providers as more cost and time effective and accurate technical solutions. The predicted benefits of intelligent agents such as Watson (e.g. immense memory space, processing of unstructured data) recommended them as viable candidates [4]. However, their technical development has tended to bypass or avoid an analysis concerned with what their role in medical care should be and whether medical staff actually needs the assistance of intelligent agents. The possible roles discussed in this chapter are replacement of the human doctor, guarantor of diagnostic accuracy or human dependent repository of data [11].

3 Impacted Parties

Health-care delivery is a highly complex environment and consists of numerous loosely connected and independent systems and subsystems which make it difficult to assess its overall business value on one side and quantifiable clinical outcomes on the other ([12], pp. 1–7).

Health care and Hospitals as Socio-Technical Systems The health-care industry and hospitals can both be seen and analysed as socio-technical systems, a heterogeneous ensemble of people, technology and legacy practices that are expected to work together for the benefit of the patient without neglecting the notion of work satisfaction for the medical personnel. Employing systemic thinking techniques can facilitate a differentiation between the system as a whole and the sum of its parts ([2], pp. 18–19).

When looking at the health-care system as a whole, the ensemble is made of inputs (patient queries), internal processes (medical interventions) and outputs (patient treatments and work satisfaction). An intelligent agent can be designed to store data inputs in one place, process them and ensure a smooth data flow through the internal processes regardless of whether they are tests performed by care staff or administrative reports for health-care management.

A comprehensive intelligent agent might face a number of challenges before ensuring a smooth transition of data across various departments and stakeholders. First of all, different stakeholders have completely different priorities.

Administrative staff and management team's jobs focus on budgets, feasibility strategy and resource allocation. The IT department's main responsibility is a viable IT strategy, security risks, upgrades and maintenance. Doctors and nurses need to think about time management, patients' care and effectiveness of treatments and also job satisfaction and work–family balance. They might have developed their own work routine and repository of data without necessarily following the policies put in place by administrative staff and the IT department. At the same time, they might need other stakeholders' permission to perform certain tests or prescribe certain treatments and definitely depend on their resource allocation. The interaction between medical personnel and their professional areas brings with it more complexity. While more tests and procedures contribute towards increased diagnostic accuracy for doctors, they increase an already strained budget and put more pressure on the administrative staff ([13], pp. 85–86; [14]). In an industry where technical skills are not distributed evenly across generations, there will always be a two-way training. Introducing an intelligent agent might put additional strain on the younger, technology-savvy generation who might feel responsible for teaching the older one how to use it [15]. However, the older generation includes the real-world experts, clinicians with many years of real-world practice who will need to teach the younger generation to develop their intuition and know when to question the intelligent agent's judgement. Another issue of this industry is the technology gap between the IT departments and medical personnel. Dr. Atul Gawande, a Harvard University surgeon, summarised this issue by explaining that "part of the bafflement occurs because the folks who know how to make such systems (i.e. intelligent agents) don't understand how the clinical encounter actually operates" [16].

To make the challenges even more complex, the health-care system is part of a constantly changing environment made up of government, regulatory bodies, technology companies, medical insurance companies and, more importantly, prospective patients. Although a clear definition and delimitation is envisaged, the system can only be analysed as part of the environment, being characterised by connectivity and a high degree of influence for external factors ([2], p. 20). In state-funded health care, the government is the main investor and the patients do not have the advantages of a competitive market.

Administrative Decision-Makers   The health-care business sector provides a hint of how the idea of profit can influence the role of technology in health care. The money flow and assumed financial motivation of using intelligent agents in health care is beyond the focus of this chapter. What remains within focus is the interaction between intelligent medical agents, management and IT support staff in health care, whose concerns include resource allocation, reporting and performance both for people and technology.

The health-care managements' motivation to support the use of intelligent agents is mentioned by Shortliffe (1979) cited by Liebowitz ([8], pp. 32-1, 32-2), who argues that an expert system should only be used if it improves the standard of quality of care at a justifiable cost in time or money or if it maintains the same level of quality by saving time or money.

Some of the technical information that appeals to political decision-makers and managers includes the following: IBM Watson is considered the first system to understand questions posed in natural language and research the entire body of medical knowledge and patient records to create a diagnosis plan in 3 s ([17], pp. 1050–1054). HP IDOL is described as recognising concepts, patterns and ideas in unstructured natural language descriptions delivering a significant impact on the productivity and efficiency of health-care professionals at the point of care. It is intended to contribute towards informing strategic decision-making, as an early warning system, or as a system to benchmark drug deployment, yielding rapid results [18]. Apart from the ability to search and interpret vast amounts of data which is virtually impossible for a human doctor, medical intelligent agents have been described as having a better diagnosis precision when it comes to known cases. IBM claims that Watson's successful diagnosis rate for lung cancer is 90 % as opposed to only 50 % for human doctors [19]. Another element that supports the use of expert systems is connectivity and integration. While previous systems such as MYCIN were operating in isolation, contemporary expert systems are being developed with the intention to be able to interact with medical equipment such as EMRs and HIS, contributing towards improvements in the quality of care and more efficient resource management ([17], pp. 1053–1059). However, there is a danger that in many cases systems might be looked upon as a silver bullet. By reducing the exploration of possible leads and replacing them with a more certain path in assigning a diagnostic, it is seen to have the potential to address the medical personnel shortage and also support financial savings [20]. This is in line with what many decision-makers strapped for staff want to hear. However, the majority of these benefits resulted from various simulations and testing activities conducted by potential software vendors in collaboration with medical institutions that have a rich expertise of technical solutions such as the Memorial Sloan Kettering Cancer Center. One of the arguments supporting this statement is the vast gap between the theoretical benefits predicted and the real-world outcomes for digitised records systems in the UK ([21], pp. 92–107). The interoperability advertised by developers must also be regarded with caution. First of all, multiple data formatting might lead to brand loyalty issues and eventually the question of market monopolisation by certain vendors. Secondly, not all medical institutions start from the same level of technology adoption. While some might have successfully implemented electronic record systems, others are still operating with paper-based ones. They support mutual learning and knowledge sharing and coordination and might not be simply replaceable by their electronic counterparts ([15], pp. 79–83; [21], pp. 105–107).

The evolution of expert information systems in general has been shaped by the advances in technology. When Watson developers first decided that health care could benefit from its capabilities, they looked at the masses of unstructured data resulting from care processes but not necessarily at how people working with that data make sense of it [22]. Doctors did not say "we need help in trying to memorise millions of medical journals" but rather factors such as misdiagnosis rate, shortage of staff or failure to achieve waiting-time targets signalled opportunities for improvement [4, 23]. This means that there may be significant mismatch between problem solution and expected outcomes.

The medical and IT professionals share a vital responsibility: the data that the intelligent agent will learn and the format they will use to redistribute the information between people and technology. Specialists with wide practical expertise tend to develop their own "language", jargon and internal collaborative code of practice (20]; [24; [25], pp. 2–3; [26]). The health-care industry is characterised by a certain level of discipline, a specific way of managing conflicting statements and an arbitrary level of detail. Barley et al. refer to the abstract models of work used in analysing a system as representations of provisional theories which might or might not capture the essence of people's activity [15]. The interpretation required to load and unload data into an intelligent agent will cause further contextual difficulties. Overcoming those contextual difficulties can ultimately dictate the efficiency of the agent ([21], p. 105 [5]).

Around 75 % of medical students and junior doctors in the UK own a smartphone and occasionally use 1–5 medical applications ([27], p. 121), but the percentage is significantly lower with more senior care providers. Before being able to use an intelligent system, medical professionals will need training and technical support which will make an IT support team an absolute necessity with a guaranteed budget share [22]. This is an investment in organisational change and requires significant resources to be successful.

The use of intelligent agents is yet to be widely spread in practice, and their real benefits and limitations are still to be identified. However, some medical institutions have pioneered their use and claimed expected benefits from informative results. A preliminary announcement from the partnership between IBM's Watson Group and Cleveland Clinic, Ohio, claimed that researchers at the clinic will use IBM's Watson Genomics Analytics to enhance the use of personalised medicine based on the patient's DNA. While doctors don't have the time or the tools to explore specific treatment alternatives for individual patients based on their unique genetic configuration, Watson is said to be able to solve this problem [28]. On the same note, Watson has already ingested all 23 million medical papers in the National Library of Medicine (MEDLINE) and can access that data in milliseconds [29].

When Watson's developers first envisaged to target the health-care industry, they regarded the patient's case as a problem scenario. The need they identified was patients and caregivers are overwhelmed with "hoards" of unstructured, ever-changing data. The initial aim of the technology they created was to provide resources needed to rationalise important medical decisions [30]. Testing showed promising results in areas such as drug prescription, drug-to-drug interaction and drug-associated complications ([4], pp. 5–10). When moving to less predictable areas, it is vital to ensure that the intelligent agent is able to cope with clinicians not following all its instructions and support them along the path dictated by their practical expertise rather than predetermined, ideal scenarios.

As senior decision-makers, the investors (private/government) and health-care management personnel carry responsibility in assigning one of the following roles to an intelligent medical agent: replacement of human doctor, guarantor of diagnostic accuracy, human dependent repository of data or support for human doctor's decision-making practices.

4 Consequences of Intelligent Agents' Implementation in Health-care Organisations

The Demand Improved living standards and advances in technology have made people more demanding over the years [20]. They want to be healthier and they want to live longer. If they get sick, they want to know the cause after being investigated for as little time as possible and to be given a quick, efficient treatment. In their view, there is no room for errors ([31], pp. 583–585).

The percentage of medical errors is situated between 3 % and 5 %, while 40 % of ambulatory malpractice claims are made for assigning an erroneous diagnosis. A study from John Hopkins University reveals that 40,500 patients die in intensive care in the USA as a result of diagnostic errors ([32], pp. 1–3).

The demographic increase and life expectancy growth have led to an increase in the number of patients whom medical bodies need to provide care to. According to a report by HSCIC [33], in 2013–2014 NHS personnel dealt with 42,400 NHS hospital admissions per day. The figure is 870 (2.1 %) more per day on average than in 2012–2013, while the greatest number of admissions by age band was for patients aged 65–69 (1.3 million, equivalent of 5.5 %). Although people tend to live longer, the healthy life expectancy has not increased at the same rate which leads to an increased need for care for an increased number of patients ([9], pp. 1–4).

These factors have led to challenges in dividing patients into categories and assessing their needs based on the affiliation to a single category. An example of the type of patients includes the elderly who represent the major consumers of health-related services including primary care (GPs), secondary care (hospitals), community (social nurses) and social care (care homes) [34]. They prefer doctors with whom they build long-lasting relationships based on patience, empathy and trust and at the same time demand relatively long and frequent consults and attention from the medical staff [35]. Other types are the younger and middle-aged patients who have very limited time and patience for health check-ups and prefer quick results to human relations and empathy. Being surrounded by smart, mobile devices many of them with built-in medical functions (i.e. applications that check blood pressure, intelligent fitness activity trackers), they tend to trust human doctors better if their view is confirmed by an app or a medical website. They also might be willing to get a second opinion, even if that is only a Google search of their symptoms and therefore might be more prone to support the utilisation of an intelligent agent such as Watson in health care ([10], pp. 516–517). However, their awareness of technology might make them more concerned regarding IS security and more demanding when it comes to their medical data handling.

Financial costs are an essential aspect to be discussed in relation to the patients' view and acceptance of intelligent agents as part of the care process. A UK-based review conducted in 2011 has revealed that in practice, patients were billed more after the introduction of clinical decision support systems because the computer recommended additional tests and also because it was easier for doctors to order them on an online-based system ([21], pp. 92–107).

The above examples show how various factors can influence patients' preferences towards intelligent medical agents. When looking at health care in general from a systemic point of view, it is vital to understand that patients are an essential stakeholder with increased decision-making responsibilities [14]. The systems thinking theory strongly argues that a contextual and holistic review of individual circumstances can be much more efficient than identifying broad categories of stakeholders and depersonalising the systems analysis ([2], p. 28; [3], pp. 3–5). Elements of disruption such as trust in technology and data security need to be taken into account in the use of intelligent agents interacting with patients. While people may be aware of intelligent medical agents through mass communication, they may have more questions when the doctor mentions, adds data or retrieves information from the agent. Additionally, doctors who have seen intelligent agents at work fear that Watson's ability to identify many possible diagnoses will encourage patients to ask for even more tests and procedures, setting off a cost-inflating "diagnostic cascade" [23]. This might distract the clinicians from the contextually relevant and truly needed health-care solutions that apply to particular circumstances.

Supply When it comes to the supply side, the users of an expert system can be divided into many categories. They can be doctors or medical support staff, and then the doctors could be researchers (professors), specialists, GPs or junior doctors; the support staff can include nurses, carers, receptionists or health advisors. They each have specific jobs, but more importantly, from a systems analysis point of view, they are individuals. They have specific work requirements, personal aspirations and ways to achieve excellence. They have different competences and abilities and may not always be able to identify contextual exceptions where the agent cannot be relied upon. The implementation of expert systems should not be dictated by how much medical literature a system can compile or its successful diagnosis rate.

As mentioned before, the key in analysing those ways is seeing patients as individuals and taking into account their particular characteristics, not classifying them as a homogeneous group. Data quality can only come under scrutiny at some point because of what is recognisable as "little data", which is personal and immediate and a context-specific alternative to Big data ([36], pp. 355–356). Trust and recognition for the experts authoring the data fed into the intelligent agent are major factors of influence for the data users. Most of the times, in medical care, information is fit for use when the doctor or nurse trusts it or knows how competent the colleague who provided it is ([15], pp. 80–86). On the other hand, doctors considered competent by their colleagues might use their practical experience and tacit knowledge in many situations and the resulting "data" stays invisible and will not be published anywhere. A major risk for the future sustainability of intelligent medical agents is that experienced doctors will not be motivated to repeatedly question the knowledge of the agent while junior doctors might get into the habit of relying on the expert agent, following a robot-like set of instructions without being incentivised to expand their individual knowledge by experimenting in practice and eventually hinder them from developing intuition ([20], [3], p. 3; [21], pp. 100–107]). The downside might be that they lose motivation to learn and remember endless variations of the same case because they know that they can access this kind of information and even more in less than 3 s ([37], p. 986; [38], pp. 188–195; [23]), resulting in the appearance of functional stupidity [39]. Conversely, more experienced doctors might find the large number of alerts and recommendations repeatedly displayed by intelligent agents disturbing and distracting, so in practice counterproductive, and start turning them off without necessarily paying attention to every single one. To find a balance in the number of reminders that an intelligent agent should flag, developers need to consider more the doctors' preferences and less the protection from lawsuits that vendors might face in the future ([21], pp. 106–107; [5]; [40], pp. 503–505).

This refers back to the actual need for an expert system; 75 % of diagnostic errors in the USA are reported to be related to cognitive factors which would translate in physician's judgement limitations ([33], pp. 1–3). At the same time, there is little known about the opposite (e.g. when cognitive factors help identify exceptions).

To link back to the patient and their view of the situation, doctors cannot be seen as IT support workers (the patient queries them; they query a database and come up with the highest probability response) and IT experts cannot be seen as replacements for doctors. There is a large category of IT-skilled patients who google their symptoms, but in the end, they all see human doctors for an accurate diagnosis and treatment. Historically, the medical profession has been highly respected because of its human interaction and trust in the healing abilities of its people [16]. Patients are not prepared, at least at the moment, to compete with the intelligent agent for the clinician's attention ([21], p. 80).

As with other computerised systems in different industries, there might be champions and there might be saboteurs. The difference in health care is highly hierarchical, based on long years of experience culture. Even if junior doctors and patients might be impressed by the technical specifications of an expert system, if a senior consultant with hundreds of hours of experience thinks the system is not viable, there are serious concerns to be considered [35].

At the same time, the number of experienced medical staff is decreasing. The figure for global health workforce shortage was 7.2 million in 2013, with a prediction to dramatically increase to 12.5 million by 2035 [38, 41]. The UK has temporarily found a solution to its shortage of medical experts by recruiting medical personnel, especially nurses from abroad ([42], pp. 558–561).

The advances in medicine and medical technology, discovery of new diseases and mutations of known ones and the enormous market of treatments represent too much information for a single doctor to learn and put into practice at the same time. Additionally, the medical knowledge generated by research and practice doubles every 7 years. The human body contains a number of variables that is simply too large for a human to monitor ([17], pp. 1051–1059). Young people who are currently studying medicine have been born in an era when a smart, mobile device is almost an extension of the human body. It is difficult to believe that they will be refractory towards technology enablement at their workplace, even if that is a hospital.

At the same time, the doctors' views are conflicting. According to Herbert Chase, a professor of clinical medicine at Columbia University and member of IBM's Watson Healthcare Advisory Board, "it's not humanly possible to practice the best possible medicine. We need machines". Given the creation rate for medical literature, a physician would need to read around 600 h per month in order to stay current ([43], pp. 21–27). Other doctors do not consider this a priority. Physician Mark Graber who heads the Society to Improve Diagnosis in Medicine thinks that "doctors have enough knowledge". On the other hand, some suggest that intelligent agents such as Watson and Autonomy could overcome difficulties linked to the soft side of the human doctors and provide unbiased second opinions [16]. But then it can also be argued that human experts are capable of making contextually relevant decisions because of the same bias [44]. Other positive predicted outcomes would include encouraging patient questions, decrease duplicate data and the solving the issue of illegible hand writing by linking the agent to an electronic record system and prescription system ([4], pp. 5–7). There are many more questions that can arise upon the actual implementation of the technology in health-care organisations. Leaving aside the natural resistance to change, doctors will want and need to understand how the technology works. This will count towards a number of training sessions and also practice ones. Additionally, the doctors will put pressure on making the processes as transparent as possible, as without seeing the internal reasoning of the intelligent agent, they will not be able to understand and validate the final diagnostic. Apart from that, technology has proven breakable over the years. Having a patient on the operating table in desperate need of support and a technical fault with the intelligent agent will leave little time tolerance for escalation and troubleshooting processes. This points to technical support once again, but as opposed to other technical industries, with potentially deadly consequences. IT support people might have serious difficulties [20].

Patients expect timely and personalised care putting pressure on physicians to see immediate results in consultation, diagnosis, treatment and recovery. Their expectations play an important part in the role that expert medical systems can be assigned over the next few years. The need for human interaction and reassurance rules out the role of replacement of human doctor. For them, care is more important than protocols and predefined care strategies. They want care personnel to be attentive to their individual needs which can be easily dismissed by a depersonalised intelligent agent ([15], pp. 80–90). The agent's role of human-dependent repository of data would not take advantage of the intelligent capabilities of the expert system, leaving the most likely role to be the guarantor of diagnostic accuracy ([25], p. 2).

As empowered as the technology might be, the ideology behind it is to simulate the cognitive capacities of the human brain. However, at least at the moment, a machine cannot be enriched with imagination, creativity or feelings. No human doctor is able to read through 23 million medical papers before providing a diagnosis, but at the same time, no computer can simulate human intuition or empathy. Modern computers have displayed outstanding results in terms of data processing, but medicine and patient care is about people, and ultimately, people should be the main decision-makers.

5 Ethical Aspects

Using an expert medical system as guarantor of diagnostic accuracy carries a sum of ethical concerns and liability issues. Bringing an intelligent agent to the medical act does not relieve medical staff from accountability and liability. As long as the people providing care are responsible for it in the patients' eyes, they should also be the ones who decide how much they can trust and rely on the intelligent agents ([45], pp. 3–6).

One of the general issues with intelligent agents is "depersonalisation". They have an inherent tendency to "empty out" the context of local interactions, specifically validity and authority, resulting in a lack of relevance. Intelligent agents capture professional expertise by formalisation—deploying impersonal knowledge, classificatory systems and procedures to shape, monitor, standardise and render calculable the work they support [34].

"Depersonalisation" leads to two follow-up concerns. The need for less medical experts might contribute towards a resistance to change showed by medical personnel who might feel excluded from the medical act. At the same time, if the intelligent agents will prove beneficial only when used by experts, it will lead to the exact opposite: more qualified experts are needed instead of mediocre personnel. Secondly, one of the major issues which has triggered long debates is the issue of liability in case of malpractice ([45], pp. 5–10). Preliminary studies suggest that intelligent agents will fall in the same category as robotic surgery or cybermedicine when it comes to regulations. Only one death has been registered in the USA after using robotic surgery where the lawsuit was settled outside the court, so at the moment, there is limited expertise ([17], pp. 1053–1055).

Even before malpractice, there might be a series of conflicts between doctors and the intelligent agents. Pointing back to the roles that intelligent agents might be assigned in this context, there will have to be clear policies in place to clarify who or what has supreme authority. If the doctor can disagree with the intelligent agent and the treatment is unsuccessful, there is a follow-up question of who takes responsibility for the action. So far, doctors who have used Watson have superficially dismissed the discussion of responsibility and best course of action. Eric Topol, a genomics professor at the Scripps Research Institute, argued that since doctors ultimately make a final diagnosis, there's no need for regulation like the one used for traditional devices used to treat patients [46].

Transparency and justifiable reasoning for the intelligent agent's processes and outputs are the key (a necessity for a doctor to be able to make a relevant judgment). However, giving doctors and support staff access to the internal structure of the intelligent agent makes the technology more vulnerable to manipulation or potentially unlawful data collection. Going a bit further and linking the agent to a pharmaceutical database through the treatments it might suggest deepens the concerns regarding data processing, data collection and sharing and, eventually, market competition issues as the agent might develop a preference for a certain medicine or producer.

Expert medical systems have been prototyped for over 50 years, but their cognitive capabilities have not appealed to physicians in practice. Recent developments in medicine generated enormous quantities of information that physicians would need to learn and update constantly. However, the time dedicated to learning would prevent them from being able to maintain the standard quality of care while dealing with their regular number of patients. At the same time, adding a piece of technology as intermediary might further increase that time and introduce additional issues with training and utilisation, therefore making the intelligent agent a suboptimal solution to the problem. Additionally, while computers are better than humans at storing, remembering and processing data, it is vital to outline that human understanding and machine understanding are significantly different. For an intelligent agent, the data it learns is a succession of symbols and its lack of consciousness prevents it from grasping how the manipulation of the data could impact a patient's life [47].

6 Conclusion

While various stakeholders in the health-care industry have very different opinions regarding the feasibility of using Watson for medical diagnosis, an essential feature distinguishes itself—that is individuality. Managers, patients and doctors can be seen as part of a system but cannot be simply divided into two basic categories: tech savvy and tech reluctant. Their particular characteristics, needs and expectations not only dictate their acceptance of intelligent agents in their daily lives (medical ones in this case) but also how they are being applied (e.g. their role in the decision-making process). Various characteristics will lead to various scenarios in real life which need to be considered before widely deploying intelligent agents.

The medical world might not be prepared to cope with an autonomous intelligent agent but, at the same time, might highly benefit from a combination of guarantor of diagnostic accuracy and human-dependent repository of data roles [16]. The intelligent agent may help with accuracy but not contextual relevance. If the artificial system proposes a decision how will the doctor sustain the ability to ensure it is the correct one? Doctors might save time by querying a machine but will waste valuable time in learning how to use it and to judge it. Perhaps the biggest difficulty will be to overcome potential functional stupidity and to sustain professional competency and capability.

Ideally, to balance the two, intelligent agents would tackle complicated and standardised problems while human doctors would focus on complex matters which require contextual deviation in decision-making as opposed to standardised assumptions. However, this would make the intelligent factor redundant and ignore stringent health-care issues such as shortage of personnel and human errors. Intelligent agents are here to stay, but expecting them to combine machine processing capabilities with emotional intelligence is an unrealistic short-term expectation. Getting them to work closely with humans, learn from experts that are dealing with people and their individual needs on a daily basis could take us one step closer to autonomous intelligent medical agents. The immediate priority is to enrich the agents with comprehensive learning capabilities, to make them able to cope with lessons that clinicians have learnt from practice not from books and, ultimately, to ensure that the agent will get this knowledge along the way by following the clinicians' path rather than distracting them by dictating a completely new one.

References

1. Patel, V. L., Shortliffe, E. H., Stefanelli, M., Szolovits, P., Berthold, M. R., Bellazzi, R., et al. (2009). Position paper: The coming of age of artificial intelligence in medicine. *Artificial Intelligence in Medicine, 46*, 5–17. doi:10.1016/j.artmed.2008.07.017.
2. Checkland, P., & Holwell, S. (1998). *Information, systems and information systems: Making sense of the field.* Chichester: Wiley.
3. Mumford, E. (1983—Revised 2013). *Designing human systems for new technology: The ETHICS method.* Manchester: Manchester Business School.
4. Castaneda, C., Nalley, K., Mannion, C., Bhattacharyya, P., Blake, P., Pecora, A., et al. (2015). Clinical decision support systems for improving diagnostic accuracy and achieving precision medicine. *Journal of Clinical Bioinformatics, 5*(1), 4.
5. Parasuraman, R., & Manzey, D. H. (2010). Complacency and bias in human use of automation: An attentional integration. *Human Factors: The Journal of the Human Factors and Ergonomics Society, 52*(3), 381–410.
6. IBM. (2015). *IBM's Watson supercomputer to speed up cancer care.* Retrieved from BBC News website: http://www.bbc.co.uk/news/technology-32607688
7. Nilsson, N. J. (2014). *Principles of artificial intelligence.* Los Altos, CA: Morgan Kaufmann.
8. Liebowitz, J. (1997). *The handbook of applied expert systems.* Boca Raton, FL: CRC Press.
9. Stubbs, E. (2015). *A season of major incidents.*
10. Porter, M. E., & Lee, T. H. (2013, October). The strategy that will fix health care. *Harvard Business Review.* Retrieved from https://hbr.org/2013/10/the-strategy-that-will-fix-health-care/
11. Wanjiku, R. (2014). *IBM pushes Watson's role in healthcare.* Retrieved from IT World website: http://www.itworld.com/article/2698674/hardware/ibm-pushes-watson-s-role-in-healthcare.html

12. Haddad, P., Gregory, M., & Wickramasinghe, N. (2014). *Evaluating business value of IT in healthcare in Australia: The case of an intelligent operational planning support tool solution.* Submitted Bled econference, Bled June.

13. Elina, V., Juhani, L., Tiina, T. J., Kari, M., Irma, V., Mauri, I., et al. (2006). Doctor-managers as decision makers in hospitals and health centres. *Journal of Health Organization and Management, 20*(2), 85–94.

14. Prahalad, C. K., & Ramaswamy, V. (2012). The new frontier of experience innovation. Image.

15. Cabitza, F., & Simone, C. (2012). "Whatever works": Making sense of information quality. In G. Viscusi, G. M. Campagnolo, & Y. Curz (Eds.), *Phenomenology, organizational politics, and it design: The social study of information systems* (p. 79). Hershey, PA: Information Science Reference.

16. Husain, I. (2011). *Why IBM's artificial intelligence "Watson" could not replace a physician.* Retrieved from: http://www.imedicalapps.com/2011/02/ibm-watson-replace-physician-artificial-intelligence/

17. Allain, J. S. (2012). From Jeopardy to Jaundice: The medical liability implications of Dr. Watson and other artificial intelligence systems. *Louisiana Law Review, 73*, 1049.

18. HP (2014). *Kainos Harnesses HP IDOL for next-generation healthcare analytics.* Retrieved from https://www.kainos.com/kainos-harnesses-hp-idol-next-generation-healthcare-analytics/

19. Ubpin, B. (2013, August 2). *IBM's Watson gets its first piece of business in healthcare.* Forbes. Retrieved from http://www.forbes.com/sites/bruceupbin/2013/02/08/ibms-watson-gets-its-first-piece-of-business-in-healthcare/

20. Cohn, J. (2013). *The robot will see you now.* Retrieved from: http://www.theatlantic.com/magazine/archive/2013/03/the-robot-will-see-you-now/309216/

21. Carr, N. G. (2015). *The glass cage: Where automation is taking us.* London: The Bodley Head.

22. Freudenheim, M. (2012). *The ups and downs of electronic medical records.* Retrieved from http://www.nytimes.com/2012/10/09/health/the-ups-and-downs-of-electronic-medical-records-the-digital-doctor.html?_r=0

23. Keim, B. (2012). *Paging Dr. Watson: Artificial intelligence as a prescription for health care.* Retrieved from http://www.wired.com/2012/10/watson-for-medicine/

24. Simonite, T. (2014). *IBM aims to make medical expertise a commodity.* Retrieved from: http://www.technologyreview.com/news/529021/ibm-aims-to-make-medical-expertise-a-commodity/

25. Bednar, P., Imrie, P., & Welch, C. (2014). Personalized support with 'little'data. In B. Bergvall-Kåreborn & P. A. Nielsen (Eds.), *Creating value for all through IT* (pp. 355–358). Berlin: Springer.

26. Imrie, P., & Bednar, P. (2014). *End user effects of centralized data control.* ItAIS2014: XI Conference of the Italian Chapter of AIS, Digital Innovation and Inclusive Knowledge in Times of Change. ItAIS, University of Genova.

27. Payne, K. F. B., Wharrad, H., & Watts, K. (2012). Smartphone and medical related App use among medical students and junior doctors in the United Kingdom (UK): A regional survey. *BMC Medical Informatics and Decision Making, 12*(1), 121.

28. Gaudin, S. (2014). *Cleveland Clinic uses IBM's Watson in the cloud to fight cancer.* Retrieved from http://www.computerworld.com/article/2840226/cleveland-clinic-uses-ibms-watson-in-the-cloud-to-fight-cancer.html.

29. The computing system that won 'Jeopardy!' is helping doctors fight cancer. (2015). Retrieved from: http://www.businessinsider.in/The-computing-system-that-won-Jeopardy-is-helping-doctors-fight-cancer/articleshow/46124256.cms

30. Ferrucci, D. A. (2012, May–June). Introduction to "This is Watson". *IBM Journal of Research and Development, 56*(3.4), 1:1,1:15.

31. Truog, R. D. (2012). Patients and doctors—The evolution of a relationship. *New England Journal of Medicine, 366*(7), 581–585.

32. Dilsizian, S. E., & Siegel, E. L. (2014). Artificial intelligence in medicine and cardiac imaging: Harnessing big data and advanced computing to provide personalized medical diagnosis and treatment. *Current Cardiology Reports, 16*(1), 1–8.

33. Hospital inpatient care: Almost 900 more admissions per day compared to previous year. (n.d.). Retrieved from: http://www.hscic.gov.uk/article/6053/Hospital-inpatient-care-almost-900-more-admissions-per-day-compared-to-previous-year

34. Greenhalgh, T., Stramer, K., Bratan, T., Byrne, E., Mohammad, Y., & Russell, J. (2008). Introduction of shared electronic records: Multi-site case study using diffusion of innovation theory. *BMJ, 337*, a1786.

35. Khosla, V. (2012). *Technology will replace 80% of what doctors do*. Retrieved from Fortune website: http://fortune.com/2012/12/04/technology-will-replace-80-of-what-doctors-do/

36. Bednar, P., Welch, C., & Imrie, P. (2014). Supporting business decision-making: One professional at a time. *DSS 2.0–Supporting Decision Making with New Technologies, 261*, 471–482.

37. Arnaout, R. (2012). Elementary, my dear doctor Watson. *Clinical Chemistry, 58*(6), 986–988.

38. Charani, E., Castro-Sanchez, E., Sevdalis, N., Kyratsis, Y., Drumright, L., Shah, N., et al. (2013). Understanding the determinants of antimicrobial prescribing within hospitals: The role of "prescribing etiquette". *Clinical Infectious Diseases, 57*(2), 188–196.

39. Alvesson, M., & Spicer, A. (2012). A stupidity-based theory of organizations. *Journal of Management Studies, 49*(7), 1072–1194. http://dx.doi.org/10.1111/j.1467-6486.2012.01072.

40. Eberhardt, J., Bilchik, A., & Stojadinovic, A. (2012). Clinical decision support systems: Potential with pitfalls. *Journal of Surgical Oncology, 105*(5), 502–510.

41. Global health workforce shortage to reach 12.9 million in coming decades. (2013). Retrieved from WHO website: http://www.who.int/mediacentre/news/releases/2013/health-workforce-shortage/en/

42. England, K., & Henry, C. (2013). Care work, migration and citizenship: International nurses in the UK. *Social and Cultural Geography, 14*(5), 558–574.

43. Duerr-Specht, M., Goebel, R., & Holzinger, A. (2015). Medicine and health care as a data problem: Will computers become better medical doctors? In A. Holzinger, C. Rocker, & M. Ziefle (Eds.), *Smart health* (pp. 21–39). Cham: Springer.

44. Bednar, P., & Welch, C. (2008). Bias, misinformation and the paradox of neutrality. *Informing Science, 11*, 85–106.

45. Luxton, D. D. (2014). Recommendations for the ethical use and design of artificial intelligent care providers. *Artificial Intelligence in Medicine, 62*(1), 1–10.

46. Edney, A. (2015). *This medical supercomputer isn't a pacemaker, IBM Tells Congress*. Retrieved from: http://www.bloomberg.com/news/articles/2015-01-29/this-medical-supercomputer-isn-t-a-pacemaker-ibm-tells-congress

47. Searle, J. (2012). Watson doesn't know it won on "Jeopardy!". *The Wall Street Journal, 23*, 15A.

Data-Mining Tools for Business Model Design: The Impact of Organizational Heterogeneity

Nicola Castellano and Roberto Del Gobbo

Abstract Business models may be considered as "cognitive" devices since a deep level of knowledge about customers, suppliers, and competitors is needed for their development. Recent studies show that data-mining tools produce a positive inter-action with business models, empowering the strategic performance capabilities that drive the achievement of competitive advantage.

The present paper aims to discuss whether the adoption in a real context of data mining in support of business modeling may be enabled or hindered by organizational heterogeneity.

The Structured Neural Network, adopted in the case study, is particularly suitable in support of strategic management, since it stimulates the convergence of personal knowledge and beliefs toward the exploitation of the key concepts and the cause-and-effect relations needed for the design of the business model. Furthermore, it provides a fact-based test for its robustness. The results provide both scientific and practical implications.

Keywords Business models • Data mining • Structured Neural Network • Decision-making support • Knowledge discovery

1 Introduction

Extant studies about business models do not express consensus about what a business model is, how it is composed, and what it is for, probably due to extreme difficulties in creating a general taxonomy which might be adaptable to every kind of environment. However, some concepts seem to be generalizable:

- Business models should explicit the value proposition that a company aims to address to its customers.

N. Castellano (✉) • R. Del Gobbo
Department of Economics and Law, University of Macerata, 62100, Via Crescimbeni 14, Macerata, Italy
e-mail: nicola.castellano@unimc.it; roberto.delgobbo@unimc.it

© Springer International Publishing AG 2017
K. Corsi et al. (eds.), *Reshaping Accounting and Management Control Systems*,
Lecture Notes in Information Systems and Organisation 20,
DOI 10.1007/978-3-319-49538-5_15

- A learning and cognitive ability is needed during the exploitation of a business model in order to detect signals that reveal the opportunity to adapt the existing model to changing environments (for established companies) or to create a new model (for start-up companies).

The adoption of business models assumes that strategy is "discovery driven" rather than planning oriented. Earlier approaches to strategy assumed that managers should have been focusing on discovering the company core competencies and consequently in searching the most profitable market opportunities. Conversely the business model approach assumes that managers should be constantly monitoring the changes in customers' need and values, in order to properly adapt the company value proposition [1].

The learning activity about customer needs and values can be intended as a knowledge discovery and, considering the massive amount of data often available, can be facilitated by the use of data-mining applications. Heinrichs and Lim [2] show that the adoption of data-mining tools creates a positive interaction with business models, improving the managers' speed to focus on the most significant opportunities and threats that require actions to develop and sustain the competitive advantage.

The research of Heinrichs and Lim is based on an experimental study which implicitly assumes that all the respondents play the same role in a virtual company environment, holding similar skills and competencies.

The present paper aims to extend the research by investigating the adoption of a data-mining tool in support of a business model design in a real context, characterized by extreme organizational differences concerning the actors involved, that can enable or hinder the effective adoption of the information tool. In particular the data-mining application is limited to the initial stage of the business model design, when a common explicit knowledge about the customer needs is required to develop a suitable value proposition accordingly.

The results obtained provide slight evidence that Structured Neural Networks (the tool adopted) may provide effective support to decision-making, even when organizational heterogeneity occurs. The paper also provide evidence that the successful adoption is conditioned by the organizational attitude to learn and discuss the managers' personal beliefs.

As practical implication, the paper also provides an example about how the information emerging from the data-mining tool may support the knowledge generation (for what concern the customer needs) and ease the design of a business model.

The remainder of the paper is structured as follows: in Sects. 2 and 3, a review of the literature about knowledge generation in support of the business models' design and data mining is summarized. The case study research is described in Sect. 4, while in Sect. 5 the main findings are discussed. Final considerations and further research directions are described in the last section.

2   Knowledge Generation and Business Modeling

Business models adopt a holistic and systemic perspective, based on activities, intended to describe dynamics, components, and linkages through which value is created and captured.

In essence a business model describes how the company intends to meet specific customer needs, how the customers will be disposed to reward the value received, and how the company is expecting to generate an adequate level of profit [3].

Despite the definitions adopted, a common issue in literature is that the design of a business model requires creativity at first, as well as a good level of knowledge about customers, suppliers, and competitors. The business models may be considered as "cognitive" devices [4]. They promote an outside-in, rather than an inside-out, focus [1], meaning that the managers should be constantly engaged in discovering and adapting to the changing customer needs and values. Internal core competencies and key resources should be developed accordingly.

In particular for what concern the customers, the questions that need to be answered are the following [3]: What do customers really value? How will the company satisfy their needs? What might the customer pay for the value received?

Reasonably, non-accurate assumptions produce uncertainty and risky future outcomes. Managers make frequently false assumptions in those areas where they believe to hold a deeper understanding and knowledge, so they don't perceive the necessity to test their thinking [5]. The only possible way to reduce the uncertainty risk is to have a clear and explicit organizational learning, able to capture the essential changes in the environment. Furthermore, it is necessary that managers are inclined to learn, to discuss, and to revise their personal beliefs and knowledge about the company and its competitive environment.

If the customer needs are clearly exploited, the managers will have the possibility to formulate a suitable value proposition. Furthermore, the knowledge about what the customers are willing to pay for is essential in order to connect the sale prices with the items perceived by customers as more valuable, thus amplifying the managers' expectations about monetization.

Assuming that lot of knowledge about these players is implicit, the managers involved in the business model design may face difficulties to fully rationalize and articulate it, and then a discovery approach based on experimentation and learning may be needed [3].

The generation of knowledge can be effectively supported by information technology, through which useful information might be produced sourcing from the massive amount of data often available in the companies' information systems and on the Internet. The adoption of information-based knowledge management tools may produce the following advantages [2]:

- Improve the managers' strategic capability, intended as the speed needed to react to environmental changes and select appropriate strategic and tactical business models.

- Develop a fact-based consensus, driving decisions without exclusively relying on personal perceptions and past experience.

Generally, the knowledge creation is supported by the following information tools: data bases, cognitive maps, decision support systems, data mining, and intranets. In particular the adoption of data mining is ever increasing.

Data-mining tools are based on statistical and machine learning theories. Their first adoptions date back to the end of the 1980s in support of marketing and other operating tasks. In the present paper, a Structured Neural Network (SNN hereafter) is adopted, since it is particularly suitable for supporting the business models' design. In the following section, the main characteristics of SNN are described.

3 Structured Neural Networks and Business Modeling

Neural Networks are inspired by biological systems and can be defined as computational models composed by a system of units (neurons) and linking connections (weights).

Every neuron is stimulated by data received as input and produces a value as output. The inputs can be generated either by external stimuli or produced by preceding neurons.

In general, the adoption of a NN is suitable when the relationships between the variables are known to be nonlinear or, not known, a priori. Additionally, a NN may be preferred over traditional parametric statistical models, when the data do not meet the assumptions required by the parametric model or when significant outliers are included in the dataset.

Usually NN applications produce results without requiring any preliminary explicit assumption about the system or the process modeled; therefore, many users, especially those not holding developed informatics skills, may perceive NN as a "black box" and may feel skeptical about the significance and reliability of the information produced.

Particularly, when supporting strategic decisions, a preliminary shared knowledge about the variables included in the model and their expected cause-and-effect relations may improve the level of trust and acceptance among the managers involved. In this context the SNN technique can be considered a valid solution for predictive modeling.

SNN is based on cognitive models that summarize the managers' beliefs and experiences about a concept [6]. Their adoption requires a preliminary exploitation and sharing of personal knowledge, converted into an explicit cause-and-effect predictive model. The SNN allows managers to test the robustness of the predictive model and provide insights about the relevance of the expected relations between the variables in terms of magnitude of the impacts produced.

The adoption of a SNN requires a top-down approach, suitable for hypothesis testing, in order to confirm existing notions and opinions about a fact [7].

Generally, the adoption of a data mining requires the integration of managerial and technical (statistic and informatics) skills, which are usually held by different actors. Consequently managerial interaction is required to generate useful insights.

In the following section, we describe the adoption of a SNN in Lube, a company operating in the kitchen furniture industry. The SNN has been adopted to support the initial step of the business model design, during which the customers' perceptions are explored in order to discover the items considered as more valuable. The information obtained will drive managers in developing a suitable value proposition.

4 Mining Through Customers' Perceptions

The Lube company is actually ranked as one of the top Italian kitchen producers. In Italy the company gets in touch with its final users by means of a wide network composed by 1500 private resellers, which are usually multi-branded licensees.

The resellers can significantly influence the final users' purchasing decision, since they have room to promote the brands of the companies they feel more satisfied with. Their level of satisfaction, in turn, is affected by multiple factors which include, of course, the product, but also extend to the operating processes (promotional, commercial, logistic, administrative, and so forth) that the resellers need to manage in strict connection with Lube.

For the above mentioned reasons, when exploring the customer needs and value perceptions in order to design an effective business model, the managers of Lube need to consider a double-layer customer perspective, centered either on the final users and the direct customers (i.e. the resellers). The direct customer perspective must help the managers to discover the needs and value perceptions of the resellers, in order to develop suitable actions and resources and activate win-win relations that may trigger shared satisfaction and profitability and a durable competitive advantage.

The Lube company does represent an interesting case study at least for two reasons. To the best of our knowledge, this paper represents the first attempt to describe the adoption of a data mining in support of a business model design. Secondly, considering the critical role of the relations between Lube and its customers, the process employed to implement the data mining and the information produced may develop the recent growing literature about network business models [8, 9].

The case study can be considered *explanatory*, since it is employed to explain how a set of (qualitative) variables impact on a complex phenomenon. The case study methodology is well suited for many kinds of information systems and software engineering research, as the objects of study are contemporary phenomena hard to study in isolation [10]. Data are collected through direct observation, adopting an action research approach. In particular one of the authors directly participated to the processes under investigation with the role of project coordinator.

The case study describes an attempt to adopt a Structured Neural Network, in support of the design of a business model. The project has been divided in three steps:

Business model design, through knowledge exploitation and sharing of personal beliefs

Data collection about customer perceptions through survey

Adoption of the data-mining technique to test the robustness of the business model

The case study may extend the extant literature on business models, by providing evidence about how the qualitative factors may enable or hinder the adoption of data mining in an organizational context characterized by heterogeneity. Summarizing, we formulate the following research questions:

RQ1: May the adoption of data-mining tools provide results perceived as useful by managers even in a context characterized by organizational heterogeneity?

RQ2: Are there any organizational factors enabling or hindering the perceived usefulness of results?

During the first step the managers of the company have been involved in creating a shared causal map in which the most significant cause-and-effect relations between customer needs, value perceptions, and level of satisfaction are represented.

According to Langfield-Smith [12], collective maps cannot be elicited by means of a structured protocol, since its determinants (the collective cognitions) are not durable and persist only during the collective encounter. Conversely, the products resulting from the collective cognitions can be investigated and so the processes needed to their development.

In particular, the collective cognitions are expressed during encounters where a group of individuals attempt to find some common ground in order to take a shared decision or agree to take some collective action. Consequently, the identity of these collective cognitions may be inferred only from the group's discussion and behavior. For that reason we decided to base our analysis only on what occurred during managers' meetings.

As an initial step, a focus group has been organized, participated by the project coordinator and by the following directors: sales, marketing, production, finance, and R&D. Furthermore, a panel of five significant customers, considered as strategic partners in terms of volume of sales and robustness of the relation with Lube, participated to the focus group in order to stimulate a discussion between managers' beliefs and customer expectations useful to elicit a more customer-oriented causal map.

To facilitate the discussion, the project coordinator asked the participants to comment the well-known ECSI framework (European Customer Satisfaction Index) and adjust it according to the peculiarities of the Lube environment (see Fig. 1).

Fig. 1 The ECSI model

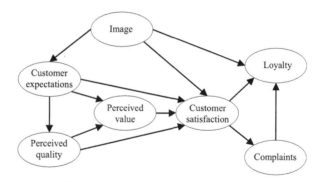

The ECSI provides an economic assessment of customer satisfaction. It derives from an adaptation of the Swedish customer satisfaction barometer [13], and its wide theoretical ground lends it to be adaptable to several different industries.

Customer satisfaction cannot be directly measured since it is developed through mental constructions. Assuming that a set of determinants produces relevant impacts on customer satisfaction, the measures about those variables might then provide a valid proxy of customer satisfaction.

During the focus group, the managers articulated the variables expected to impact on customers satisfaction and loyalty.

As a result, the satisfaction framework shown in Fig. 2 has been developed. For matters of privacy only, a simplified version is shown.

The Lube framework includes the latent variables (LV), customer expectations (CE), perceived quality (PQ), image, perceived value, satisfaction, and profitability.

Either CE or PQ is connected to a group of 11 manifest variables (MV), representing the technical/functional features, sellout support, and operating relations.

The technical/functional features determine the efficiency of the operating processes, in which the company and the customers are involved, and include accuracy and on-time delivery to final users, rapidity in replacing defective or nonconforming products, and availability and ease of use of the configurator software employed by the customers to design the kitchen project on the base of the requests received by the final users and to submit the order to the headquarter.

Sellout support includes all the activities undertaken in order to increase the likelihood for the customers to successfully sell the kitchens produced by Lube. The following variables are considered: richness and detail of catalogs, merchandising initiatives organized by the headquarter (products promotions, advertising material, and so forth), and specific training initiatives directed toward the customers.

Operating relations represent the human side of the relation between Lube and its customers and include courtesy, promptness of the headquarter staff in providing answers and solutions to the customers' requests and problems, and technical assistance.

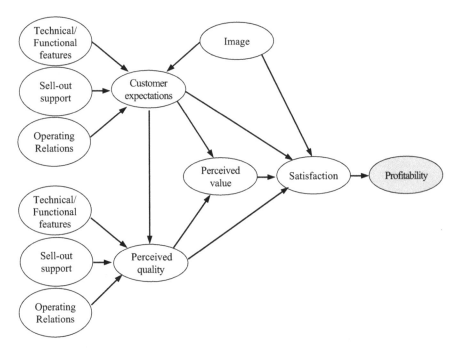

Fig. 2 The (direct) customer perspective of Lube business model

The CE expresses how customers consider relevant the three drivers, whereas PQ measures the perceptions of customers about how Lube produces quality and satisfaction when managing issues relating to the three drivers.

The perceived value is connected to the quality/price ratio and to a qualitative assessment about the value of products and services provided by Lube in comparison with those of the main competitors.

The architecture of the network defines how the nodes are interconnected. In total the developed framework considered 34 manifest variables. The construction of the SNN was conducted by following the structured process described by Coakley and Brown [11]. The software "STATISTICA Data Miner" (StatSoft) was employed to support the analysis.

In the following step, a sample of customers has been involved in a survey and has been asked to evaluate, through a questionnaire, the 34 manifest variables by means of a 10-level qualitative scale, where 1 expresses a "very negative" and 10 a "very positive" opinion about the item.

The sample was composed by 600 sales outlets randomly selected. The sample was stratified by level of sales and by geographical area. The survey consisted of items related to each LV shown in Fig. 2. As input variables for the model, 24 questions have been identified. All items were scaled from 1 to 10. The data collected allowed to develop a Structured Neural Network (SNN) to measure the significance of the stimuli produced by the variables included in the framework (the arrows in Fig. 2).

As described above, SNN are particularly suitable in this context, since they allow to model nonlinear relations between variables in the absence of any a priori information about their shape and nature, as in the case of customer satisfaction and its determinants.

Moreover, since the customer perspective of Lube business model has been developed as a cognitive representation of the managers' knowledge, exploited and shared, the SNN may provide a test of robustness based on data sourced directly from customers and representing their needs and beliefs. The SNN provides, then, a fact-based support to the managers' assumptions and provide a focus on the variables which should be more sensitive in improving satisfaction and profitability.

The inclusion of profitability in the network allows to quantify the importance of a latent variable in creating monetary value and allows managers to evaluate whether the costs generated by the initiatives aimed to improve satisfaction might be covered by the expected revenue streams.

Figure 3 shows the results produced by the adoption of the SNN: the weights reflect the importance of the stimuli produced on the neurons. When a weight is negative, the connection produces an "inhibitory" effect. As an example, customer expectation produces an inhibitory effect on perceived value. This means in practical terms that the customers' expectations do not produce a direct impact on

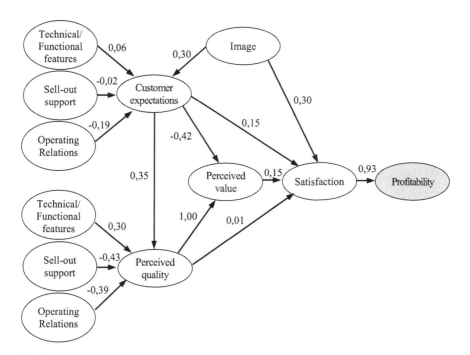

Fig. 3 Results produced by the Structured Neural Network

perceived value but produce a stimulus on perceived quality that, in turn, stimulates perceived value and satisfaction. Conversely, when the weights are positive, the highest the value, the highest the magnitude of the stimulus produced on the neuron.

5 Discussion of Results and Managerial Implications

The results produced by the SNN have been discussed during a meeting participated by the CEO, the project coordinator, and all the managers involved in the focus group. The managers hold extremely different profiles for what concern the past working experience and educational background (see Table 1).

The CEO did not attend university; he got a high school certificate in accounting and worked in the company since the early 1970s. He developed a really high experience in the industry and he is one of the elder managers.

The directors of marketing and finance are both graduated in economic disciplines and have been working in their actual role for more than 20 years. The directors of R&D and production also have been working in Lube for more than 30 years covering different positions that let them develop a high on-the-job experience and technical skills on production planning and product development.

The sales director developed past experiences in different companies of the same industry, and once in the company, he covered different roles in the sales department, such as the head of the sales orders processing office. None of the managers involved have developed competencies related to the management information systems.

The project coordinator is the youngest in the group; he is graduated in economic disciplines, got a PhD in management, and developed deep mathematic, statistic,

Table 1 Managers' profile: working experience and educational background

Managers	Level of instruction	Experience in the company	Previous working experiences	Information systems skills
CEO	High School Certificate	>40 years	No	Low
Sales	High School Certificate	> 25 years	Yes	Low
Marketing	Degree in Economics	> 20 years	Yes	Low
Production	High School Certificate	> 30 years	Yes	Low
Finance	Degree in Economics	> 20 years	No	Low
R&D	High School Certificate	> 30 years	No	Low
Project Coordinator	PhD in Management	< 15 years	No	High

and informatics skills. His experience in the company is relatively low (compared to that of other managers). He represents the company intelligence, since he is appointed to produce almost all the information needed in support of strategic and tactical decision-making.

Despite the differences between the managers, they all considered as reliable the results obtained and did not show any skepticism, neither when the results, unexpectedly, did not confirm their individual or collective expectations and prior beliefs.

The results obtained are in line with extant literature [2], but in addition our study provides an empiric slight evidence that the adoption of data-mining tools may provide an effective support to strategic planning and business model design, even when the operating managers do not hold similar competencies, past experiences, and educational background.

It's worth noting that the CEO played a key role in determining the tool effectiveness in terms of support to decision-making. During the meeting he never showed any doubt about the reliability of the results produced by the SNN and always considered them as accurate and reasonable. His mind-set positively influenced all the participants that aligned their mental attitudes with that of the CEO. We may then argue that the company attitude to learn, either if shared between managers or produced by a top-down persuasion, is necessary to determine the effectiveness of the information tool.

For what concern the managerial implications, the managers agreed that the image was the main driver of customer satisfaction since it showed the largest positive weight in connection to the satisfaction neuron. After the discussion the managers decided to align their decision to what revealed by the SSN: the corporate and product image needed to be strengthened, in order to positively impact on satisfaction and foster profitability. Surprisingly, before the meeting the image was generally perceived as one of the less significant drivers of customer satisfaction.

6 Conclusions

Summarizing, the present paper shows how a SNN may support the business model design and its managerial implications in terms of knowledge generated.

The paper extends literature on business models since it shows that data-mining tools, and Structured Neural Networks in particular, may improve the managers' strategic capability even when they do not hold similar competencies and educational background. The successful adoption of the SNN has been positively conditioned by the mental attitude of the CEO that played a key role in determining the general acceptance of the results by all other managers and the effectiveness of information produced in driving decision-making.

The paper also provides several managerial implications. It shows that the preliminary design of the network can be considered as a knowledge creation step, where managers' experience and perceptions are converted into collective explicit knowledge through externalization.

The cognitive map developed, which represents the architecture of the SNN, can be considered an explicit vehicle of information that allow to transfer, share, and discuss company knowledge throughout the organization and foster a general consensus about company policies and strategies.

The quantitative results, expressed in terms of magnitude of the impact that a variable is expected to produce, allow to test the robustness of managers' perceptions and provide a model that facilitate decision-making and strategic planning.

Finally, it's worth noting that the considerations drawn in the case study are context specific and may not necessarily be generalizable to other companies. Further applications of data-mining tools both in similar and different organizational and competitive environments might provide further comparable evidences.

References

1. Gunter Mc Grath, R. (2010). Business models: A discovery driven approach. *Long Range Planning, 43*(2010), 247–261.
2. Heinrichs, J. H., & Lim, J. S. (2003). Integrating web-based data mining tools with business models for knowledge management. *Decision Support Systems, 35*, 103–112.
3. Teece, D. J. (2010). Business models. *Business Strategy and Innovation, Long Range Planning, 43*, 172–194.
4. Baden-Fuller, C., & Haefliger, S. (2013). Business models and technological innovation. *Long Range Planning, 46*, 419–426.
5. Bertels, H. M., Koen, P. A., & Elsum, I. (2015). *Business models outside the core. Lessons learned from success and failure.* Research-Technology Management, March–April, pp. 20-29.
6. Lee, C., Rey, T., Mentele, J., & Garver, M. (2005). *Structured neural network techniques for modeling loyalty and profitability.* SAS SUGI, 30.
7. Berry, M., & Lynoff, G. (1997). *Data mining techniques for marketing, sales, and customer support.* New York: Wiley.
8. Heikkilä, M., & Heikkilä, J. (2010). Conscription of network business models. *IUP Journal of Business Strategy, 7*(4), 7–23.
9. Liu, R. (2015). Management learning in business networks: The process and the effects. *Management Learning, 46*(3), 337–360.
10. Runeson, P., & Höst, M. (2008). Guidelines for conducting and reporting case study research in software engineering. *An International Journal. Empirical Software Engineering.* doi:10. 1007/s10664-008-9102-8.
11. Coakley, J. R., & Brown, C. E. (2000). Artificial Neural Networks in accounting and finance: Modeling issues. *International Journal of Intelligent Systems in Accounting, Finance and Management, 9*, 119–144.
12. Langfield-Smith, K. (1996). Exploring the need for a shared cognitive map. *Journal of Management Studies, 29*(3), 349–368.
13. Fornell, C. (1992). A national customer satisfaction barometer: The Swedish experience. *Journal of Marketing, 56*, 6–21.

Accounting Information System and Transparency: A Theoretical Framework

Daniela Mancini and Rita Lamboglia

Abstract This article contributes to the growing literature on transparency by developing a theoretical framework to analyse the relation between the AIS integration level and the transparency level in the Italian public sector. Based on the literature review regarding transparency and IIS, a research model is proposed. The AIS integration level is measured through three dimensions: part integration, full system integration and full information integration. The transparency level is assessed by the following dimensions: formal transparency, quality transparency and full transparency. The framework shows how different AIS integration levels match with various transparency characteristics. Higher levels of AIS integration enable an increase in the characteristics of transparency and guarantee its effectiveness and interactivity. In contrast, lower levels of AIS integration determine a sufficient and minimum degree of transparency that is evaluated only through the existence or the nonexistence of the information on the public organisation website.

Keywords Transparency • Accounting information systems • Public administration • Integrated information systems

1 Introduction

This study provides an analysis of the relation between the accounting information system (AIS) integration level and the transparency level in Italian public organisations.

Over the last two decades, transparency has become a relevant issue as a result of recent legislation [1]. Many governments have introduced norms of transparency as a key component of their efficiency and reform programmes to improve performance and accountability in the public sector (e.g. transparency agenda in the UK 2010, open government in the USA 2009, Dlgs. 33/2013 in Italy).

D. Mancini (✉) • R. Lamboglia
Parthenope University of Naples, Naples, Italy
e-mail: daniela.mancini@uniparthenope.it; rita.lamboglia@uniparthenope.it

© Springer International Publishing AG 2017
K. Corsi et al. (eds.), *Reshaping Accounting and Management Control Systems*,
Lecture Notes in Information Systems and Organisation 20,
DOI 10.1007/978-3-319-49538-5_16

According to the transparency laws, public organisations must publish the key data set on their websites in specified, open data standards to disclose information to many parties and make public data more accessible, interesting and dynamic via websites, mobile device apps and other platforms.

In this context, AIS integration appears to play a pivotal role by providing assurance and support on how to improve and manage transparency.

Transparency in regulation's growing significance has stimulated a call for additional research.

Many studies have focused on the advantages and disadvantages of transparency and on the descriptions of specific transparency initiatives [1–5]; however, they do not consider the dynamics of this phenomenon [6]. These dynamics are very complex because the transparency results from the interactions between many and different actors and the rapid changes in technologies. Therefore, there are large differences in the characteristics of transparency initiatives and in the degree to which transparency is applied.

The construction of transparency involves a variety of actors. Public organisations make decisions on and apply a transparency programme; however, in this process, they are influenced by different stakeholders that are crucial for the success or the failure of the process [7]. Moreover, these relations between public organisations and stakeholders are developed in different cultural settings and in complex national and international policy contexts. In addition, the decisions and the implementation of the transparency are influenced by new and constantly evolving new technologies.

The dynamics and changes regarding transparency can be examined in terms of these features. To begin, the institutional relations between public organisations and stakeholders may be developed in terms of what are considered to be correct actions and which external actors could access the information. Second, information exchanges may be analysed in terms of speed, ease of use and accessibility.

All of these aspects need to be explained further.

To date, a growing number of studies have been conducted on the construction of transparency in interactions between the public sector and stakeholders (transparency as an institutional relation) [6, 8] and on the interaction between transparency and new technologies (transparency as information exchange). However, these studies use a reductionist approach because they focus only on short-term changes and ignore the fact that transparency is a phenomenon that is built and rebuilt over time through a social and political process as well as information exchanges. Public disclosure is related to information system and, more specifically, AIS because the information that public organisations must publish, at least in Italy, concerns mainly financial data. Despite this aspect, the literature is nearly silent on the relations between transparency and AIS.

Therefore, considering these research gaps, we need further studies to analyse transparency.

This article fits in the research area concerning transparency as an information exchange.

The key goals of this paper are as follows:

- To contribute and expand the literature on transparency that explores the relation between AIS integration and transparency. Specifically, this work analyses whether and how the integration level of AIS influences the level of transparency in terms of regulatory compliance and access to information in public organisations.
- To develop a theoretical model to analyse whether and how different levels of AIS integration contribute to improve transparency's effectiveness.

The remainder of this paper is structured as follows: the next section analyses the literature and formulates the research question, and the third section presents and analyses the theoretical model. Finally, conclusions and future implications of the research follow.

2   Literature Review

2.1   Concepts of Transparency in the Public Sector

Although transparency in public sector organisations has been the object of several studies, particularly since the 1990s [1], there is not yet a mutually agreed-upon definition for transparency [6]. Transparency is defined and analysed in a variety of forms, which reflects the fact that researchers often have different perceptions of transparency and examine it from different perspectives.

The literature on transparency in the public sector can be articulated in two main research areas.

In the first area, transparency is considered a tool to curb corruption and is confused with "good government" and accountability [9]. Some of these studies analyse government corruption and accountability from the principal-agent theory perspective and consider transparency to be the principal means to reduce information asymmetries between citizens (principals) and the government (agent). The principal-agent theory presupposes that information asymmetries are the main obstacle that prevents principals from monitoring agents. Therefore, if agents create and operate in transparent organisations, principals are more enabled to evaluate the extent to which their interests are being served by government and to encourage accountability and deter abuses by officials. In contrast, "if agent creates an opaque organisation, principals are largely obstructed from exercising accountability" [9].

Transparency is often used as synonymous to accountability; however, Bovens [11] considers this definition a reductionist approach because he believes that transparency "is not enough to qualify as a genuine form of accountability". Accountability is a complex concept composed of five different dimensions: transparency, liability, controllability, responsibility and responsiveness. According to this broader conceptualisation, transparency appears to represent only one element of accountability that is instrumental for the success of the accountability process [10, 11].

Furthermore, this first research area shows that transparency and accountability require changes in the public administration culture [12]. When political leaders and public managers promote more transparency, this request often produces a negative reaction from others. Citizens, for example, view these initiatives solely as vehicles for politicians to seek re-election. However, public employees consider these initiatives to be signs of mistrust and think that they waste time and effort in reporting what they do rather than doing more. To change the work culture and resolve this conflict, certain suggestions appear to be relevant [12]. First, to develop and rebuild the trust in citizens, electors, the media and employees, governments must work to safeguard organisations' integrity and reputation. Second, to develop trust means to reduce suspicion. Public managers must be able to communicate that the requirements for accountability do not indicate that managers have lost trust but that they attempt to minimise the corruption risks. Furthermore, managers must spread this message to others: "Even if a report is not read, writing it can be of value" [12]. Providing updates may modify work approaches and make people more competent to improve the products and services provided.

The second research area defines transparency as the public disclosure of information. Transparency refers to the ability to disclose information to relevant parties, thus reducing uncertainty by developing trust. This definition of transparency considers three elements: the act of disclosure, the information disclosed and the agents that either disclose the information or are its recipients [1]. All of these elements are management practices that reduce corruption and contribute to the stabilisation of the government organisation. In accordance with this definition, transparency can be analysed from three different perspectives [1]. From a market perspective, transparency is considered a tool to reduce the risk of exposure and vulnerability. From a political perspective, transparency represents the characteristic of a well-functioning government that follows democratic and empowering principles. From an international perspective, transparency makes a "platform for international trust and for better assessment and implementation of international treaties; a lack of disclosure implies a weakening, if not sabotage, of the international regime" [1].

In fact, the literature discusses two other distinct approaches to information disclosure related to transparency: a "functional rationale" approach and a "cultural rationale" approach.

The first focuses on the utilitarian benefits of transparency and attributes to transparency the functional role of developing trust in both government and democracy, of improving confidence in a country's economy and of leading to major economic prosperity and political stability. This approach can be applied at both the national and international levels. A national level of transparency is related to policy compliance; however, the international levels are associated with the formation of international treaties.

The second approach focuses on transparency as a norm of appropriateness. The country's transparency level permits the measurement of its embeddedness in the world polity. The requirement of transparency is not only based on mandatory regulations, but appears to be based on a cultural model of proper governance. In accordance with this approach, transparency is considered a new transnational norm that can be matched to the principles of social progress and social justice. Government organisations explain what they do and who they are by providing data and information to their broadly defined stakeholders. These organisations can develop transparency in several social spheres that are composed of human rights, local politics, defence, democracy, welfare and family relations. In this context, transparency permits governments to achieve two goals: organisational efficiency (often called "development") and empowered social involvement (often called "democracy").

The analysis of the transparency literature shows that many studies have focused on the advantages and disadvantages of the phenomenon, the impacts that it produces on the democracy and the accountability factors that influence transparency.

Therefore, the existing literature is very silent on the dynamics that guide and determine the transparency level in the public sector. These dynamics are several and complex and regard the interactions between people and the continuous development of information and communication technologies (ICT).

Focusing on the dynamics between transparency and ICT, a growing number of studies [13, 14] are primarily focused on analysing the potential contribution of electronic government (E-government) to enhance interactivity and transparency as well as the openness of the public sector to promote new forms of accountability. E-government has been defined as the "use of ICTs, and particularly the internet as a tool to achieve better government" [15]. "It is considered as a mechanism to transform public sector organisations through the use of ICTs" [16]. The literature [14, 16] shows that the main benefit of these technologies is the enhancement of citizen participation. The creation of blogs, collaborative websites (e.g. Wikipedia), social networking sites (e.g. Facebook), microblogging services (e.g. Twitter) and multimedia sharing services (e.g. Flickr, YouTube) permits all users to participate directly in the process of communication through the contribution of contents, comments regarding social and political problems and tagging.

The analysis of E-government studies and Italian transparency regulations (Dlgs. 33/2013, CIVIT deliberation 105/2010, Commissione Anticorruzione deliberation 50/2013) has enabled the identification of the following transparency characteristics: publication of information, accessibility, information quality, usability and interactivity [4, 17–26].

In this paper, the compliance level with the transparency process is measured through these variables, which are described in Sect. 4.

2.2 Accounting Information System and Transparency

AIS is considered a relevant component of the general information system that has the role of collecting, processing and communicating accounting information [27]. Studies reveal that the first use of information systems (ISs) was in relation to accounting [28].

Although a growing number of studies highlight the relevance that accounting information has in the transparency process [29–33], the literature is actually nearly silent on the relation between AIS and transparency.

In recent years, scholars have conducted theoretical and conceptual studies that generically consider the link between AIS and transparency.

Dillard and Yuthas [34] reveal the importance to construct new AIS to respond to the needs of an increasingly pluralistic society. The authors consider "critical dialogics" and "agonistic pluralism" to be two relevant theories for AIS design and implementation. Critical dialogics refers to the power of accounting information to facilitate democratic mechanisms. Agonistic pluralism is a branch of democratic theory, in which AIS must provide a starting point to enable and support pluralistic discussion and decision-making. Based on these considerations, the authors require an expansion of the traditional AIS with regard to system development and use. AIS must incorporate tools and techniques that promote the dialogue among multiple stakeholders, enhance transparency and generate consensus on values, interests and beliefs.

Darabos [29] conducted a theoretical study in which the main article and books that have approached the study of "accounting information" from a decisional perspective are reviewed. At the end of the analysis, the paper shows the relevance of AIS to achieving the consistency, usefulness, transparency and unambiguousness of information.

Empirical studies focus primarily on the capital market [31] or inter-organisational relationships. This research shows that the adoption of new information technology, such as a real-time business reporting technology (RBRT), increases transparency and enables the attainment of capital at a lower cost than rivals; in addition, it can lead to the creation of organisational capabilities and the realisation of relational capital.

The literature review reveals none of the existing theories, and the framework considers if and how the integration level of AIS influences the transparency process in the public sector.

The motivation of this research project is derived from this research gap. Therefore, the purpose of this study is to develop a better understanding of the relation between the integration levels of AIS and transparency levels. There appears to be the potential for government organisations to make better use of integrated AIS when performing a transparency activity. This research project will attempt to uncover how integrated AIS can offer support to transparency and how it can be exploited.

The next section presents the research model developed to analyse the relation.

3 Developing a Research Model to Analyse the Relation Between AIS Integration and Transparency

The model, which the authors developed on the basis of the literature to explore the relation between the AIS integration and transparency in government organisations, focuses on the following areas:

- Integrated information systems (IISs)
- Transparency in public organisations

Public transparency has been analysed in the previous sections of this paper. Therefore, in this section, we focus on the aspects regarding the IIS (how previous studies have examined and evaluated the IIS) and on the model construction.

IS integration consists of an integrated technology by which data and applications, through different communication networks, can be shared and accessed for organisational use [35]. The main scope of IIS is to provide significant information support in the organisation to react to continuous challenges in the market.

IS integration is also considered a process that develops step by step and in different firm levels. According to this definition, IS integration is considered not only a tool to facilitate the use of data and applications "but also provide the flexibility to meet future business demands in information and applications" [35].

Research on IIS has evolved in recent years, and it has principally analysed the impacts of enterprise resource planning (ERP) systems on IS quality. Other studies have attempted to analyse the impact of ERP systems on managerial reporting and control [36–38].

IIS can be described by components and characteristics [28].

IIS components represent all the elements that enable the support of management accounting. Examples of components are ERP systems, data warehouses as well as executive portals.

IIS characteristics instead are analysed by utilising two different approaches.

A first approach considers the general characteristics of integration: flexibility, system scope, complexity, functionality, user-friendliness and the level of effort needed to implement the system. A second approach analyses the characteristics of integration that consider different dimensions.

Booth et al. [39] identify three dimensions of integration: data integration, hardware/software integration and information integration. The first refers to the feature of IIS in which data are stored and maintained in one place only. Hardware/software integration regards the technical aspects of integration, whereas information integration refers to the business aspects and the interchange of information between different departments.

In examining the role of IS integration on business process improvement, Bhatt and Troutt [35] re-elaborate the model of Booth et al. [39] and examine two interrelated dimensions of IS integration: data integration and communication network integration. Communication network integration can be further separated into different parts: communication network connectivity and communication network flexibility. Therefore, IS integration is valuated through three elements: data integration, communication network connectivity and communication network flexibility.

Data integration refers to data standards and logical coding schemes. The firms need to develop common data resource management policies to share data in the organisation and between suppliers and customers. An organisation can gradually improve integrated systems by using standards in data definition, logical coding and data structure.

By using integrated communication networks, information can be easily transmitted.

The communication level between two or more integrated information systems (ISs) depends on two factors: communication network connectivity and communication network flexibility. Communication network connectivity regards the level in which various systems, in and between different firms, are connected to sharing information. To geographically connect ISs, a firm can use, for example, local area communication networks (LAN) and wide area networks (WAN). Communication network flexibility refers to the level to which an organisation utilises common standards and protocols to promote compatibility between various ISs. The compatibility between systems enables companies to meet the existing information needs and helps to address future demands (alliances with several other companies).

Considering the literature review, the framework used to assess if and how the AIS integration influences the transparency level in public organisations is shown in Fig. 1.

The framework articulates AIS integration and transparency on three levels and defines hypothetical relations that could be developed between the different levels.

A starting point to analyse the three AIS integration levels is to define the following dimensions of AIS integration [35, 39]:

- Data integration
- Network connectivity
- Network flexibility

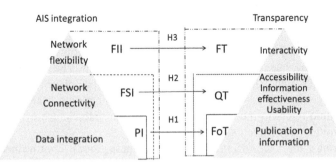

Fig. 1 Research model

"Data integration" is the first integration dimension; it refers to two features of IIS. The first concerns the existence of one common database for all applications, by which data are stored and maintained in one place only. The second features relate to the use of standards in data definition, logical coding and data structure, which permit sharing data both inside and outside the organisation. This aspect requires the development of data resource management policies.

"Network connectivity" is the second integration dimension. Network connectivity consists of hardware and software integration and considers only the technical dimensions of information management. On this level, the integration refers to the degree to which various systems, in and between different firms, connect to share information.

"Network flexibility" represents the third integration dimension. Although "network connectivity" considers only the technical aspects of integration, this level also considers the quality of information. In the model, we introduce the "network flexibility" as synonymous to information integration to describe the scope of interchange and the use of data and information generated by enterprise applications and functional areas. Network flexibility refers to the degree to which organisations utilise standards and protocols to promote compatibility between various IISs.

To define the AIS integration levels, a three-point ordinal scale was developed by considering the feasible combinations of these dimensions.

The AIS integration levels are the following, defined from lowest to highest:

- Part Integration (PI): a high level for "data integration" but a low level for the other two dimensions
- Full System Integration (FSI): a high level for "data integration" and "network connectivity" but a low level for "network flexibility"
- Full Information Integration (FII): a high level for all the dimensions

To define the transparency levels, we begin with three dimensions. According to the literature analysed, the authors consider transparency not only as the publication of information on the website but also other information characteristics that can guarantee effectiveness and interactivity. Therefore, we considered the following dimensions:

- Publication of information
- Accessibility, information effectiveness and usability
- Interactivity

The first dimension refers to the existence or the nonexistence of the information that the public administration must publish on the website, according to the regulation. "[...] for publication means the publication in the public administration web sites of documents, information and data relating to the organisation and activities of public authorities [...]" (Dlgs. 33/2013, art. 2).

Accessibility regards the facility to achieve specific information that the law requires local governments to publish. To increase the access to the information disclosed on the websites, we adopt Decree No. 33/2013, which states the following: "For the full accessibility of the information published on the home page of the institutional websites has placed a special section called 'Transparent administration', in which are contained data, information and documents published under the current legislation" (Dlgs 33/2013, art. 9). Information effectiveness refers to all of the characteristics that each data item that is published must have. Usability regards the possibility to directly download data from a website in a format that permits its reuse and aggregation.

Interactivity regards the existence of tools on the website that ensure a direct and mutual interaction between users and the public administration. In addition to the integration levels, a three-point ordinal scale was developed by considering the feasible combinations of these dimensions.

The three transparency levels are the following:

- Formal Transparency (FoT): a high level for "public information" but a low level for the other two
- Quality Transparency (QT): a high level for "public information" and "accessibility, information effectiveness and usability" but a low level for "interactivity"
- Full Transparency (FT): a high level for "public information", "accessibility, information effectiveness and usability" and "interactivity"

The theoretical framework supposes the existence of specific relations between the AIS integration levels and the transparency levels. According to previous studies, we hypothesise the following:

- A part integration (PI) matches with a formal transparency (FT).
- A full system integration (FSI) matches with a quality transparency (QT).
- A full information integration (FII) matches with a full transparency (FT).

The model emphasises these relations, which highlights that higher levels of AIS integration enhance the performance characteristics of transparency, whereas a lower AIS integration level determines the minimum requirements of transparency. Greater success in the transparency initiatives is achieved when we have a high level of "data integration", "network connectivity" and "network flexibility".

4   Conclusions and Future Research

This paper set out to enhance our understanding of the relation between AIS integration and transparency. Based on the literature review, a theoretical framework has been presented to analyse if and how the integration level of AIS influences the process of compliance to the transparency regulation in the public organisations. The AIS integration level is assessed through three dimensions: data integration, network connectivity and network flexibility. To define the AIS integration levels, a three-point ordinal scale was developed by considering the feasible combinations of these dimensions. The AIS integration levels are the following, defined from lowest to highest: part integration (PI), a high level for "data integration" but a low level for the other two dimensions; full system integration (FSI), a high level for "data integration" and "network connectivity" but a low level for "network flexibility"; and full information integration (FII), a high level for all the dimensions.

The transparency level is measured through the following dimensions: publication of information; accessibility, effectiveness and usability; and interactivity. In addition, for the integration levels, a three-point ordinal scale was developed by considering the feasible combinations of these dimensions. The three transparency levels are the following: formal transparency (FoT), a high level for "public information" but a low level for the other two; quality transparency (QT), a high level for "public information" and "accessibility, information effectiveness and usability", but a low level for "interactivity"; and full transparency (FT), a high level for "public information", "accessibility, information effectiveness and usability" and "interactivity".

The framework shows how different AIS integration levels match with various transparency characteristics. Higher levels of AIS integration enable an increase in the characteristics of transparency and guarantee its effectiveness and interactivity.

In contrast, lower levels of AIS integration determine a sufficient and minimum degree of transparency, evaluated only through the existence or the nonexistence of the information on the public organisation's website.

Transparency is an active and ongoing research field. The goal of this article was to provide a theoretical framework based on the literature review, with which to analyse how AIS integration levels contribute to transparency effectiveness. In future research steps, we will consider case studies to test the research project and the validity of the framework. Those cases that will be selected will differ in terms of policy domains, level of government and external actors and be highly relevant in terms of the significant changes in government transparency over the past two decades.

References

1. Jang, Y. S., Cho, M., & Drori, G. S. (2014). National transparency: Global trends and national variations. *International Journal of Comparative Sociology, 70,* 1–24.
2. Bannister, F., & Connolly, R. (2011). The trouble with transparency: A critical review of opened in E-government. *Policy and Internet, 3*(1), 1–30.
3. Etzioni, A. (2010). Is transparency the best disinfectant? *Journal of Political Philosophy, 18* (4), 389–404.
4. Grimmelikhuijsen, S. (2012). Linking transparency, knowledge and citizen trust in government: An experiment. *International Review of Administrative Sciences, 78*(I), 50–73.
5. Meijer, A. (2009). Understanding modern transparency. *International Review of Administrative Science, 78*(2), 255–269.
6. Meijer, A. (2013). Understanding the complex dynamics of transparency. *Public Administration Review, 73*(3), 429–439.
7. Roberts, A. (2006). *Blacked out: Government secrecy in the information age.* New York: Cambridge University Press.

8. Hood, C., & Heald, D. (2006). Transparency: The key to better governance? *Public Administration, 86*(2), 591–618.
9. Relly, J. E., & Sabharwal, M. (2009). Perceptions of transparency of government policymaking: A cross-national study. *Government Information Quarterly, 26*, 148–157.
10. Bauhr, M., & Grimes, M. (2014). Indignation or resignation: The implications of transparency for societal accountability, governance. *An International Journal of Policy, Administration and Institution, 27*(2), 291–320.
11. Bovens, M. (2007). Analysing and assessing accountability: A conceptual framework. *European Law Journal, 13*(4), 447–468.
12. Koppel, J. (2005). Pathologies of accountability: ICANN and the challenge of "Multiple accountabilities disorder. *Public Administration Review, 65*(1), 94–108.
13. Osborne, D. (2004). Transparency and accountability reconsidered. *Journal of Financial Crime, 11*(3), 292–300.
14. Al-Jabri, I. M., & Roztocki, N. (2015). Adoption of ERP systems: Does information transparency matter? *Telematics and Informatics, 32*, 300–310.
15. Bertot, J. C., Jaeger, P. T., & Grimes, J. M. (2010). Using ICTs to creates a culture of transparency: E-government and social media as openness and anti-corruption tools for societies. *Government Information Quarterly, 27*, 264–271.
16. OECD. (2003). *The e-government imperative: Main findings*. Paris: OECD.
17. Bonson, E., Torres, L., Royo, S., & Flores, F. (2012). Local e-government 2.0: Social media and corporate transparency in municipalities. *Government Information Quarterly, 29*, 123–132.
18. Cucciniello, M., Nasi, G., & Valotti, G. (2012), *Assessing transparency in government: Rhetoric, reality and desire*. 45th Conference on system science, pp. 2451–2461.
19. Glassey, O., & Glaseey, O. F. (2004). A proximity indicator for e-government: The smallest number of clicks. *Journal of E-Government, 1*(4), 1–12.
20. Grimmelikhuijsen, S., & Welch, E. W. (2012). Developing and testing a theoretical framework for computer-mediated transparency of local governments. *Public Administration Review, 72* (4), 562–571.
21. Jorge, S., Sá, P. M., Pattaro, A. F., & Lourenço, R. P. (2011). *Local government financial transparency in Portugal and Italy: A comparative exploratory study on its determinants*. In: 13th Biennial CIGAR Conference, Bridging Public Sector and Non-Profit Sector Accounting, Ghent (Belgium).
22. Searson, E. M., & Johnson, M. A. (2010). Transparency laws and interactive public relations: An analysis of Latin American government web sites. *Public Relations Review, 36*, 120–126.
23. Karsten, S., Visscher, A. J., Dijkstra, A. B., & Veenstra, R. (2010). Towards standards for the publication of performance indicators in the public sector: The case of schools. *Public Administration, 88*(1), 90–112.
24. Liem, S. I. (2007). *Costituents of transparency in public administration with reference to empirical findings from Estonia*. Dissertation of the University of St. Gallen, Graduate School of Business Administration, Economics, Law and Social Sciences (HSG).
25. Pina, V., Torres, L., & Royo, S. (2007). Are ICTs improving transparency and accountability in the EU regional and local governments? An empirical study. *Public Administration, 85*(2), 449–472.
26. Curtin, D., & Meijer, A. J. (2006). Does transparency strengthen legitimacy? A critical analysis of European Union policy documents. *Information Policy, 11*, 109–122.
27. Welch, E. W., & Wong, W. (2001). Global information technology pressure and government accountability: The mediating effect of domestic context on website openness. *Journal of Public Administration Research and Theory, 11*, 509–538.
28. Gelinas, U. J., Sutton, S. G., & Hunton, J. E. (2005). *Accounting informations systems*, (6th ed., International edition). Thomson, OH: South-Western.
29. Rom, A., & Rohade, C. (2007). Management accounting and integrated information systems: A literature review. *International Journal of Accounting Information Systems, 8*(1), 40–68.

30. Darabos, E. (2014). Accounting systems and their convergences nowadays. *Economic Science Series, 23*(1), 604–610.
31. Dillard, J., & Yuthas, K. (2013). Critical dialogics, agonistic pluralism, and accounting information systems. *International Journal of Accounting Information Systems, 14*, 113–119.
32. Kimbro, M. (2002). A cross-country empirical investigation of corruption and its relationship to economic, cultural, and monitoring institutions: An examination of the role of accounting and financial statements quality. *Journal of Accounting, Auditing and Finance, 17*(4), 325–349.
33. Mistry, J. J. (2012). The role of e-governance in mitigating corruption. *Accounting and Public interest, 12*, 137–159.
34. Stein, M., Salterio, S., & Shearer, T. (2015). "Transparency" in accounting and corporate governance: Making sense of multiple meaning, ssrn.
35. Shaomin, L., & Pinsker, R. (2005). Modelling RBRT adoption and its effects on cost capital. *International Journal of accounting information systems, 6*(3), 196–215.
36. Bhatt, G. D., & Troutt, M. D. (2005). Examining the relationship between business process improvement initiatives, information systems integration and customer focus: an empirical study. *Business Process Management Journal, 11*(5), 532–558.
37. Granlund, M., & Malmi, T. (2002). Moderate impacts of ERPS on management accounting: A lag or permanent outcome? *Management Accounting Research, 13*, 299–321.
38. Scapens, R. W., & Jazayeri, M. (2003). ERP systems and management accounting change: opportunities or impacts? A research note. *European Accounting Review, 12*(1), 201–233.
39. Booth, P., Matolcsy, Z., & Bernhard, W. (2000). The impacts of enterprise resource planning systems onaccounting practice. The Australian experience. *Australian Accounting Review, 103*, 4–17.

Factors Influencing Mandatory and Voluntary e-Disclosure Diffusion by Municipalities

Benedetta Gesuele and Concetta Metallo

Abstract This study takes a first step toward understanding the diffusion of e-disclosure tools by Italian municipalities. We construct a synthetic indicator for measuring mandatory disclosure through website and an indicator for voluntary disclosure through social media usage, such as Facebook and Twitter. Moreover, we propose a research model to analyze the determinants of e-disclosure tools diffusion in order to underline any differences for mandatory and voluntary e-disclosure. We use OLS regression modeling on 93 Italian municipalities' data during 2012. The central idea is that determinants can influence in different ways the mandatory and voluntary e-disclosure tools diffusion.

Keywords e-Disclosure municipality • Facebook • Twitter • Website

1 Introduction

Nowadays, characterized by profound economic and financial crisis, citizens need to control the public activities and public entities' performance. Consequently, public entities have the need to disclosure information concerning their activities. New technologies can help governments in information provision, and the Internet has become an important tool to increase the public transparency and accountability [1], key drivers for good governance in the public sector. The Web 2.0 applications, and social media in particular, represent the last step in Internet development usage by the government. Social media provide new and innovative methods to improve the interaction between the government and citizens about policy issue and to enable citizens to participate the democratic process [2].

B. Gesuele (✉)
Department of Law, Pegaso University, Naples, Italy
e-mail: benedettagesuele@gmail.com

C. Metallo
Department of Sciences and Technology, Parthenope University, Naples, Italy
e-mail: concetta.metallo@uniparthenope.it

© Springer International Publishing AG 2017   263
K. Corsi et al. (eds.), *Reshaping Accounting and Management Control Systems*,
Lecture Notes in Information Systems and Organisation 20,
DOI 10.1007/978-3-319-49538-5_17

In the last years, many municipalities have added to their official website (e-disclosure) also several social media to communicate with citizens, as an additional form of online communication (such as Facebook, Twitter, and YouTube). Our study focuses on Web 2.0 application usage by municipalities because of their rising adoption and the small amount of academic research on the topic. These issues have become an interesting area of inquiry for Public Management scholars and Information Systems researchers. In fact, Mossberger and colleagues [3] have shown that local government is an important subject for the study of social media because of traditions of citizen participation at the local level. The Italian context is an interesting field of investigation of these phenomena because in Italy the importance of mandatory e-disclosure through municipality's website is recognized (with legislative decrees 150/2009 and 33/2013). Despite this, voluntary e-disclosure through social media is becoming more and more established.

This study takes a first step toward understanding the diffusion of Web 2.0 tools by Italian municipalities. In particular, we constructed a synthetic indicator to measure web and social media diffusion, such as Facebook and Twitter, by local government. Moreover, based on agency theory and neo-institutional framework, we propose a research model to analyze the determinants of social media diffusion in order to underline any differences for mandatory and voluntary e-disclosure. The structure of this paper is as follows. In the next section, we introduce the literature review on e-disclosure and social media usage by municipalities. In Sect. 3, we describe the research model and hypotheses, and then we outline the research methodology and the results of the analysis (Sect. 4). Finally, in Sect. 5, we discuss findings.

2 Literature Review

The disclosure via web (e-disclosure) by municipalities has received much attention among researchers. Agency theory and neo-institutional framework represent the most commonly applied theoretical backgrounds for understanding the impacts of web application on the public communication by local government.

Many research on e-disclosure have focused on disclosure via website [4–6], while only a very few have investigated social media adoption [2, 5, 7, 8]. Most of these studies were aimed to the realization of an e-disclosure index, summarizing the information disclosure on municipalities' website and identification of e-disclosure determinants. For example, Serrano-Cinca [6] investigated the determinants of voluntary Internet financial reporting by local administrations. In their study, size, political will, and citizens' income level affect e-disclosure. Gandia [9] analyzed the websites of several municipalities for understanding e-disclosure determinants and showed that political competition, public media visibility, and citizens' educational levels affect voluntary disclosure levels. Yu [10] highlighted how the size, wealth, local authority' organization, pro-capita income, and financial condition affect the e-disclosure. García and García-García [11] analyzed determinants of nonfinancial reporting in the Spanish municipalities, such as level of citizens' economic development, life quality level, size, municipality's budgetary, political stability, political strength, and political rivalry. Similarly, Garcia-Sanchez [12] assessed the determinants of sustainability disclosure practices in Spanish municipalities, considering as variables the level of citizens' economic development, life quality level, size, municipality's budgetary, political stability, political strength, and political rivalry.

The rapid diffusion of social media applications is ushering new ways for the government to communicate with and engage the public, and social media usage by municipalities represents an additional form of e-disclosure. Norris and Reddick's [13] survey on social media adoption of local governments (e.g., Facebook, Twitter, and YouTube) in the United States highlighted an amazing adoption rates; two-thirds of local governments had adopted at least one social media. Bonsón and colleagues' research [2] on the use of Web 2.0 and social media tools in EU local governments has shown that most local governments are using social media although the use of these applications to promote e-participation is still in their infancy at the local level. Klang and Nolin [14] investigated several Swedish social media policies produced by municipalities in order to recommend practical guidelines for improving transparency and interaction through social media. Kavanaugh [15] analyzed social media use by local governments for managing crisis situations from the routine (e.g., traffic, weather crises) to the critical (e.g., earthquakes, floods). Feeney and Welch [16] investigated whether different e-participation technologies and the intensity of e-participation technology use are associated with managers' perceptions of outcomes in the local governments. Mossberger [3] examined the use of social media and other interactive tools in the 75 largest US cities between 2009 and 2011, constructing an index of interactivity. Oliveira and Welch [17] have shown patterns of social media application for particular purposes, highlighting that social media tools are not a monolithic group. Ma [18] examined the diffusion of police microblogging (e.g., Twitter) and its determinants in Chinese municipal police bureaus through the perspective of organizational innovation diffusion. Her findings have shown that government size, Internet penetration rate, regional diffusion effects, and upper-tier pressure are positively and significantly associated with the adoption and earliness of police microblogging.

3 Research Model and Hypotheses

This study is aimed to analyze the determinants of mandatory (trough website) and voluntary e-disclosure (trough social media such as Facebook and Twitter) by Italian municipalities. In this research, we propose a research model to analyze the determinants of e-disclosure tools diffusion in order to underline any differences for mandatory and voluntary e-disclosure.

We built two e-disclosure indices: e-disclosure website index (eDI) measures the mandatory disclosure through municipalities' websites; social media usage index (smI) measures the voluntary disclosure via social media such as Facebook and Twitter. The use of synthetic indicator to measure website and social media diffusion among municipalities has been developed in some previous studies [2, 19, 20].

Fig. 1 Research model

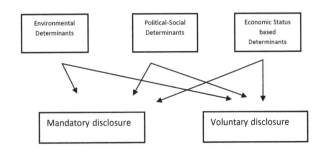

Several empirical studies [5, 31] have found evidence that social determinants, such as municipalities' size, are able to influence the use of web applications for mandatory and voluntary disclosure tools. Other scholars highlighted the role of economic and political factors as the key drivers of web application adoption by local government [6, 20]. In this study, we chose to identify three types of determinants that can affect e-disclosure: environmental determinants (size, municipality's type, and geographical position), political–social determinants (gender of mayor and political position), and economic status determinants (financial autonomy and citizens' wealth). We developed a research model in order to investigate determinants of mandatory and voluntary e-disclosure by Italian municipalities in order to underline the existence of different types of determinants; see Fig. 1.

The scholars agree that [4, 6, 11, 19–21] there is a positive relationship between size and usage of strategic communication tools by municipalities. In line with the agency theory, we consider the organization size as e-disclosure determinants, in the biggest municipalities people have less face-to-face contacts and use more web application as communication tools, that can be consider as showcase for municipalities activities [11]. Large municipalities would show greater information asymmetries among managers and citizens, and the social media usage can be considered as a strategic tool for reducing the agency costs [6]. Consequently, we proposed the following hypothesis:

H1: There is a positive relationship between municipality's size and e-disclosure tools (eDI and smI).

Several authors [20, 22–24] considered the geographical position and regional differences as a determinant in the development of e-government activities. The scholars considered that the regional differences could influence also differences in political culture and governance styles [25] as patterns of accounting and disclosure [6, 7, 26]. Thus, the following hypothesis was proposed:

H2: There is a relationship between municipalities' geographical position and e-disclosure tools (eDI and smI).

Previous research investigated about the relationship between municipality's type as urban district (small town) or city (large town) and e-disclosure propensity [2, 4]. e-Government tools usage requires specific technical and administrative structure [21] and availability of financial, technical, or personnel capacities [27, 28]. Several authors agreed that cities have more resources and tend to be more inclined to e-disclosure tools [29, 30]. Thus, the following hypothesis was proposed:

H3: There is a positive relationship between municipality's type and e-disclosure tools (eDI and smI).

Municipalities are governed by politicians, and their political ideology may influence disclosure practices, because different ideologies usually suggest different situations facing local authorities [6, 12]. The ruling party's political ideology may support different e-government styles and influence some aspects of administration culture such as e-disclosure propensity. The previous empirical studies have shown different results. For example, Tolbert and colleagues [32] highlighted the positive influence of left-wing ideology on e-government development. Similarly, other studies showed that municipalities governed by left-wing majorities are more transparent than those ruled by conservative mayors [4, 12]. On the contrary, other scholars found opposite results [5]. In this study, we hypothesized that political position may influence disclosure practices through website or social media by municipality. Thus, we proposed the following hypothesis:

H4: There is a relationship between political position and e-disclosure tools (eDI and smI).

In literature there are different studies that include the gender of mayor as political determinant [3, 22, 31]. The scholars investigated participatory inequality between men and women, showing that the gender is related to political activity [3, 33, 34].Thus, we proposed the following hypothesis:

H5: There is a relationship between gender of mayor and e-disclosure tools (eDI and smI).

Many studies [4, 11, 30, 34, 35] considered the relationship between municipalities' financial condition and disclosure. The central idea is that financial condition reveals the ability of municipality's management to benefit from considerable proper revenues (essentially taxes and fees) [5]. Consequently, local government has an increased responsibility to give citizens explanations on where and how is spending such revenues [5] and tends to highlight more the results of municipalities' activities. Thus, we proposed the following hypothesis:

H6: There is a positive relationship between financial autonomy and e-disclosure tools (eDI and smI).

In different studies, citizens' wealth is considered as a disclosure determinant [10, 19, 20, 22]. People that have higher economic status have more access to new technology [10] and greater user experience [9]. In fact, Yo [10] shown that people with a lower per capita income are less inclined to web usage. Moreover, citizens with higher income per capita expect more services and performance information [6, 9, 10, 18]. Thus, we proposed the following hypothesis:

H7: There is a positive relationship between citizens' wealth and e-disclosure tools (eDI and smI).

4 Methodology

This section introduces the information about the sample, measurement, and data analysis.

4.1 The Research Context: The Italian Municipalities

The Italian public sector is divided into three levels: state, 20 regional governments, 101 cities (such as large town), and 9.195 urban districts (small town). In Italy, there are several acts about the e-disclosure. The last acts are legislative decrees 150/2009 and 33/2013. In 2009, the legislative decree 150 proposed the extend control on municipalities' activities in order to improve performances. This reform predicted that the local government discloses some information on their activity, such as objectives, organization, performance indicators, and data about resources spent to deliver public services. The legislative decree 33/2013 established the mandatory disclosure and outlined the information to publish on the website.

To test the proposed model, we used ordinary least squares (OLS) regression modeling on 93 Italian municipalities' data during 2012. The sample is composed by Italian municipalities that use both Facebook and Twitter for voluntary disclosure.

4.2 Measurement

e-Disclosure website index (eDI) measures interaction level among citizens and municipalities using official/mandatory disclosure channel [2]. For e-disclosure website index, we considered some items based on previous literature. In particular, we analyzed the website of each local government and looked for the following 13 items (i): organization (i1), governing body (i2), consults (i3), wage body (i4), management (i5), controlled company (i6), internal auditing (i7), performance (i8), balance (i9), balance controlled company (i10), economic planning (i11), support planning (i12), and assets (i13). They are collected manually. For every item, we analyzed the presence that was scored with a binary variable (presence, 1; no presence, 0). It is calculated by the following equation (Equation 1):

$$eDI = \sum_{k=1}^{13} i_k$$

The social media usage index (smI) is constructed using Facebook information, which describes municipalities' Fb activity, and Twitter information, which describes municipalities' Twitter activity. The use of a synthetic indicator to measure the level of Fb and Tw usage by municipalities has been developed in some previous studies [2, 19, 20, 36]. The Fb index is composed of seven items (i) collected from Arata's (2012) report [37] and manually from municipalities' Fb Homepage. The items chosen are the number of friends (i1), up data frequency (i2), reply to comment (i3), replay to link or video (i4), import by official page (i5), presence of specific type of contents (i6), and type of account (i7). For every item, we analyzed the presence that was scored with a binary variable (presence, 1; no presence, 0). The Tw index is composed of eight items (i) collected from Arata's (2012) report [38]: total tweet (i1), following (i2), followers (i3), recognizability (i4), Twitter frequency (i5), tweet number to others in the last 12 months (i6), mean number of retweets (RT) to our tweet in the last 12 months (i7), and specific contents (i8). For item number 3, 4, and 7, we analyzed the presence that was scored with a binary variable (presence, 1; no presence, 0). The item numbers 1, 2, 5, and 6 have been measured in natural logarithm (LN). The smI is one synthetic indicator that we construct adding up two indicators, Fb index and Tw index, and calculated by the following equation (Equation 2):

$$smI = FbI \sum_{K=1}^{7} i + TwI \sum_{K=1}^{8} i$$

For the determinants, many data are collected from comuniverso.it. comuniverso.it is a free web portal on Italian municipalities that publics data about political, economic, and geographic information on the municipalities. Determinants are described in the following table (Table 1).

Table 2 shows descriptive statistics.

4.3 Data Analysis

We analyzed the correlation among variables in order to use OLS regression model. The following table (Table 3) shows that there is not a strong correlation among the independent variables.

Table 1 Determinant description

Variable	Tag	Definition	Measurement	Literature	Sources
Size	Size	The number of municipality's population	Number (Natural 1) Number (1: Nord; 2: Centro; 3: South; 4: Island)	Laswad, Fisher, and Oyelere (2005), Alvarez et al. (2010), Guillimòn, Bastida, and Benito (2011), Albalate (2013), Serrano-Cinca, Rueda-Tomas, and Portillo-Tarragona et al. (2008), and Garcia and Garcia (2010)	www. comuniverso. it
Geographical Position	GeoPos	The Municipalities' geographical location The type of local government: municipality (such as urban district) or city (Such as large town)		Norris and Moon (2005), Albalate (2013)	www. comuniverso. it
Municipalities' type	Mtype		Number (0: municipality; 1: city)	Laswad Fisher, and Ovelere (2005)	www. comuniverso. it
Political position	PolPos	The political ideology of municipal ruling parties	Number (1: left; 2: right; 3: center-left; 4: center-right; 5: center)	Guillimòn Bastida and Benito (2011)	www. comuniverso. it
Gender	Gender	The mayor's gender	Number (1: woman: 0: men)	Guillimòn Bastida and Benito (2011)	www. comuniverso. it
Index of financial autonomy	FinAut	Index of financial autonomy	Number	Laswad Fisher, and Oyelere et al. (2005), Styles and Tennyson (2007),	www.istat.it

(continued)

Table 1 (continued)

Variable	Tag	Definition	Measurement	Literature	Sources
				Guillimòn et al. (2011), and García et al. (2010)	
Citizens' Wealth	CitWealth	The value of economic activity per capita	Number	Laswad Fisher, and Oyelere et al. (2005), Styles and Tennyson (2007), Guillimòn et al. (2011), and García et al. (2011)	www.istat.it

Table 2 Descriptive statistics

Variables	Mean	Median	Min	Max
Size	9.76522	9.74373	5.18178	13.8046
GeoPos	2.02151	2.00000	1.00000	4.00000
MType	0.774194	1.00000	0.00000	1.00000
PolPos	3.82796	3.00000	2.00000	10.0000
Gender	0.043478	0.00000	0.00000	1.00000
AutFin	59.7097	62.0000	15.0000	86.0000
CitWealth	9.97551	9.96133	9.61820	10.3227
eDI	8.81720	9.00000	0.00000	13.0000
smI	40.2714	34.0865	13.5756	112.528

Table 3 Correlation

Size	GeoPas	MType	Pol_Pos	Gender	AutFin	CitWealth	
1.0000	−0.0713	−0.6902	−0.2375	−0.1221	0.1031	0.6033	Size
	1.0000	0.1762	0.0549	−0.1534	−0.4108	−0.4883	GeoPos
		1.0000	0.1439	0.1124	0.1099	−0.5949	MType
			1.0000	−0.0589	0.0071	−0.1647	PolPos
				1.0000	0.2242	−0.0089	Gender
					1.0000	0.2801	AutFin
						1.0000	CitWealth

Table 4 OLS regression model (e-disclosure website determinants)

	Coefficient	Error Std.	T Student	p-value	
const	−103.306	24.5274	−4.2119	0.00006	***
Size	0.543515	0.228585	2.3777	0.01969	**
GeoPos	0.205635	0.278213	0.7391	0.46189	
MType	0.755022	0.883971	0.8541	0.39546	
PolPos	−0.186127	0.214482	−0.8678	0.38798	
Gender	0.800325	1.20059	0.6666	0.50685	
AutFin	0.0140757	0.0190251	0.7398	0.46146	
CitWealth	10.589	2.49437	4.2452	0.00006	***
R^2	0.481509				
R^2 adjusted	0.438301				

***, error $<1\%$; **, error $<5\%$; *, error $<10\%$

Then, using regression analysis, OLS performed the data analysis for testing the hypothesized relationships among constructs. The two models listed below show the contribution of independent variables (environmental, political–social, and economic status-based determinants) to dependent variables (e-disclosure website index and social media usage index).

In particular, we tested the hypotheses concerning on the relationship on determinants and eDI through the following OLS regression model (Equation 3):

$$eDI = \alpha + \beta(\ln)Size + \beta GeoPos + \beta MType + \beta PolPos + \beta Gen + \beta AutFin + \beta CitWealth$$

Table 4 shows the findings of the first OLS regression model. Findings highlight that size and citizen's wealth affect to e-disclosure website index; thus, hypotheses 1 and 7 are supported.

Then, we tested the hypotheses concerning on the relationship on determinants and smI through the following OLS regression model (Equation 4):

$$smI = \alpha + \beta(\ln)Size + \beta GeoPos + \beta MType + \beta PolPos + \beta Gen + \beta AutFin + \beta CitWealth$$

Table 5 shows the findings of the second OLS regression model. Findings highlight that size and political position are positively related to social media index; thus, hypotheses 1 and 4 are supported. Moreover, Table 5 shows that the geographical position and municipalities' type affect social media index, supporting hypotheses 2 and 3.

Table 5 OLS regression model (social media usage determinants)

	Coefficient	Error Std.	T Student	p-value	
const	−25.5858	153.784	−0.1664	0.86826	
Size	5.54602	1.4332	3.8697	0.00021	***
GeoPos	−3.66365	1.74436	−2.1003	0.03870	**
MType	−9.82247	5.54238	−1.7722	0.07998	*
PolPos	2.3832	1.34477	1.7722	0.07999	*
Gender	1.02161	7.52753	0.1357	0.89237	
AutFin	−0.13246	0.119285	−1.1104	0.26998	
CitWealth	2.54882	15.6394	0.1630	0.87093	
R^2	0.475005				
R^2 adjusted	0.431256				

***, error $<1\%$; **, error $<5\%$; *, error $<10\%$

5 Discussion of Results

In line with previous studies [19, 20, 30], our findings have shown a positive relationship between municipality's size and e-disclosure. Large municipalities are more likely to use website and social media, where a higher number and variety of stakeholders might encourage the information disclosure [12].

Our results have also highlighted that citizens' wealth affect e-disclosure through website, in accord with several studies [10, 26, 31]. Domínguez [21] have argued that higher income per capita is directly linked to purchases of computers and technological devices, as well as access to the Internet; consequently, these features influence demand for e-disclosure. Conversely, findings have not shown a significant relationship between citizens' wealth and social media usage. Twitter and Facebook are the most popular social media tools because they are entirely free and with open access and user-friendly, used for professional and personal purposes in both workplace and "out-of-office" environments, and individuals can access on their computers, phones, or both. For these reasons, we believe that citizens' wealth is not an important prerequisite of their adoption. Moreover, Facebook and Twitter are increasingly gaining currency for both younger and older people, regardless of economic or social status and geographic position. In fact, our results have highlighted that municipalities' type and geographical position have a negative influence on social media usage, in contrast to other studies [9, 25, 39]. We justify these results considering the characteristics of the sample investigated. While the previous research analyzed national governments of several countries, our study is focused on municipalities of a single country, such as Italy, where regional differences in administrative culture are minor. Findings showed a significant relationship between political position and social media usage by municipality, consistently with previous studies [6, 19, 36]. Governing party's political ideology may support different e-government styles and influence some aspects of administration culture such as e-disclosure propensity. Bonsón and colleagues ([2], p. 12) have shown that "the development of an active presence in social media platforms is not country-related but dependent on the political will and specific circumstances of each local government."

This study presents several limitations. One limitation stems from the size of the sample with respect to the determinants investigated. Second, literature of traditional disclosure (not web) indices is abundant and detailed, but the new disclosure (via web or social media) indices present specific problems that may involve a certain degree of subjectivity. Moreover, the e-disclosure index considered in this work (eDI and smI) seems heterogeneous: the first is simple, and it can vary from 0 to 13; the second is more complex, and it is composed of dichotomous items and not. Future research would be appropriate to make a validity test of this index.

Despite some limitations, this research contributes to the existing knowledge on e-disclosure, highlighting the growing importance of voluntary disclosure through social media. Findings from 93 Italian municipalities showed the presence of different determinates for e-disclosure website and social media usage, pointing out that large municipalities characterized by high income per capita are more likely to use website to information disclosure. Moreover, municipality's size and political position are able to influence the use of social media as strategic communication channel. Moreover, the geographical position and municipality's type negatively affect e-disclosure through social media, differing from the results of the most previous research.

References

1. Bonson, E., Torres, L., Rayo, S., & Flores, F. (2012). Local e-government 2.0: Social Media and corporate transparency in municipalities. *Government Information Quarterly, 29*(12), 123–132.
2. Reddick, C. G., & Aikins, S. K. (2012). *Web 2.0 Technologies and democratic governance* (Political, policy and management implications). New York: Springer.
3. Mossberger, K., Wu, Y., & Crawford, J. (2013). Connecting citizens and local governments? Social media and interactivity in major US cities. *Government Information Quarterly, 30*(4), 351–358.
4. Guillimòn, M. D., Bastida, F., & Benito, B. (2011). The determinants of Local Government's financial transparency. *Local Government Studies, 37*(4), 391–406.
5. Jorge, S., Moura, Sá P., Pattaro, A. F., & Lourenço, R. P. (2011). *Local government financial transparency in Portugal and Italy: A comparative exploratory study on its determinants.* In: 13th Biennial CIGAR conference, Ghent, Belgium.
6. Serrano-Cinca, C., Rueda-Tomas, M., & Portillo-Tarragona, P. (2008). *Factors influencing e-disclosure in local public administrations.* In: Documento de Trabajo 2008-03, Facultad de CienciasEconomicas y Empresariales, Universidad de Zaragoza.
7. Perez, C. C., Rodriguez, B., Manuel, P., & Lopez Hernandez, A. M. (2008). e-Government process and incentives for online public financial information. *On line Information Review, 32*(3), 379–400.
8. Magro, M. J. (2012). A review of social media use in e-government. *Administrative Sciences, 2*, 148–161.

9. Gandia, J. L., & Archidona, C. (2008). Determinants of web site information by Spanish city councils. *On line Information Review, 32*(1), 35–57.

10. Yu, H. (2010). *On the determinants of internet-based disclosure of government financial information.* Conference Proceeding of Management and Service Science (MASS): 09/2010.

11. García, A. C., & García-García, J. (2010). Determinants of online reporting of accounting information by Spanish local government authorities. *Local Government Studies, 36*(5), 679–695.

12. García-Sánchez, I. M., Frías-Aceituno, J. V., & Rodríguez-Domínguez, L. (2013). Determinants of corporate social disclosure in Spanish local governments. *Journal of Cleaner Production, 39*, 60–72.

13. Norris, D. F., & Reddick, C. G. (2013). Local e-government in the United States: Transformation or incremental change? *Public Administration Review, 73*(1), 165–175.

14. Klang, M., & Nolin, J. (2011). Disciplining social media: An analysis of social media policies in 26 Swedish municipalities. *First Monday, 16*(8).

15. Kavanaugh, A. L., Fox, E. A., Sheetz, S. D., Yang, S., Li, L. T., Shoemaker, D. J., et al. (2012). Social media use by government: From the routine to the critical. *Government Information Quarterly, 29*(4), 480–491.

16. Feeney, M. K., & Welch, E. W. (2012). Electronic participation technologies and perceived outcomes for local government managers. *Public Management Review, 14*(6), 815–833.

17. Oliveira, G. H. M., & Welch, E. W. (2013). Social media use in local government: Linkage of technology, task, and organizational context. *Government Information Quarterly, 30*(4), 397–405.

18. Ma, L. (2013). The diffusion of government microblogging: Evidence from Chinese municipal police bureaus. *Public Management Review, 15*(2), 288–309.

19. Bonsón, E., Royo, S., & Ratkai, M. (2014). *Facebook practices in Western European municipalities an empirical analysis of activity and citizens' engagement.* Administration & Society, 0095399714544945.

20. Gibby, A., Smith, S., Pang, V., & Toorn, C. V., (2014). *The impact of WEB 2.0 (GOV 2.0) and social media technologies on engagement in local government.* PACIS 2014 Proceedings. Paper 120.

21. Alvarez, I. G., Dominiquez, L. R., & Sanchez, I. M. G. (2010). Are determining factors of municipal e-government common to a worldwide municipal view? An intra-comparison. *Government Information Quarterly, 27*(4), 423–430.

22. Gesuele, B., & Alvino, F. (2014). Social determinants and e-disclosure. Empirical Evidence from the Spain. *Journal of USA- CHINA Public Administration, 11*(7), 557–563.

23. Pina, T., Rayo, V., Torres, L., & Rayo, S. (2009). E-government evolution in EU local governments: A comparative perspective. *Online Information Review, 33*(6), 1137–1168.

24. Hammerschmid, G., & Meyer, R. E. (2005). New public management in Austria: Local variation of a global theme. *Public Administration, 83*(3), 709–734.

25. Piotrowski, S. J., & Van Ryzin, G. G. (2007). Citizen attitudes toward transparency in local government. *The American Review of Public Administration, 37*(3), 306–323.

26. McNeal, R., Schmeida, M., & Hale, K. (2007). E-disclosure laws and electronic campaign finance reform: Lessons from the diffusion of e-government policies in the States. *Government Information Quarterly, 24*(2), 312–325.

27. Moon, M. J., & Norris, D. F. (2005). Does managerial orientation matter? The adoption of reinventing government and e- government at the municipal level. *Information Systems Journal, 15*(1), 43–60.

28. Bertot, J. C., Jaeger, P. T., & Grimes, J. M. (2010). Using ICTs to create a culture of transparency: E-government and social media as openness and anti-corruption tools for societies. *Government Information Quarterly, 27*(3), 264–271.

29. Ingram, R. W. (1984). Economic incentives and the choice of state government accounting practices. *Journal of Accounting Research, 22*(1), 126–144.

30. Laswad, F., Fisher, R., & Oyelere, P. (2005). Determinants of voluntary Internet financial reporting by LGA. *Journal of Accounting and Public Policy, 24*, 101–121.
31. Albalate, D. (2010). *The institutional, economic and social determinants of local government transparency*. W.P. IREARP.
32. Tolbert, C. J., Mossberger, K., & McNeal, R. (2008). Institutions, policy and E-government in the American States. *Public Administration Review, 68*(3), 549–563.
33. Verba, S., Norman, H. N., & Joe, O. K. (1978). *Participation and political equality. A several nation comparison*. Cambridge: Cambridge University Press.
34. Andersen, K. (1975). Working woman and political participation. *American Journal of Political Science, 19*(3), 439–453.
35. Styles, A., & Tennyson, M. (2005). *The accessibility of financial of U.S. Municipalities on the Internet*. Paper Presented at The American Accounting Association Mid-Atlantic Regional Meeting, March 25, Philadelphia, PA.
36. Mergel, I., & Bretschneider, S. I. (2013). Three stage adoption process for social media use in government. *Public Administration Review, 73*(3), 390–400.
37. Arata, G. (2012). *TwitterPA 2012/1. Quanti sono e cosa fanno gli enti locali su Twitter*. www.scribd.com/giovanniarata.
38. Arata, G. (2012). *FacebookPA 2012/1. Quanti sono e cosa fanno gli enti locali su Facebook*. www.scribd.com/giovanniarata.
39. Debreceny, R., Gray, G. L., & Mock, J. (2001). Financial reporting web sites: What users want in terms of form and content. *The International Journal of Digital Accounting Research, 1*(1), 1–23.

Accountability and Performance of Italian Local Government Authorities: How Does e-Disclosure Affect Performance?

Luigi Lepore and Sabrina Pisano

Abstract The Internet has become the most important channel to disclose information and to reduce the distance between local government authorities and its stakeholders, in order to maintain politicians, managers and public administrations accountable. The study examines the relationship between accountability and performance of Italian Local Government Authorities that are obliged to disclose performance data on their website, in order to enhance transparency and participation for improving public performance. Findings show no significant relationship between e-disclosure and performance, underlining that the greater transparency is only symbolic, and a positive and significant relationship between media interest and performance, highlighting the relevant role that media could have in stimulating citizens to control ways through which politicians and public managers spent money and create public value.

Keywords Disclosure • Accountability • Performance • Media

1 Introduction

In the last two decades, many European countries have realized different public management reforms to strengthen public accountability arrangements and to design new ones, in order to improve public performance at both central and local levels.

Research about the relationship between accountability and performance are often based on agency theory framework, because it is useful to explain the information asymmetry between local government authorities (LGAs) and stakeholders and consequently the potential free riding of politicians and manager that could choose a way to use public money that expropriates citizens, that are taxpayers and so the lenders of public administrations.

L. Lepore (✉) • S. Pisano
Department of Law, Parthenope University, Naples, Italy
e-mail: luigi.lepore@uniparthenope.it; sabrina.pisano@uniparthenope.it

© Springer International Publishing AG 2017
K. Corsi et al. (eds.), *Reshaping Accounting and Management Control Systems*,
Lecture Notes in Information Systems and Organisation 20,
DOI 10.1007/978-3-319-49538-5_18

This research explores the relationship between accountability and performance of Italian LGAs after the reform issued in 2009, which requires Italian LGAs to disclose performance data on their website, in order to enhance transparency and, as a consequence, improve their performance. The objective is to understand how the accountability arrangements defined for LGAs actually work.

We also investigate the role of media that, spreading information about public performance, could facilitate citizens in making judgments about the ways public administrations spend public money to deliver public services.

2 Accountability and Performance of Local Government Authorities

Public management reforms realized in the last two decades call for the introduction at both central and local government level of more transparency and accountability, in order to improve effectiveness and efficiency. The concept of accountability could be defined as the state of being answerable, responsible and or accountable for results in the own area of responsibility. Accountability goes beyond rendering an account of the resources used, but also includes the efficient use of those resources and the ability of policy decisions and managerial activities to satisfy public needs [1].

The state of being responsible can be referred both to the organizational level—in this case, for example, we speak about accountability of LGAs—and at the individual level - i.e. the accountability of manager or politicians [2].

These reform processes originated from the assumption that to improve public performances it is necessary to ensure transparency on performance data that allows citizens to make judgments about the ways public administrations spend public money to deliver public services (social control). Citizens, that are the electorate, have the right to be informed about the actions and expenditures of the executive and legislative arms of the government [3, 4]. Transparency enhances engagement, involvement and participation in political and public issue by a large part of stakeholder group, and this is important for keeping politicians and managers accountable [5].

Research about the relationship between accountability and performance are often based on agency theory framework [6]. There are, however, also other theoretical approaches that have been used to investigate the implementation of mandatory performance measurement system in government organizations, including institutional theory. Cavalluzzo and Ittner [7], for example, refer to institutional theory to explain implementation success of performance measurement system in government activities.

Voters, citizens and other stakeholders are considered the principals, and politicians and managers are considered the agents. The relationship between principal and agent in public sector is not easier to define, because here there are different accountability relationships: those between elected officials and managers, those between elected officials and citizens and those between citizens and managers [8].

Consistent with what happened in other European countries, whose most emblematic case is represented by the UK, the reform of Italian LGAs issued in 2009 by the Law 15/2009 and implemented by the Legislative Decree 150/2009 requires LGAs to disclose their objectives, performance indicators and data about resources spent to deliver public services, as well as information about organization, on their website (hereafter e-disclosure) in order to improve performances.

Despite considerable interest of researchers all around the world, relatively few studies have been conducted on the effect of this kind of reforms on the efficiency and effectiveness of LGAs. Convincing and homogeneous evidence that these reforms will lead to better performance has not yet been found, particularly in Italy and in that countries that are characterized by a public administration style affected by structures, principles, logics and instruments inherited from a bureaucratic, hierarchical, Weberian public administration based on administrative law [9, 10].

In this research, we explore the relationship between accountability and performance of Italian LGAs after the reform issued in 2009, considering the accountability relationships between citizens and elected officials and those between citizens and managers. In particular, we try to analyse in which way more transparency and accountability, enhancing the social control, influence performance at organizational level. We address prevalently to the agency theory, because it better explains the information asymmetry between LGAs and stakeholders that inhibits the supervision of government activities by citizens and consequently the performance improvement.

Agency theory suggests that information asymmetry between citizens and politicians and managers pushes agents to free ride. So, in order to reduce the opportunity of free riding and improve LGAs' overall performance, it is necessary to enhance social control.

The progresses in the use of Internet made more easy the diffusion of information about performance and, in general, the interaction between LGAs and stakeholders. So, the Internet became the most important "highway" to disclose information, to reduce the distance between LGAs and its stakeholders and so to maintain politicians, managers and public administrations accountable.

Many authors have highlighted the fundamental contribution of the Internet to promote new forms of accountability, enhancing interactivity, transparency and openness of LGAs [11–14]. These are all considered as positive values to increase social control and so to strengthen citizen trust in governments [12, 15]. So, the following hypothesis has been formulated:

H_1 e-Disclosure is positively associated with LGAs' performance.

However, the presence of the information on Internet does not assure that citizens receive and use that information to exercise the social control. So, it becomes important that media and newspaper disclose that information about the performance. The relevant role of media and newspapers in stimulating public opinion and social control is clear if we consider the case of the UK, where the

LGAs' score about the performance related to the delivery of public service and the use of public money was published not only on the Audit Commission website, but it was also disclosed by media and newspapers. According to these considerations, we hypothesize that:

H₂ Media interest is positively associated with LGAs' performance.

3 Method

This study is part of a wider research aiming at testing the relationship between accountability and performance in a longitudinal period (2010–2015), using panel analysis. We decided to start the analysis from the year 2010 in order to test the effects of the potential greater transparency of LGAs derived from the mandatory implementation of accountability measures resulting from the issuing of Legislative Decree 150/2009 and Law 15/2009. From that data set, this paper reports the results of just the first year, i.e. 2010.

3.1 Sample

We empirically test the previous hypotheses on a sample of 162 Italian LGAs in 2010. Our sample is composed of all LGAs which responded to a questionnaire that we sent during 2011 in order to collect data on our variables. We chose to investigate LGAs because they are responsible for the provision of the most immediate public services to citizens. In this sense, it is important to examine how many information they release and how disclosure affects their performances. We decided to analyse the information released in 2010 because the reform required LGAs to disclose performance data starting from this year.

3.2 Measurement

Our dependent variable is the LGAs' performance. The concept of performance, in the public sector, is very complex and multidimensional. More specifically, the financial aspect (i.e. profitability, costs, revenues) can be considered only one dimension that composes the overall performance of a public institution. However, in this paper we decided to use the financial autonomy (*FAut*) as a proxy of the LGAs' performance, on the basis that the financial crisis started in 2008 had a relevant impact on the LGAs' financial dimension.

We calculated *FAut* as the ratio between revenues obtained from local taxes and tariffs to total current revenues. If this ratio is high, it means that LGA is little

Table 1 The items identified

Items
Mandatory informative documents
Organizational aspects
Performance indicators
Resource use indicators
Output of the measurement activities
Output of the assessment activities
Remunerations
Curriculum vitae
Information about managers and administrative clerks
Employee absence rates
Information about other administrative clerks

dependent on other public administrations for sources of financing. We collected data on our dependent variable from the ANCI website.

We had two independent variables: e-disclosure released during 2010 (*e-Disc*) and media interest (*MedInt*).

e-Disc was measured developing an unweighted disclosure index. The research method was organized as follows. Firstly, we selected the performance data that LGAs should disclose on the Internet on the basis of the reform issued in 2009. We identified 11 items that mainly concern outcome, output and processes measures, as well as information about the organization.

Table 1 reports the items identified.

Then, we inserted this performance information in the questionnaire sent to LGAs and collected data for each item. A score of 1 was assigned to each item if the LGA affirmed it was disclosed and a score of 0 otherwise. We verified the answers received to the questionnaire by analysing the LGAs' website, in order to control if they were correct, and we did not find errors. The final score assigned to each LGA was measured by an index, which varies from 0 to 1 and is equal to the ratio between the number of items released and the total amount of items identified ex ante.

We also used the questionnaire to collect data on our second independent variable: *MedInt*. We measured *MedInt* using a 4-point scale varying from 0 to 3 according to the degree of media interest perceived by each LGA, on the basis of the consideration that public organizations are prompted to work better if they feel to be more evaluated.

3.3 Control Variables

We considered six control variables. We analysed the traditional disclosure released by LGAs (*TradDisc*), and we measured this variable as the number of both mandatory and voluntary reports drawn up by each LGA in 2010, using the questionnaire. Size (*Size*) was measured as the number of LGA inhabitants [16, 17]. Employment (*Empl*) was computed as the percentage of inhabitants that has a job. Both *Size* and *Empl* were collected from ISTAT website. Press visibility (*PressVis*) was calculated as the number of items in the print press in which LGA appeared during 2010 by a count search on Google [18]. Internet visibility (*IntVis*) was measured as the number of incoming links to LGA website according to Google [16]. Finally, citizens' wealth (*CiWeal*) was measured as the disposal income per LGA inhabitant [16, 19], and we collected data on this variable on the ANCI website.

3.4 Descriptive Statistics

Table 2 provides descriptive statistics. The LGAs investigated are mainly small: the average *Size* is 10,676.60 inhabitants. Moreover, only 55 % of inhabitants has a job. These LGAs present medium levels of *FAut*: on average 43 % of current revenues is obtained from local taxes and tariffs.

Passing to *e-Disc*, it emerges that the LGAs investigated released 53 % of the performance data identified on average, that is equal to six items. The mean of *MedInt* is 0.88; it means that the LGAs studied consider media to be not really interested in their performances.

TradDisc is very low (16 %), because most LGAs do not draw up voluntary reports. Those LGAs that prepare voluntary reports draw up at most three documents that are mainly social accountability reports. Both *PressVis* and *IntVis* present low values (16.27 and 11.43). These findings could be due to the dimension of the LGAs included in the sample. In other words, it could be that media are not very interested in the events occurring in smaller LGAs.

We checked for any possible collinear issues among the variables through the correlation matrix, variance inflation factors and condition indices.

Table 3 provides the correlation coefficients between *FAut* and the independent and control variables.

FAut shows significant positive correlations with *e-Disc*, *TradDisc*, *Empl* and *IntVis*. Furthermore, Table 3 shows that *e-Disc* is negatively correlated to *MedInt* and positively correlated to *TradDisc* and *IntVis*.

In general, the analysis indicates that LGAs with a high level of *e-Disc* have higher performance and that LGAs with high *e-Disc* perceive a lower degree of media interest, maybe because they consider that these mechanisms act as substitutes for social control, draw up a higher number of both mandatory and voluntary reports and have a higher number of incoming links to their website according to Google.

Table 2 Descriptive statistics

Variables	Mean	Std.d.	Min.	5th pct.	50th pct.	95th pct.	Max.
FAut	0.434	0.140	0.090	0.220	0.440	0.660	0.820
e-Disc	0.534	0.196	0.000	0.100	0.600	0.800	1.000
MedInt	0.888	1.015	0.000	0.000	1.000	3.000	3.000
TradDisc	0.159	0.144	0.000	0.000	0.166	0.500	0.666
Size	10676.600	11948.400	533.000	1328.050	8298.000	30756.800	90288.000
Empl	55.863	10.372	36.900	37.900	61.800	67.595	69.100
PressVis	16.277	75.657	0.000	0.000	4.000	50.050	926.000
IntVis	11.438	13.635	0.000	0.000	7.000	40.850	92.000
CiWeal	23058.300	19346.700	14747.000	16487.900	20440.000	27866.900	233730.000

Table 3 Correlation matrix

	(1)	(2)	(3)	(4)	(5)	(6)	(7)	(8)	(9)
FAut (1)	1.000	0.141*	0.078	0.157**	0.107	0.452***	0.097	0.158**	−0.071
e-Disc (2)		1.000	−0.126*	0.337***	0.116	0.242***	0.107	0.194***	−0.009*
MedInt (3)			1.000	−0.062	−0.000	−0.037	−0.014	0.061	0.058
TradDisc (4)				1.000	0.160**	0.195**	0.064	0.253**	−0.127
Size (5)					1.000	−0.039	0.555***	0.599****	−0.014
Empl (6)						1.000	0.088	0.224****	−0.007
PressVis (7)							1.000	0.436***	0.020
IntVis (8)								1.000	0.020
CiWeal (9)									1.000

*** $= p < 0.01$, ** $= p < 0.05$, * $= p < 0.10$

Table 4 Results from OLS regression

Dependent variable: financial autonomy		
Variables	Estimated coefficient	t-Statistic
e-Disc	0.011	0.218
MedInt	0.017	1.820*
TradDisc	0.045	0.602
Size	2.164	1.847*
Empl	0.006	6.382***
PressVis	−2.922	−0.185
IntVis	−0.000	−0.754
CiWeal	−4.320	−0.845
Observations	162	
R^2	0.265	
Adjusted R^2	0.225	
F-statistic	6.722***	

$*** = p < 0.01$, $* = p < 0.10$

4 Regression Analysis

To test our hypotheses, we used the following OLS regression model:

$$
\begin{aligned}
FAut = \quad & \alpha + \beta_1 e\text{-}Disc + \beta_2 MedInt + \beta_3 TradDisc \\
& + \beta_4 Size + \beta_5 Empl + \beta_6 PressVis + \beta_7 IntVis \\
& + \beta_8 CiWeal + \varepsilon
\end{aligned}
\tag{1}
$$

This econometric model investigates the influence of the independent variables identified on LGAs' performance.

Table 4 shows findings from OLS regression.

The results provide support for hypothesis H_2, showing a positive relationship between MedInt and FAut ($\beta = 0.017$, $p < 0.10$). The findings also show a positive association both between Size and FAut ($\beta = 2.164$, $p < 0.10$) and between *Empl* and *FAut* ($\beta = 0.006$, $p < 0.01$). However, considering the adjusted R^2, the model explains a mild proportion of the variation in *FAut*.

5 Discussion and Conclusions

In this study we have investigated the relationship between e-disclosure and performance of Italian LGAs using the framework of agency theory.

Our results provide partial support for the hypotheses developed. In particular, we found no significant relationship between e-disclosure and performance. The mechanism of social control does not work, and so increased e-disclosure does not mean better performance. In other words, in Italy the reform did not bring to an increase in the performance; it could be because this variable is not related to disclosure. Probably, holding LGAs accountable for results will only lead to improved performance if certain external conditions are fulfilled. Our result is different from those of previous research showing a positive relationship between accountability and performance. Schaltegger and Torgler [6], for example, found empirical evidence that government accountability is crucial for public indebtedness and fiscal discipline. However, our result is consistent with studies that do not find evidence of benefits, in terms of performance improvement, from mandated increase in performance measurement and accountability in government organization. Cavalluzzo and Ittner [7] argue that organizations gain legitimacy by conforming to external expectations regarding appropriate management control systems in order to appear modern, rational and efficient to external observers but tend to separate their internal activities from the externally focused symbolic systems.

Government organizations implement the required practices, but the changes will tend to be only symbolic: it is superficial and loosely tied to employees' actions. Different empirical studies found that government organizations that implement management accounting systems to satisfy legislative requirements make little use of the systems for internal purposes [20–22]. These practices were used by LGAs more as political strategies for controlling controversy than as tools for improving accountability or decision-making [23]. These studies suggest that the compulsory performance measurement systems may increase the development of result-oriented performance measures but have little effect on accountability, use or performance.

Moreover, we found a positive and significant relationship between media interest and performance. Our result highlights the relevant role that media could have in stimulating citizens to control ways through which politicians and public managers spent money to create public value. The importance of this role was emphasized in the UK during the reform process of LGAs' control system in the period 1997–2010. In the UK, the ranking of LGAs, defined according to the methodology defined Comprehensive Performance Assessment, was made public every year in mid-December on the website of the Audit Commission, and press releases and conferences were reserved to the media a few days before publication online, in order to stimulate public opinion and social control.

In a comparative perspective, the British LGAs are characterized by a high level of professionalism, guaranteed by competitive mechanisms of recruitment and career advancement from which spring both the clear distinction between politics and administration and the widespread presence in government of managerial and organizational skills and therefore not prevalently legal like in Italy.

The lack of a market for "local government control" prevents the operation of the mechanism of social control. In practice, if in the underperforming LGAs, managers and politicians responsible for the poor performance are not replaced, the accountability mechanism, which assures that greater transparency is accompanied by a performance improvement of LGAs, obviously, cannot operate.

Therefore, reforms like that one implemented in Italy that try to strengthen accountability mechanisms could fail because of the lack of instruments for the protection of stakeholders, such as a market for "local government control" or a valid system of incentives that push underperforming managers and/or politicians to improve the results of the organization.

Moreover, often the information provided to citizens do not reach the recipient, or it is difficult to read and interpret, and therefore this information must be diffused, "reinterpreted" and made more readable, for example, through the action of the media.

The study presents some limits. First, it only reports the results of the first year of accountability measures' implementation, i.e. 2010. However, as discussed above, this is part of a wider research, but until now we have only collected the data for 1 year. In future development of this study, we will extend our sample, and we will also try to check for reverse relationship and problems eventually arising from outliers. Second, the use of self-respondent questionnaire to measure different variables is a limitation because it is subject to criticism of respondent bias. Third, we used financial autonomy as a proxy of the overall LGAs' performance, but this is only a possible way to measure performance. To better test our hypotheses, we could use other measures of performance, such as the level of LGAs' indebtness, the fiscal discipline and so on. Finally, we merely referred to the agency theory, but there are other theories that can be used in order to better explain the relationship between accountability and performance, for example institutional theory.

Acknowledgements The research has been published thanks to the financial support received by the Parthenope University, Naples, entitled "Bando di sostegno alla ricerca individuale per il triennio 2015–2017. Annualità 2015".

References

1. Osborne, D., & Gaebler, T. (1993). *Reinventing Governament: How the enterpreneurial spiritis transforming the public sector*. New York: Penguin Book.
2. Royle, M. T., Hall, A. T., Hochwarter, W. A., Perrewé, P. L., & Ferris, G. R. (2005). The interactive effects of accountability and job self-efficacy on organizational citizenship behavior and political behavior. *Organizational Analysis, 13*(1), 53–71.
3. Fountain, J. (1991). Service efforts and accomplishment reporting. *Public Productivity and Management Review, 15*(2), 191–198.
4. Lepore, L., & Pisano, S. (2013). Determinants of Internet-based performance reporting released by Italian local government authorities. In D. Mancini, E. Vaassen, & R. P. Dameri (Eds), *Accounting information systems for decision making*. Vol. 3 of Springer series: Lecture Notes in Information Systems and Organisation. Berlin: Springer Physica-Verlag.
5. Farneti, G. (2011). *Ragioneria pubblica. Il "nuovo" sistema informativo delle aziende pubbliche*. Milano: FrancoAngeli.
6. Schaltegger, C. A., & Torgler, B. (2007). Government accountability and fiscal discipline: A panel analysis using Swiss data. *Journal of Public Economics, 91*(1), 117–140.
7. Cavalluzzo, K. S., & Ittner, C. D. (2004). Implementing performance measurement innovations: Evidence from government. *Accounting, Organizations and Society, 29*, 243–267.

8. Kluvers, R. (2003). Accountability for performance in local government. *Australian Journal of Public Administration, 62*(1), 57–69.
9. Dunleavy, P., & Hood, C. (1994). From old public-administration to new public management. *Public Money & Management, 14*(3), 9–16.
10. Pollitt, C., & Bouckaert, G. (2000). *Public management reform: A comparative analysis.* Oxford: Oxford University Press.
11. Cyberspace Public Research Group. (2001). *Web attribute evaluation system (WAES).* http:// www.cyprg.arizona.edu
12. Demchak, C. C., Friis, C., & La Porte, T. M. (2000). Webbing governance: National differences in constructing the public face. In G. D. Garson (Ed.), *Handbook of public information systems* (pp. 179–196). New York: Marcel Dekker.
13. Drüke, H. (2007). Can e-government make public governance more accountable? In A. Shah (Ed.), *Performance accountability and combating corruption* (pp. 59–87). Washington, DC: The World Bank.
14. La Porte, T. M., Demchak, C. C., & De Jong, M. (2002). Democracy and bureaucracy in the age of the web. Empirical findings and theoretical speculations. *Administration & Society, 34* (4), 411–446.
15. Kim, P. S., Halligan, J., Cho, N., Oh, C. H., & Eikenberry, A. M. (2005). Toward participatory and transparent governance: Report on the sixth global forum on reinventing government. *Public Administration Review, 65*(6), 646–654.
16. Serrano-Cinca, C., Rueda-Tomas, M., & Portillo-Tarragona, P. (2008). Factors influencing e-disclosure in local public administrations. In Documento de Trabajo 2008-03, Facultad de Ciencias Economicas y Empresariales, Universidad de Zaragoza.
17. Garcìa, A. C., & García-García, J. (2010). Determinants of online reporting of accounting information by Spanish LGAs. *Local Government Studies, 36*(5), 679–695.
18. Laswad, F., Fisher, R., & Oyelere, P. (2005). Determinants of voluntary Internet financial reporting by LGA. *Journal of Accounting and Public Policy, 24*, 101–121.
19. Yu, H. (2010). On the determinants of Internet-based Disclosure of Government Financial Information. In Conference Proceeding of Management and Service Science (MASS).
20. Ansari, S., & Euske, K. J. (1987). Rational, rationalizing, and reifying uses of accounting data in organizations. *Accounting, Organizations and Society, 12*(6), 549–579.
21. Brignall, S., & Modell, S. (2000). An institutional perspective on performance measurement and management in the 'new public sector'. *Management Accounting Research, 11*(3), 281–306.
22. Geiger, D. R., & Ittner, C. D. (1996). The influence of funding source and legislative requirements on government cost accounting practices. *Accounting, Organizations and Society, 21*(6), 549–567.
23. Dirsmith, M. W., Jablonsky, S. F., & Luzi, A. D. (1980). Planning and control in the U.S. government: A critical analysis of PPB, MBO and ZBB. *Strategic Management Journal, 1*(4), 303–329.

Italian Web-Based Disclosure: A New Index to Measure the Information Released on Human Capital

Sabrina Pisano, Luigi Lepore, and Federico Alvino

Abstract This paper investigates the human capital (HC) disclosure provided by a sample of Italian nonfinancial listed companies on their website. Different from previous studies on HC disclosure, which mainly referred to Sveiby's model, our disclosure index includes items concerning both the stock of knowledge and capabilities of employees and the human resource management practices. Unlike prior researches, we found a higher level of HC disclosure released by firms, demonstrating that the use of a wider index permits a better understanding of the companies' disclosure behavior. This study contributes to the literature on HC disclosure in different ways. First, we develop a wider HC disclosure index, which could be used in future studies, and compare our results with findings of previous research. Moreover, this is the first study, to the best of our knowledge, examining HC disclosure provided by Italian companies on their website.

Keywords Human capital disclosure • Website • Italian companies

1 Introduction

Over the last decades the relevance of HC disclosure has been widely recognized by standards setters, regulators and scholars for different reasons. Releasing HC information permits to increase the transparency to capital markets [1], informing stakeholders on the company's ability to create economic value, to establish trustworthiness with stakeholders [2], to appear legitimate in the eyes of society [3, 4], and so on.

Standards setters issued several guidance encouraging firms to improve their business reporting by making extensive voluntary disclosures of information about intellectual capital (IC) [5–9], and from the regulator's perspective, instead, in 2003

S. Pisano (✉) • L. Lepore • F. Alvino
Department of Law, Parthenope University, Naples, Italy
e-mail: sabrina.pisano@uniparthenope.it; luigi.lepore@uniparthenope.it; federico.alvino@uniparthenope.it

© Springer International Publishing AG 2017
K. Corsi et al. (eds.), *Reshaping Accounting and Management Control Systems*,
Lecture Notes in Information Systems and Organisation 20,
DOI 10.1007/978-3-319-49538-5_19

the EU issued Directive 2003/51/EC, which required companies to provide in their management discussion and analysis statement information relating to HC.

Researchers conducted several studies aiming at analyzing the amount of HC disclosure and, more generally, of IC disclosure voluntarily released by firms operating in different countries. Most of the previous research conceptualized HC using Sveiby's [10] classification of IC, which comprises the following three components: structural/internal capital, relational/external capital, and HC. The overriding conclusion from these studies is that, although HC is considered the most valuable asset within the three IC categories [11], this is the component less disclosed.

According to Abhayawansa and Abeysekera [12], the low level of HC disclosure, compared to the results concerning both external and internal capital disclosures, is the consequence of the framework used to construct the disclosure indices. HC disclosure indices developed using Sveiby's [10] IC tripartite only consider the stock of knowledge and capabilities of the employees, but do not take into account the human resource practices implemented within the company to motivate and leverage these knowledge resources. As a consequence, the authors suggested developing new HC disclosure indices that consider both the stock of knowledge and the human resource management practices involved within the firm. To our knowledge, so far few studies have developed such wider indices [13–18].

In this paper, we responded to the call for research of Abhayawansa and Abeysekera [12], developing a HC disclosure index that includes items concerning both the stock of knowledge and capabilities of employees and the human resource management practices.

This study is part of a wider research aiming at investigating the HC disclosure provided by companies listed in different countries and its determinants, developing a regression model. In this study, however, we describe the HC disclosure index developed and report the findings of the HC disclosure practices adopted by a sample of companies listed in just one country.

We conducted our analysis on a sample of Italian nonfinancial listed companies and, consistent with Cormier et al. [1], decided to focus on web-based HC disclosure. The Internet has been widely recognized as the best channel for release information to stakeholders [19] and, more specifically, HC disclosure. The research conducted by Beattie and Smith [3] on a sample of UK firms' human resource directors showed that about 46 % of them indicated the company web page as an effective channel of HC external disclosure, mainly because it is able to reach potential employees. However, the authors also found other incentives to HC external disclosure, such as demonstrating that the company is socially responsible, providing important information to investors that is not included in mandatory financial disclosures, or helping to create trustworthiness with other stakeholders in general and employees in particular.

The remainder of the paper is organized as follows. The next section reviews previous studies on HC disclosure. Section 3 describes the sample and the research model. Section 4 reports and discusses the results of the study. Finally, Sect. 5 draws some conclusions and limits of the study.

2   Literature Review

The HC is a category of most IC models developed by academics and practitioners [10, 20–24] (see [25] for a review of the principal guidelines and frameworks developed with a focus in reporting IC). More precisely, HC is considered the most valuable asset within the three IC categories [11], so that Roslender and Fincham [26] defined HC as the primary IC and the other two categories as the secondary IC, promoting an HC-centered perspective on IC.

During the years, different definitions of HC have been developed. Most of these consider that HC (or employee competence used by Petty and Guthrie [11]) comprises the knowledge, skills, and capabilities that individuals own and use. The most complete definition was developed by Abeysekera and Guthrie [14], which defined HC as "A combination of factors possessed by individuals and the collective workforce of a firm. It can encompass knowledge, skills and technical ability; personal traits such as intelligence, energy, attitude, reliability, commitment; ability to learn, including aptitude, imagination and creativity; desire to share information, participate in a team and focus on the goals of the organization."

The authors also identified three streams of research on HC: (1) developing HC measurement for financial reporting, (2) understanding how users make decisions using HC measurement information, and (3) exploring how HC is measured and reported by firms.

This paper contributes to the third stream of research, by analyzing HC disclosure provided by a sample of Italian listed firms.

Companies release HC information for several reasons: to create an image of its hidden value [27], to communicate the link between HC and performance to stakeholders [14], to mimic the "best practice" firms [11], to achieve an effective management of the critical resources [3], and to reduce tension between firms and their constituents in the interest of further capital accumulation [13].

Several studies have analyzed the amount of voluntary HC disclosure and, more generally, IC disclosure provided by firms in Australia [28–30], Ireland [31], the UK [17, 32], Italy [33], Sri Lanka [14, 15], Singapore [34], Hong Kong [35], Malaysia [36], and New Zealand [37]. Some studies specifically focused on HC disclosure [13, 38–41], while others conducted international comparative studies [42–44]. The main document that has been analyzed is the annual report, but there are also studies focusing on specific sections of the annual report, i.e., the management discussion and analysis and the chairman's letter [18], or other documents, such as the reports of presentations to financial analysts [45, 46], the IPO prospectuses [16, 47], or the sustainability report [48]. Very few studies have analyzed the HC disclosure provided by companies on their website [1]. A small number of longitudinal studies have been conducted and have found a slight improvement in the amount of HC information disclosed during the years [49]. All previous studies used a framework developed by the IC literature, mainly Sveiby's [10] model, to analyze the amount of disclosure provided by companies.

Table 1 IC categories by frequency of reporting

Study	Country	Year/s	IC disclosure		
			External structure	Internal structure	Human capital
Guthrie and Petty [28]	Australia	1998	40 %	30 %	30 %
Bozzolan et al. [33]	Italy	2001	49 %	30 %	21 %
Abeysekera and Guthrie [14, 15]	Sri Lanka	1998–1999	41 %	24 %	35 %
		1999–2000	44 %	20 %	36 %
Cerbioni and Parbonetti [44]	European countries	2002, 2003, 2004	32 %	50 %	18 %
Sujan and Abeysekera [29]	Australia	2004	53 %	28 %	19 %
Li et al. [17]	UK	2004–2005	38 %	34 %	28 %
Cinquini et al. [48]	Italy	2005	38 %	24 %	38 %
		2006	37 %	25 %	38 %

The overriding conclusion from previous studies is that HC is the least frequently reported IC category. By the way of example, Bukh et al. [16] found that only 17.8 % of companies provided HC information; Bozzolan et al. [33] found that 6 out of 30 firms investigated did not disclose HC information. When disclosed, most studies found that HC is generally presented in a qualitative form [29] and that the amount of HC information released is very small, compared to the information disclosed on both external and internal capital (see Table 1).

In other words, although HC has been widely recognized as the most important asset of the firm [15], the findings of most prior studies on IC disclosure in annual report do not confirm this assumption, showing that the most reported category is external capital. This result could be due to the lack of an established and generally accepted framework for IC reporting [28], to the risk of such information being used by competitors [33], to the lack of perception by firms that employees may be relevant as value drivers, or to the risk of losing HC [45].

According to Abhayawansa and Abeysekera [12], the low level of HC disclosure is the consequence of the framework used to construct the disclosure indices, which mainly considers the stock of knowledge and capabilities of the employees, but does not take into account the human resource management practices implemented within the company to motivate and leverage these knowledge resources. As noted by Bontis and Fitz-enz [50], both training and employee satisfaction have positive effects on HC, and Roslender et al. [51] suggested that employee wellness should be a component of primary IC.

Table 2 The sample

Company	Industry	Sales (€/ 000000)	Company	Industry	Sales (€/ 000000)
Aedes	Real estate	42.37	Gabetti	Real estate	29.74
Best Union Company	Technology	50.08	I Grandi Viaggi	Tourism-leisure	70.18
Biesse	Manufacturing	427.14	Immsi	Automobile	1274.58
Boero Bartolomeo	Manufacturing	95.94	Isagro	Chemistry	145.94
Brunello Cucinelli	Clothing	357.38	Italmobiliare	Manufacturing	4451.30
Buzzi Unicem	Manufacturing	2506.35	Mondadori Editore	Telecommunications	1.18
Csp International	Clothing	127033.00	Mondo Tv	Telecommunications	18.26
Dada	Technology	67.45	Ovs	Clothing	689.71
D'Amico	Manufacturing	212.48	Panariagroup	Manufacturing	272.97
Digital Bros	Technology	141.57	Piquadro	Clothing	63.05
Emak	Technology	354.76	Reply	Technology	632.18
Enel Green Power	Utility	2920.00	Retelit	Telecommunications	37.16
Esprinet	Technology	2291.14	Roma	Tourism-leisure	128.44
Finmeccanica	Manufacturing	14663.00	Seat Pagine Gialle	Telecommunications	408.18
Fnm	Tourism-leisure	295.87	Servizi Italia	Manufacturing	234.35

3 Sample and Research Method

3.1 Sample Selection and Data Source

Our sample is composed of 30 Italian nonfinancial companies listed at 31 December 2014. Our population was composed of all Italian nonfinancial companies listed at the MTA market. The complete list consisted of 197 organizations. We used a simple random procedure to define the final sample.

Table 2 shows the list of the companies included in the sample. The table also reports the industry and the value of the sales in 2014 for each firm, as a proxy of their size.

Most of the sampled companies belong to the manufacturing industry (26 %). It follows the technology industry (20 %), the clothing (13 %), and the telecommunications (13 %) industries.

The companies analyzed differ each other in terms of size, ranging from a minimum value of the sales of € 1.18 (Mondadori Editore) to a maximum of € 127033.00 (Csp International).

Our data sources were the web-based HC disclosure voluntarily provided by companies. As in Cormier et al. [1], we focused on the information on a firm's website provided in an HTML format, excluding documents in PDF format linked to the website, such as financial statement, management discussion and analysis, or other reports, both voluntarily and mandatorily drawn up. We analyzed every sections of the firm's website and we collected data in one week during the month of May in 2015.

3.2 Research Method

To collect data on web-based HC disclosure, we used content analysis [52], which is the research method most used in IC disclosure studies [53].

The coding procedure was organized as follows. Firstly, we identified the items of HC disclosure using the IC literature. We decided to not define too many items in order to avoid the possibility of coding errors deriving from a great number of content categories [4]. As a consequence, we identified 9 HC disclosure items and grouped these items in two categories: (1) the stock of knowledge and capabilities of employees and (2) the human resource management practices (see Table 3), as suggested by Abhayawansa and Abeysekera [12].

Once the HC disclosure items were identified, the website of each sampled company was analyzed and data were collected for each item of information.

Table 3 HC disclosure items

HC disclosure item	Definition and examples of information
Stock of knowledge and capabilities	
Employee-related measurements	Number of employees, median age distribution of employees, racial distribution of employees, gender distribution of employees, number of disabled employees, employee breakdown by job function, value added per employee, revenue per employee
Education	Education of directors as well as other employees
Know-how and experience	Knowledge, know-how, expertise, or skills of directors and other employees, employee work-related competences and knowledge
Human resource management practices	
Recruitment	Recruitment policies, description of job requirements
Training	Training policies, description of training programs, training expenses, number of training programs, number of training days per employee, share of employees participating in training programs
Career development	Employee development policies and programs, internal promotion
Welfare and motivation	Remuneration and incentives systems, pension, insurance policies, employee share option scheme, employee benefits, employee satisfaction, employee motivation, job rotation opportunities, employee turnover, flexibility, absence
Health and safety	Safety policies, number of accidents at work
Union activity	Trade union activities

The analysis was conducted by an assistant researcher and an associate professor. The text units have been chosen as the recording units, in order to avoid the limits deriving from the use of sentences. The use of sentence, in fact, requires to determine which item dominates if different items are mentioned in the same sentence. With the text unit, instead, we broke down the sentences according to how many pieces of information they contain, and, then, we coded each text unit to an HC disclosure item.

Each text unit was coded with a score of 0 if the company did not provide information, with a score of 1 if the information was released in a qualitative form and with a score of 2 if the information was disclosed in a quantitative form. We decided to weight quantitative information more heavily than qualitative information because precise information is considered more useful and able to enhance the firm's reputation and credibility [54]. If the same information was repeated, we considered all the repetitions, because the extent to which HC disclosures are repeated is also of interest [4]. We also coded the tables and considered each table cell as a piece of information [36]. The amount of HC disclosure was measured by counting the frequency of occurrence for each item. An overall score was assigned to each firm in relation to the total amount of HC disclosure released in both the categories identified by the following formula:

$$HCD_j = \sum_{i=1}^{2} TextUnit_{ij}$$

The score (HCD) awarded to firm j is equal to the sum of text units disclosed across the two categories i identified. This ordinal measure of HC disclosure level will permit us to rank the sampled companies and make comparison between them.

To verify inter-coder reliability, the two coders firstly defined a set of coding rules. Then, each researcher independently coded two websites, in order to identify the differences between coders. Finally, these differences were discussed and, on the basis of this discussion, the final set of coding rules was defined. To quantify the level of inter-coder reliability, the Krippendorff alpha was calculated, obtaining an acceptable result (78 %).

4 Results and Discussion

Table 4 reports the web-based HC disclosure released by the sampled companies.

The percentage of firms providing information for each item identified shows the richness, in absolute terms, of the HC disclosure released on their website by Italian companies. As Table 4 shows, there are no items for which all the sampled companies provided information. Moreover, 5 out of 30 companies investigated

Table 4 Italian listed companies web-based HC disclosure

| HC disclosure item | % of firms | Breakdown of total number of text units | | Total N. of text units | % of text Units |
		N. of text units in qualitative form	N. of text units in quantitative form		
Stock of knowledge and capabilities	*73%*	*1111*	*378*	*1489*	*54%*
Employee-related measurements	46%	6	376	382	14%
Education	53%	225	2	227	8%
Know-how and experience	53%	880	0	880	32%
Human resource management practices	*66%*	*935*	*357*	*1292*	*46%*
Recruitment	56%	477	0	477	17%
Training	33%	118	60	178	6%
Career development	10%	58	34	92	3%
Welfare and motivation	33%	174	184	358	13%
Health and safety	23%	93	79	172	6%
Union activity	6%	15	0	15	1%
Total		2046	735	2781	100%
Mean				92.70	
Standard deviation				153.63	

(Aedes, Csp International, Mondo TV, Piquadro, Roma) did not release information on HC. Although we investigated the website, rather than consider the annual report, which is the source of information mainly used in IC studies, our results are in line, among others, with those of Bozzolan et al. [33], Bukh et al. [16], and Garcìa-Meca [45] and could be explained using different arguments: these findings could be due to the lack of an established and generally accepted framework for IC reporting [28] or to the risk of such information being used by competitors [33]. The item disclosed by the majority of firms is *Recruitment* (56%). In line with this finding, almost all companies have the section "Work with us" on their website. This result confirms the finding of Beattie and Smith [3], showing that 46% of firms' human resource directors considered the website as an effective channel of HC external disclosure to reach potential employees.

With respect to the information released for each item, the last two columns of Table 4 illustrate the total amount of text units (in absolute value and in percentage) disclosed by all the sampled companies. The third and fourth columns, instead, show for each item the number of text units disclosed both in qualitative (column 3) and in quantitative form (column 4).

The total amount of HC information provided is 2781 text units. Companies gave importance to the items concerning both the stock of knowledge and capabilities of employees (54%) and the human resource management practices (46%).

On average the sampled companies disclosed 92.70 text units. This result is partially different from the findings of previous studies showing low levels of HC disclosure for companies operating both in Italy [33] and in other countries [29]. Our different result, compared to those of previous studies, could be the consequence of the framework used to construct our index. Unlike previous researches, our HC disclosure index does not exclusively consider the stock of knowledge and capabilities of the employees, but, according to the suggestion of Abhayawansa and Abeysekera [12], we also took into account the human resource management practices implemented within the company to motivate and leverage the knowledge resources. In fact, when we compare our finding with those of other studies whose HC disclosure indices also include the human resource management practices, we find similar results. Abeysekera [13], for example, found that companies provided 937 HC items in 2001 and 784 in 2002; Abeysekera and Guthrie [14, 15] showed that firms released 596 HC information in 1998–1999 and 790 in 1999–2000, although they used the sentence as recording unit. However, there are other two reasons that could justify our result: first, we used the text unit as recording unit, rather than the sentence. So, we broke down the sentences into several text units. As a consequence, it was very likely to find a higher amount of HC disclosure. Second, we investigated the website, rather than the annual report, as most previous research did. If we analyze diverse documents, we obtain different results. Cinquini et al. [48], for example, analyzed the Italian companies' sustainability reports and found results similar to ours: the amount of HC disclosure provided was 1566 in 2005 and 1668 in 2006; however, they used the sentences, graphics, charts, and tables as recording units.

The item with the highest percentage of text units is *Know-how and experience*. This result is due to an extended and detailed description of the knowledge, know-how, expertise, or skills of the firm's directors. The second item most disclosed is *Recruitment*, showing that Italian companies mainly use their website for recruitment purposes like UK firms [3]. This kind of information, in fact, is mainly released in the section "Work with us," demonstrating that potential employees are the prime stakeholders addressed by the sampled companies. It follows the *Employee-related measurements* item and the *Welfare and motivation* item. In the *Employee-related measurements*, the sampled companies mainly reported the number of employees; this result is not unexpected, considering that Art. 2427 of the Italian civil code requires companies to release information on the number of employees in the note of the financial statement. So, the sampled firms repeated the information contained in the note in their website. Few companies (Buzzi Unicem, Finmeccanica, and Mondadori Editore) reported data on the distribution of employees per age, race, gender, geographical area, or job function. Only Seat Pagine Gialle provided information on the revenue per employee and exclusively Buzzi Unicem reported the value added per employee. The high amount of text units released in the *Welfare and motivation* item is due to the Mondadori Editore company, which described its remuneration and incentives systems, as well as the employee benefits.

The standard deviation shows a relatively high value (153.63), revealing that the disclosure behaviors adopted by Italian firms have not been homogeneous. As stated, this could be due to the lack of an established and generally accepted framework for IC reporting [28].

Finally, Table 4 reveals that Italian companies mainly reported web-based HC disclosure in a qualitative form. This result is in line with the findings of previous studies [18, 29, 46]. Some quantitative information is reported in the following items: *Employee-related measurements*, *Welfare and motivation* (mainly due to the indication of the management's remuneration and stock option by Mondadori Editori), *Health and safety* (mainly due to the description of the accidents at work by Buzzi Unicem and Mondadori Editore), and *Training* (mainly due to an extended description of the training programs, expenses, and numbers by Mondadori Editore).

Table 5 ranks the sampled companies according to their score.

The company that received the highest score was Mondadori Editore, while there are five firms (Aedes, Csp International, Mondo TV, Piquadro, Roma) that did not release HC information on their website. Considering the size of these companies reported in Table 2, it seems that there is no relation between size and HC disclosure, although previous studies suggested that size is an important determinant of IC disclosure [18, 33, 43, 46]. However, this assumption needs to be empirically verified with further analysis.

Table 5 The companies' rank

Company	HCD	Company	HCD
Aedes	0	I Grandi Viaggi	37
Csp International	0	Emak	38
Mondo Tv	0	Brunello Cucinelli	61
Piquadro	0	Dada	70
Roma	0	Best Union Company	86
Digital Bros	2	Biesse	94
Fnm	7	Ovs	99
Boero Bartolomeo	8	D'Amico	113
Panariagroup Industrie Ceramiche	8	Gabetti	124
Esprinet	15	Italmobiliare	134
Immsi	24	Seat Pagine Gialle	266
Reply	24	Enel Green Power	289
Retelit	26	Finmeccanica	319
Isagro	30	Buzzi Unicem	423
Servizi Italia	32	Mondadori Editore	1187

5 Conclusions

This paper contributes to existing literature on HC reporting by developing a disclosure index that includes items concerning both the stock of knowledge and capabilities of employees and the human resource management practices.

We used the abovementioned index to investigate the HC information released by a sample of Italian nonfinancial listed companies on their website, and, unlike previous research, we found a higher level of HC disclosure, demonstrating that the use of a wider index, compared to those mainly referred to Sveiby's model, permits a better understanding of the companies' disclosure behavior.

The study is exploratory in nature and presents some limitation. So, further work needs to be done in several ways. First, the sample includes only 30 listed companies; hence, the results may not be generalized to all Italian firms. However, this study is part of a wider research aiming at investigating the HC disclosure provided by companies listed in different countries and its determinants, developing a regression model. In addition, it could be interesting both to examine the HC disclosure provided over a longitudinal period in order to better understand its development and to compare the characteristics of HC disclosure via website to HC disclosure released via traditional media, such as the annual report, in order to shed some lights on possible differences or similarities and understand the reasons for that. Finally, it could be interesting to analyze further attributes of disclosure, such as the time orientation (forward looking or present or past) and the type (financial or nonfinancial) of the HC information disclosed.

References

1. Cormier, D., Aerts, W., Ledoux, M. J., & Magnan, M. (2009). Attributes of social and human capital disclosure and information asymmetry between managers and investors. *Canadian Journal of Administrative Sciences, 26*(1), 71–88.
2. Van der Meer-Koistra, J., & Zijlstra, S. M. (2001). Reporting on intellectual capital. *Accounting, Auditing & Accountability Journal, 14*(4), 456–476.
3. Beattie, V., & Smith, S. J. (2010). Human capital, value creation and disclosure. *Journal of Human Resource Costing & Accounting, 14*(4), 262–285.
4. Beattie, V., & Thomson, S. J. (2007). Lifting the lid on the use of content analysis to investigate intellectual capital disclosures. *Accounting Forum, 31*(2), 129–163.
5. AICPA. (1994). *Improving business reporting—a customer focus.* Meeting the information need of investors and creditors, comprehensive report of the special committee on financial reporting (the Jenkins report). AICPA, New York.
6. FASB. (2001). *Improving business reporting: Insights into enhancing voluntary disclosures.* Steering Committee Report, Business Reporting Research Project. FASB, Norwalk.
7. IASB. (2010). Management commentary, IFRS Practice Statement. IASB, London.
8. ICAEW. (2000). *Intellectual capital: Issue and practice.* London: ICAEW.
9. ICAEW. (2000). *Human capital and corporate reputation: The boardroom agenda.* London: ICAEW.

10. Sveiby, K. (1997). *The new organizational wealth. Managing and measuring knowledge-based assets*. San Francisco: Berret-Koehler.
11. Petty, R., & Guthrie, J. (2000). Intellectual capital literature review. Measurement, reporting and management. *Journal of Intellectual Capital, 1*(2), 155–176.
12. Abhayawansa, S., & Abeysekera, I. (2008). An explanation of human capital disclosure from the resource based perspective. *Journal of Human Resource Costing & Accounting, 12*(1), 51–64.
13. Abeysekera, I. (2008). Motivations behind human capital disclosure in annual reports. *Accounting Forum, 32*(1), 1–13.
14. Abeysekera, I., & Guthrie, J. (2004). Human capital reporting in a developing nation. *British Accounting Review, 36*(3), 251–268.
15. Abeysekera, I., & Guthrie, J. (2005). An empirical investigation of annual reporting trends of intellectual capital in Sri Lanka. *Critical Perspective on Accounting, 16*(3), 151–163.
16. Bukh, P. N., Nielsen, C., Gormsen, P., & Mouritsen, J. (2005). Disclosure of information on intellectual capital in Danish IPO prospectuses. *Accounting, Auditing & Accountability Journal, 18*(6), 713–732.
17. Li, J., Pike, R., & Haniffa, R. (2008). Intellectual capital disclosure and corporate governance structure in UK firms. *Accounting and Business Research, 38*(2), 137–159.
18. Oliveira, L., Rodrigues, L. L., & Craig, R. (2006). Firm-specific determinants of intangibles reporting: Evidence from the Portuguese stock market. *Journal of Human Resource Costing & Accounting, 10*(1), 11–33.
19. Marston, C. L., & Polei, A. (2004). Corporate reporting on the internet by German companies. *International Journal of Accounting Information Systems, 5*(3), 285–311.
20. Brooking, A. (1996). *Intellectual capital. Core asset for the third millennium enterprice*. London: International Thomson Business Press.
21. Edvinsson, L., & Malone, M. S. (1997). *Intellectual capital*. New York: Harper.
22. Kaplan, R. S., & Norton, D.P. (1992). The balanced scorecard. Measures that drive performance. Harvard Business Review. January-February.
23. Kaplan, R. S., & Norton, D. P. (1996). Using the balanced scorecard as a strategic management system. Harvard Business Review. January-February.
24. Kaplan, R. S., & Norton, D. P. (2000). Having trouble with your strategy? Then map it. Harvard Business Review. September-October.
25. Asanga Abhayawansa, S. (2014). A review of guidelines and frameworks on external reporting of intellectual capital. *Journal of Intellectual Capital, 15*(1), 100–141.
26. Roslender, R., & Fincham, R. (2004). Intellectual capital: Who counts, controls? *Accounting and the Public Interest, 4*(1), 1–23.
27. De Pablos, P. O. (2002). Evidence of intellectual capital measurement from Asia, Europe, and the Middle East. *Journal of Intellectual Capital, 3*(3), 146–193.
28. Guthrie, J., & Petty, R. (2000). Intellectual capital: Australian annual reporting practices. *Journal of Intellectual Capital, 1*(3), 241–251.
29. Sujan, A., & Abeysekera, I. (2007). Intellectual capital reporting practices of the top Australian firms. *Australian Accounting Review, 17*(2), 71–83.
30. White, G., Lee, A., & Tower, G. (2007). Drivers of voluntary intellectual capital disclosure in listed biotechnology companies. *Journal of Intellectual Capital, 8*(3), 517–537.
31. Brennan, N. (2001). Reporting intellectual capital in annual reports: Evidence from Ireland. *Accounting, Auditing & Accountability Journal, 14*(4), 423–436.
32. Williams, S. M. (2001). Is intellectual capital performance and disclosure practices related? *Journal of Intellectual Capital, 2*(3), 192–203.
33. Bozzolan, S., Favotto, F., & Ricceri, F. (2003). Italian annual intellectual capital disclosure. An empirical analysis. *Journal of Intellectual Capital, 4*(4), 543–558.
34. Firer, S., & Williams, S. M. (2005). Firm ownership structure and intellectual capital disclosures. *Journal of Accounting Research, 19*(1), 1–18.

35. Petty, R., & Cuganesan, S. (2005). Voluntary disclosure of intellectual capital by Hong Kong companies: Examining size. Industry and growth effects over time. *Australian Accounting Review, 15*(2), 40–50.

36. Husin, N. M., Hooper, K., & Olesen, K. (2012). Analysis of intellectual capital disclosure—an illustrative example. *Journal of Intellectual Capital, 13*(2), 196–220.

37. Whiting, R. H., & Miller, J. C. (2008). Voluntary disclosure of intellectual capital in New Zealand annual reports and the "hidden value". *Journal of Human Resource Costing & Accounting, 12*(1), 26–50.

38. Khan, H. U. Z., & Khan, R. (2010). Human capital disclosure practices of top Bangladeshi companies. *Journal of Human Resource Costing & Accounting, 14*(4), 329–349.

39. Lin, L. S., Huang, I. C., Du, P. L., & Lin, T. F. (2012). Human capital disclosure and organizational performance. The moderating effects of knowledge intensity and organizational size. *Management Decision, 50*(10), 1790–1799.

40. Olsson, B. (2001). Annual reporting practices: Information about human resources in corporate annual reports in major Swedish companies. *Journal of Human Resource Costing and Accounting, 6*(1), 39–52.

41. Pisano, S. (2015). Human capital disclosure in the MD&A statement: An analysis on Italian public utilities. *Journal of Human Resource Management.* Special Issue: Challenges and Opportunities in the Performance Measurement and Control Systems of Human Resources Management for the Services Industry, *3*(2–1), 39–46.

42. Alvino, F. (2000). *Le competenze e la valutazione del capital umano in economia aziendale.* Torino: Giappichelli.

43. Bozzolan, S., O'Regan, P., & Ricceri, F. (2006). Intellectual capital disclosure (ICD). A comparison of Italy and the UK. *Journal of Human Resource Costing & Accounting., 10*(2), 92–113.

44. Cerbioni, F., & Parbonetti, A. (2007). Exploring the effects of corporate governance on intellectual capital disclosure: An analysis of European biotechnology companies. *European Accounting Review, 16*(4), 791–826.

45. Garcìa-Meca, E. (2005). Bridging the gap between disclosure and use of intellectual capital information. *Journal of Intellectual Capital, 6*(3), 427–440.

46. Garcìa-Meca, E., & Martìnez, I. (2005). Assessing the quality of disclosure on intangibles in the Spanish capital market. *European Business Review, 17*(4), 305–313.

47. Singh, I., & Van der Zahn, J.-L. W. M. (2008). Determinants of intellectual capital disclosure in prospectuses of initial public offerings. *Accounting and Business Research, 38*(5), 409–431.

48. Cinquini, L., Passetti, E., Tenucci, A., & Frey, M. (2012). Analyzing intellectual capital information in sustainability reports: Some empirical evidence. *Journal of Intellectual Capital, 13*(4), 531–561.

49. De Silva, T. A., Stratford, M., & Clark, M. (2014). Intellectual capital reporting: A longitudinal study of New Zealand companies. *Journal of Intellectual Capital, 15*(1), 157–172.

50. Bontis, N., & Fitz-enz, J. (2002). Intellectual capital ROI: A causal map of human capital antecedents and consequents. *Journal of Intellectual Capital, 3*(3), 223–247.

51. Roslender, R., Stevenson, J., & Kahn, H. (2006). Employee wellness as intellectual capital: An accounting perspective. *Journal of Human Resource Costing & Accounting, 10*(1), 48–64.

52. Krippendorf, K. (1980). *Content analysis: An introduction to its methodology.* Beverly Hills, CA: Sage.

53. Guthrie, J., Petty, R., Yongvanich, K., & Ricceri, F. (2004). Using content analysis as a research method to inquire into intellectual capital reporting. *Journal of Intellectual Capital, 5*(2), 282–293.

54. Botosan, C. A. (1997). Disclosure level and the cost of equity capital. *The Accounting Review, 72*(3), 323–349.

Intellectual Capital Management and Information Risk

Chiara Demartini, Delio Panaro, and Sara Trucco

Abstract The value relevance of intellectual capital (IC) disclosure has been vastly investigated in different countries and settings. Prior studies investigate the effect that IC has on different organisational performance dimensions. In particular some scholars found that IC information is able to provide valuable information for issuing positive recommendations on listed companies. However, to date the literature lacks in providing evidence of the effect of IC management on a company's information risk, defined as the analyst's recommendations to buy, hold or sell stocks. The aim of this research is thus to analyse the effect that IC performance may have on the information risk, measured as the way in which the market is informed about the firm performance. To test our main research question, we ran panel data regressions applied to a sample of 3027 US listed companies, which disclosed IC information on a stand-alone social or IC statement over the period 2008–2012. Empirical results may be of interest for both academics and practitioners, since it allows to reduce a gap in the literature about the contribution of the IC performance on firms' reputation and to give support to managers to properly understand the potential of both beneficial and unintended effects of such voluntary disclosure.

Keywords Intellectual capital • Voluntary disclosure • Information risk • American firms • Panel data

C. Demartini
University of Pavia, Pavia, Italy
e-mail: mariachiara.demartini@unipv.it

D. Panaro
iBe, Rome, Italy
e-mail: d.panaro@be-tse.it

S. Trucco (✉)
Rome University of International Studies, Rome, Italy
e-mail: sara.trucco@unint.eu

1 Introduction

The value relevance of intellectual capital (IC) disclosure has been vastly investigated in different countries and settings [1–4]. In this framework, prior studies investigate the effect that IC has on different organisational performance dimensions. In particular some scholars found that IC information is able to provide valuable information for issuing positive recommendations on listed companies [5]. However, to date, the literature lacks in providing evidence of the effect of IC management on a company's information risk, defined as the analyst's recommendations to buy, hold or sell stocks.

Based on the previous considerations, we attempt to answer the main research question, "Does IC management impact on a company's information risk?", by testing whether the IC management reflects into a company's information risk. To answer the main research question, we used a "cross-sectional dominant" pooled OLS regression model on a sample of 3027 US listed firms that issued stand-alone social and IC statements over the period 2008–2012.

Empirical results may be of interest for both academics and practitioners, since they allow to reduce the gap in the literature about the contribution of the IC performance on firms' reputation and to give support to managers to properly understand the potential both beneficial and unintended effects of such voluntary disclosure.

The remainder of the paper is organised as follows. The second and the third sections will provide a review of the literature and the theoretical development of the conceptual framework. The fourth section will discuss sample selection and data collection. The fifth section will present the statistical model. The sixth section will analyse results from the sample. A discussion of empirical findings and concluding remarks are outlined in the final section.

2 Literature Analysis

2.1 Information Risk and Asset Pricing

Asset pricing literature stresses the role of information risk in setting an asset price [6]. In an equilibrium-state market, indeed, individuals have common beliefs and an asset price should be insensitive of information other than these beliefs. Nonetheless, differential information issued through public or private channels may affect stock market prices.

Information risk, indeed, refers to private or public information, which can affect asset prices. It is usually defined as the analyst's recommendations to buy, hold or sell stocks [5]. Other scholars investigated the information risk, by taking into account the financial analysts' report, such as [7, 8] In particular, they examined, through a content-analysis approach, sell-side analyst company report, by finding interesting considerations about the role of the narrative section of the annual report on the investment recommendation by analysts. Furthermore, other scholars carried out a survey to financial analysts in order to analyse priority measures in their reports [9, 10].

2.2 Intellectual Capital

Amongst the very different definitions of IC reported into the literature [11–13], this study adapts the broad definition by Hsu and Fang [14] and defines IC as the dynamic set of knowledge, capabilities, networks, operation processes and individual and organisational relations that contribute to creating a company's long-lasting value. Such a definition encompasses most of the characteristics that prior definitions put forward in that it is grounded on the most widespread classification of IC components, which categorises three types of IC: human competencies, "the knowledge embedded in people"; structural or organisational capital, "the knowledge embedded in the organisation and its systems"; and relational capital, "the knowledge embedded in customers and other relationships external to the organisation" [4, 15, p. 70]. Furthermore, it accounts also for capabilities [11, 16, 17] and organisational relations as part of the firm's IC.

The IC literature increased significantly over the last three decades and addressed some new knowledge into the managerial [18, 19], accounting [15, 20–22], leadership [23] and organisational literature [24]. The increasing interest in this topic is related to the positive effect that IC has on different organisational performance dimensions, amongst which organisational learning and new product development [14], incremental and innovative capabilities [19] and the orchestration and configuration effects of top executives' capabilities [25] are some of the most cited ones. Although prior studies could not achieve a consensus on a shared IC theoretical framework yet [4], the concept of IC states that knowledge management is at the core of competitive advantage.

2.3 Information Risk and IC Management

Since mandatory financial information is getting less relevant in the decision issued by financial analysts regarding a company's recommendation consensus, more and more voluntary and non-financial information provides support to this decision [26–28]. In particular, some scholars, by using a survey of Belgian financial analysts, found that firms which disclose more forward-looking information and more internal-structure information have more accurate forecasts by financial analysts [29]. Amongst non-financial voluntary information, IC information has been found to provide valuable information for issuing positive recommendations on listed companies [5, 30] As a matter of fact, [30] found that financial analysts are more willing to consider good news, such as an increase in the costumer satisfactions for their firm's forecast than bad news. García-Meca and Martínez [5], through a sample of listed Spanish companies, demonstrated that financial analysts usually convey some kinds of IC information in their recommendations, such as information regarding a firm's strategy, customers and processes. However, the extant literature on the relationship between intellectual capital and information risk focuses primarily on the quantity and quality of the voluntary information disclosed by firms [1, 2, 5] without investigating whether IC management would affect financial analysts' recommendation. Thus, in this paper we attempt to empirically test whether the IC management reflects into a company's information risk, which can be stated into the following main research question: Does IC management impact on a company's information risk?

3 Hypothesis Development

In order to reply to our main research question, Does IC management impact on a company's information risk?, we grounded our theoretical development on both the general asset pricing theory [31, 32] and the resource-based view of the firm [33, 34]. Indeed, since firms seek to survive over time, they have to build a sustainable competitive advantage based upon a financially viable positioning in the capital market. IC literature found that the management of intangible assets, other than those considered by the international accounting standards, contributes to the development of a sound strategy [5] and a long-run competitive advantage [18, 22, 35].

However, the value of non-conventional intangible assets is neither easily accessible to financial investors nor always professionally audited. Thus, financial investors have both to look for such kind of information through more expensive systems, than the publicly audited financial information, and to check the extent to which this information is reliable in making their investment decisions. Therefore, there is a lack of correlation between the firm's capability to generate future earnings and its financial risk, as represented by capital markets. The value relevance of intellectual capital disclosure has been vastly investigated in different countries and settings [1–4]. However, to date the literature lacks in providing evidence of the effect of IC management and a company's information risk. Empirical evidence of that could support more efficient capital market decisions. On the other hand, IC management could become less trivial and more focused on those components and items, which are supposed to provide better recommendations [5]. Some studies investigate the quality and amount of IC information reported on analysts' recommendation report and found that analysts are more willing to use IC information in their "buy" rather than "sell" recommendations.

When checking for the effect of each IC component on the overall report issued by analysts, human capital information fell short in providing valuable insights to financial analysts. This result could be due to the fact that employees' capabilities are not firm owned [36]. However, other streams of literature suggest that more experienced and well-trained personnel drive higher organisational performance, thus reducing the firm's information risk [37, 38]. Moreover, lower levels of turnover of employees allow the personnel competences to increase over time and generate productivity improvements, which result in higher organisational performance. Human capital management has also been found to support the implementation of a company's strategy, when it is performed at the average. Indeed, an early investment in human capital is not able to offset the costs for it [39]. Financial analysts might take this information into account when issuing their recommendation report. Therefore, we would like to test the following hypothesis.

HP1. Higher human capital performance positively affects a company's information risk.

Structural capital performance has to do with the company hard and soft infrastructure supporting the firm's core business. Effectiveness and degree of access to the networks, information technology systems, production system, safety procedures and so forth are all examples of organisational capital items. Prior literature found that when such systems are in place, organisational performance improves too [40]. Quality systems, such as Six Sigma, and safety systems, such as those aimed at reducing the lost time for injury rate, have also been found to improve organisational performance [41, 42]. Moreover, costs linked to innovation activities, which are aimed at enhancing the structural capital contributes to the quality and productivity levels displayed by the company [43]. Structural capital has also been found to contribute to a determinant of a firm's information risk, i.e. management accounting practices [44]. For instance, prior literature found that traditional capital budgeting practices are strongly related to structural capital management. Indeed, companies showing a strong budget emphasis should put in place suitable structural assets to support managerial activity. This, in turn, leads to the development of reliable private and public information, thus reducing information risk. Therefore, financial analysts that are aware of the company's performance related to such kind of capital might well reduce the information asymmetry between the company and the capital market by issuing a more favourable recommendation on the company under investigation. We are therefore testing the following hypothesis.

HP2. Higher structural capital performance positively affects a company's information risk.

Relational capital component oversees the relationship between the company and its customers as well as other external stakeholders. It also includes corporate reputation [45]. Prior literature found that profitable and loyal customers are supposed to generate sustainable revenues in the long term [46, 47]. However, these relationships are not easily captured and valued by traditional financial reporting frameworks [48]. Thus, investors might take misleading investment decisions, whether they are not able to gauge the relevance of such intellectual assets. Analysts might reduce the asymmetry between the company and the financial market by issuing a recommendation, which reports such information also.

HP3. Higher relational capital performance positively affects a company's information risk.

4   Sample Selection and Data Collection

We selected all the US industrial listed firms from ESG Asset4 database (Thomson Reuters Datastream). We excluded financial institutions, as they have particular features and they need a separate treatment. We identified 3027 US listed firms that issued stand-alone social and intellectual capital statements.

According to the literature, the information risk is measured by a proxy, which is the analyst stock recommendations. A higher value issued by analysts indicates a higher information risk [5].

To measure the quality of IC management, we first reviewed the literature on IC [3] and identified eight items, which refer to performance of three components— relational capital, human capital and structural capital—of IC. Data on the eight items was gathered from Thomson Reuters Datastream, which provides the item value on a scale from 0 to 100.

For the IC management, we identified, according to some scholars, the following items: average training, client loyalty, turnover of employees, training hours total, Six Sigma and quality management systems, lost time for injury rate, score performance and internal promotion [3].

For each component of IC, the following items were included:

– Relational capital (RC): Client loyalty
– Human capital (HC): Average training, turnover of employees and training hours total
– Structural capital (SC): Internal promotion, lost time for injury rate, Six Sigma and quality management systems and score performance/cost innovations

As control variables and to test the firm's complexity, we used total inventories, total receivables and total assets.

Our sample time period goes from 2008 to 2012, ending up with 15,135 observations for each variable ($N = 181,620$).

5   Statistical Model

Table 1 shows some descriptive statistics of our research variables; correlation matrix and Pearson index in order to check for the presence of multicollinearity are presented in Table 2. Correlation matrix entries allow us to reject the hypothesis of the presence of multicollinearity.

In order to test our research hypotheses, we used a "cross-sectional dominant" pooled OLS regression model [49]. The linear model, based on panel data analysis, is drawn as follows:

$$Y_{it} = \beta_0 + \beta_1(X1_{it}) + \beta_2(X2_{it}) + \ldots + \beta_n(Xn_{it}) + \varepsilon_{it}$$

Table 1 Descriptive statistics of the research variables ($N = 181{,}620$)

Variable	Min	Max	Mean	Standard deviation
Information risk	1	5	2.45	0.56
Average training	0.06	297	34.99	13.01
Client loyalty	38.61	100	44.37	14.71
Turnover of employees	0.00	84.52	11.49	3.99
Training hours total	138.50	3.6240e+07	1.2767e+06	1.1138e+06
Six Sigma and quality management systems	−1	1	−0.65	0.66
Lost time for injury rate	0.00	67	4.14	2.64
Score performance/cost innovations	0.06	63.21	56.91	15.65
Internal promotion	−1	1	−0.17	0.85
Total assets	645	6.3165e+11	2.4026e+09	1.9426e+10
Inventory	−9.54	2.8106e+10	9.7180e+07	6.9707e+08
Receivables	0.00	4.6291e+10	1.5777e+08	1.0463e+09

where $i = 1, \ldots, 3027$ for each firm in the panel data and $t = 2008, \ldots, 2012$ refers to the sample time period.

The dependent variable (y) is the information risk, whereas the independent variables are average training, client loyalty, turnover of employees, training hours total, Six Sigma and quality management systems, lost time for injury rate, score performance and internal promotion, which together measure the performance of IC.

In order to reduce data heterogeneity, which could affect analysis results, before running the pooled data analysis, each variable has been normalised.

6 Empirical Findings

The results of the pooled regression analysis for the whole set of firms are reported in Table 3.

Empirical findings show that if the average training, the training hours total and the Six Sigma and quality management systems increase, the information risk that analysts perceive decreases and vice versa.

Furthermore, results highlight that, if the client loyalty, the score performance and the internal promotion increase, the information risk measured through the recommendation consensus increases and vice versa.

Nothing can be said about the relationship between information risk and (1) turnover of employees and (2) lost time for injury rate.

Table 2 Correlation matrix and Pearson index

	IR	CL	IP	SS	AT	TE	TH	CI	LTI
Information risk (IR)	1								
Client loyalty (CL)	0.019* 0.018	1							
Internal promotion (IP)	0.041** 0.000	0.159** 0.000	1						
Six Sigma (SS)	−0.013 0.122	0.047** 0.000	0.146** 1.721E-72	1					
Average training (AT)	−0.048** 0.000	0.095** 0.000	0.000 0.624	0.070** 0.000	1				
Turnover of employees (TE)	−0.002 0.838	0.004 0.633	0.058** 8.7823E-13	−0.017* 0.039	−0.090** 0.000	1			
Training hours (TH)	−0.043** 0.000	0.017* 0.031	0.037** 4.3071E-06	0.051** 0.000	0.342** 0.000	0.028** 0.001	1		
Cost innovations (CI)	0.044** 0.000	0.060** 0.000	0.156** 7.7785E-83	0.079** 0.000	−0.018* 0.027	0.003 0.756	−0.005 0.508	1	
Lost time injury (LTI)	0.003 0.717	0.004 0.582	0.037** 4.3254E-06	−0.017* 0.033	−0.075** 0.000	0.002 0.814	0.004 0.619	0.013 0.120	1

The first entry of each cell shows the Pearson index, and the last entry shows the sign (two tailed)

*Correlation is significant at 0.05 (two tails)

**Correlation is significant at 0.01 (two tails)

Table 3 Results of the pooled OLS regression analysis (information risk is the dependent variable)

	β	P value	Standard error
Average training	−0.074	0.001***	0.022
Client loyalty	0.014	0.027**	0.006
Turnover of employees	−0.216	0.263	0.019
Training hours total	−0.106	0.001***	0.031
Six Sigma and quality management systems	−0.005	0.069*	0.003
Lost time for injury rate	−0.008	0.731	0.023
Score performance/cost innovations	0.017	0.000***	0.004
Internal promotion	0.009	0.000***	0.002
Total assets	−0.151	0.000***	0.031
Inventory	−0.035	0.485	0.050
Receivables	−0.200	0.000***	0.056

$R^2 = 1.18\%$

*, ** and *** indicate a significance degree between 0.10 and 0.05, between 0.05 and 0.01 and between 0.01 and 0, respectively

Therefore, the HP1 (higher human capital performance positively affects a company's information risk) is partially supported since both the average training and the training hours total affect the management of the IC.

The HP2 (higher structural capital performance positively affects a company's information risk) is partially confirmed since the Six Sigma and quality management systems increase and the information risk decreases. However, internal promotions and cost innovations move both in the opposite direction that we predicted. Even if they deserve further investigation, the sign of cost of innovations could be interpreted as a proxy of projects' riskiness; therefore, they could be recognised as intangible assets and increase, for this reason, the corporate risk.

Finally, the HP3 (higher relational capital performance positively affects a company's information risk) is not supported, even if the relationship is statistically significant (the sign is positive, therefore opposite to our expectations).

Amongst control variables, total assets and receivables are statistically significant (β are both negative); therefore, if total assets and receivables increase, the information risk decreases and vice versa.

7 Conclusions

Empirical results carried out in the US sample allow us to reply to our main research question: "How does IC management impact on a company's information risk?" As a matter of fact, the extant literature on the relationship between IC and information risk focuses primarily on the quantity and quality of the voluntary information disclosed by firms [1, 2, 5] without investigating whether IC management would affect financial analysts' recommendation. Therefore, performing a pooled OLS, we try to fill the literature gap, by testing whether the IC management reflects into a company's information risk.

In particular, we found that higher human capital performance positively affects information risk of a company, since the IC performance related to average training and the training hours total positively affect the information risk. These results confirmed previous literature about this topic [36]. This is because lower levels of turnover of employees and higher training hours allow the personnel competences to increase over time and generate productivity improvements, which result in higher organisational performance.

Surprisingly, the relationship between relational capital performance and information risk shows an opposite sign with respect to the predicted one.

Furthermore, we found that higher levels of one component of the structural capital performance positively affect company's information risk; as a matter of fact, the Six Sigma and quality management systems increases; and the information risk decreases. However, internal promotions and cost innovations move both in the opposite direction that we predicted. Even if they deserve further investigation, the sign of cost of innovations could be interpreted as a proxy of projects' riskiness; therefore, they could be recognised as intangible assets, thereby increasing the corporate risk. These particular results open interesting avenues of research.

Empirical results may be of interest to both academics and practitioners, since they allow to reduce the gap in the literature about the contribution of the IC performance on firms' reputation and to give support to managers to properly understand the potential both beneficial and unintended effects of such voluntary disclosure.

This study is not without its limitations. First, the study sample is cross-sectional so our analysis lacks any industry-specific focus or comparison between different industries. As for control variables, we have controlled complexity with the amount of accruals only, without taking into account merger and acquisitions, the number of foreign subsidiaries and markets served, etc. Furthermore, the sample is large but the research is focused only on the US market; thereby, it could be interesting to extend the analysis to other countries and propose comparisons amongst them.

References

1. Abeysekera, I., & Guthrie, J. (2005). An empirical investigation of annual reporting trends of intellectual capital in Sri Lanka. *Critical Perspectives on Account, 16*(3), 151–163.
2. Beattie, V., & Smith, S. J. (2012). Evaluating disclosure theory using the views of UK finance directors in the intellectual capital context. *Accounting and Business Research, 42*(5), 471–494.
3. Bozzolan, S., O'Regan, P., & Ricceri, F. (2006). Intellectual capital disclosure (ICD): A comparison of Italy and the UK. *Journal of Human Resource Costing & Accounting, 10*(2), 92–113.

4. Guthrie, J., Ricceri, F., & Dumay, J. (2012). Reflections and projections: A decade of Intellectual Capital Accounting Research. *The British Accounting Review, 44*(2), 68–82.
5. García-Meca, E., & Martínez, I. (2007). The use of intellectual capital information in investment decisions: An empirical study using analyst reports. *The International Journal of Accounting, 42*(1), 57–81.
6. Easley, D., Hvidkjaer, S., & O'Hara, M. (2002). Is information risk a determinant of asset returns? *The Journal of Finance, 57*(5), 2185–2221.
7. Breton, G., & Taffler, R. J. (2001). Accounting information and analyst stock recommendation decisions: A content analysis approach. *Accounting and Business Research, 31*(2), 91–101.
8. Rogers, R. K., & Grant, J. (1997). Content analysis of information cited in reports of sell-side financial analysts. *Journal of Financial Statement Analysis, 3*(1), 17–30.
9. Beattie, V. (1999). *Business reporting: The inevitable change?* [Internet]. Institute of Chartered Accountants of Scotland Edinburgh. Cited September 5, 2015, from http://www.opengrey.eu/item/display/10068/385822
10. Dempsey, S. J., Gatti, J. F., Grinnell, D. J., & Cats-Baril, W. L. (1997). *The use of strategic performance variables as leading indicators in financial analyst's forecasts*. Available SSRN 2346 [Internet]. Cited September 5, 2015, from http://papers.ssrn.com/sol3/papers.cfm?abstract_id=2346
11. Edvinsson, L., & Sullivan, P. (1996). Developing a model for managing intellectual capital. *European Management Journal, 14*(4), 356–364.
12. Guthrie, J., & Petty, R. (2000). Intellectual capital: Australian annual reporting practices. *Journal of Intellectual Capital, 1*(3), 241–251.
13. Guthrie, J. (2001). The management, measurement and the reporting of intellectual capital. *Journal of Intellectual Capital, 2*(1), 27–41.
14. Hsu, Y.-H., & Fang, W. (2009). Intellectual capital and new product development performance: The mediating role of organizational learning capability. *Technological Forecasting Social Change, 76*(5), 664–677.
15. Bontis, N. (1998). Intellectual capital: An exploratory study that develops measures and models. *Management Decision, 36*(2), 63–76.
16. Choo, C. W, & Bontis, N. (2002). *The strategic management of intellectual capital and organizational knowledge* [Internet]. Oxford University Press. Cited June 20, 2015, from: https://books.google.it/books?hl=it&lr=&id=MrqqutgQydEC&oi=fnd&pg=PR17&dq=The+Strategic+Management+of+Intellectual+Capital+and+Organizational+Knowledge&ots=xMtsd7EM2M&sig=qyJ_K-Cc8tZbSyfngMbT6hw6DaQ
17. Hsu, I., & Sabherwal, R. (2012). Relationship between intellectual capital and knowledge management: An empirical investigation. *Decision Sciences, 43*(3), 489–524.
18. Nahapiet, J., & Ghoshal, S. (1998). Social capital, intellectual capital, and the organizational advantage. *Academy of Management Review, 23*(2), 242–266.
19. Subramaniam, M., & Youndt, M. A. (2005). The influence of intellectual capital on the types of innovative capabilities. *Academy of Management Journal, 48*(3), 450–463.
20. Marr, B., Gray, D., & Neely, A. (2003). Why do firms measure their intellectual capital? *Journal of Intellectual Capital, 4*(4), 441–464.
21. Mouritsen, J., Larsen, H. T., & Bukh, P. N. (2001). Valuing the future: Intellectual capital supplements at Skandia. *Accounting, Auditing & Accountability Journal, 14*(4), 399–422.
22. Roos, G., & Roos, J. (1997). Measuring your company's intellectual performance. *Long Range Planning, 30*(3), 413–426.
23. Bontis, N., & Nikitopoulos, D. (2001). Thought leadership on intellectual capital. *Journal Intellectual Capital, 2*(3), 183–191.
24. Leana, C. R., & Van Buren, H. J. (1999). Organizational social capital and employment practices. *Academy Management Review, 24*(3), 538–555.
25. Kor, Y. Y., & Mesko, A. (2013). Dynamic managerial capabilities: Configuration and orchestration of top executives' capabilities and the firm's dominant logic. *Strategic Management Journal, 34*(2), 233–244.

26. Anderson, G. M. (1988). Mr. Smith and the preachers: The economics of religion in the wealth of nations. *Journal of Political Economy, 96*(5), 1066–1088.

27. Ball, R., Jayaraman, S., & Shivakumar, L. (2012). Audited financial reporting and voluntary disclosure as complements: A test of the confirmation hypothesis. *Journal of Accounting and Economics, 53*(1–2), 136–166.

28. Dhaliwal, D. S., Li, O. Z., Tsang, A., & Yang, Y. G. (2012). Voluntary nonfinancial disclosure and the cost of equity capital: The initiation of corporate social responsibility reporting. *The Accounting Review, 86*(1), 59–100.

29. Orens, R., & Lybaert, N. (2007). Does the financial analysts' usage of non-financial information influence the analysts' forecast accuracy? Some evidence from the Belgian sell-side financial analyst. *The International Journal of Accounting, 42*(3), 237–271.

30. Ngobo, P.-V., Casta, J.-F., & Ramond, O. (2012). Is customer satisfaction a relevant metric for financial analysts? *Journal of the Academy Marketing Science, 40*(3), 480–508.

31. Blume, M. E., & Friend, I. (1973). A new look at the capital asset pricing model. *The Journal of Finance, 28*(1), 19–34.

32. Ross, S. A. (1976). The arbitrage theory of capital asset pricing. *Journal of Economic Theory, 13*(3), 341–360.

33. Peteraf, M. A. (1993). The cornerstones of competitive advantage: A resource-based view. *Strategic Management Journal, 14*(3), 179–191.

34. Wernerfelt, B. (1984). A resource-based view of the firm. *Strategic Management Journal, 5*(2), 171–180.

35. Bontis, N. (2001). Assessing knowledge assets: A review of the models used to measure intellectual capital. *International Journal of Management Reviews, 3*(1), 41–60.

36. Ui, J. (2003). Why are capital market actors ambivalent to information about certain indicators on intellectual capital? *Accounting, Auditing & Accountability Journal, 16*(1), 31–38.

37. Huselid, M. A. (1995). The impact of human resource management practices on turnover, productivity, and corporate financial performance. *Academy of Management Journal, 38*(3), 635–672.

38. Storey, D. J. (2004). Exploring the link, among small firms, between management training and firm performance: A comparison between the UK and other OECD countries. *International Journal of Human Resource Management, 15*(1), 112–130.

39. Hitt, M., Duane Ireland, R., Michael Camp, S., & Sexton, D. L. (2001). Guest editors' introduction to the special issue, strategic entrepreneurship: Entrepreneurial strategies for wealth creation. *Strategic Management Journal, 22*, 479–491.

40. Black, S. E., & Lynch, L. M. (2001). How to compete: The impact of workplace practices and information technology on productivity. *The Review of Economics and Statistics, 83*(3), 434–445.

41. Antony, J., & Banuelas, R. (2002). Key ingredients for the effective implementation of Six Sigma program. *Measuring Business Excellence, 6*(4), 20–27.

42. Vredenburgh, A. G. (2002). Organizational safety: Which management practices are most effective in reducing employee injury rates? *Journal of Safety Research, 33*(2), 259–276.

43. Rothwell, R. (1994). Towards the fifth-generation innovation process. *International Marketing Review, 11*(1), 7–31.

44. Tayles, M., Pike, R. H., & Sofian, S. (2007). Intellectual capital, management accounting practices and corporate performance: Perceptions of managers. *Accounting, Auditing and Accountability Journal, 20*(4), 522–548.

45. Grasenick, K., & Low, J. (2004). Shaken, not stirred: Defining and connecting indicators for the measurement and valuation of intangibles. *Journal of Intellectual Capital, 5*(2), 268–281.

46. Reinartz, W. J., & Kumar, V. (2000). On the profitability of long-life customers in a non-contractual setting: An empirical investigation and implications for marketing. *Journal of Marketing, 64*(4), 17–35.

47. Storbacka, K., Strandvik, T., & Grönroos, C. (1994). Managing customer relationships for profit: The dynamics of relationship quality. *International Journal of Service Industry Management, 5*(5), 21–38.

48. Andrikopoulos, A. (2009, May). *Accounting for intellectual capital: on the elusive path from theory to practice* [Internet]. Report No.: ID 1399333. Rochester, NY: Social Science Research Network. Cited September 4, 2015, from http://papers.ssrn.com/abstract=1399333

49. Stimson, J. A. (1985). Regression in space and time: A statistical essay. *American Journal of Political Science, 29*(4), 914–947.

XBRL Adoption in Public Organizations: Criticalities and Perspectives

Elisa Bonollo

Abstract Last years have been characterized by an increasing need for transparency towards public organizations with a pressing request for publishing on line official documents and financial data. In this context scholars and operators opened a discussion on the adoption of XBRL in public organizations to promote wide diffusion and timely use of financial data. The aim of this paper is to conduct a theoretical analysis to understand whether XBRL could be easily adopted by Italian public organizations. The analysis highlights criticalities related to the definition of the XBRL taxonomy due to the heterogeneity of accounting information systems of public organizations. It shows also that the coding system of the mandatory integrated chart of accounts could offer perspectives to XBRL adoption.

Keywords XBRL • Public organizations • Accounting information systems

1 Introduction

Financial reporting in public organizations has once again become a significant topic in the scientific debate especially following the public finance crisis of the last decades. This crisis has produced a growing attention of the community on the use of public resources and, consequently, an increasing request for accountability and transparency [1–3].

Accountability and transparency are, at the same time, "old" and "new" concepts. They are "old" because the public organizations have always accounted for their use of financial resources, but, at the same time, they are "new" concepts as they now mainly refer to releasing official documents and relevant data on institutional websites of public organizations [4–6].

In this context, scholars and operators opened a discussion on the adoption of XBRL (eXtensible Business Reporting Language) in public organizations to promote the diffusion and use of financial data. XBRL is a digital and open

E. Bonollo (✉)
Department of Economics and Business Studies, University of Genoa, Genoa, Italy
e-mail: bonollo@economia.unige.it

© Springer International Publishing AG 2017
K. Corsi et al. (eds.), *Reshaping Accounting and Management Control Systems*,
Lecture Notes in Information Systems and Organisation 20,
DOI 10.1007/978-3-319-49538-5_21

standardized language used for business disclosure [7–11]. Surprisingly, there are few studies on its use in public organizations, particularly with reference to Italy.

This paper aims to analyse criticalities in adopting XBRL in Italian public organizations. The implementation of XBRL in public organizations is rather complex, and the first major issue is the development of an XBRL taxonomy that harmonizes the use of financial terms [12–14]. Consequently, the paper focuses on pros and cons of the existing coding systems used by public organizations in Italy (e.g. SIOPE—Information System on Public Organizations' Operations) to understand whether they could be used as a basis for the development of an XBRL taxonomy.

Consistently with the relative scarcity of XBRL research focused on public organizations, this paper will conduct a theoretical analysis, mainly descriptive, and is structured as follows. The next section begins with basic information on the XBRL and reviews the prior literature on the subject in public organizations; Sects. 3 and 4 describe the main criticalities for the adoption of XBRL in public organizations by considering the heterogeneity of accounting information systems and the definition of the taxonomy; the final section will draw some conclusions.

2 XBRL for Public Organizations: A Brief Overview and a Bit of Literature

XBRL is a markup language that makes financial data readable and understandable by any software [15]. In summary, when an XBRL file is created (by converting a file originated in other formats or by directly entering data by using an *ad hoc* software), the financial data to be disclosed are tagged, thus allowing their users to promptly and easily process them by using traditional management software [8]. XBRL makes information usable in a standard digital format, regardless of their original viewing, with consequent savings in terms of time, costs, resources and error risks.

In other words, during the creation of a financial document file (an annual report, a table, a report for a website, etc.), financial data are tagged with labels similar to a bar code [16]. These "tags" remain permanently connected to financial data and associated to a set of other information, making them univocal financial data. When data are subsequently "recalled" by using these tags, they can be processed immediately, without having to enter them again manually.

Precisely like a real language, XBRL is based on a grammar, "XBRL specification", and a vocabulary, called "XBRL taxonomy" [17]. The specification is a document that describes how to create an XBRL document in technical terms; it is univocal and is defined by the International XBRL Consortium. The taxonomy indicates how to describe financial information and provides a standard classification system in a hierarchical order. It is a list of financial elements (called "concepts") that can be potentially used in a report and of the related attributes and connections (called "fields") that identify information allowing the encoding in the XBRL language (e.g. code, name in Italian, data type, period, regulatory reference or accounting standard, mathematical and definitional relationships among data, text labels in multiple languages) [18]. The taxonomy varies depending on the country where it is used. Indeed, local jurisdictions have been created at national level (in Italy, in 2006, XBRL Italy was founded with the task of developing and validating taxonomies in compliance with the guidelines of the International XBRL Consortium) [17, 19].

Prior research on this topic mainly deal with the adoption of XBRL in enterprises [20–23], whereas there are very few specific contributions on the use of XBRL in public organizations. Literature concerning public organizations can be found mainly in professional journals, conference papers and book chapters, regards normative issues and focuses on the potential benefits and criticalities of adopting XBRL [19, 24–27] and on the actual costs and benefits demonstrated by the first public organization adopters [26, 28–32].

In detail, some authors observed that the adoption of XBRL can bring benefits for public organizations because they have to prepare many reports, often containing similar or identical financial information but with different formats, timeframes and targets; thus, XBRL adoption can eliminate costs, times and errors due to re-entering data [33]. In other words, XBRL can be implemented to better enable public organizations to manage their data and thus to offer better services to their communities [21].

Furthermore, XBRL adoption could reduce the administrative burden also for enterprises that are often required to report financial information to different public organizations in different ways [34].

XBRL adoption by public organizations means also a higher level of accountability and transparency for external stakeholders. The introduction of XBRL can reduce financial manipulations with a full and fair disclosure of financial data [35]. In this regard, some authors highlighted how the stakeholder financial information needs could be met much more effectively by using XBRL [17, 19, 24]. Indeed, XBRL gives the opportunity of downloading and immediately analysing data of budgets and annual reports in the case of mandatory control (just think of the activities of the Supreme Audit Institution, the Ministry of Finance, etc.) or in the case of any form of political control (carried out by individuals, lobbies, political parties, associations, etc.). Consequently XBRL is expected to improve the accountability of public managers and so the community trust [36].

In addition to this, as already said, XBRL improves the transparency of public organizations by allowing access to relevant and user-friendly financial information that could be used by individuals or entities in support of decision-making processes (suppliers, potential investors, employees, etc.). Indeed, XBRL can make reported financial information machine readable and comparable and, in this way, can also support the development of e-government [12, 37].

Again, other authors highlighted some criticalities such as the heterogeneity of the accounting information systems of public organizations. This accounting heterogeneity means that we have different types of budget and reporting documents and so different types of data according to the public organization considered (state central administration, regional and local governments, healthcare organizations, universities, etc.). Furthermore, the same authors reveal also the criticalities related to the initial investment and the well-known public employees' resistance to change [19, 37].

In this context, this research has been developed to look more deeply into the Italian situation and understand whether the disharmony in Italian public accounting information systems, combined with the existence of different coding systems already in use in public organizations, could prevent the adoption of XBRL or even make it useless or redundant.

3   Accounting Information System in Italian Public Organizations

In order to understand the complexity of adopting XBRL in Italian public organizations, we should first outline the main features of their different budgeting and accounting information systems.

We could identify five "models" of budgeting and accounting information systems, going from the traditional public model to models very similar to those of enterprises [38–42]:

- State central administration, where the accounting information system is based on traditional public accounting, the so-called cash- and commitment-based accounting system. The state annual authorizing budget contains a classification of expenses by missions and programs (that are the institutional purposes and the activities to be carried out); at year end the "general statement of state account" consists of the traditional public annual report (with revenues and expenses) and the "general asset account" (which is not built on the basis of accounting and includes several information sheets on assets and liabilities).
- Regional and local governments and their controlled entities (except healthcare organizations and the so-called centralized healthcare management) with the traditional cash- and commitment-based accounting system with authorization function. These public organizations adopt common accounting standards and common budgeting and reporting schemes, with a classification of expenses by missions and programs. As to final reporting, the "general report" will include the traditional public annual report, the income statement, the statement of assets and liabilities and, as of 2016, also the consolidated financial statement. Starting from 2016, the traditional public accounting system will be based on a common integrated chart of accounts (standardized at national level) and will be supplemented, just for information, by accrual accounting (that will be introduced only in 2018 for local governments with a population of less than 5000 inhabitants).

- Universities use only accrual accounting and, based on ministerial accounting standards and schemes, prepare the authorizing consolidated economic and investment budget, the table of reclassification of expenses by missions and programs and at year end the consolidated financial statement. The common chart of accounts at national level, even if required by the legislation, has not yet been prepared [43].
- Local healthcare organizations, hospitals and the so-called centralized healthcare management use only accrual accounting, with an annual economic budget (with no authorization power), and at year end they prepare the financial statement. Since 2012, financial statement schemes and accounting standards have been introduced at national level. Moreover, since then, the table of classification of expenses by missions and programs and the consolidated financial statement of the regional healthcare system have been mandatorily adopted.
- Other public organizations adopt an integrated system of traditional public accounting and accrual accounting; this accounting information system has been based, since 2014, on accounting standards and on a common integrated chart of accounts. The budget includes the authorizing financial budget (with expenses reclassified by missions and programs) and the economic budget. At year end, in addition to the traditional annual report, they prepare the statement of assets and liabilities, the income statement and accompanying notes.

The accounting framework of public organizations is therefore extremely complex, as it includes both traditional and accrual accounting systems and different reporting documents.

The recent accounting harmonization process reduced but did not eliminate the heterogeneity of accounting information systems among the different types of public organizations. On the contrary, within each type of public organization, the lawmaker requires the use of common budget and annual report schemes, identical valuation criteria, a common integrated chart of accounts and identical accounting rules to record management facts. In this regard, Mussari [44] pointed out how, in spite of the use of the term harmonization by the lawmaker, public organizations of the same type seem to be heading towards a total unification of accounting. Complete homologation, at least within the same type of public organization, could actually provide an excellent basis for the possible adoption of XBRL.

4 XBRL Taxonomy for Public Organizations

At present, in the Italian context, it is not possible to create a single XBRL taxonomy for all public organizations due to the aforementioned accounting heterogeneity. A specific taxonomy could be arranged at least for each type of public organization.

The creation of a taxonomy for the use of XBRL involves, as a first step, the classification of the possible financial data of a public organization by creating a list of all the financial items that could be processed to meet a wide range of disclosure requirements.

Defining the taxonomy is a critical step that will affect all the subsequent reprocessing of data, because users will be enabled to use only those existing in the taxonomy. About this, some authors said that the standardization required by a taxonomy involves the risk of flattening the information capacity of financial documents [44].

Each item ("concept") will be associated to an identification code and to different "fields" (categories of information that are provided for the identification and comprehension of the elements of the taxonomy) to specify their meaning univocally and to enhance their information capacity by increasing the types of reports and analyses the users may create.

The list of financial items and the corresponding fields will then be shared among the potential stakeholders involved and subsequently validated by XBRL Italy to become an XBRL taxonomy.

In Italy, the existing XBRL taxonomies ("Italian accounting standards taxonomy version 2014-11-17" for non-listed companies and "International accounting standards IAS-IFRS taxonomy" for listed companies) can be used only by private and public enterprises.

Public organizations need specific initiatives mainly due to the already said heterogeneity of budgeting and accounting information systems, which means data having different nature, and also to the existence of different coding systems of financial data already being used in the public organizations for different purposes. About this last point, there is the need to prevent XBRL from becoming perceived as a further bureaucratic requirement. However, we should point out that there could be the possibility of taking advantage of the aforementioned existing coding systems to create an XBRL taxonomy.

In order to investigate this option, we will analyse the features and the diffusion of these coding systems.

4.1   SIOPE: Sistema Informativo sulle Operazioni degli Enti Pubblici (Information System on Public Organizations' Operations)

The Information System on Public Organizations' Operations (SIOPE) is a coding system to log financial data regarding the cash flow operations of public organizations. More specifically a SIOPE code must be added by public organizations to each revenue and expense item at the moment of receipts and payments. Its main purpose is to allow the State General Accounting Department to constantly monitor public revenues and expenses and facilitate the process of consolidation of public accounts.

SIOPE coded data are transmitted by the cash manager of each public organization to the Bank of Italy, on a daily basis. There are nine distinct coding systems used for different public organizations: state central administration, regional and local governments, universities, research agencies, healthcare organizations, social security institutions, park authorities and chambers of commerce.

Gradually introduced starting from 2003, the SIOPE is consistent with the European System of National and Regional Accounts (ESA) and is the result of a collaboration of the State General Accounting Department, ISTAT (Italian National Institute of Statistics), the Bank of Italy and the public organizations involved.

The items of this code depend on which accounting information system has been adopted by the specific public organization considered and are continuously updated following the evolution of the accounting legislation. Conversely, its layout has remained virtually unchanged and includes a numerical code, a description of the item and a brief definition.

Since June 2014, the collected information have been made available for the involved public organizations and for all the citizens through a specific freely accessible web application (www.siope.it). This website contains:

- Daily and monthly coded data referred to the individual public organizations
- National, regional and provincial monthly aggregates of the coded data of each type of public organization
- Monthly processing of the coded data referred to the individual public organizations
- National, regional and provincial monthly aggregates of the processed data indicated in the previous point
- Coded data regarding the payments made by the state central administration with an electronic mandate on a daily and monthly basis

The data can be downloaded in Excel format referred to an individual public organization or to multiple public organizations and can be aggregated in summary tables organized by geographic or demographic variables. In addition, space and time comparisons between public organizations can be provided.

Always based on SIOPE data, the website www.soldipubblici.gov.it allows semantic searches among the payments of public organizations. The reference coding is always SIOPE, but, unlike with www.siope.it, these data cannot be extracted.

In short, SIOPE information concerns almost all public organizations. For the singular public organization, the SIOPE code is a bureaucratic requirement, but the State General Accounting Department can monitor through it the public expenditure, and citizens can read and/or download in Excel format financial data through specific websites.

It would be possible to use the SIOPE code as a work basis for the creation of an XBRL taxonomy for each type of public organization. The adoption of a such XBRL taxonomy would be useful for the users that could avoid the process of re-entering data. The criticality of such a use of the SIOPE is that it concerns only the monetary aspect of management and that it has a fragmentary nature, leading to the use of nine different XBRL taxonomies, therefore not a single, unified language.

4.2   ESA (European System of National and Regional Accounts), COFOG (Classification of the Functions of Government) and New Classification of Expenses by Missions and Programs

The European System of National and Regional Accounts (ESA 2010) is the European Union accounting framework for a systematic and detailed description of the activities of an economy, its components and the relations between them. This is the basic coding through which each member state of the European Union sends information to the European Commission for monitoring public finance trends [46].

The ESA 2010, implemented in September 2014 to replace the previous ESA 95, is the result of a close cooperation between the Statistical Office of the European Commission (EUROSTAT) and the statistical offices of the member states. Indeed, at European level consolidated reporting has a statistical nature. The ESA 2010 has been adopted with Regulation no. 549 of the Council of the European Union (Official Journal "G.U." 26/06/2013), which defined in detail the data reporting methodologies to be used and their subsequent transmission by governments to EUROSTAT.

In the ESA 2010 coding, which concerns the entire economic system, public organizations are distinguished into state central administrations (ministries and autonomous public agencies), local governments (regional and local governments, healthcare organizations, other public organizations whose competence extends to a part of the national territory) and social security institutions.

The ESA 2010 adopted, as part of public finance statistics, a coding system of expenses classified by public policies, developed in 1997 by the OECD and called Classification of the Functions of Government (COFOG). The COFOG code is the same for all public organizations of the member states of the European Union.

The COFOG, which highlights the aims of activities of public organizations [47, 48], includes three levels of analysis for expenses:

- Divisions or first-tier functions representing the primary goals pursued by the public organizations (totalling a number of 10)
- Groups or second-tier functions concerning the specific areas of intervention of public policies (totalling a number of 68)
- Classes or third-tier functions identifying the single objectives that include the areas of intervention of public organizations (totalling a number of 106)

In this respect we should point out that in Italy, after the accounting harmonization process, in the budget and annual report, the new classification of expenses by missions and programs (requested to all public organizations) is in line with the COFOG code. Missions and programs are identified by a progressive number, thus creating a coding system of expenses by destination.

More specifically, public organizations must indicate in their budgets and in their annual reports the corresponding second-tier function of COFOG for each "program". There are different mission and program codes according to different budgets and annual reports of public organizations, such as regional and local governments, universities, healthcare organizations and other public organizations. Conversely, at present there is not a predefined mission and program scheme for the state central administration, so every year state budget and state annual report must indicate the corresponding COFOG for each "program".

The set of information is reported in two free access and very user-friendly websites (www.finanzalocale.interno.it, www.openbilanci.it), but their data cannot be copied into a file.

The codes of missions and programs could be used as a basis for the creation of an XBRL taxonomy. In this case, data in XBRL format would increase the information potential of the aforementioned websites, as in this way they would offer visitors the opportunity to download data in a format that can be immediately reprocessed.

In this regard, the major criticalities are that this code only concerns the expenses classified by destination and that the number of mission and program items is rather limited, with the risk of reducing the possibilities for users to process data.

4.3   The Integrated Chart of Accounts

The integrated chart of accounts (standardized at national level) is one of the main instruments for the public accounting harmonization process in Italy. It is required for all public organizations, except for the state and healthcare organizations, and ensures the possibility of connecting accounts with the international classification COFOG.

At present we can distinguish:

- Chart of accounts at national level for public organizations, such as regional and local governments and other public organizations with traditional public accounting to be supplemented in the future with the accrual accounting; the charts of accounts of these different types of public organizations are substantially the same, even if introduced with different legislative initiatives in different times (in the state central administration, the integrated chart of accounts, even if contemplated, has not yet been prepared).
- Chart of accounts of public organizations with only accrual accounting, for which it has not yet been prepared (this is the case of universities) or is not presently required (it is the case of healthcare organizations with a uniform chart of accounts at regional level).

In all the public organizations where the integrated chart of accounts exists, this must be attached to the budget and the annual report with all its items and relative values.

The integrated chart of accounts is the result of a voluntary testing carried out by some public organizations, and it includes the following parts:

- Financial chart of accounts (for the cash- and commitment-based accounting system)
- Economic chart of accounts (for the accrual accounting)
- Chart of accounts of asset, liability and equity items (for the accrual accounting)

The chart of accounts for the traditional public accounting is a table divided into two sections (revenues and expenses) in turn divided into five levels. The economic chart of accounts is a representation in six levels of items of revenues and costs. Finally, the third part of the integrated chart of accounts is composed of a scheme to seven levels of balance sheet items.

Due to its extremely analytical nature (with almost 9000 items in the case of regional and local governments), the integrated chart of accounts could be a possible XBRL taxonomy, with more effectiveness than the SIOPE code (which, at the moment, is more fragmentary) and the mission and program code (which is too short).

Table 1 shows a comparison among the existing coding systems considered in this paper. The integrated chart of accounts appears as the preferred option because it is shared, very detailed and linked with the COFOG code. The criticality is that, at present, there is an integrated chart of accounts only for some public organizations. State central administration, universities and healthcare organizations are, at the moment, excluded.

On the basis of the observations reported, the XBRL taxonomy could be built by using the items of the integrated chart of accounts associated with other information ("fields"). Table 2 is a proposal with different types of information to collect for

Table 1 Code comparison

Codes	Pros	Cons
SIOPE	– Shared – Tested for years – Mandatory – Almost all public organizations involved (regardless of the accounting information system adopted)	– Too many types of codes – Only monetary items (related to receipts and payments)
Missions-Programs-COFOG	– Linked with international classification of expenses (COFOG) – Mandatory – All public organizations involved (regardless of the accounting information system adopted)	– Rather synthetic – Only expenses classified by destination
Integrated chart of accounts	– Shared – Very detailed – Mandatory – Including financial, economic, asset, liability, equity items – Linked with international classification of expenses (COFOG) – Almost all public organizations involved	– Not yet created for public organizations adopting only accrual accounting system

Table 2 A proposal

| ID | Concept | Data type | Unit of measure | Value | Context | | |
					Public organization	*Period*	*Scenario*
Italian label	**English label**	**SIOPE code**	**COFOG code**	**Mission code**	**Program code**	**Accounting standard**	

each item of the taxonomy. Here the "technical" content of the XBRL taxonomy are not considered; the focus is on the contents that characterize the taxonomy of Italian public organizations. For example, the field "scenario" can consider the different phases of revenues and expenditure reported in the annual report of public organizations adopting the traditional public accounting. Alternatively, it can consider the different stages (planning, programming and reporting) of revenues and costs in the case of public organizations that adopt the accrual accounting.

5 Conclusions

An increasing interest for accountability and transparency requirements has emerged in public organizations over the last few years. Consequently, public organizations have begun to exploit the potential of the Internet by making their official documents and/or significant information available in the World Wide Web. In such a context, the possible use of the XBRL language has started to be considered by scholars and operators. XBRL can be a potential instrument for public organizations' transparency and not a useless bureaucratic requirement if it is used for enhancing information towards stakeholders. If, for example, the institutional website of a public organization reports a file of financial data in XBRL format, users can obtain and process information saving costs and time compared to the past.

This paper highlighted, through a theoretical study, that the adoption of XBRL in Italian public organizations presents some criticalities, essentially due to the heterogeneity of the budgeting and accounting information systems used, thus making it impossible to create a univocal XBRL taxonomy. Moreover, different coding systems already in use could lead to the risk of seeing the creation of the XBRL file as just another bureaucratic fulfilment.

However, these coding systems could be used as a basis for the development of an XBRL taxonomy. More specifically, our investigation highlighted how the most appropriate taxonomy, at least for public organizations using the cash- and commitment-based accounting system, could be the new integrated chart of accounts, which is sufficiently analytical and shared to become a list of items for the taxonomy.

The road towards the adoption of XBRL in public organizations is still long, and there are also criticalities regarding the resistance to change and the cost of initial investment not considered in this paper. A possible extension of this study could be an international comparison in order to understand in which way other countries of European Union are developing their XBRL taxonomy for public organizations.

References

1. Gray, A., & Jenkins, W. (1993). Codes of accountability in the new public sector. *Accounting Auditing and Accountability Journal, 6*, 52–67.
2. Mulgan, R. (2000). Accountability: An ever-expanding concept? *Public Organization, 78*, 555–573.
3. Romzek, B. S. (2000). Dynamics of public sector accountability in an era of reform. *International Review of Administrative Sciences, 66*, 21–44.
4. Meijer, A. (2014). Transparency. In M. Bovens, R. E. Goodin, & T. Schillemans (Eds.), *Public accountability*. Oxford: Oxford University Press.
5. Mussari, R., & Steccolini, I. (2006). Using the internet for communicating performance information. *Public Money & Management, 26*, 193–196.
6. Quagli, A. (Ed.). (2001). *Internet e la comunicazione finanziaria*. Milano: FrancoAngeli.
7. Bonson, E. (2001). The role of Xbrl in Europe. *International Journal of Digital Accounting Research, 1*, 101–110.
8. Debreceny, R., & Gray, G. L. (2001). The production and use of semantically rich accounting reports on the internet: XML and Xbrl. *International Journal of Accounting Information Systems, 2*, 47–74.
9. Hodge, F. D., Kennedy, J. J., & Maines, L. A. (2004). Does search-facilitating technology improve the transparency of financial reporting? *The Accounting Review, 79*, 687–703.
10. Pinsker, R., & Li, S. (2008). Costs and benefits of Xbrl adoption: Early evidence. *Communications of the ACM, 51*, 47–50.
11. Troshani, I., Parker, L. D., & Lymer, A. (2015). Institutionalising XBRL for financial reporting: resorting to regulation. *Accounting and Business Research, 45*, 196–228.
12. Chen, Y. C. (2013). Improving transparency in the financial sector. *Public Performance & Management Review, 37*, 241–262.
13. Quagli, A., & Ramassa, P. (2011). L'efficienza delle tassonomie tra esigenze di standardizzazione e prassi aziendale. In S. Zambon (Ed.), *XBRL e informativa aziendale. Traiettorie, innovazioni e sfide*. Milano: Franco Angeli.
14. Locke, J., & Lowe, A. (2007). An (open) source of enlightenment or disillusion? *European Accounting Review, 16*, 585–623.
15. Bergeron, B. (2003). *Essentials of Xbrl, financial reporting in the 21st century*. Hoboken, NJ: Wiley.
16. Petacchi, P. (2006). Nuovi strumenti per le comunicazioni economico-finanziarie: l'extensible business reporting language (XBRL). In AAVV, Riferimenti storici e processi evolutivi dell'informativa di bilancio tra dottrina e prassi. Rirea, Roma.
17. Fredeani, A. (2011). *Il bilancio di esercizio in Xbrl*. Milano: Ipsoa.
18. Bovee, M., Ettredge, M., Srivastava, R. P., & Vasarhelyi, M. A. (2002). Does the year 2000 XBRL taxonomy accommodate current business financial reporting practice? *Journal of Information Systems, 16*, 165–182.
19. Soverchia, M. (2009). XBRL ed il sistema informativo-contabile delle amministrazioni pubbliche. In A. Fredeani (Ed.), *XBRL. Il presente ed il futuro della comunicazione economico finanziaria*. Milano: Giuffrè.
20. Alles, M., & Debreceny, R. S. (2012). The evolution and future of XBRL research. *International Journal of Accounting Information Systems, 13*, 83–90.

21. Perdana, A., Robb, A., & Rohde, F. (2015). An integrative review and synthesis of XBRL research in academic journals. *Journal of Information Systems, 29*, 115–153.
22. Roohani, S., Xianming, Z., Capozzoli, E. A., & Lamberton, B. (2010). Analysis of XBRL literature: A decade of progress and puzzle. *International Journal of Digital Accounting Research, 10*, 131–147.
23. Valentinetti, D., & Rea, M. A. (2011). Adopting XBRL in Italy: Early evidence of fit between Italian GAAP taxonomy and current reporting practices of non-listed companies. *International Journal of Digital Accounting Research, 11*, 45–67.
24. Abdolmohammadi, M., Harris, J., & Smith, K. (2002). Government financial reporting on the internet: The potential revolutionary effects of Xbrl. *Journal of Government Financial Management, 51*, 24–31.
25. Ball, C. (2007). Better information better management. *Journal of Government Financial Management, 56*, 16–19.
26. Kull, J., & Abraham, C. (2008). Xbrl and public sector financial reporting. *Journal of Government Financial Management, 57*, 28–32.
27. Rezaee, Z., & Turner, J. L. (2002). Xbrl-based financial reporting: Challenges and opportunities for government accountants. *Journal of Government Financial Management, 51*, 16–22.
28. Chen, Y. C. (2012). A comparative study of e-government XBRL implementations: The potential of improving information transparency and efficiency. *Government Information Quarterly, 29*, 553–563.
29. Kull, J. (2008). Oregon State XBRL Report Forthcoming. *Journal of Government Financial Management, 57*, 36.
30. Smith, K., Abdolmohammadi, M., & Harris, J. (2001). Extensible Markup Language: A new technology tool for the public sector. *Government Finance Review, 17*, 20–25.
31. Ida, M. (2012) *XBRL financial database for higher education institutions.* Proceedings of the 14th International Conference on Advanced Communication Technology, PyeongChang South Korea, pp. 318–322.
32. Hulstijn, J., de Winne, N., Janssen, M., Van Wijk, R., Bharosa, N., & Tan, Y. H. (2011). *Public process management: A method for introducing standard business reporting.* Proceeding of the 12th Annual International Conference on Digital Government Research, pp. 141–150.
33. Mauss, V. C., Bleil, C., Vanti, A. A., & Balloni, A. J. (2008). Xbrl in public organization as a way to evince and scale the use of information. In K. Elleithy (Ed.), *Innovations and advanced techniques in systems* (Computing Sciences and Software Engineering). Bridgeport: Springer.
34. De Winne, N., Janssen, M., Bharosa, N., Van Wijk, R., & Hulstijn, J. (2011). Transforming public-private networks: An XBRL-based infrastructure for transforming business-to-government information exchange. *International Journal of Electronic Government Research, 7*, 35–45.
35. Roohani, S., Furusho, Y., & Koizumi, M. (2009). XBRL: Improving transparency and monitoring functions of corporate governance. *International Journal of Disclosure and Governance, 6*, 355–369.
36. Dawes, S., Cresswell, A., & Pardo, T. (2009). From 'need to know' to 'need to share': tangled problems, information boundaries, and building of public sector knowledge networks. *Public Administration Review, 69*, 392–402.
37. Soverchia, M. (2015). How can technology improve government financial transparency? The answer of the eXtensible business reporting language (XBRL). *International Journal of Public organization in the Digital Age, 2*, 24–38.
38. Anessi Pessina, E. (2007). *L'evoluzione dei sistemi contabili pubblici: aspetti critici nella prospettiva aziendale.* Milano: Egea.
39. Anselmi, L. (2003). *Percorsi aziendali per le pubbliche amministrazioni.* Torino: Giappichelli.
40. Borgonovi, E. (2002). *Principi e sistemi aziendali per le amministrazioni pubbliche.* Milano: Egea.
41. Lapsley, I., Mussari, R., & Paulsson, G. (2009). On the adoption of accrual accounting in the public sector: A self-evident and problematic reform. *European Accounting Review, 18*, 719–723.

42. Steccolini, I. (2009). *Cambiamento e innovazione nei sistemi contabili pubblici*. Milano: Egea.
43. Bonollo, E., Lazzini, S., & Zuccardi Merli, M. (2016). Innovations in accounting information system in the public sector. Evidences from Italian Public Universities. In D. Mancini, R. P. Dameri, & E. Bonollo (Eds.), *Strengthening information and control systems* (The synergy between information technology and accounting models). London: Springer.
44. Mussari, R. (2012). Brevi considerazioni sui mutamenti in atto nei sistemi di contabilità pubblica. *Azienda pubblica, 25*, 11–21.
45. Fredeani, A. (2008). Xbrl: il nuovo linguaggio della comunicazione economico-finanziaria. *Pratica contabile, 4*, 10–13.
46. Giovanelli, L. (2005). *I modelli contabili pubblici nel processo di integrazione europea*. Milano: Giuffrè.
47. Giovanelli, L. (2000). *Modelli contabili e di bilancio in uno Stato che cambia*. Milano: Giuffrè.
48. Pavan, A., & Reginato, E. (2004). *Programmazione e controllo nello Stato e nelle altre amministrazioni pubbliche: gestione per obiettivi e contabilità economica*. Milano: Giuffrè.

Implementation of Mandatory IFRS Financial Disclosures in a Voluntary Format: Evidence from the Italian XBRL Project

Andrea Fradeani, Carlo Regoliosi, Alessandro D'Eri, and Francesco Campanari

Abstract Recent research has highlighted how intensely accounting literature has focused on the potential benefits of XBRL for improving the efficiency and effectiveness of communication between companies and their internal and external stakeholders. Some studies have analyzed ex ante the degree of compatibility between the existing XBRL Taxonomies and actual corporate financial reporting practices, in order to identify the degree of potential misfit between these taxonomies and the related reported items in company financial statements. Other works have addressed the structural characteristics of voluntary XBRL adopters, particularly in the USA, based on the voluntary filing program of the Securities and Exchange Commission (SEC). Finally, some papers consider the relevant impacts of XBRL technology in one of two ways: either (a) once its formal implementation has already occurred (on a voluntary or mandatory basis) or (b), even before then, by assessing ex ante the potential impacts of this technology.

Based on existing research on the motivation and characteristics of companies providing voluntary disclosures, our work takes a third way, by considering a pilot project activated in 2011 to implement the IFRS Taxonomy in the Italian market, thanks to an initiative of XBRL Italy. This empirical study was conducted over a fairly limited sample of both listed and non-listed Italian companies using a case study methodology and applying the 2011 IFRS Taxonomy to the main quantitative financial statements of the surveyed companies (statement of financial position, statement of comprehensive income, cash flow statement, and statement of changes in equity), which we globally refer to as "face financials." The results of each application were then grouped together to derive qualitative considerations on the extent to which the 2011 IFRS Taxonomy fitted the actual needs of preparers. This study is qualitative in nature and represents the first step of a multiyear project to

A. Fradeani (✉) • F. Campanari
Department of Economics and Law, University of Macerata, Macerata, Italy
e-mail: a.fradeani@unimc.it; f.campanari@unimc.it

C. Regoliosi • A. D'Eri
Department of Business Studies, Roma Tre University, Rome, Italy
e-mail: carlo.regoliosi@uniroma3.it; alessandro.deri@uniroma3.it

© Springer International Publishing AG 2017
K. Corsi et al. (eds.), *Reshaping Accounting and Management Control Systems*,
Lecture Notes in Information Systems and Organisation 20,
DOI 10.1007/978-3-319-49538-5_22

improve the IFRS Taxonomy by identifying the labels that need to be adjusted to match the local Italian accounting requirements.

Keywords IFRS • XBRL • IFRS Taxonomy • Financial reporting • Digital accounting

1 Introduction

Recent research has highlighted how intensely accounting literature has focused on the potential benefits of XBRL[1] for improving the efficiency and effectiveness of communication between companies and their internal and external stakeholders [1]. Some studies have analyzed ex ante the degree of compatibility between the existing XBRL Taxonomies[2] and actual corporate financial reporting practices, in order to identify the degree of potential misfit between these taxonomies and the related reported items in corporate financial statements [2]. Other works have addressed the structural characteristics of voluntary XBRL adopters, particularly in the USA, based on the SEC's voluntary filing program [3]. Thus, in general, previous research has considered the relevant impacts of XBRL technology in one of two ways: either (a) once its formal implementation has already occurred (on a voluntary or mandatory basis) or (b), even before then, by assessing ex ante the potential impacts of this technology. Based on existing research on the motivation and characteristics of companies providing voluntary disclosures, our work takes a third way, by considering the Italian XBRL Pilot Project—launched in 2011 by XBRL Italy—involving, on a voluntary basis, companies adopting IFRS (mainly listed) that were asked to make an assessment of the viability of the IFRS XBRL Taxonomy for their external and internal financial communication needs.

The paper (a) considers the characteristics of the firms that volunteered to take part in the project and their motivation to undertake such an exercise and (b) presents the actual degree of compatibility between the given taxonomy and existing financial reporting practices adopted for traditional statements. We find that actual implementation results are partially in line with those expected in previous studies on Italian listed companies. The paper contributes to the existing accounting literature in two ways: (a) it considers the adoption of XBRL

---

[1]XBRL is a markup language designed to code, use, and exchange business data in a way that computers can directly manage it. It's an open standard, free of license fees, derived from XML and promoted by XBRL International Inc. Thanks to XBRL accountants, auditors and users can share, reuse, and analyze data in a new interactive way. XBRL is either mandated or voluntarily used for filing accounts in several countries including Australia, Belgium, Canada, China, Denmark, France, Germany, Israel, Italy, Korea, the Netherlands, Spain, Sweden, Singapore, the United Kingdom, India, Brazil, Japan, and the USA.

[2]An XBRL Taxonomy is a list of concepts with their corresponding tags for a specific reporting purpose, such as filing financial information under IFRS or US GAAP. Similar to a dictionary, it defines each concept and describes its attributes and relationships. Each concept used in an XBRL document must be defined in the corresponding XBRL Taxonomy.

technology—although in the context of a pilot project—in light of the wider literature on voluntary disclosures to assess if the findings of previous literature addressing the "voluntary content" of disclosures are applicable and consistent to the case of a "voluntary format" for mandatory disclosures, and (b) it considers, for the first time, the pro forma implementation of XBRL for a sample of Italian companies adopting IFRS.

Last but not least, we wish to acknowledge the contribution of the IFRS Working Group, established within XBRL Italy, which has enabled us to develop this research idea and conduct this study.

2 Literature Review

The potential benefits of XBRL for improving the efficiency and effectiveness of communication between companies and their internal and external stakeholders have long been debated in the academic literature [1, 4] as well as their impact on investors' trading behavior [5]. In other works, the role of XBRL as a facilitator for transparency in corporate reporting is discussed [6–10]. Some studies have investigated the degree of compatibility between the existing XBRL Taxonomies and actual corporate financial reporting practices, in order to identify the degree of potential misfit between these taxonomies and the related reported items in corporate financial statements [2]. Other works have addressed the structural characteristics of voluntary XBRL adopters, particularly in the USA, based on the SEC's voluntary filing program [3, 11]. Recent studies have also addressed more in detail the quality and types of extensions to the XBRL (IFRS) Taxonomy in order to understand the degree of accuracy of such disclosures, thus testifying that a learning curve exists for the preparation of XBRL disclosures [12, 13]. A more limited number of studies as so far investigated the XBRL voluntary disclosure space. Existing research in this area includes regression analysis on the characteristics of firms which have decided to adopt XBRL on a voluntary basis [14]. In a recent review of existing literature on XBRL [15], the research conducted on XBRL-related topics and the issues and impacts being highlighted (as identified in terms of occurrences) have been analyzed in order to identify what areas of XBRL impacts and issues have been made subject to only limited or no research at all. Research on taxonomy extensions can be linked to at least three major XBRL-related issues: tagging process and accuracy [16, 17] and implementation efforts needed to implement extensions [18–22]. One additional XBRL impact being investigated most recently refers to the potential of XBRL to reduce information asymmetry in financial markets [23, 24].

Thus, in general, previous research has considered the relevant impacts of XBRL application to corporate reporting in one of two ways: either (a) once its formal implementation has already occurred (either on a voluntary or mandatory basis) or (b), even before then, by assessing ex ante the potential impacts of this technology. Particularly, this paper enters the discussions regarding the quality of extensions when XBRL reports are prepared in the specific setting of the Italian market, whereas the degree of experience in extending XBRL Taxonomies is at its initial steps.

3 The IFRS Taxonomy Pilot Project

In December 2011, XBRL Italy—the entity affiliated with XBRL International in charge of the Italian jurisdiction—started a working group focusing on companies adopting IFRS (mainly listed) and their XBRL implementation challenges. This working group represents a voluntary experiment to test to what degree the 2011 IFRS Taxonomy meets the needs of local preparers (IFRS Taxonomy 2011).

Companies were invited to take part in a specific exercise: verifying whether the elements contained in the 2011 IFRS Taxonomy (i.e., the most recent version of the IFRS Taxonomy available in the Italian language) are able to adequately represent the information contained in the 2011 consolidated financial statements of the surveyed entities. The adequacy was qualitatively tested based on the outcome of the interviews with senior financial officers of the surveyed entities who expressed their judgment on the XBRL elements based on their experience and on the need to comply with the general principles of faithful representations, clarity, and correctness. Also, entities were asked to express their views on the quality of the Italian translation of the 2011 IFRS Taxonomy.

There are two reasons for choosing consolidated financial statements instead of separate or individual financial statements:

1. Consolidated financial statements are the most relevant statements with respect to informative power about a group of entities in its entirety.
2. They are less influenced by country-specific issues (such as local tax rules) than are individual and separate financial statements.

Furthermore, the project considered the adequacy of the 2011 IFRS Taxonomy for 2010 consolidated financial statements for two reasons:

1. The 2011 IFRS Taxonomy includes the XBRL translation of IFRSs as issued on 1 January 2011.
2. We found it less burdensome for the participants to test 2010 financial statements than those of 2011, which were still being prepared at the beginning of the pilot project.

The project followed a two-step process: in the first step, one entity was tested for purposes of fine-tuning the model, and, in the second step, all other entities joined the exercise. Two meetings were convened during 2012: the first was in Rome (June 21) to discuss the results of the pilot application of the model to one entity; the second meeting was split into two—one in Rome (December 18) and one in Milan (December 19)—to analyze the Excel files filled in by the participants.

4 The Participants

The pilot project involved a limited, though significant, number of entities. Particularly, the participants were among the most relevant—by size and type of operations—Italian IFRS adopters, most of which are listed in the Italian stock exchange.

The sample does not include entities belonging to the financial industry (i.e., insurance, banking, etc.) because:

1. These entities are subject to a peculiar regulatory regime that also involves specific adjustments to the IFRS accounts.
2. The 2011 IFRS Taxonomy does not include industry-specific elements for those types of entities.

The list of the nine participants is presented in Table 1 below.

We note that this exercise is particularly relevant for entities that may be willing to file their financial statements in foreign markets, such as Eni e Telecom Italia, which may apply to be admitted as a *foreign private issuer* to the US stock exchange (via *Form 20-F*) by the SEC.

5 The Methodology

The participants were given a package with the Italian version of the 2011 IFRS Taxonomy and an Excel file containing the 2545 elements of the IFRS XBRL dictionary, sorted by type of statement they belong to (balance sheet, income statement, cash flow statement, statement of changes in equity, and related disclosures).

As shown in Fig. 1 below, for each item—identified by type and legal reference—participants were asked to express a judgment (column "Val") on the ability of the specific element to represent the corresponding concept presented in their 2010 consolidated financial statements. Where an item was considered as not properly reflecting the concept used in the consolidated financial statements,

Table 1 Study participants

Group name	Industry	Listed/not listed
Atlantia	Construction	Listed
Enel	Energy	Listed
Eni	Oil and gas	Listed
Fiat	Automotive	Listed
Prysmian	Energy and ICT cables	Listed
RCS	Publishing	Listed
Telecom Italia	ICT	Listed
Ferrovie dello Stato	Railways	Not listed
Heineken	Beverage	Not listed

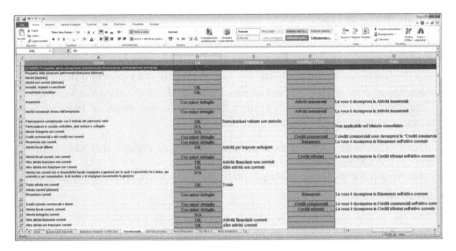

Fig. 1 The ability of specific elements to represent a corresponding concept

participants were asked to indicate whether the IFRS XBRL elements needed to achieve either a higher or a lower level of detail to faithfully represent the source concept. For this purpose, columns "Modifica ITEM" and "Nota" were provided to suggest an alternative solution to the IFRS label. Participants could also indicate (by using the specific column "Traduzione") an alternative translation when they felt that the existing translation was not satisfactory.

This exercise has produced nine Excel packages that a working group of preparers and researchers tasked with reporting the outcomes of these meetings to the IFRS XBRL team discussed directly with the participant entities at the meetings mentioned above.

6 The Translation

In the short run, the project aimed to test and, if necessary, improve the only public output of the IFRS Working Group: the Italian translation of the IFRS Taxonomy 2011. In the following Tables 2 and 3, we present some relevant modification proposals suggested by working group members.

We show here the *desiderata* (things wanted or needed), limited to the balance sheet (in its current/noncurrent version) and to the income statement (either by type of item or by purpose), focusing on both the referenced reporting standard and, when possible, on its translation.

Before illustrating the *desiderata*, we offer some considerations about the accounting terminology used:

1. It is strongly influenced by the socioeconomic context of the country where it was developed.

Table 2 Modification proposals for the balance sheet

Label	Desiderata	Reference	Official translation
Prospetto della situazione patrimoniale-finanziaria	Stato patrimoniale, Situazione patrimoniale-finanziaria consolidata	IAS 1.10.a	Prospetto della situazione patrimoniale-finanziaria
Attività immateriali diverse dall'avviamento	Attività immateriali, Immobilizzazioni immateriali	IAS 1.54.c	n/a
Attività fiscali differite	Attività per imposte anticipate {4}	IAS 1.54. o/1.56	Attività per imposte differite, Attività fiscali differite
Altre attività non finanziarie non correnti	Altre attività non correnti {4}	Common practice	n/a
Altre attività non finanziarie correnti	Altre attività correnti {3}, Crediti diversi e altre attività correnti	Common practice	n/a
Capitale sociale emesso	Capitale sociale {4}, Capitale emesso	IAS 1.54. r/1.78.e/1. IG	Capitale emesso, Capitale sottoscritto
Utili portati a nuovo	Utili (perdite) portati a nuovo {2}, Utili e perdite accumulati	IAS 1.54. r/1.78.e	Riserve
Totale patrimonio netto attribuibile ai soci della controllante	Patrimonio netto del gruppo {3}, Capitale e riserve di pertinenza del gruppo	IAS 1.54.r	Capitale emesso e riserve attribuibili ai soci della controllante
Partecipazioni di minoranza	Interessenze di terzi {3}, Patrimonio netto di terzi {2}	IAS 1.54.q	Partecipazioni di minoranza
Accantonamenti non correnti per benefici per i dipendenti	Fondi per benefici ai dipendenti, TFR e altri benefici ai dipendenti, Benefici ai dipendenti non correnti, Fondi del personale, Benefici relativi al personale	IAS 1.78.d	Accantonamenti non correnti per i benefici per i dipendenti
Passività fiscali differite	Passività per imposte differite {5}, Imposte differite passive	IAS 1.54. o/1.56	Passività per imposte differite, Passività fiscali differite
Altre passività non finanziarie non correnti	Altre passività non correnti	Common practice	n/a
Accantonamenti correnti per benefici per i dipendenti	Benefici ai dipendenti correnti, Fondi del personale	IAS 1.78.d	Accantonamenti correnti per i benefici per i dipendenti
Altri accantonamenti correnti	Quota a breve dei Fondi rischi e oneri, Fondi correnti, Fondi rischi ed oneri	IAS 1.78.d	Altri accantonamenti correnti
Passività fiscali correnti, correnti	Debiti per imposte correnti {3}, Debiti per imposte sul reddito	IAS 1.54.n	Passività per imposte correnti, correnti
Altre passività non finanziarie correnti	Altre passività correnti, Debiti diversi e altre passività correnti	Common practice	n/a

Note: frequency of *desiderata* is in curly brackets

Table 3 Modification proposals for the income statement

Label	Desiderata	Reference	Official translation
Ricavi	Ricavi delle vendite e delle prestazioni {3}, Ricavi delle vendite, Ricavi della gestione caratteristica	IAS 1.82.a	Ricavi
Utile lordo	Margine lordo	IAS 1.103	Utile lordo
Costi per benefici ai dipendenti	Costo del personale {3}, Spese del personale, Costo lavoro	IAS 1.102	Costi per benefici ai dipendenti
Utile (perdita) da attività operative	Risultato operativo {3}, Utile (perdita) operativo {2}	IAS 32.IE33	n/a
Utile (perdita) al lordo delle imposte	Risultato prima delle imposte {3}, Utile/perdita ante imposte, Risultato ante imposte, Utile (perdita) prima delle imposte	IAS 1.102/1.103	Utile prima delle imposte
Proventi (oneri) fiscali	Imposte sul reddito {4}, Imposte {2}	IAS 1.82.d/12.79	Oneri tributari, Oneri (proventi) fiscali
Utile (perdita)	Risultato netto dell'esercizio (gruppo e terzi) {2}, Utile (perdita) d'esercizio {2}, Risultato dell'esercizio, Utile netto	IAS 1.82.f	Utile (perdita) d'esercizio
Utile (perdita), attribuibile ai soci della controllante	Quota di interessenza del gruppo, Risultato di gruppo, Risultato netto di gruppo, Soci della capogruppo	IAS 1.83.a.ii	Risultato economico d'esercizio attribuibile ai soci della controllante
Utile (perdita), attribuibile a partecipazioni di minoranza	Utile (perdita) di competenza di interessenze di terzi {2}, Quota di interessenza di terzi, Risultato di terzi, Risultato netto di terzi, Interessi di terzi	IAS 1.83.a.i	Risultato economico d'esercizio attribuibile a partecipazioni di minoranza

Note: frequency of *desiderata* is in curly brackets

2. It derives, especially in Latin countries (including Italy), from both the Italian accounting tradition and the tax and legal-specific terminology [25].

On the contrary, the jargon of IFRS has a different and peculiar origin; international financial reporting standards are intended for global application and do not take single jurisdictions into consideration (especially those not relevant for financial markets). Furthermore, IFRS are the result of an inherent cultural compromise dominated by Anglo-American financial accounting (starting from the use of English as the official language). In the light of this, the translation of IFRS is not an easy task. As the IASB knows, this applies not only to Italy; the literature clearly shows that translation can be an issue when a country has a radically different accounting culture from others. Any student, researcher, or professional who has attempted to handle the corpus of the IFRS has had to face this problem. The official Italian version of the Taxonomy often looks odd and misleading, sometimes requiring the support of the original version. As said above, we believe that this is not only an issue of translation. In fact, the problem arises because of a mix of cultural differences and the need to maintain a rigid systemic coherence between the original text and its multiple translations. The IFRS Taxonomy has shed some light on this issue. The possibility to personalize the accounting systems permitted by international financial reporting standards allows preparers (we refer to the written version of the financial statements) to bypass completely the problem. In fact, the official translation does not imply the use of a specific language or terminology or a specific level of detail. The IFRS Taxonomy only obliges preparers to attribute a specific meaning to each element of the financial statement.

The use of XBRL—without the possibility of creating extensions even when the taxonomy is the outcome of a wide consultation process—results in a contradictory situation where a means for delivering financial information, created to be flexible and fully customizable, becomes an element of rigidity in the overall financial reporting process. In this respect, an unreliable translation is a limit that preparers cannot overcome unless they are able to extend the taxonomy. Taxonomy extensions are a hard topic to cope with, but there is now a trend toward using extensions that is one of the results from the pilot project.

Particularly, Tables 2 and 3 illustrate that there is a trend toward a translation that better reflects the Italian accounting tradition. In our view, although many of the comments received from preparers are meaningful, they should not necessarily trigger taxonomy changes. We refer, in particular, to the situation where the label translation is identical to the official Italian text of the IFRS Bound Volume (the IFRS translation published by the Official Journal of the European Union, as endorsed following European Regulation (CE) 1606/2002). A significant example is the costs associated with employee benefits (in Italian *Costi per benefici ai dipendenti*), which is quite new in the Italian context but perfectly reflects what is written in the Italian version of IAS 1 (par. 102). Other translations may be preferred (such as *Costo del personale*, *Spese del personale*, or *Costo del lavoro*), which reflect the *desiderata* expressed by participants. We note, however, that the IFRS Taxonomy cannot be expected to correct issues inherent in the text of a standard itself.

The IFRS Working Group will certainly try, also thanks to XBRL Italy, to raise the translation issue and eventually trigger a revision of the translated versions of the taxonomy. Participants also expressed other *desiderata*, which could be considered as part of the IFRS Taxonomy revisions. These are instances where a proposed XBRL label allows for better adherence of the IFRS Taxonomy to the core text of the IFRS Bound Volume as officially translated in Italian. This is the case, for example, of the label referring to deferred tax liabilities (in Italian *Passività fiscali differite*). Five of nine entities suggested revising the label to mean liabilities for deferred taxes (in Italian *Passività per imposte differite*). This label would not only be more familiar to the surveyed entities, but it would also better reflect the text of paragraph 54 in IAS 1. In other words, where an official translation provides more solutions, it is certainly possible to adopt the translation that more closely meets local accounting practices. Similarly, the labels derived from the common practice analysis. When they do not rely on different degrees of detail, the lack of official references allows for more flexibility. Although, in the 2011 IFRS Taxonomy, these instances are not frequent, due to the IASB's Industry Practice Project, they will be more relevant in the future.

One of the translation issues identified by the participants is the lack of taxonomy items for deferral and integration items (in Italian *Ratei e risconti*). This lack may also reflect the diversity between the Italian and the Anglo-Saxon accounting traditions. Particularly, the detail of the disclosure items No. 800100 does not include positive integration items (in Italian *Ratei attivi*), which could be inserted by means of modifying the labels "Other noncurrent receivables" and "Other current receivables" (in Italian, respectively, *Altri crediti non correnti* and *Altri crediti correnti*) in the following "Positive integrations and Other noncurrent receivables" and "Positive integrations and Other current receivables" (in Italian, respectively, *Ratei e altri crediti non correnti* and *Ratei e altri crediti correnti*).

7 The Mapping Process

The IFRS reporting model is based on the wide ability for preparer to customize their financial statements. In fact, notwithstanding the large amount of requirements indicated in each standard (quite often these requirements can be met by either providing the related information in the quantitative statements or in the notes), the principles indicated in IAS 1 Presentation of Financial Statements merely represent a starting point. Each preparer will then adjust these requirements to its own specific needs to get to a "final product" that is represented by the bundle of quantitative and qualitative information provided in the financial statements. These adjustments will try to reflect the industry- and entity-specific needs, which in a certain time frame are deemed to represent the economic and financial position of each entity.

Therefore, in the paper format of their financial statements, preparers have a certain degree of "freedom," as also mentioned when discussing translation-related issues. This freedom involves both the structure and the content that, together with the disclosures, comprise the financial statements. This freedom—in a "perfect" IFRS-compliant world—is meant to offer preparers a tool for better communicating with their stakeholders and providing them with a faithful representation of the entity itself.

The adoption of XBRL intends to boost this flexibility-freedom concept thanks to the "extensibility" of the taxonomy. Furthermore, XBRL as a means to communicate business-related information should support the capability of customizing IFRS financial statements. Filing financial statements in XBRL format implies, as shown in Fig. 2, finding the best match between the information included in the financial statements and the XBRL elements provided by the taxonomy.

Sometimes, certain financial items cannot be mapped, either because of limitations in the XBRL dictionary or due to the extreme specificity of a filing entity. In those cases, it will be necessary to create extensions to the standard XBRL dictionary. The customization required will depend on three main drivers:

Fig. 2 Preparing financial statements in XBRL format (Source: IFRS Foundation, The IFRS Taxonomy 2013 Guide, p. 27)

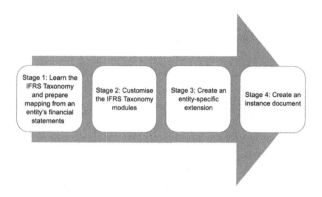

1. The quality and completeness of the taxonomy
2. The degree of freedom of the accounting standards
3. The degree of complexity and peculiarity of the phenomena to be represented

A set of accounting standards, such as IFRS, which is principles based and has customizable reporting schemes, represents an important benchmark for the process that results in the production of an XBRL instance, especially when this document tries to represent the financial statements of large and complex entities operating in the international environment.

While it is not possible to manipulate the degree of freedom offered by accounting standards and the peculiarities of the phenomena that financial statements purport to represent, it is possible to try to improve the quality of the taxonomies. Therefore, the target is to reduce the number of extensions, not only to limit the costs of digitally codifying financial statements but also, primarily, to reduce the potential problems of coherence and comparability (in this respect, consider the experience of the US stock exchange, where filing financial statements in XBRL is compulsory, which has shown how the use of extensions—notwithstanding the availability of a richer taxonomy—has created significant difficulties in terms of comparability).

Lastly, regarding the impact of XBRL as a tool, it is largely unavoidable that the taxonomy will influence the choices of preparers who will almost certainly tend to sacrifice their personal interpretation to make use of the available elements. We note that, in this respect, the role of auditing and assurance in the mapping process between the financial statement and the XBRL Taxonomy will become increasingly relevant.

8   XBRL Schemes Relating to the Balance Sheet and Income Statement

Mapping the quantitative statements to the 2011 IFRS Taxonomy elements has certainly been a delicate issue but has turned out to be a less burdensome task than expected. This is probably the result of the effectiveness and the degree of "administrative maturity" of the preparers involved in the exercise.

Apart from one entity, which has been adopting XBRL for quite some time, all other participants asked for a number of amendments to the original XBRL dictionary being tested. On average, they asked for changes to about 25 % of the balance sheet items and to about 15 % of those related to the income statement. Some entities, in particular, found specific issues in the mapping process due to the peculiarities of their business. This is the case, for example, of entities in the oil and gas and railway industries. For those entities, the 2011 IFRS Taxonomy lacked several basic concepts that have now been added, at least partially, in the latest releases of the IFRS Taxonomy (e.g., the 2012 IFRS Taxonomy includes 3769 items, 1224 more than the 2011 Taxonomy used in our pilot project; these additional elements came largely from the Common Practice Project, which tries to identify the most common items included in the financial statements of industrial and commercial entities. The 2013 IFRS Taxonomy has been further improved, with 114 additional elements, 76 of which came from the Industry Practice Project related to the financial and extractive industries).

Table 4 outlines the most significant *desiderata* for the level of detail in the balance sheet (in both current and noncurrent versions of the IFRS Taxonomy). In

Table 4 Most significant *desiderata* for the level of detail in the balance sheet

Label	Desiderata
Avviamento	Uso di un minor dettaglio {5}
Attività immateriali diverse dall'avviamento	Uso di un minor dettaglio {4}
Crediti commerciali e altri crediti non correnti	Uso di un minor dettaglio {2}, Uso di un maggior dettaglio {1}
Attività fiscali correnti, non correnti	Uso di un minor dettaglio {4}
Altre attività finanziarie correnti	Uso di un maggior dettaglio {3}
Utili portati a nuovo	Uso di un minor dettaglio {3}
Riserva sovrapprezzo azioni	Uso di un minor dettaglio {4}
Altre riserve	Uso di un minor dettaglio {4}
Debiti commerciali e altri debiti non correnti	Uso di un minor dettaglio {2}, Uso di un maggior dettaglio {1}
Passività fiscali correnti, non correnti	Uso di un minor dettaglio {4}
Accantonamenti correnti per benefici per i dipendenti	Uso di un minor dettaglio {3}
Altri accantonamenti correnti	Uso di un minor dettaglio {3}
Altre passività finanziarie correnti	Uso di un maggior dettaglio {4}

Note: frequency of *desiderata* is in curly brackets

most cases, entities want less detail than that described in the 2011 IFRS Taxonomy. The content of the balance sheet scheme that the IASB has envisioned is more expansive than the one required in practice. We highlight two instances:

1. Most participants were surprised about the split into "Goodwill" and "Intangible Assets Other Than Goodwill" (in Italian *Avviamento and Attività immateriali diverse dall'avviamento*), as this level of detail was meant to be more relevant for disclosures than for the face financials. Similarly, the level of detail used in the analysis of equity identifies six items (as opposed to the minimalistic approach taken in IAS 1 at par. 54).

2. Less frequently, entities have requested a higher level of detail. In this respect, entities suggested splitting "Other Current Liabilities" (in Italian *Altre passività finanziarie correnti*) into two elements to identify separately short-term financing from mid- to long-term financing facilities.

When entities discovered that certain specific items were missing or not described (excluding those in the oil and gas and railway industries), this is largely due to the unification into one single item of elements not included in the reference taxonomy.

Table 5 indicates the most significant *desiderata* for the level of detail for items in the income statements (in the version of this statement that sorts elements by type of item). The *desiderata* are, in this case, more concentrated and bring out the higher level of detail most entities applied to the residual item "Other Costs" (in Italian *Altri costi*). In the income statement, participants would favor the distinction of items such as "Services Expense" (in Italian *Costi per servizi*), "Lease Expense" (in Italian *Costi per godimento beni di terzi*), "Other Expense" (in Italian *Oneri diversi di gestione*), "Provisions" (in Italian *Accantonamenti*), and "Impairment Charges on Receivables" (in Italian *Svalutazione crediti commerciali e diversi*).

As previously discussed with reference to the balance sheet, for the income statement, the oil and gas and railway industries also seem to be largely penalized by the lack of specific items that are able to reflect the peculiarities of their business.

Table 5 Most significant *desiderata* for the level of detail in income statement items

Label	Desiderata
Incremento (decremento) in rimanenze di prodotti finiti e lavori in corso	Uso di un minor dettaglio {3}, Uso di un maggior dettaglio {1}
Ammortamenti	Uso di un minor dettaglio {2}, Uso di un maggior dettaglio {2}
Altri costi	Uso di un maggior dettaglio {5}

Note: frequency of *desiderata* is in curly brackets

9   The Outcome of the Pilot Project

We believe that the pilot project, notwithstanding its inherent limitations due to the small sample considered, has been mutually beneficial for both XBRL Italy and the participants. The latter have been able to better analyze the implementation challenges posed by XBRL to their long-standing and well-consolidated accounting practices. On the other hand, XBRL Italy has activated, as one of the first jurisdictions in the world to operate in this field, a project to simulate the implementation of the IFRS Taxonomy to directly test its most relevant issues, providing an important feedback to the IASB itself.

We also believe that this pilot project represents a seminal fieldwork in Italy that may trigger a more in-depth analysis of the following considerations.

First, the 2011 IFRS Taxonomy has not shown the degrees of quality and completeness needed to make its application compulsory. In other words, it would have been possible to apply the taxonomy but at the expense of significant changes in the financial statements or by means of an intensive use of extensions. In this respect, we want to note what the Center for Audit Quality expressed with reference to the 2011 IFRS Taxonomy in its March 29, 2011, letter to the US Securities and Exchange Commission. The SEC shared these views to substantiate its choice to temporarily "freeze" the use of XBRL for foreign private issuers that are IFRS filers: "We acknowledge the IFRS Foundation's efforts to further develop its IFRS taxonomy and the improvements that have been made to date; however, it is our understanding that users of the IFRS Taxonomy 2011 still may need to create numerous extensions for their interactive data exhibits, which may limit the usefulness of such interactive data to users of financial statements. Such extensions may be needed because IFRS Taxonomy 2011 does not yet fully address common reporting practice or industry specific disclosures and does not include standard definitions. In addition, absent significant development of the IFRS taxonomy for footnote disclosures, the need to create a significant number of extensions may continue in year two of the phase-in period, when detailed tagging is required. Until these issues are addressed in future taxonomy enhancements, we believe the benefits achieved by requiring certain FPI's to submit interactive data based on IFRS Taxonomy 2011 may not outweigh the cost and effort to be expended and that additional time is necessary to further develop the IFRS taxonomy."

We commend the IASB's choice to enrich the subsequent releases of the taxonomies thanks to the Common Practice Project and the Industry Practice Project, which have significantly improved the situation. Particularly, as noted earlier, the Industry Practice Project has introduced, in the 2013 IFRS Taxonomy, items that are specific to the financial (including insurance) and extractive industries. The 2014 IFRS Taxonomy will introduce items related to the pharmaceutical, real estate and ICT, and transportation industries.

Second, if the compulsory adoption of XBRL is to become operational for IFRS filers, preparers should be free to extend the taxonomy. This is a necessary precondition to ensure the high degree of customization that is inherent in international financial reporting standards themselves. The improvement of the future releases of the IFRS Taxonomy may mitigate the need for extensions, but cannot totally eliminate it.

In our view, reaching these objectives will require entities to acquire a better knowledge of the reference taxonomy—this knowledge could be enhanced by the initiatives of XBRL Italy—and their availability to discuss, review, and, if necessary, change their accounting practices, to improve the degree of consistency between local practices and international practices, which the taxonomy tries to represent.

Finally, we would like to raise the issue of the importance of reaching a certain consistency between the translation of the IFRS Bound Volume and the IFRS XBRL labels. No translation issues seem to have occurred, however, with respect to the need for better coordination between IFRS Taxonomy items and issues that are specific to the Italian economic and legal context. In this respect, it will be important for Italian jurisdictions to involve a larger number of entities in a future testing project to also extend the scope of the exercise to the separate financial statements.

10 Looking Ahead

In the coming months, the IFRS Working Group, established within XBRL Italy, will prioritize the following three XBRL-related areas of activities:

1. Synchronizing the translation activities of IFRSs and XBRL: the latest Italian version of the IFRS Taxonomy is the 2011 version; during 2014, the working group should work on the translation of the 2014 IFRS Taxonomy and, at the same time, on an acceptable degree of synchronization between the IASB's issuance of new labels and the translation by XBRL Italy.
2. A new and wider testing exercise: the working group should focus in 2014 on a larger sample, with wider institutional and technological support. We believe that more input from the regulators will increase not only the number of entities taking part in this exercise but also the quality and the relevance of the testing itself.
3. Create synergies with other jurisdictions and with other international initiatives: the working group will need to improve its international presence so that it can disseminate the results achieved with its testing exercises and share its views in the international arena to eventually influence the decision-making process in the EU where necessary.
4. Provide extensions for regulatory purposes: given the aim of achieving a wider mandate to adopt XBRL, it will be important to implement an extension module for regulatory purposes.

References

1. Debreceny, R. S. (2012). The evolution and future of XBRL research. *International Journal of Accounting Information Systems, 13*, 83–90.
2. Valentinetti, D., & Rea, M. A. (2012). IFRS Taxonomy and financial reporting practices: The case of Italian listed companies. *International Journal of Accounting Information Systems, 13*, 163–180.
3. Debreceny, R. S., Chandra, A., Cheh, J. J., Guithues-Amrhein, D., Hannon, N. J., Hutchison, P. D., et al. (2005). Financial reporting in XBRL on the SEC's EDGAR system: A critique and evaluation. *Journal of Information Systems, 19*, 191.
4. Bonson, E., Cortijo, V., & Escobar, T. (2008). The role of XBRL in enhanced business reporting (EBR). *Journal of Emerging Technologies in Accounting, 5*, 161–173.
5. Blankespoor, E., Miller, B. P., & White, H. D. (2011). *XBRL and transition period market frictions*. Ann Arbor, MI: University of Michigan.
6. Premuroso, R. F., & Bhattacharya, S. (2008). Do early and voluntary filers of financial information in XBRL format signal superior corporate governance and operating performance? *International Journal of Accounting Information Systems, 9*, 1–20.
7. Piechocki, M. C., Felden, A., Graning, C., & Debreceny, R. (2009). Design and standardization of XBRL solutions for governance and transparency. *International Journal of Disclosure and Governance, 6*, 224–240.
8. Cho, Y. J., Bhattacharya, N., & Kim, J. B. (2014). *XBRL Mandate and access to information: Evidence from reactions of financial analysts and institutional investors*. American Accounting Association Annual Meeting. Research Collection School of Accountancy.
9. Wang, T., Wen, C. Y., & Seng, J. L. (2014). The association between the mandatory adoption of XBRL and the performance of listed state-owned enterprises and non-state-owned enterprises in China. *Information & Management, 51*(3), 336–346.
10. Liu, C., Yao, L. J., Sia, C. L., & Wei, K. K. (2014). The impact of early XBRL adoption on analysts' forecast accuracy-empirical evidence from China. *Electronic Markets, 24*(1), 47–55.
11. Kaya, D. (2014). The influence of firm-specific characteristics on the extent of voluntary disclosure in XBRL: Empirical analysis of SEC filings. *International Journal of Accounting and Information Management, 22*(1), 2–17.
12. Boritz, J. E. (2009). Assurance on XBRL-related documents: The case of United Technologies Corporation. *Journal of Information Systems, 23*(2), 49–78.
13. Debreceny, R. S., Farewell, S. M., Piechocki, M., Felden, C., Graning, A., & d'Eri, A. (2011). Flex or break? Extensions in XBRL disclosures to the SEC. *Accounting Horizons, 25*(4), 631–657.
14. Ragothama, S. (2012). Voluntary XBRL adopters and firm characteristics: An empirical analysis. *The International Journal of Digital Accounting Research, 12*, 93–119.
15. Müller-Wickop, N., Schultz, M., & Nüttgens, M. (2013). *XBRL: Impacts, issues and future research directions*. Enterprise Applications and Services in the Finance Industry, Volume 135 of the series Lecture Notes in Business Information Processing (pp. 112–130). Springer.
16. Pinsker, R., & Li, S. (2008). Costs and benefits of XBRL adoption: Early evidence. *Communications of the ACM, 51*, 47–50. Association for Computing Machinery.
17. Plumlee, R. D., & Plumlee, M. A. (2008). Assurance on XBRL for financial reporting. *Accounting Horizons, 22*, 353–368.
18. Doolin, B., & Troshani, I. (2007). Organizational adoption of XBRL. *Electronic Markets, 17*(3), 199–209.
19. Boritz, J. E., & No, W. G. (2008). The SEC's XBRL voluntary filing program on EDGAR: A case for quality assurance. *Current Issues in Auditing, 2*(2), A36–A50.
20. Bartley, J., Chen, Y., & Taylor, E. (2010). Avoiding common errors of XBRL implementation. *Journal of Accountancy, 209*, 46–51.
21. Bartley, J., Chen, A. Y. S., & Taylor, E. Z. (2011). A comparison of XBRL filings to corporate 10-Ks-evidence from the voluntary filing program. *Accounting Horizons, 25*(2), 227–245.

22. Harris, T., & Morsfield, S. (2012). *An evaluation of the current state and future of XBRL and interactive data for investors and analysts.* White Paper. Columbia Business School.
23. Blankespoor, E., Miller, B. P., & White, H. D. (2014). Initial evidence on the market impact of the XBRL mandate. *Review of Accounting Studies, 19*(4), 1468–1503.
24. Yen, J. C., & Wang, T. (2015). The Association between XBRL adoption and market reactions to earnings surprises. *Journal of Information Systems, 29*(3), 51–71.
25. Nobes, C. (1998). Towards a general model of the reasons for International differences in financial reporting. *Abacus, 34*(2), 162–187.

Printed in the United States
By Bookmasters